Japa-Yoga

Other books by the same Author

1. **Cyclic Universe**: Cycles of the Creation, Evolution, Involution and Dissolution of the Universe; **2 vols.**; Vol. 1: The Unsolved Riddle: Eternal, Created or Evolved Universe; Vol. 2: Integral Cosmology: Cosmic Creation, Evolution and Dissolution in Cycles; ISBN 81-246-0190-9 (set)
2. **Meditation**: Science and Practice; ISBN 81-246-0211-5
3. **Mind and Supermind**; **2 vols.**; Vol. 1: Indian Perspective; Vol. 2: Western Perspective; ISBN 81-246-0053-8 (set)
4. **Yoga Nidrā — Yogic Trance**: Theory, Practice and Applications; ISBN 81-246-0242-5

Japa-Yoga

(Mantra-Yoga)

Theory, Practice and Applications

N.C. Panda

D.K. Printworld (P) Ltd.
New Delhi

Cataloging in Publication Data — DK
Courtesy: D.K. Agencies (P) Ltd. <docinfo@dkagencies.com>

Panda, N.C. (Nrusingh Charan), 1929 –
Japa-yoga (Mantra-yoga) : theory, practice and applications / N.C. Panda.
xxvi, 362 p., 23 cm.
English and Sanskrit (Sanskrit in Devanagari and roman)
Includes bibliographical references (p.)
Includes index.
ISBN 812460388X

1. Yoga. 2. Hindu mantras. 3. Meditation — Hinduism. 4. Yoga — Therapeutic use. I. Title.

DDC 181.45 22

ISBN 81-246-0388-X (Hardbound)
81-246-0389-8 (Paperback)
First published in India 2007

Published and printed by:
D.K. Printworld (P) Ltd.
Regd. office : *'Sri Kunj'*, F-52, Bali Nagar
Ramesh Nagar Metro Station
New Delhi - 110 015
Phones : (011) 2545-3975; 2546-6019; *Fax* : (011) 2546-5926
E-mail: dkprintworld@vsnl.net
Web : www.dkprintworld.com

To
my son, Bikash
and
daughter-in-law, Snigdhā (Mānu)
with blessings
and
prayer to God
for their peace and prosperity

Prologue

THE *yoga* of devotion (*bhakti-yoga*) lays a great deal of importance on the *japa* (the repeated utterance — silent, whispering or vocal — of the name of God), which appeals to the religious persons. The *Bhagavad-Gītā* has eulogized the *japa*. As a matter of fact, all religions hold similar opinions on the benefits obtained from the repeated utterance of God's name. The philosophy related to *bhakti-yoga* is mostly dualistic in some sense or other.

The *yoga* of the realization of the Reality (*jñāna-yoga*) uses the *praṇava-japa* and the *praṇava-dhyāna* as a ladder to ascend the steps to reach the summit. Philosophically speaking, the *jñāna-yoga* is primarily non-dualistic. None the less, the *oṁkāra-japa* plays a prominent role in the spiritual practices of non-dualism.

The *Pātañjala-yoga* of eight limbs, otherwise known as the *aṣṭāṅga yoga* or the *rāja-yoga*, advocates the *japa* of the *praṇava*, the *oṁ* that designates *Īśvara* (God). If properly done, the *japa* becomes *dhyāna*, one of the higher limbs of the eightfold *yoga*.

Mantra-japa is vitally important in Tantra. Although Tantra-Yoga is an important branch of *yoga*, a few realize that Tantra has anything to do with *yoga*. The *Kuṇḍalinī Yoga* is an exclusive branch of Tantra. One can hardly separate *haṭha-yoga* and Tantra. *Bandhas*, *mudrās* and *nyāsas* are the contributions of Tantra-Yoga. A *tāntrika* can hardly achieve anything without the *puraścaraṇa japa*. Notwithstanding these facts, any book on *japa* rarely deals with any *tāntrika japa*.

It is heartening to note that *yoga* has been popularized throughout the world. Most *yoga* schools limit their activities to physical postures (*yogāsana*s), sometimes with a little addition of *prāṇāyāma* and meditation. Most *yoga* schools do not give much emphasis on the three higher limbs of the yogic practices, namely, *dhāraṇā*, *dhyāna* and *samādhi*. Yoga practices, for the improvement of physical health and for preventing and curing diseases, are not discredited here. At the same time, it is emphasized that the mental and the spiritual health can hardly be neglected. Further, it is to be noted that the primary goal of Yoga is spiritulization of oneself and that liberation (*mokṣa*) is to be sought by making Yoga a means.

We have a conviction that the *japa* technique of Yoga is comparatively easier than the other ones. In spite of this fact, many *yoga* schools hardly give any importance to this technique.

We went through the scanty number of *yoga* books on *japa*. A few of them are reasonably good and we have been immensely benefitted by them. Nevertheless, we have a feeling that a lacuna does exist and it is to be got over. And hence is this attempt to write this book.

With regard to *japa-yoga*, our approach has been holistic and synthetic. Essentially, we are non-dualistic and monotheistic in a wider frame which binds diverse theories of dualism, polytheism and pantheism. We are firm and steadfast about the fact that Being is formless and a single one only. At the same time, we do accept forms and multiplicity by accepting the phenomenon of manifestation from the Unmanifest and also by recognizing the psychological need of forms for avoiding abstractions and for better mental concretization. Thus, we have drawn no line of demarcation between *yoga* and *tantra*, Vedic and non-Vedic systems, dualism and non-dualism, form-worship and formless worship, devotion and knowledge, science and spirituality and the sundries.

This book on *japa-yoga* has systemetized *japa*s of diverse systems. It has elaborated the techniques in simplified ways. It focuses on the methods of doing the *japa*. It is up to the reader to choose one or more of the techniques of *japa* for his/her adoption out of the cafetaria-presentation.

The *japa* is usually regarded as a religious activity. We have not denied that. But we have philosophized it and that is the reason for short discourses here and there on different philosophical systems. As a religious activity, it is based on faith. As part of philosophy, it is based on rationality, logicality and analysis. We have leaned more on spirituality than on religion.

It is hard for some people to accept the *japa* as a science. We do not agree with them. This book on *japa-yoga* has a lot of science, especially medical science with special reference to the treatment of diseases. Any reader can practise the *japa* methods and ascertain the benefits obtained. Any medical scientist may do experimentation on the efficacy of the *japa*-methods for preventing and curing diseases. It is hoped that doctors, in the future, may prescribe the *japa*-techniques in addition to their medical and/or surgical therapies.

The *japa-sādhanā* is partly subjective and partly objective. Objectivity which is a key-word in scientific experimentation may not wisely exclude this partial subjectivity while evaluating the experimental results.

The *Pātañjala-yoga* does recognize the importance of the *japa*. But many *yoga* schools hardly include *japa* in their teaching. We have tried to associate the *japa* with the yogic *saṁyama* — the *dhāraṇā, dhyāna* and *samādhi,* done together. We have used the *japa* technique to achieve the status of *brāhmī-sthiti* (stay in *Brahman*), as recommended by the *Bhagavad-Gītā. Japa,* if sincerely and regularly practised, would be able to keep the body and mind healthy, to release the self (*apparently* bound *ātmā*) from bondage, to spiritualize the person and finally to attain liberation (to become *Brahman,* the Pure Consciousness).

We have designed the *japa* techniques for both *bhukti* (wordly fulfilment of benign types) and *mukti* (spiritual liberation). For the average person, it is wise to strike a balance. For a person who has already ascended many rungs of the spiritual ladder, *mukti* may be the only goal and the *japa,* along with other spiritual methods, may be the means.

The *japa-yoga* is simple in comparison with some of the other methods of *yoga*. A few methods other than the *japa* have also been associated with it. We hope, the readers will not only read this book, but also practise any of its techniques which they like most. If salvation is a far goal, mental peace should be a near one. And a tension-free, still and creative mind is not a small achievement. *Oṁ śāntiḥ śāntiḥ śāntiḥ.*

Sep. 5, 2006 **N.C. Panda**
(*Ācārya Śaktipāda*)

Acknowledgement

KNOWLEDGE leads to devotion, that, in turn, leads to salvation. Simple devotion, without knowledge, has the chance of ending in superstition. *Bhagavān* Vyāsa, the great, ancient Indian seer, after compiling the spoken Vedic literature (*śruti*) and writing the great epic, *The Mahābhārata*, wrote *The Bhāgavatam*, a superb piece of devotional scripture. *Ṛṣi* Patañjali adopted the main tenets of the Sāṅkhya philosophy. His contribution of the *Yoga-Sūtras* to the humanity is unparalleled in the annals of history. In this Yoga philosophy, he added the concept of *Īśvara* (God) to the atheistic Sāṅkhya metaphysics. He prescribed "merging and staying in *Īśvara* (*īśvara-praṇidhāna*)." This author has been very much inspired by revered Vyāsa and Patañjali. After writing the *jñāna-kāṇḍa* on cosmology and cosmogony, the fundamental Being and the phenomenal becomings (in *Māyā in Physics, The Vibrating Universe, Mind and Supermind, Cyclic Universe*), this author changed the direction of his mental journey to books like *Meditation, Yoga-Nidrā* and *Japa-Yoga*. He pays his obeisance to honourable Vyāsa, Patañjali and many others whose names are not mentioned here.

Sri Susheel Kumar Mittal, the Director of D.K. Printworld, has helped me a lot in publishing my books (except the first two, published by Motilal Banarsidass). I am very much grateful to Mittal Jee and his Publishing Organization.

My sincere thanks are due to Prof. Abhinna Chandra Sahu (my disciple) and Śrī Rabi Narayan Pradhan for their invaluable assistance in the production of the manuscript. I shall fail in my duty if I do not record my appreciation for the invaluable help rendered by Sri Amitabh Sahu, Sri Kahnu Charan Sahu, Sri Shambhunath Sahu, Smt. Sujata Sahu, Smt. Amita Sahu and Smt. Smita Sahu (all of them being my disciples). I also thank Shakuntala (my disciple and a staunch devotee of God), her son Bishwadeb and her daughter-in-law Minati for their whole-hearted support in the prodcution of this manuscript. I thankfully appreciate the secretarial assistance rendered by Sri Dhruba Charan Dehury, and the photography assistance rendered by Sri Bijoy Kumar Sahoo. My blessings are showered on Dwijesh (Dr. Dwijesh Kumar Panda), my youngest brother, who contributed some reference medical books.

Retinal detachment in both the eyes has deprived the author of 100 per cent vision in the right eye and 70 per cent vision in the left eye. His writing career still continues by the support of his family members: Prakash, Bikash and Bibhas — sons, and Smita (Ilu), Snigdha (Manu) and Arati (Runi) — daughters-in-law. He thanks and blesses them.

The author is a poet and a fiction writer. He loves God through loving His creation, both inanimate and animate. He feels that this life is not worth living without love. He thanks his granddaughters (Disha — Divyasha, Lisa — Anwesha, Soma — Arpita, Lopa — Lopamudra, Mita — Madhusmita, Nita — Nivedita) and his only one grandson (Munu — Siddharth) for their love which intensely enriches his emotional life. He thanks his daughter (Prema — Shephali) and son-in-law (Sudhir) for their affection mixed with reverence. Last but not the least, his special thanks are due to his wife (Manorama) who provides the motor power to this senile author whose physique is dry like the winter-fallen-leaves and whose mind is green like the spring-emerging-bud.

Sep. 5, 2006 **Nrusingh Charan Panda**
(*Ācārya Śaktipāda*)

Khanduali Mandir Road
Agastya Bhavan, 712 Sahid Nagar
Bhubaneswar-751 007
Orissa, India

Key to Transliteration

VOWELS

अ *a*	आ *ā*	इ *i*	ई *ī*	उ *u*	ऊ *ū*
(but)	(palm)	(it)	(beet)	(put)	(pool)
ऋ *ṛ*	ए *e*	ऐ *ai*	ओ *o*	औ *au*	
(rhythm)	(play)	(air)	(toe)	(loud)	

CONSONANTS

Guttural	क *ka*	ख* *kha*	ग *ga*	घ *gha*	ङ *ṅa*
	(skate)	(blockhead)	(gate)	(ghost)	(sing)
Palatal	च *ca*	छ* *cha*	ज *ja*	झ *jha*	ञ *ña*
	(chunk)	(catch him)	(john)	(hedgehog)	(bunch)
Cerebral	ट *ṭa*	ठ* *ṭha*	ड *ḍa*	ढ* *ḍha*	ण* *ṇa*
	(start)	(anthill)	(dart)	(godhead)	(under)
Dental	त *ta*	थ *tha*	द *da*	ध* *dha*	न *na*
	(path)	(thunder)	(that)	(breathe)	(numb)
Labial	प *pa*	फ* *pha*	ब *ba*	भ *bha*	म *ma*
	(spin)	(philosophy)	(bin)	(abhor)	(much)
Semi-	य *ya*	र *ra*	ल *la*	व *va*	
vowels	(young)	(drama)	(luck)	(vile)	
Sibilants	श *śa*	ष *ṣa*	स *sa*	ह *ha*	
	(shove)	(bushel)	(so)	(hum)	
Others	क्ष *kṣa*	त्र *tra*	ज्ञ *jña*	ळ* *ḷ*	ॠ* *ṝ*
(*kṣatriya*)	(*triśūla*)	(*jñānī*)	(*play*)		

अं (ं) *ṁ anusvāra* (nasalisation of preceding vowel) like *saṁskṛti*

अः *visarga* = *ḥ* (aspiration of preceding vowel) like (*prātaḥ*)

ऽ *Avagraha* consonant #'consonant (like:- *ime 'vasthitā*)

Anusvāra at the end of a line is presented by m (म्) and not ṁ

* No exact English equivalents for these letters.

Contents

Prologue vii

Acknowledgement xi

Key to Transliteration xiv

Abbreviations xxi

List of Figures xxiii

Chapter 1
Theoretical Introduction to Japa-yoga

The Meaning of the Term Japa-Yoga 2
Japa-Yajña, the Best One among Sacrifices 2
Japa-Yoga in Yoga-Vedānta 3
Pātañjala Japa-Yoga 3
The Vedic and Vedāntic Sanctification of Praṇava 4
Four Pādas and three Mātrās of Oṁ 8
Oṅkāra — the Forerunner of all Mantras 9
Oṅkāra-Japa 9
Three Varieties of Japa 10
Īśvara-Praṇidhāna 11
Mantra-japa in the Framework of Pātañjala Yoga 13
Japa in yoga-Vedānta 19
The Need for the Repetition of the Mantra 20

Prescriptions & Proscriptions in Pātañjala Yoga 22
Japa in the Yoga of Devotion **28**
Bhakti-Yoga in Non-Dualism 31
Symbol-Worship in Bhakti-Yoga 32
Monotheism versus Polytheism 34
Forms of Japa in Bhakti-Yoga 38
Nāma-Japa 38
Mantra-Japa 38
Likhita-Japa 39
Kīrtana 39
Devotion — the Key Factor in Bhakti-Yoga 40
Japa at the Terminal Stage of Life 45
Japa-Yoga in Tantra **46**
Deities in Tantra 47
The Right-path (Dakṣiṇācārī) Tantra 47
The Śākta and the Tāntrika 48
The Special Features of Tantra 49
Tāntric Mantras 60
The Mechanism of Action of Mantra-Japa **63**
The Mechanism of Action of the Praṇava-Japa and the Ajapā-Japa 63
The Mechanism of Action of the Devotional Japa 66
The Mechanism of Action of the Tāntric Japa 71
The Psychological and the Physiological Mechanism of the Action of Japa 77

Chapter 2
Practice of Japa-Yoga

Preliminary Preparations and Prerequisites for Mantra-Japa **93**
Preparation 93
Prerequisites 98

- Observances of Yama and Niyama 99
- The Need of a Guru 101
- Guru-Vāda 103
- The Choice of a Mantra 107
- Number of Japa and Counting Technique 110
- Type of Japa Recommended 118

The Practice of Mantra-Japa in Yoga-Vedānta 120

- Oṅkāra Japa 120
- Ajapā-Japa 123
- The Japa of the Gāyatrī-Mantra 125
  - The Gāyatrī-Mantra and its Interpretation 125
  - The Deity of the Gāyatrī Mantra 129
  - The Japa of the Gāyatrī-mantra in the Vedic System 134
  - Benefits from the Gāyatrī Japa 137

The Tantricization of the Gāyatrī Mantra 137

- Ācamana 140
- Prāṇāyāma 141
- Saṅkalpa 141
- Kara-Nyāsaḥ 143
- Ṣaḍaṅga-Nyāsaḥ 144
- Pre-Japa and Post-Japa Mudrās 145
- Worshipping Mother Gāyatrī before Japa 159
- Japa of the Gāyatrī-Mantra 159
- Conclusoin of the Gāyatrī Sādhanā 159
- The Practice of Mantra-Japa in Bhakti-Yoga 160
- Purāṇic Gāyatrī-Mantras 160
  - Gaṇeśa-Gāyatrī 160
  - Brahmā-Gāyatrī 161
  - Viṣṇu Gāyatrī 161
  - Nṛsiṁha-Gāyatrī 162
  - Kṛṣṇa-Gāyatrī 162
  - Rāma-Gāyatrī 163

Rudra-Gāyatrī 163
Sūrya-Gāyatrī 163
Hanumat-Gāyatrī 164
Durgā-Gāyatrī 164
Lakṣmī-Gāyatrī 165
Kālī-Gāyatrī 166
Sarasvatī-Gāyatrī 166
Śakti-Gāyatrī 167
Nāma-Japa 167
Some Mantras for Japa 167
The Practice of Mantra-Japa in Tantra 171
Mānasa Pūjā of Mother Durgā 171
Some Tāntric Mantras for Japa 173
Gaṇeśa Mantra 173
Durgā Mantra 173
Lakṣmī Mantra 173
Sarasvatī Mantra 173
Kālī Mantra 173
Dakṣiṇa-Kālī Mantra 174
Gaurī Mantra 174
Parameśvarī Mantra 174
Cāmuṇḍā Mantra 174
Navārṇa Mantra 174
Mahā-Mṛtyuñjaya-Mantra 181
Tryakṣara-Mṛtyuñjaya-Mantra 184
Dvādaśākṣara-Mṛtyuñjaya-Mantra 184
Mahā-Mṛtyuñjaya-Mantra-Japa-Sādhanā 184
Kīrtana 191
Vedic and Vedāntic Kīrtana 192
Kīrtana of Bhakti-Yoga 193
Anuṣṭhāna 196
Japa-Yoga for all Religions 198
The Application of the Practices 199

Chapter 3
Applications of the Mantras of Yoga-Vedānta

Oṁ the Easiest and the Best Mantra for Everybody 202
God-Realization 202
Oṅkāra-japa in Karma-Yoga 204
Oṅkāra-japa for Mental Peace and Tranquillity 205
Oṅkāra-japa for Correcting Psychiatric Problems 207
Oṅkāra-japa for Curing Psychosomatic Diseases 209
Oṅkāra-japa in the Treatment of Hypertension 211
Oṅkāra-japa Focused on Diseased Organs 212
Oṅkāra-japa for the Fulfilment of a Worldly Desire 217
Oṅkāra-kīrtana 219
Ajapā-Japa 220
So 'haṁ Kīrtana 223
Gāyatrī-Japa 224
Niṣkāma Gāyatrī-Japa 224
Sakāma Gāyatrī-japa 225
Mantras of Bhakti-Yoga 229
Tāntrika Mantras 232
Sampuṭīkaraṇa of a Tāntrik Mantra 232
The Japa of a Vedic cum Tāntric Mantra 235
Japa in Āsanas for the Cure of Joint and Spinal Problems 239
Bīja-Japa in Vīrāsana (Vīryāsana) 244
Bīja-Japa in Makarāsana 247

Japa in Ūrdhvamukhī Tāḍāsana 249
Japa in Meru-Agra-Vakrāsana 250
Japa in Meru-Pārśva-Vakrāsana 251
Japa in Bhujaṅgāsana 251
Japa in Śalabhāsana 253
Japa in Paścimottānāsana 255
Japa with Mudrās for Specific Health Problems **257**
Immuno-Fortification 257
Mudrā-Japa for Curing Sinus-Infection and Migraine 263
Mudrā-japa for Relief from Hypertension 266
Mudrā-Japa for Relief from Heart Diseases 269
Mudrā-Japa to Control the Disease of Diabetes 274
Mudrā-Japa for Relief from Hepatic Disorders 280
Mudrā-japa for Relief from Chronic Constipation 283
Japa-Therapy in Cancer 291
SOS in Yoga-Tantra **295**
The Japa of Sampuṭa-Mantras 296
The Japa of Some other Trāṇa (SOS)-Mantras 297
Japa for Mukti and Bhukti **299**

Glossary **305**

Bibliography **339**

Index **345**

Abbreviations

AV	:	*Atharvaveda*
BG	:	*Bhagavad-Gītā*
Bhā	:	*Bhāgavatam*
BS	:	*Brahma-Sūtram*
BU	:	*Bṛhadāraṇyaka Upaniṣad*
CU	:	*Chāndogyopaniṣad*
DBhā	:	*Devī-Bhāgavatam*
KTU	:	*Kaṭhopaniṣad*
MAU	:	*Māṇḍūkyopaniṣad*
Mbhā	:	*Mahābhārata*
MKG	:	*Māṇḍūkya Kārikā* of Gauḍapāda
MS	:	*Manu-Smṛti*
MSJ	:	*Mīmāṁsā-Sūtra* of Jaimini
MTU	:	*Maitrī Upaniṣad*
MUU	:	*Muṇḍakopaniṣad*
PST	:	*Prapañcasāra-Tantram* of Śaṅkarācārya
PŚTCM	:	Pūrṇānanda's *Śrītattvacintāmaṇi*
PU	:	*Praśnopaniṣad*

PYD	:	*Pātañjala-Yoga-Darśanam*
PYDVB	:	*Pātañjala-Yoga-Darśanam, Vyāsa-Bhāṣyam*
R̥V	:	*R̥gveda*
ŚB	:	*Śāṅkara Bhāṣyam*
ŚBrā	:	*Śatapatha Brāhmaṇa*
SL	:	*Saundarya-laharī* of Śaṅkarācārya
SPS	:	*Sāṅkhya-Pravacana-Sūtra*
ŚT	:	*Śāradā-Tilaka*
ŚU	:	*Śvetāśvatara Upaniṣad*
TĀ	:	*Taittirīya Āraṇyaka*
VC	:	*Vivekacūḍāmaṇi* of Śaṅkarācārya
Vāpu	:	*Vāyu Purāṇa*
YV	:	*Yajurveda*

List of Figures

fig. 1.1 : The courses of the *suṣumṇā*, the *iḍā* and the *piṅgalā*

fig. 1.2 : The web-structure of the *nāḍīs* in the subtle body

fig. 1.3 : The seven *cakra*s in the subtle body

fig. 2.1 : *Siddhāsana*

fig. 2.2 : *Padmāsana*

fig. 2.3 : *Svastikāsana*

fig. 2.4 : *Vajrāsana*

fig. 2.5 : *Sukhāsana*

fig. 2.6 : *Cin-mudrā*

fig. 2.7 : *Jñāna-mudrā*

fig. 2.8 : Clockwise and anticlockwise sliding of the rosary beads

fig. 2.9 : The positions of the fingers and the thumb in rolling the rosary beads

fig. 2.10 : The rosary inside the hanging *gomukhī*

fig. 2.11 : The use of the *uttarīya* while counting the rosary beads

fig. 2.12 : *Karamālā* counting of a *deva-mantra*, with two *meru*s in the middle finger
(a) Counting of ten (b) Counting of eight

fig. 2.13 : *Karamālā* counting of a *śakti-mantra*, with two *meru*s in the index finger
(a) Counting of ten (b) Counting of eight

fig. 2.14 : The *oṅkāra* symbol

fig. 2.15 : The picture of mother Sarasvatī (Purāṇic)
fig. 2.16 : The picture of mother Gāyatrī (*tāntrika*)
fig. 2.17 : *Mudrā* : *sumukham*
fig. 2.18 : *Mudrā* : *sampuṭam*
fig. 2.19 : *Mudrā* : *vitatam*
fig. 2.20 : *Mudrā* : *vistṛtam*
fig. 2.21 : *Mudrā* : *dvimukham*
fig. 2.22 : *Mudrā* : *trimukham*
fig. 2.23 : *Mudrā* : *caturmukham*
fig. 2.24 : *Mudrā* : *pañcamukham*
fig. 2.25 : *Mudrā* : *ṣaṇmukham*
fig. 2.26 : *Mudrā* : *adhomukham*
fig. 2.27 : *Mudrā* : *vyāpakāñjalim*
fig. 2.28 : *Mudrā* : *śakaṭam*
fig. 2.29 : *Mudrā* : *yamapāśam*
fig. 2.30 : *Mudrā* : *grathitam*
fig. 2.31 : *Mudrā* : *unmukhonmukham*
fig. 2.32 : *Mudrā* : *pralambam*
fig. 2.33 : *Mudrā* : *muṣṭikam*
fig. 2.34 : *Mudrā* : *matsyaḥ*
fig. 2.35 : *Mudrā* : *kūrmaḥ*
fig. 2.36 : *Mudrā* : *vārāhakam*
fig. 2.37 : *Mudrā* : *siṁhākrāntam*
fig. 2.38 : *Mudrā* : *mahākrāntam*
fig. 2.39 : *Mudrā* : *mudgara*
fig. 2.40 : *Mudrā* : *pallavam*
fig. 2.41 : *Mudrā* : *surabhiḥ*
fig. 2.42 : *Mudrā* : *cetanā*
fig. 2.43 : *Mudrā* : *vairāgyam*
fig. 2.44 : *Mudrā* : *yoniḥ*

fig. 2.45 : *Mudrā* : *śaṅkhaḥ*
fig. 2.46 : *Mudrā* : *paṅkajam*
fig. 2.47 : *Mudrā* : *liṅgam*
fig. 2.48 : *Mudrā* : *nirvāṇam*
fig. 2.49 : *Śrīdurgā-navārṇa-mantra-yantra*
(a) *Durgā-yantra* (b) *Navārṇa-yantra*
fig. 2.50 : *Muṣṭi-mudrā*
fig. 2.51 : *Śakti-mudrā*
fig. 2.52 : *Mṛga* or *sāraṅga-mudrā*
fig. 2.53 : *Pañcānana-mudrā*
fig. 3.1 : *Śavāsana*
fig. 3.2 : *Mātṛ-mudrā*
fig. 3.3 : *Vīrāsana*
(a) with *cin-mudrā* (b) with palms facing downward, resting on the knees
fig. 3.4 : *Makarāsana*
(a) Front view (b) Side view
fig. 3.5 : *Ūrdhvamukhī tāḍāsana*
fig. 3.6 : *Meru-agra-vakrāsana*
fig. 3.7 : *Meru-pārśva-vakrāsana*
(a) Left spinal twist (b) Right spinal twist
fig. 3.8 : *Bhujaṅgāsana*
fig. 3.9 : *Ardha-śalabhāsana*
(a) Right (b) Left
fig. 3.10 : *Śalabhāsana*
fig. 3.11 : *Paścimottānāsana*
fig. 3.12 : *Kāma-mudrā*
fig. 3.13 : *Kaṇṭha-mudrā*
fig. 3.14 : *Nīlakaṇṭhī-mudrā*
fig. 3.15 : *Ākāśī-mudrā*

fig. 3.16 : *Dhenu-mudrā*
fig. 3.17 : *Agrasparśī tāḍāsana*
fig. 3.18 : *Bhadrāsana*
fig. 3.19 : *Madhyabhedī-prāṇāsana*
fig. 3.20 : *Prāṇa-mudrā*
fig. 3.21 : *Vāyu-mudrā*
fig. 3.22 : *Hasta-ṭaṅka-mudrā*
fig. 3.23 : *Pada-ṭaṅka-mudrā*
fig. 3.24 : *Piṇḍadā-mudrā*
fig. 3.25 : *Kuja-mudrā*
fig. 3.26 : *Sūrya-mudrā*
fig. 3.27 : *Kulīra* (*pādāgni*)*-mudrā*
fig. 3.28 : *Samāna-mudrā*
fig. 3.29 : *Samāna-nābhi mudrā*
fig. 3.30 : *Bahupadī-mudrā*
fig. 3.31 : *Kara-pārśva-mudrā*
(a) *Mukulita* (b) *Ardha-mukulita* (c) *Vistārita*
fig. 3.32 : *Varuṇa-mudrā* (*Jala-mudrā, Āpo-mudrā*)
fig. 3.33 : *Pavana-muktāsana*
(a) Right leg (b) Left leg (c) Both legs
fig. 3.34 : *Pṛthvī-mudrā*
fig. 3.35 : *Apāna-mudrā*
fig. 3.36 : *Upastha-mudrā*
fig. 3.37 : *Dvināḍa-paṅkaja-mudrā*
fig. 3.38 : *Pārṣṇi-mudrā*
fig. 3.39 : *Tattva-mudrā*
fig. 3.40 : *Kleśahā-mudrā*
fig. 3.41 : *Nakha-vidīrṇa-mudrā*

1

Theoretical Introduction to Japa-Yoga

JAPA-YOGA is mainly a *bhakti-yoga* (the *yoga* of devotion). Believers in God, a fundamental, spiritual Being, who is the foundation of the entire universe (*viśvādhāra*), its creator, sustainer and annihilator, and the all-controller (*sarveśvara*) are most likely to be benefitted by the *japa-yoga*. Steadfastness in faith with true, sincere love and respect for the fundamental Being is the primary prerequisite for this type of *yoga*. This sort of mental preparedness may be expressed by the Sanskrit word *niṣṭhā*.

It is not a fact that atheists (*nāstika*s) or doubters (*saṁśayavādin*s) or agnostics cannot be at all benefitted by the *japa-yoga*. Here it may be relevant to refer to a classical legend. Ratnākara was a robber. Circumstantially, he realized that he had to give up robbery and adopt a spiritual life. He sat in meditation, with Lord Rāma's *nāma-japa* (*nāma* = name; *japa* = repetition). Ratnākara could not utter the sacred name, Rāma. He started with *marā* (meaning "corpse"). After many days of the repetition of this word, he automatically uttered Rāma. He became the Holy Saint, Vālmīki, the author of the Epic, the *Rāmāyaṇa*. This legend clearly states that the transformation of a person is possible and that the *nāma-japa* has the capacity to convert a die-hard atheist into a theist.

The Meaning of the Term Japa-Yoga

The Sanskrit word *yoga* has been derived from the verb-root √*yuj*, meaning "the act of yoking, adding, joining, attaching, harnessing." Contextually, it means the act of yoking the mind and/or the self (*ātmā*) with God or the Super-Self (*Paramātmā*). The Sanskrit word *japa* has been derived from the verb-root √*jap*, meaning "to repetitively utter in a low voice; to mutter/whisper especially prayers or incantations; to pray in a low voice; to invoke or call upon in a low voice; to whisper repeatedly; to mutter prayers, repeating, in a murmuring tone, passages from a scripture or charms, spells or names of a deity."

Japa-Yajña, the Best One among Sacrifices

The Sanskrit word *yajña* has been derived from the verb root √*yaj*, meaning "to worship, adore, honour." The word *yajña* is a comprehensive term which encompasses a variety of devotional rituals such as worship, devotion, prayer, oblation, offering. Any selfless action for the benefit of others and the welfare of God's creation is a sacrifice (The killing of animals, birds and human beings for offering to a deity, practised in some primitive cults is a superstition, a blind faith, a social evil and a heinous crime. It is sometimes wrongly termed as a sacrifice.). When the word sacrifice is used with reference to *yajña*, it has the connotation of the Vedic oblation, sacred offering with love, devotion, altruism and self-denial. The Sanskrit word *tyāga* has some relevance, in meaning, to "sacrifice." When the word *yajña* is used as "sacrifice" in general, it may carry the usual religious and ritual meaning, or it may carry a secular meaning with reference to self-denial or self-abnegation for the welfare of others, for that of the society or of the whole universe.

We come across the term *japa-yajña* in the *Bhagavad-Gītā*.[1] Lord Śrīkṛṣṇa says to Arjuna: "I am the *japa-yajña* among the *yajña*s." This clearly shows that the *japa-yajña* is the best among all forms of *yajña*s. The word *yajñānām* is the genitive plural of the word *yajña*. Contextually, the *Gītā* uses the word *yajña* in a theistic context. It is obvious from this use that forms of *yajña* are many. The best form of *yajña*, according to the *Gītā*, is *japa-yajña*.

Japa-Yoga in Yoga-Vedānta

Pātañjala Japa-Yoga

Ṛṣi Patañjali, in his aphorisms on his Yoga Philosophy, has recognised *japa* as a form of *yoga*.[2] He emphasizes that one has to think of the meaning of the *japa-mantra* while mentally or verbally repeating the *mantra*.[3] Simply mechanical repetition, without thinking of the meaning of the *mantra*, has little usefulness.

Some Western medical research workers, while experimenting on *mantra-japa* done at the beginning of meditation, have substituted *oṁ* with monosyllables such as "one," "kat," "gab," "ku," et cetera, and have claimed that the *yoga*-practitioners have obtained equal success. For persons who do not have realization of the meaning of *oṁ*, they take it for granted that *oṁ* and "one" or any other meaningless monosyllable are equivalent for this purpose. It is, however, not a fact. The Western *yoga*-practitioners on whom research experiments were conducted mechanically accepted *oṁ*, "one" and other monosyllables as equivalents without pondering over the meaning of *oṁ*. Hence, was the non-difference in the effects produced by *yoga*.

Some *tāntrika mantra*s have mystical seed-syllables (*bīja*s) that have *apparently* no meanings. The utterance of these seed-syllables, with proper pronunciation, however, produces profound effects. In such cases too, the referential meaning of the *bīja* is to be pondered over. Here we cite some examples. The monosyllable *bīja*s *aiṁ*, *śrīṁ* and *krīṁ* refer to Mother Sarasvatī, Lakṣmī and Kālī, respectively. The monosyllable *bīja*s *oṁ*, *haṁ*, *yaṁ*, *raṁ*, *vaṁ* and *laṁ* refer to the *cakra*s *ājñā*, *viśuddhi*, *anāhata*, *maṇipūra*, *svādhiṣṭhāna* and *mūlādhāra*, respectively. Patañjali's insistence on the reflection on the meaning of the *mantra* while doing *japa* has no exception.

Patañjali's aphorisms, antecedent to his reference to *japa* (*PYD*, I.28), may be mentioned here. He generally accepts the metaphysics of Kapila's Sāṅkhya. But, the former's philosophy is theistic whereas the latter's is atheistic (although not materialistic). Patañjali recommends a complete surrender to God (*Īśvara*).[4] *Īśvara* is designated by the *praṇava* or *oṁ*.[5] If *Īśvara* is *vācya* (nameable, predicable), His *vācaka* (name or designation) is *oṁ* (otherwise called *praṇava*). In the Yoga of Patañjali, *japa* is a form of *yoga*, and it is the repetitive utterance of *oṁ*, with meditative thought on its meaning.

The Vedic and Vedāntic Sanctification of Praṇava

The monosyllable *oṁ*, the *praṇava* and the *udgītha* are not different. The etymological meaning of the word *praṇava* is indicative of its significance.[6] Any Vedic *mantra*, at the time of fire sacrifice (*agnihotra*), is recited with *oṁ* in the beginning and *svāhā* in the end. No *mantra* is sanctified, if not begun with *oṁ*. The *Chāndogya Upaniṣad* has a number of references to the *praṇu* or *praṇava*, the *oṅkāra* and the *udgītha*, which carry the same meaning.[7] The monosyllable *oṁ* is the essence of the Vedas.[8] It is the *praṇu*, the *oṅkāra* and the *udgītha*.[9] It is to be worshipped and to be meditated upon.[10] One is to take refuge in this monosyllable.[11] It is mentioned elsewhere in this book that the inanimate world (macro and micro) is continually sounding *oṁ* in a very subtle tone. This fact has been corroborated by the Upaniṣad.[12] The *ajapā-japa* is very important for a treatise like this on the *japa-yoga*. The Upaniṣad mentions that the heart sings[13] (*hṛd gāyati*) and the *prāṇa* continually sounds *oṁ* in a subtle manner.[14]

The solid, the liquid and the gaseous states of matter and energy are in decreasing order of grossness or in increasing order of subtlety. Space (*ākāśa*) is the subtlest material existence among the *bhūta*s. It is material and full; it is not a void or a vacuum. This Vedāntic concept of space is in contrast with the ancient Greek philosophical concept which deemed space as an absolute void. Only in the last half of the twentieth century did the particle physicists and the quantum physicists realize that, in super-heated condition, hot space can generate micro-particles and particles. This fact was, however, recognized by the Vedāntists and the Vaiśeṣika philosophers of India. In the expanding phase of the universe, *ākāśa* is the origin of all the materiality; in the contracting phase, it is the final goal.[15] This is not the whole truth, however. *Praṇava* (*oṁ*) is the source of *ākāśa*. *Oṅkāra*, verily, is all this[16] and is to be worshipped and meditated.

Some other Vedāntic references on the *praṇava* are worth mentioning here. The *Gītā* declares that the *praṇava* is the essence of all the Vedas (*praṇavaḥ sarvavedeṣu*)[17] and that the *Ṛgveda*, the *Sāmaveda* and the *Yajurveda* are to be known as the sacred *oṅkāra*.[18] The *Maitrī Upaniṣad* eulogizes the *oṅkāra*[19] and states that the *praṇava* is the *udgītha* and that the *udgītha* is the *praṇava*.[20] The *Muṇḍaka Upaniṣad* compares the *praṇava*, the self (*ātmā*) and *Brahman* with the bow, the arrow and the target, respectively. Through the help of the *praṇava*, if correctly hit, one becomes united with *Brahman*.[21] The *Praśnopaniṣad* states that *oṁ* is both God (*Īśvara*) and the attributeless *Brahman*.[22] The *Śvetāśvatara Upaniṣad* categorically says that the vision of *Īśvara* (God) can be achieved by means of *oṁ*, the *praṇava*. It presents a simile of a lower friction stick (the body) and an upper friction stick (*oṁ*). It compares the operation of friction with meditation through which one gets a vision of God.[23]

Śaṅkara says that the *oṁ* is represented as the symbol (*pratīka*) of the Supreme (*paramātmā*) and therefore the means of the meditation of the Supreme.[24]

Śaṅkara uses the word *svādhyāya* in his interpretation of the *udgītha*.[25] This word has gained immense importance in Yoga. Patañjali has included in his *niyama*s.[26] Radhakrishnan has quoted a Sanskrit verse in connection with *svādhyāya* and *praṇava-japa*.[27] He defines *svādhyāya* as the study of the scriptures dealing with liberation or the repetition of the *praṇava*.[28] It is the study of the scriptures and recitation of *mantra*s which lead to purity of mind (*cittaśuddhi*).

The *Māṇḍūkyopaniṣad* gives all the significance of the *praṇava* (*oṁ*) in a nutshell as follows:

> The syllable *oṁ* is all this. Its explanation follows. All the past, the present and the future are encompassed in the syllable *oṁ* only. And whatever else exists beyond the threefold time is the syllable *oṁ* only.[29]

In other words, this statement may be paraphrased: The syllable *oṁ*, which symbolizes *Brahman*, stands for the manifested universe of matter and energy, the past, the present and the future, as well as the unmanifested Absolute.

There is also the mention of the *praṇava* (*oṅkāra*) in a number of places in the *Bhagavad-Gītā*. This *oṁ* is the quintessence of all the four Vedas.[30] The *Gītā* prescribes to utter the monosyllable *oṁ* and contemplate on its meaning at the beginning of any sacred function. It unavoidably precedes all *mantras*.[31] The sacredness of *oṁ* has been emphasized in the *Gītā*; this monosyllable purifies the body and the mind.[32]

Sarasvatī, the consort or power (*śakti*) of Brahmā (God, one and the only one, who takes the role of the creation of the universe), plays her musical string instrument (*vīṇā*) which generates the primal sound *oṁ* with innumerable musical notes. The notes are produced by the three strings (*guṇas*: *sattva, rajas, tamas*) of the *vīṇā*. The Vedic scriptures[33] make use of Mother Sarasvatī's *vīṇā* as a symbol (*pratīka*) for the modern superstring theory of physics. According to this theory, the universe of diversity is the product of the vibrations of the strings of the *vīṇā*, played by Mother Sarasvatī.[34]

Four Pādas and three Mātrās of Oṁ

The *Māṇḍūkyopaniṣad* states: "All this, verily, is *Brahman*. This self is *Brahman*. It has four quarters (*pāda*s)."[35] "This self is designated by the sacred syllable *oṁ*, consisting of three *mātrā*s. The *pāda*s are the *mātrā*s and the *mātrā*s are the *pāda*s. The *mātrā*s are *a*, *u*, and *ṁ*."[36]

The common meaning of *mātrā* is "measure." Here the word contextually means "constituent units." According to the conjunction rule of Sanskrit grammar, *a* and *u* combine to form *o*. The three *guṇa*s (attributes, strings), namely, *sattva*, *raja*s and *tama*s, are represented by *a*, *u*, and *ṁ*, respectively.

The four *pāda*s (quarters) have been described by the *Māṇḍūkyopaniṣad*. The first *pāda* is *vaiśvānara* whose sphere of activity is the waking (*jāgarita*) state.[37] The second *pāda* is *taijasa* whose sphere of activity is the dream (*svapna*) state.[38] The third *pāda* is *prājña* whose sphere of activity is the state of deep sleep (*suṣupti*).[39] The fourth *pāda* is the *turīya* (literally meaning "fourth"). It is the state of the Absolute *Brahman*, formless, attributeless, functionless, non-relational, non-dual, non-cosmic, Saccidānanda (*Sat* = Existence; *Cit* = Pure Consciousness; *Ānanda* = Pure Bliss).[40]

These are the four states of the Self (*Ātmā*). The first two states, namely, the *vaiśvānara* and the *taijasa*, refer to the activities of the individual self (*jīvātmā*). The external world is experienced in the *vaiśvānara* state. The internal world (impressions printed in the *antaḥkaraṇa*) is experienced in the *taijasa* state. The *prājña* state refers to *Īśvara* (God or *Paramātmā*).[41] It may not, however, be misconstrued that *vaiśvānara*, *taijasa* and *prājña* are different. Gauḍapāda says: "It is the one alone who is known in the three states."[42]

The fourth state (*turīya*) is devoid of *mātrā* (*amātra*).[43] It cannot be made use of (*avyavahārya*). The whole universe is resolved into it (*prapañcopaśama*). In *turīya*, neither is there the sense-perceptible, external world, nor is there the inner world of the *antaḥkaraṇa*. This a fully non-dual state (*advaita*), benign (*śiva*) and absolutely peaceful (*śānta*). In both *suṣupti* and *turīya*, the consciousness of the external objects and the mental impressions (*smṛti* and *saṁskāra*s) vanishes. But the *prājña* in *suṣupti* is associated with a latent seed of consciousness while this does not exist in *turīya*.[44]

The four *pāda*s and the three *mātrā*s have already been referred to. *Vaiśvānara*, in the waking state, is the *mātrā a*.[45] *Taijasa*, in the dream state, is the *mātrā u*.[46] *Prājña*, in the deep sleep, is the *mātrā ṁ*.[47] *Turīya*, the *amātra* (devoid of *mātrā*) state, is the whole of the monosyllable *oṁ*.[48]

Oṅkāra — the Forerunner of all Mantras

Oṅkāra (*oṁ*) itself is the monosyllable (*ekākṣara*) *mantra*. This is the best one among all *mantra*s. One does not need any other *mantra* if one sincerely and steadfastly meditates on it.

Praṇava (*oṁ*) is the bridge among *mantra*s. A *mantra* does not gain its full sanctity unless the *praṇava* precedes it.[49] The *Chāndogya Upaniṣad*[50] recommends that one should sound out *oṁ* while reciting the *mantra*s of the Vedas.

Oṅkāra-Japa

The Pātañjala Yoga Darśanam has two aphorisms in connection with the *praṇava* (*oṁ*). The first one says that

Īśvara (God) is designated by the symbol *oṁ*.[51] In this *sūtra*, *tasya* (his) refers to *Īśvara* (God). The comprehension of two preceding *sūtras*[52] is a prerequisite for the full understanding of this *sūtra*. The second *sūtra*[53] with reference to the *praṇava* prescribes the *japa* of the *praṇava*, with the concurrent reflection on its meaning. Previously, it has been mentioned that complete surrender to God is *Īśvara-praṇidhāna*. This meaning is not denied here. But the actual significance and the elaborate meaning of *Īśvara-praṇidhāna* are being given here with reference to Patañjali's *sūtras* (*PYD*, I.23 and I.28). Before we proceed further, we would like to present the three varieties of *japa*.

THREE VARIETIES OF JAPA

Mantra-japa is done in one out of three ways, namely, *vaikharī*, *upāṁśu* and *mānasika*. The variety is known as *vaikharī* when the *mantra* is pronounced and repeated verbally. Persons in the immediate surrounding can hear the *vaikharī japa*. In the *upāṁśu* variety, the *japa* is done in a whisper or humming, with the movement of the lips. To other persons present in the vicinity, the *japa* is inaudible. The *japa* is *mānasika*, when it is mentally repeated, without producing any sound, either loud or humming. In any of the three varieties, simply mechanical repetition of the *mantra* is not enough. While doing the *japa*, meditation on the meaning of the *mantra* is to be done, as recommended by Maharṣi Patañjali.

Pratyāhāra (the withdrawal of the senses) is one out of the eight limbs of *Pātañjala Yoga*. This can be achieved through a number of means, and *vaikharī japa* is one of the many means. Of course, the main purpose of *japa* is not for practising *pratyāhāra*. For non-adepts in *yoga*, *vaikharī japa* is recommended in the initial stage. The loudness of the *japa* is conducive to concentration on the meaning of the *mantra*. It shuts out all extraneous thoughts and stops them from re-entering into the mind. In the course of practice, one may proceed from the *vaikharī* to the *upāṁśu* variety and finally to the *mānasika* variety.

The *upāṁśu japa* is better than the *vaikharī* variety and the *mānasika japa* is better than the *upāṁśu* variety. Although the *mānasika* variety is the best among the three, it is not very suitable for the beginner since his mind is prone to distractions during the *japa* in silence. Some tāntric *mantras*, especially with seeds (*bīja*), produce better effects if pronounced verbally. The waves they produce, the height of the waves, the wavelengths and their frequency have significance in producing the desired effects. Hence, it is recommended that the *vaikharī* variety is to be adopted for such special purposes.

The *praṇava-japa* recommended in the *Pātañjala Yoga* should be done mentally in silence. The *mānasika* variety of the *japa* is indispensable especially for *saṁyama* (*dhāraṇā*, *dhyāna* and *samādhi* done together).

Īśvara-Praṇidhāna

The Sanskrit word *Īśvara* means the Ruler or the Controller of the universe or God. The Sanskrit word *praṇidhāna* (*pra-ni-√dhā + lyuṭ*) means to give the whole attention to, attention paid to or profoundly meditate upon. The relevant *yoga*-aphorism[54] has already been interpreted as complete surrender to God. This interpretation is popular, but, strictly from etymological point of view, it is not precisely correct.

Since God is designated by the syllable *oṁ*, for fixing one's attention on God, one has to repeat this syllable, with full contemplation on its meaning. Here lies the significance of the *yoga-sūtra* on the *mantra-japa*.[55] The repetition of the *mantra* may be verbal (*vaikharī*), humming (*upāṁśu*) or silent and mental (*mānasika*).

One who does the *oṅkāra-japa* should have strong faith in God and one-pointedness in concentration (*ekāgratā*). In the course of the repetition of the monosyllable, with concomitant contemplation on its meaning, one gradually plunges into *tanmayatā* (the action of plunging and immersing into God; *tat* + *mayaṭ*, *tat* meaning that (God) and *mayaṭ* meaning filled or full). In the final state of the *oṅkāra-japa*, one reaches the fourth state (*turīya*) in which the difference between the object and the subject is obliterated and the attributeless state of the absolute *Brahman* is attained.

In fact, in the course of *oṅkāra-japa*, one progressively experiences four states of existence. One starts from the *vaiśvānara* state, in which the external world (including one's body and internal gross organs) is experienced. Next, the transition takes place from the *vaiśvānara* to the *taijasa*, in which the *saṁskāra*s in the *antaḥkaraṇa* and the *smṛti* (memory store) are experienced. The *prājña* is the next transitional state, in which the individual self (*jīvātmā*) merges in *Īśvara* (God), like sugar crystals in an unsaturated aqueous solution. In spite of the solution, the invisible sugar has its own identity, although not manifested to the naked eye. Duality still exists between the individual self and the Supreme Self; the former is still in the possession of the experience of "I am" (*asmitā*). Finally, this *asmitā* is lost, and the individual self becomes *Brahman*, without the distinction of object and subject. This is the *turīya* state, in which complete non-duality is established.

Through *oṅkāra-japa*, the progression from the state of the *vaiśvānara* to that of the *turīya* can be achieved by practice. In this connection, the *Muṇḍakopaniṣad*[56] may be referred to. *Praṇava* (*oṁ*) is the bow. The individual self is, indeed, the arrow. *Brahman* is spoken of as the target of that (arrow). It is to be hit unmistakably. If done so, the self becomes one with *Brahman* like the arrow with the target.

The *Śvetāśvatara Upaniṣad*[57] compares the body with a piece of wood and the individual self with the latent fire in wood. Ordinarily, the hidden self is not graspable. Friction through drilling is necessary to render the latent fire visible. Similarly, the self is to be realized through the *japa* of the *praṇava*. By making the body the lower friction-stick (*araṇi*) and the *praṇava* the upper friction-stick (*uttarāraṇi*), one has to practise the drill (friction) of meditation in order to realize God, otherwise hidden and unrealized.

Thus, the philosophy of *Pātañjala Yoga* and that of the Upaniṣads converge on the focal point that the *praṇava-japa* is an effective technique of attaining to Godhead and *Brahman* hood.

MANTRA-JAPA IN THE FRAMEWORK OF PĀTAÑJALA YOGA

The *japa* of God's name (*nāma-japa*) has been recommended and is in practice in most religions of the world. This is part of the *bhakti-yoga* (the *yoga* of devotion) which is not strictly relevant to *Pātañjala Yoga*. The *bhakti-yoga* will be discussed later in this chapter. The Tantra recommends the *japa* of so many *mantras*, many of which contain seed (*bīja*) syllables (*akṣara*). The tāntric *japa* is also unconnected with the *Pātañjala Yoga*. The *mantra-japa* of the tāntric system will also be discussed later in this chapter.

The Vedic *mantras*, while being recited, are preceded by the *praṇava* (*praṇu*). The *mantra* is sanctified by this process. The purpose is slightly different from that of the Yoga-Vedānta.

The *Pātañjala Yoga* has started its second chapter with the *sūtra* on *kriyā-yoga*, which includes *tapaḥ*, *svādhyāya* and *Īśvara-praṇidhāna*.[58] *Svādhyāya* and *Īśvara-praṇidhāna* have already been explained in this chapter. Since the *praṇava-japa* is inseparably connected with *Īśvara-praṇidhāna*, the *japa* of *oṁ*, with concomitant and constant reflection on its meaning, is a form of *kriyā-yoga*.

Maharṣi Patañjali has prescribed eight limbs of Yoga (*aṣṭāṅga-yoga*) in his Yoga philosophy.[59] These limbs are: *yama*, *niyama*, *āsana*, *prāṇāyāma*, *pratyāhāra*, *dhāraṇā*, *dhyāna*, and *samādhi*. If the *japa* can be established as a form of *Pātañjala Yoga*, it must conform to one or more of these eight limbs.

In the yogic process of *pratyāhāra*, the senses (*indriyas*) are withdrawn. They are rendered non-functional during meditation. They may be coming in contact with the external world. They may be connected with the internal mental world. Still they neither transmit any input data to the *antaḥkaraṇa* nor do they receive any output data from the *antaḥkaraṇa*.

The *praṇava-japa* is one of the multiple techniques of creating the state of *pratyāhāra*. This *pratyāhāra* state, brought about by *japa*, is conducive to *dhāraṇā* and *dhyāna*. How it assists *samādhi* will be elaborated later.

Patañjali has defined *pratyāhāra* in one of his aphorisms.[60] In this state, the senses are withdrawn into the *citta* (mind-stuff), as if they are dissolved in the latter. This results in the non-transmission of any information from the external world to the *citta*. Thereby all the doors of the *citta* are closed.

In *dhāraṇā*, the *yogī* concentrates on a location.[61] He fixes his *citta* on a location which may be outside or inside his body. The spot of concentration may be the written syllable *oṁ*; it may be a black spot on a paper, a lighted spot on a crystal, the picture or the statue of a deity, any spot in his own body or the spot between his two eyebrows (the *ājñā cakra*). Generally, in meditation or in *mantra-japa*, he fixes his *citta* on the *ājñā cakra* whose *bījākṣara* (seed-syllable) is *oṁ*. We would deal with the applications of *mantra-japa* in the third chapter of this book, where we would recommend *dhāraṇā* on specific organs of one's body, or on the pictures of other persons, or on other persons whose pictures are mentally conceived.

The *japa* of the *praṇava* (*oṁ*) or any other *mantra* is a form of *dhyāna*. Patañjali defines *dhyāna*[62] in the following way:

> While fixing the *citta* on the meditated object or spot (*dhyeya*), *dhyāna* is done on a single thought which flows continuously, without break and without admixture of any other thought, like the continuous flow of a stream of oil from one pot above to another pot below.

A reference has already been made to *Īśvara-praṇidhāna*, which is achieved through *oṅkāra-japa*. The Sanskrit word *nidhāna* means "a receptacle" or "a shelter (*āśraya-sthala*)."

The prefix *pra* contextually means "supreme." A *yogī*'s *citta* rests in God, finds the supreme shelter in God. This can be achieved through *oṅkāra-japa* and other yogic techniques. While doing the *japa*, one's *citta* is fully occupied with the meaning of the *japa-mantra*. This has also been referred to. The thought on *Īśvara* (God), with his attributes, should continuously flow in the *citta* while doing the *praṇava-japa*. Thus, the *japa* becomes *dhyāna* in the *Pātañjala Yoga*.

The *Bhagavad-Gītā* has a concept of *brāhmī sthiti* (stay in *Brahman* or *Īśvara*).[63] The *yogī*, while doing *oṅkāra-japa*, really stays in *Īśvara* (God). In this process, *oṁ* serves as a vehicle and also as an *ālambana* (support).

Oṁ is not only a vehicle and/or a support, but also a sacred syllable which is the foundation of the empirical universe. Brahmā (One and only One God who takes the role of the creator of the universe) creates the universe through His Power (Consort) Sarasvatī. She plays her *vīṇā*, with three strings. These are the super-strings of the string-theory of modern physics. The strings vibrate to produce the primal sound *oṁ*. Hence Mother Sarasvatī is known as the Vāgdevī (the goddess of speech, sound or voice). The primal sound (*oṁ*) is produced in the form of innumerable musical notes. Each note is a micro-particle or a macro-object. Thus, the sound is not an ordinary sound like any other. Its sacredness is fundamental and cannot be expressed by any language.

Maharṣi Patañjali recommends the *japa* of *oṁ*. In reality, the whole universe and every entity (micro or macro, and non-living or living) of the universe are constantly and continuously engaged in doing the *praṇava-japa* by echoing the primal vibrations of *oṁ*. This is not a mere speculation.

It can be experimentally verified by everybody if he/she practises *dhyāna*. The *oṅkāra dhvani* (*dhvani* = sound) of nature is clearly audible in a low, synchronous tone after a certain degree of success in meditation is achieved. Not only *oṁ* initially generates, but it continuously generates the universe and also it sustains it. No material entity (including energy-quanta) can be sustained without the spontaneous repetition of the primal *mantra, oṁ*.

In reality, the primal vibrations (*spandana* or *kampana* or *nāda*)[64] of the three strings of the *vīṇā* of Mother Sarasvatī did not and do not produce any sound. The perception of sound needs a medium to transport the sound-waves, some type of auditory apparatus and a brain containing an auditory centre. These requisites were not available before the universe was created and even after the creation until advanced animals and humans evolved. The primal vibrations were, in fact, in conformity with those of the sound *oṁ*. The first evolute was *virāḍ*[65] (*mahat* or *buddhi* or the Cosmic Mind) from which evolved *āpaḥ* or *nāra*[66] (the subtlest Cosmic Fluid or Cosmic Water which supercondensed as a *bindu*[67] (singularity).

In the *bindu* state, the vibrations were concentrated and did not radially move. When *prāṇa*[68] evolved from *āpaḥ* and the Cosmic Egg exploded[69] with the concurrent evolution of *ākāśa*[70] or aditi,[71] the vibrations could get the mediums of *āpaḥ* and *ākāśa* for transmission.

The *yogī* goes on repeating *oṁ* mentally. Thereby he passes on from the *vaiśvānara* to the *taijasa* and then from the *taijasa* to the *prājña*. In the *prājña* state, his *ātmā* (self) plunges into *Paramātmā* (the Great Self, the Supreme *Īśvara*, God). This state is attained in the highest intensity of *dhyāna*.

Still, in this state, complete non-duality is not established. A seed-consciousness of "I" (*ahaṅkāra, asmitā*) persists. This "I" is the worshipper (*upāsaka*) and *Īśvara* (God) is the worshipped (*upāsya*). And, hence is the duality. The subject-object relationship is still not obliterated in the *prājña* state.

Saṁyama[72] is a yogic process in the *Pātañjala Yoga*. When *dhāraṇā, dhyāna* and *samādhi* are done simultaneously, the combined process is known as *saṁyama*. Through the *japa* of the *praṇava*, a *yogī* can practise *saṁyama*. For the *samādhi* to be included in *saṁyama*, elucidation may be made on the type of *samādhi* known as *samprajñāta*.[73]

What is this *samprajñāta samādhi*? In this type of preliminary *samādhi*, the consciousness (1) of the gross and the subtle objects perceived by the senses (*indriyas*), (2) of the senses and the subtle, mental, internal instrument (*antaḥkaraṇa*) or the instrumental agency of perception, and (3) of the self, falsely identified with the intellect (*buddhi*), does persist. These three are technically termed as perceivable (*grāhya*), perceiving instruments (*grahaṇa*) and perceiver (*grahītā*), respectively. In this whole process, *vitarka* (alternative), *vicāra* (mentation), *ānanda* (experience) and *asmitā* (ego-sense) operate.

We have already discussed the four *pādas* (quarters) and the three *mātrās* (*a, u, ṁ*) of the *praṇava*, as given in the *Māṇḍūkyopaniṣad*. In the fourth *pāda* (*turīya*), there is the cessation (*virāma*) of the *mātrās*. In other words, the *turīya* state is devoid of *mātrās*. This is the state of full *samādhi*, devoid of forms, attributes, functions and dualities. The self (*ātmā*) and the Self (*Paramātmā, Īśvara, Brahman*) are completely identified in the *turīya*, the state of full quiescence. For the *yogī*, in the *turīya* state, the phenomenal universe does not exist.

Maharṣi Patañjali has defined *samādhi* which may be compared with the *turīya* state of the *Māṇḍūkyopaniṣad*. His definition is: In the *samādhi* state, the *yogī*'s own existence becomes void-like (*svarūpaśūnyamiva*) and his consciousness is identified with the Cosmic Consciousness which is meditated upon (*dhyeya*).[74]

In order to reach the *turīya* or the full *samādhi* state, one has to suspend the *oṅkāra-japa* and remain in a thoughtless condition. While explaining the *japa-sūtra* (I.28) of Patañjali, Vyāsa says: "*Samādhi-yoga* follows the *praṇava-japa* and then the *praṇava-japa* follows the *samādhi-yoga* and, by this process, the Supreme Self is realized."[75]

What has been given in the foregoing paragraph is the key to meditation. In the beginning stage of meditation, one does *mānasika oṅkāra-japa* slowly and steadily in synchronization with one's slow breath. One continues this *japa* for some time. Then one stops the *japa* and remains in thoughtless condition. If and when extraneous thoughts trespass upon the mind, one again resorts to *oṅkāra-japa*, after which the thoughtless condition is restored. In the process of meditation, the *oṅkāra-japa* serves as a support (*ālamba*).

JAPA IN YOGA-VEDĀNTA

Oṁ is a verbal symbol that names (*vācaka*) *Brahman* or *Īśvara*. For this purpose, *Brahman* or *Īśvara* is *vācya* (that which is named). This *vācaka* (*oṁ*) is used in any form of Yoga; it is not necessarily reserved for *jñāna-yoga* (the *yoga* of knowledge) only. However, the *praṇava* (*oṁ*) plays an important role in the *japa* of the Yoga-Vedānta.

In the Yoga-Vedānta system, the *oṅkāra-japa* may be *vaikharī* (loud), *upāṁśu* (humming or whispering) or *mānasika* (silent). When it is loud, its protraction may be too long, long, medium, or short. Adepts in *yoga* use the silent variety. They synchronize the *oṅkāra-japa* with the rhythms of inhalations and exhalations which are slow and steady. In order to get the best effects, this synchronization is unavoidable.

There is a second type of *japa* in Yoga-Vedānta. This is *so 'ham japa*, or otherwise known as *ajapā-japa* (spontaneous *japa*). Śaṅkarācārya, the eighth-century famous exponent of the Advaita (Non-Dualistic) Vedānta, has emphasized this *so 'ham japa*. This term is a conjunction of two words, *saḥ* + *aham*. The former means "He" (God) and the latter "I." The total expression means "He is I." All living creatures breathe *so 'ham* unconsciously. Man also breathes it unconsciously, 21,600 times in a day of 24 hours. With each inhalation, he unconsciously utters *so* (*saḥ*), and with each exhalation, he unconsciously utters *ham* (*aham*). Śaṅkara, however, advises that man should repeat it consciously. Then only, does the *ajapā-japa* become *yoga*.

THE NEED FOR THE REPETITION OF THE MANTRA

The word *japa* has an in-built meaning that a *mantra* is uttered (silently, hummingly, or verbally), with deep reflection on its meaning, and that this utterance is repeated. Some *mantra*s are repeated 108 times or multiples thereof. Sometimes, in order to save time, a *mantra* is repeated 54 or 27 (28) or 10 times. Tāntric *mantra*s are sometimes recommended to be repeated 0.1 or 1.0 or 10 million times.

Why are *mantra*s repeated? Cannot repetition be dispensed with? The answer to the second question is "No." We have to answer the first question then.

We have to take two common examples in order to explain the matter. We memorise a song or a *mantra* or a mathematical formula by repeating it several times. We draw a figure or paint a piece of art. We bring the lines of the figure into prominence by tracing over the lines several times. We touch the colour-brush several times in order to get our desired shade. From these two examples, we get some general clue to the answer to our question. Still we do not get our precise answer.

The brain and the mind are different. The former is a gross organ like the liver, kidneys, heart and lungs. The mind is invisible. The brain is the apparatus of the mind. No instrumental experimentation can be done on the mind whereas it can be done on the brain. We get knowledge on the mind indirectly and inferentially. We do not know the location of the long-term memory store and how exactly information are stored in the memory. Ancient Indian seers have told us that the store-house of *saṁskāra*s (both *vāsanā-saṁskāra*s and non-*vāsanā-saṁskāra*s) is the *antaḥkaraṇa*. New *saṁskāra*s are stored and some old *saṁskāra*s are erased. The repetition of a *mantra* helps store a new *saṁskāra* and erase an old *saṁskāra*. The exact scientific mechanism is, however, unknown to us.

A *mantra* can influence one's own mind and other minds too. It can also influence the Supermind which is the Cosmic Mind. This is brought about by the repetition of the *mantra*. The minds of other persons can be better influenced through the mediation of the Supermind. Non-living material entities have also their respective minds. Each material entity, micro or macro, is conscious. Matter (including energy) can be influenced through *mantra*s and this influence is fortified through repetition.

Our body cells, tissues and organs are material. They can be influenced, favourably or unfavourably, through *mantra*s. Mind rules over matter, although the reverse pathway is not altogether ineffective. There is interaction between mind and matter. Through the repetition of a *mantra* (if properly designed and worded), the body's physiological and biochemical functions can be altered. For such purposes also, the *mantra-japa* is to be repeated.

PRESCRIPTIONS AND PROSCRIPTIONS IN PĀTAÑJALA YOGA

There is a saying: The Vedas do not make a person virtuous if his conduct is bad.[76] Just reverse is the opinion in many popular religions. Accordingly, one may perform any number of sinful acts, one's life may be unethical, and still one may be pious by uttering the name of Hari (God). Yoga condemns the second version and accepts the first one.

In the twentieth century and later, *yoga* has been popular throughout the world. Many yogic institutions have been built in many countries, both East and West. But very few yogic institutions have laid much (or any) emphasis on the yogic *yama*s and *niyama*s. *Yoga* has often been identified with yogic *āsana*s. Sometimes, some *prāṇāyāma* and some sort of *dhyāna* are added to the yogic postures. *Yoga* which is purely spiritual has been rendered to a discipline of acrobatics. There is no doubt that acrobatics are secular and do give some benefits to the physical body. But even *dhyāna* cannot give mental peace to a person if he does not live an ethical life. One must try to be a good man. There is no substitute for goodness. Without the observance of *yama* and *niyama*, the *japa-yoga* and any other type of *yoga* are almost useless.

It has already been stated that the *Pātañjala Yoga* has eight limbs, namely, *yama, niyama, āsana, prāṇāyāma, pratyāhāra, dhāraṇā, dhyāna* and *samādhi*. Out of these, the first two (*yama* and *niyama*) are the foundations; the middle three (*āsana, prāṇāyāma, pratyāhāra*) are the useful techniques to achieve the goal; and the last three (*dhāraṇā, dhyāna* and *samādhi*) occupy the apex structure of the temple of Yoga. The superstructure cannot stand without the foundation which is mostly underground.

Yama includes five proscriptions.[77] These are: 1. Do not do violence (*ahiṁsā* = non-violence). 2. Do not tell lies (*satya* = truthfulness). 3. Do not steal, do not misappropriate (*asteya* = non-stealing). 4. Do not make sexual abuse and avoid sexual indulgence and excess (*brahmacarya* = sex-abstinence; ethical sex-conduct). 5. Do not accept unearned cash and kind and do not accumulate property at the deprivation of others and by exploiting others (*aparigraha* = Non-accumulation).

The benefits of *ahiṁsā*,[78] *satya*,[79] *asteya*,[80] *brahmacarya*[81] and *aparigraha*[82] have been given by Patañjali in five aphorisms. Non-violence should be practised in thought, speech and action. Complete sexual abstinence is recommended for an ascetic (*saṁnyāsī*) who has renounced the world, who lives for a higher and nobler purpose of life and who devotes his full time for spiritual attainment. Such a person can be able to sublimate sex, if he is determined to do so. Spiritual persons, living in the social world and working for the benefit of the society, may marry and have regulated sex in life. All or most of the ancient Indian seers (*ṛṣi*s) married and produced children. But their sex-life was very much regulated. A priest, with excessive, uncontrollable sex-urge, a tendency for sexual indulgence and a secret extra-marital sex (hetero or homo) relationship, is a social criminal. He should better marry, and religious institutions should allow such a marriage. Marriage is not unholy. Sex is not a sin and sex-life is a biological and emotional necessity. If a higher spiritual life can sublimate sex, then only can full sexual abstinence be ideal for devoting full time to spirituality, for getting rid of family entanglement, for keeping the nervous system calm and for avoiding the *citta-vṛtti*s arising out of sex-sensuality. For householders, the issue is different, however. They can marry and experience married sex-life, with the avoidance of excess, of course. They should refrain from extra-marital sex. If they do that, they would be householder (*gṛhastha*) *brahmacārī*. Yoga approves of it.

Patañjali's *niyama* incorporates five prescriptions.[83] These are: (1) cleanliness (*śauca*), (2) contentment (*santoṣa*), (3) austerities (*tapaḥ*), (4) study of spiritual scriptures for liberation (*mokṣa-śāstra-adhyayana*), leading to the practice of scriptural instructions in life and the mental *japa* of the *praṇava* or *oṁ* (*svādhyāya*), and (5) stay in God (*brāhmī sthiti*) through the *praṇava-japa* (*Īśvara-praṇidhāna*) or popularly interpreted as complete surrender to God.

The body, the speech and the mind should be clean. A dirty body, with dirty clothes and dirty environment, breeds diseases and is not aesthetic. A diseased body is unsuitable for the performance of *yoga*. A *yogī*'s speech should be free from obscenity and vulgarity. It should not be cruel so as to hurt others. It should be soft and polite. The mind of the *yogī* should be clean. He should not harbour dirty thoughts in his mind. The mind should be free from malice, envy, ill will and inimical, destructive thoughts. The *antaḥkaraṇa* is to be cleansed in order to get success in *yoga*. Patañjali has given two aphorisms[84] with reference to the benefits from cleanliness.

The important role played by contentment (*santoṣa*)[85] in *yoga* cannot be over-emphasized. One has to establish the equanimity[86] of mind in opposite conditions such as states of sorrowfulness and joyfulness, profit and loss, victory and defeat, success and failure. One has to get rid of opposites and contradictions (*nirdvandva*).[87] If one develops these mental traits, one gets the key to contentment.

It is very often argued that dissatisfaction provides a potent stimulus to prosperity, progress and affluence. If one is satisfied with whatever little one gets, one develops the trait of slothfulness and inertia. Such a person can hardly prosper and progress. "Be dissatisfied with the utmost you get. Make efforts for further improvements and progress. Keep the sky as the limit. Or pierce the sky and go farther. Never put a full stop to your marching ahead. The path of progress is infinite. Ascend vertically or spirally, but always upwards. Dissatisfaction is the stimulant to upward progress."

The theorisers of what has been given in the foregoing paragraph have a total misunderstanding of the yogic *santoṣa*. This theory is responsible for the modern rat-race in the economic, social and political fields. For this theory only, many persons of the modern world superficially enjoy affluence; but they are deprived of inner *santoṣa*; they are unhappy and agonized; they find meaninglessness in their lives; sometimes they prefer suicide to living this wretched life.

The *Gītā* and the Yoga do not recommend inaction and indolence. In the war-field, Arjuna preferred inaction to action. Śrīkṛṣṇa advised him to act. This is the beginning of the *Gītā*. There is one significant characteristic of the action recommended by the *Gītā*, however. It should be detached action, without any attachment to the fruits thereof. It has not been advised to reject the fruits of action. In spite of the best efforts in performing the actions, the results may be bad or may not be so good as per expectation. In such a situation, only detachment (*anāsakti*) can save the person from frustration and agony.

Any action (*karma*) may end in success, partial success or failure. The last two conditions make a person unhappy if he is not detached. How can one be free from contradictions? How can one have equanimity of mind in both success and failure? How can one have *santoṣa* in loss and defeat? Is there any skill in action that can bring about the equanimity of mind and *santoṣa* in opposite situations? The skill is to constantly yoke the intellect (*buddhi*) with God.[88] This is called *buddhi-yoga*.[89] There are many techniques in Yoga which can be adopted to attain to *buddhi-yoga*. And the *japa* of the *praṇava* is one of those techniques.

What has been described with reference to *buddhi-yoga* can be practicable for a *sthitaprajña* (one whose *prajñā* or *buddhi* constantly stays in *Īśvara* or God).[90] Such a person is in *brāhmī sthiti* (stay in *Brahman*).[91] He is otherwise called *sthitadhī*.[92] A *yogī* in *brāhmī sthiti* can be compared with an ocean which is always full and does not swell up further even if water from many rivers constantly flows into it. Similarly, a *yogī*'s mind is always peaceful and contented even if desires enter into his ever-full mind.[93] He is ever super-saturated with peace and contentment. For attaining to this mental status, the *japa* of *praṇava* is one of the many yogic tools.

Tapaḥ is the third yogic prescription.[94] Many writers on Yoga have translated this word as austerities. We would translate it as the acceptance of pain and suffering willingly for the performance of one's own duties (for *svadharma-pālana*).

Some *yogī*s unnecessarily torture their body for their *yoga-sādhanā*. They stand in shoulder-deep, cold water in the midnight of the winter season and do *mantra-japa*. They look at the scorching sun to meditate at the midday of the hot summer while standing on a spot surrounded by burning fire. They lie on thorn-beds and pierce their tongues with nails to perform austerity-rituals. Such practices are *kṛcchra-sādhanā*s which are to be condemned. The body is to be protected. Unnecessary discomforts to it must be avoided.

What is *tapaḥ* then? If physical suffering is necessary for a *noble* cause, the *yogī* should be glad to undertake the suffering without any mental resentment. Periodical, but regular, fasting may be necessary. Of course, such fastings (*upavāsa*) must not be too frequent to adversely affect the health. The observance of some vows (*vrata*s) such as the maintenance of silence for some hours (*mauna-vrata*) may be beneficial.

Impurity is got rid of by *tapas*. As a result, the body and the mind become purer. Sometimes, *tapas* serves as a *prāyaścitta* (a penance or an act of self-punishment as reparation for guilt).

We have already discussed *svādhyāya* and *Īśvara-praṇidhāna* which are the fourth and the fifth yogic prescriptions, respectively. Through the scriptural studies, *mantra-japa* and the recitation of the *praṇava*, one can get a direct perception of one's *iṣṭa-devatā* (chosen deity of whom one is the ardent devotee).[95] Through the mental repetition of the *praṇava*, one may constantly be in union with God to whom one fully surrenders. By this, the obstacles to *samādhi* are removed and the success for attaining to *samādhi* is accelerated.[96]

This completes the theoretical discussion on the *japa* of Yoga-Vedānta. Next, we take up the theory of the *japa* in *Bhakti-Yoga* (the Yoga of Devotion).

Japa in the Yoga of Devotion

In the Vedānta of the Indian philosophical systems, *dvaita-vāda* (dualism) and *advaita-vāda* (non-dualism) are the two main branches among many. Among the followers of the two systems, there is often bitter conflict. Such conflicts are rooted in sheer misunderstanding. At the start, we would devote some time to clarify some allied concepts and to dispel the misunderstanding.

Monotheism (*ekeśvara-vāda*) is the doctrine that there is only one God in the whole universe and that He is the creator and the sustainer. Monotheism of the religions of the Middle-East and the West rigidly distinguishes the subject from the objects. If God is compared with a carpenter, the universe and all component entities of the universe are furniture like chairs, tables and sofa, et cetera. The former is the subject and the latter are the objects. An object can never be converted into the subject.

It is a general misconception that Hinduism is polytheistic rather than monotheistic. A Hindu is supposed to believe in many gods and goddesses. Such an idea is not totally unfounded, so far as the mass is concerned. But, essentially, if we go to the root of Hinduism, namely, the Vedas, and the Vedānta, we find in Hinduism an empirical polytheism or even pantheism in the total framework of monotheism. The Vedas are the first to declare the concept of *Brahman*, one only, formless, undifferentiated, all-pervasive, and the fundamental Consciousness. Nowhere in the world, except in the Vedas and the Vedānta, is found the concept of *Brahman*. The Vedas and the *Prasthāna-Traya* (the Upaniṣads, the *Brahmasūtra* and the *Bhagavad-Gītā*) unambiguously prescribe monotheism.

Monotheism and non-dualism are not identical, however. In the concept of non-dualism, Reality (*Brahman*) is non-dual and there is no multiplicity, whatsoever. The phenomenal universe is empirical and, in the strict sense, not real. Being a reflection of *Brahman*, it has apparent existence. It is still not nothing. With forms, qualities and functions, it is meaningful empirically. Only *Brahman* is absolute and real. The difference between the subject and the object(s) disappears in non-dualism. From the non-dualistic point of view, the universe is not different from *Brahman*, although an identity cannot be established. Apart from *Brahman*, the universe cannot exist as a second and separate entity. Non-dualism further asserts that the individual self is not essentially different from the Universal Self (*Brahman* or *Īśvara* or God). This last concept is totally rejected by the Western monotheism and the Indian dualism. According to the Western monotheism, the soul is created by God, at the time of conception, from nothing. It further holds that, on the day of the final judgement, God sends the souls to the heaven or the hell, for final and eternal stay there, in eternal bliss in the heaven and in eternal damnation in the hell. God gives His verdict after judging the pious or impious actions of the individual soul in his/her life, the only single life he/she had. Rebirth is not accepted in all religions, not born in India.

The Indian dualists regard the individual selves as eternal, without beginnings and ends. They are reborn again and again until someone gets final salvation. In the released state, the self happily stays in the divine sphere in the company of God. But, the dualists never agree to the idea that an individual self can ever be the Universal Self (God).

The non-dualists hold that no self is permanently damned, that he is not different from *Brahman* from which he is alienated due to his ignorance (*avidyā*), his false association with his body, his bondage with his karmic *saṁskāra*s and that, one day or the other, every self must have his home-coming (his re-union and re-identification with *Brahman*). The non-dualist asserts that there is nothing in the universe which is *really* different from *Brahman*. The water (H_2O) in the blood, urine, stool, sewage, a dirty pool, river and sea looks differently due to the acquisition of filth and extraneous materials, possesses different colours and odours, and sometimes toxins, poisons, bacteria, protozoa and viruses. But, on distillation and re-distillation, pure H_2O can be had, irrespective of the source.

We steadfastly subscribe to non-dualism. But, irrespective of any ism (monotheism, polytheism, dualism, etc.), the *yoga* of devotion is equally effective in all faiths. Hence, any conflict is unnecessary. The question pops up: where is the place of *bhakti-yoga* in non-dualism? The statement "*Brahman* prays to *Brahman*" seems to be meaningless.

Bhakti-Yoga in Non-Dualism

In the first section of this chapter, we have already discussed the four quarters of the self, as given in the *Māṇḍūkyopaniṣad*. They are: the *vaiśvānara*, the *taijasa*, the *prājña* and the *turīya*. The first one is functional in the wakeful state and experiences the gross objects of the universe. The second one is functional in the dream state and experiences the stored impressions in the memory and the *saṁskāra*s. The third one is functional in the stage of deep sleep and experiences neither the gross nor the subtle objects. In this *prājña* state, the individual self almost approaches the Universal Self (*Īśvara* or God). Nevertheless, duality is not fully obliterated even in this third state. The "I" (*aham*), separate from "He" (God), still persists at a deep level. Thus, even in non-dualism, dualism is an empirical fact in the three states of *vaiśvānara, taijasa* and *prājña*. Only when one goes to the *turīya* state, does dualism disappear and pure non-dualism prevail.

Śaṅkara, the advocate of non-dualism, has composed prayer-songs for God in the monotheistic system and gods and goddesses in the polytheistic system. At the same time, he gives a philosophy of pure non-dualism. Is he confused due to mental deficiency? Is he inconsistent? Is he not intellectually honest? These questions are profane for

Hindus who regard Śaṅkara as an incarnation of Lord Śiva. The great sage is more often misunderstood than understood. Modern-world-thought and modern science are still to evolve to a higher level to comprehend Śaṅkara's non-dualism. In the *Vivekacūḍāmaṇi*, he sings:

> I am God. I am the destroyer of the hell. I am the destroyer of the three worlds. I am the Supreme Person. I am the Ruler and the Controller. I am the unbroken whole. I am the last Witness. Nobody else is my Lord to control me. I am I-less; I am my-less.[97]

The attention may be drawn to the concluding part of the verse quoted in the foregoing paragraph. One becomes a non-dualist only when one is I-less and my-less. In that state of non-dualism, devotion (*bhakti*), prayer (*prārthanā*) and *japa* (the repetition of God's name) are not necessary. In the dualistic state, however, these are necessary. As a matter of fact, it is not ordinarily possible to reach the I-less and my-less state without the prior *bhakti-yoga*.

Symbol-Worship in Bhakti-Yoga

The Vedas and the Upaniṣads were to declare in the world for the first time that God is formless. The Vedic *Ārya*s did not have temples and were not using icons for worshipping. The Mauryan emperor Aśoka engaged Greek and Arabic sculptors for erecting pillars in different parts of his empire. The Buddhists were the first in India to introduce icon-worship (the worship of Lord Buddha's statue). Hindus started icon-worship in the fourth or fifth century CE. Of course, the worship of the phallus (*liṅga*) and the female generative organ (*śakti*) was very ancient by the aboriginal communities. The Vedas unambiguously condemned this phallus worship.[98] At a later period, the Hindus assimilated the concept of the worship of the *liṅga* (phallus) and the *yoni* (female generative organ), with a change of meaning, of course. The aborigines got the idea of their origin by direct perception of copulation and parental generation and so they worshipped the *liṅga* and the *yoni* as the divine father and the divine mother, respectively. The later Hindus also worshipped the stone-*liṅga* and the stone-*yoni* as symbols for the divine Father and the divine Mother, respectively. At the post-Vedic period, the Hindus adopted symbol-worship and might have appreciated the meaningful symbols of the pre-Vedic people.

A devotee can dispense with symbols for worshipping. Advanced *yogī*s among Hindus do not need any icon. For psychological need, of course, icons serve as visual aids. Hence, the *Bhagavad-Gītā* has prescribed both formless and form worship, with preference on the latter for the spiritual non-adepts.[99]

There is nothing wrong with icon-worship. The worshipper is psychologically better satisfied with his higher concentration on icons which serve as visual aids. But, the system of icon-worship is apt to mislead the common mass. Very often, the symbol (icon) and the symbolized (God) are equated. The map of India cannot be India. The plastic model of a methane (CH_4) molecule cannot be the methane molecule itself.

The use of symbols is ubiquitous in the world both for religious and non-religious purposes. The flag of every nation in the world is a sacred symbol of the concerned nation. A soldier in the army, the navy and the air force gladly sacrifices his life to protect the symbol. A sports team uses a symbol. An institution has its own symbol. Those religions who claim to do formless worship do use symbols. We may take the glaring example of Christianity. Without the concept of the cross-symbol and the symbol of crucified Christ, it is almost impossible for a Christian to effectively pray. Symbols are necessary in religions. If we accept it as a fact, the use of icons in *bhakti-yoga* cannot be discredited. However, the limitation should be properly understood. An icon is like the map of a country, and not the country itself.

Monotheism versus Polytheism

Judaism, Christianity and Islam are monotheistic. In the monotheism of Christianity are contained the Father (God), the Son (Jesus Christ) and the Holy Ghost or Holy Spirit, combinedly known as the Trinity.

The Vedic religion is undoubtedly monotheistic.[100] The Vedas make a clear distinction between *Īśvara* (God) who is one and only one and the multiple *devatā*s (shining deities). The *Ṛgveda* clearly mentions that the *deva*s (gods) were born after the creation.[101] God is formless (*arūpa*) and cannot be perceived by our usual five senses of perception. To sing the glory of Unmanifest (*avyakta*) God, the Vedic seers had to resort to praising the magnificent, the beautiful, the marvellous, the splendent and the splendid manifestations of Nature as *devatā*s. They also did something else. They praised the glory of one and only one God by different names, depending upon the functions and attributes of God described in the relevant Vedic verse. When forms are made use of in the description of the formless, the world-image (*viśva-rūpa*) is the only technique. This technique has been exactly followed in the eleventh chapter of the *Bhagavad-Gītā* when Arjuna saw the world-image in Śrīkṛṣṇa.[102]

The Hindu religion, as practised today, has evolved and changed considerably from the original Vedic religion, without basic changes, however. It has no founder-preacher. It is not institutionalized. It has not a single scripture. It follows thousands of scriptures written by seers down the ages. There is full freedom, without any regimentation, in the religion.

In the epic and the Purāṇic age, one and only one God (*Parameśvara*) was conceived as the Hindu Trinity (*trimūrti*). When God is conceived as the Creator, He is Brahmā. When He is conceived as the sustainer and the nourisher of the universe, He is Viṣṇu (the all-pervader, the Sanskrit word having been derived from the verb-root *√viś*, meaning to pervade). When He is conceived as the destroyer and annihilator, He is Rudra (the terrible one). Even the same Rudra is worshipped as Śiva (the benevolent and auspicious) as people of all religions worship the merciful God.

The Hindu religion is unique in one respect that God is a bipolar Reality, being both the Father and the Mother of the universe. *Brahman* is neutral. Still its Power (*Śakti*) is *Māyā*, the feminine principle. *Brahman* is non-dual, its *Māyā* being inseparable from it like fire and heat. *Brahman* associated with *Māyā* that serves as the *upādhi* (limiting adjunct), is *Īśvara* (God). *Īśvara, Paramātmā* (the Great Self) or *Parameśvara* (the Supreme Lord) is masculine in gender. In the analogy of a neutron (neutral in charge or with no charge) becoming a proton (with positive charge) and an electron (with negative charge), *Brahman* becomes *Īśvara* (God) and *Īśvarī (Māyā)* unavoidably. The former is the

Father of the universe and the latter the Mother. The Father functions as the Chairperson (*adhyakṣa*);[103] the Mother as the Executive Agent.[104]

When we come to the Hindu Trinity, one Father becomes three, namely, Brahmā, Viṣṇu and Rudra, and one Mother also becomes three, namely, Sarasvatī, Lakṣmī and Gaurī or Kālī. The consorts of Brahmā, Viṣṇu and Rudra are Sarasvatī, Lakṣmī and Gaurī or Kālī, respectively. The three Mothers are combinedly known as Durgā or Caṇḍī. The Vedas do make a reference to the three Mothers (*tri ambā = tryambā*), with different names, of course.[105] Thus, according to the Hindu religion, the universe is a product out of the union of one divine Father and one divine Mother.

Some say that Christianity has also the concept of one divine Mother. Mother Mary is human like mother Devakī. The former is Jesus Christ's virgin mother. The latter is Śrīkṛṣṇa's mother, the wife of Vasudeva, Śrīkṛṣṇa's father. Devakī is not a goddess and Vasudeva is not a god. Any human father or human mother cannot play the role of the creator, the sustainer and the destroyer of the universe. He or she cannot be omnipotent, omniscient and omnipresent. Thus, any mortal human being cannot become God or Goddess.

In our opinion, Hindu religion should have stopped with *Brahman, Māyā, Parameśvara* and the masculine and feminine Trinity. But it *created* and is still *creating* multiple gods and goddesses. Only the symbol *oṁ* (ॐ) would have been enough. The composite symbol *Śiva-Śakti* (the *liṅga* and the *yoni*), which is not anthropomorphic, could have satisfied the psychological needs of the devotees. At best, the visual representations of the Hindu Trinity (both masculine and feminine) should have sufficed. Notwithstanding this fact, the multiplicity of images do not confuse the enlightened Hindu, who is a monotheist. Different, however, is the case with the mass, not expected to ascend the higher rungs of the spiritual ladder. In spite of all these critical comments on the metaphysics of Hinduism, it is asserted that even the common Hindu is *essentially* a monotheist. Hinduism is a cafetaria-type of religion with free option to choose for everybody.

Very often in *japa-yoga*, some devotees keep an image (an idol or a picture) in front for better concentration. That is why we deliberated on this topic here. With icon or no icon, one can do *japa*. The metaphysical differences among the various religions do not pose hurdles at all. The basic theory of the *japa-yoga* is the same for people of all religions. Changes in formalities are followed to suit individuals.

Problems should not arise for variations in the use of God's name in *japa*. God has no name. Human beings name Him. Differences in religious concepts, languages and cultures are responsible for the different names of God. Animals, birds and human beings all over the world drink water (H_2O). We do not know if animals and birds have names for water, since they do not use languages. Each language which human beings use has word(s) for water. Irrespective of the differences in the words for water, the substance of water does not change from area to area and from language to language. Similarly, the use of different names for one God only does not alter God Himself. It is not wise to think that there is a Hindu God, a Muslim God, a Christian God, and so on. God is one, not only for the earth, but also for the whole universe.

The Upaniṣads use the term *nāma-rūpa*. Whenever there is a *rūpa* (form), there is a *nāma* (name). The Hindus conceive of many forms of the formless Reality. Hence, they use a name for each form. Religions that do not admit forms for God also use names for God. These names do not stand for forms, but for concepts (the concepts of a Divine Being).

Forms of Japa in Bhakti-Yoga

NĀMA-JAPA

God's name may be repeated. This is called *nāma-japa*. A Christian may repeat the name of Jesus Christ. A Muslim may use the sacred name Allah. A Hindu may use the name of the God or Goddess whom he loves most. Examples of his *nāma-japa* may be as follows: 1. Rāma Rāma Rāma Rāma . . . . 2. Kṛṣṇa Kṛṣṇa Kṛṣṇa Kṛṣṇa . . . . 3. Hari Hari Hari Hari . . . . 4. Nārāyaṇa Nārāyaṇa Nārāyaṇa Nārāyaṇa . . . . 5. Sītā Rāma Sītā Rāma . . . . 6. Rādhe Kṛṣṇa Rādhe Kṛṣṇa . . . . 7. Hare Rāma Hare Rāma Rāma Rāma Hare Hare; Hare Kṛṣṇa Hare Kṛṣṇa Kṛṣṇa Kṛṣṇa Hare Hare. Depending on his/her mood at a particular time, the *name* may change. If someone has a chosen or a tutelary deity (*iṣṭa-devatā*), one may repeat his or her name for the *japa*.

MANTRA-JAPA

Instead of only the name of God or Goddess, a *mantra* may be repeated. This is called *mantra-japa*. What is a *mantra*? It has already been stated that the word *mantra* has been derived from the verb-root √*man* (meaning to think). The literal meaning of *mantra* is "an instrument of thought." A thought is generated by it. The generated thought may be transmitted by it to a targeted organ of one's body or another targeted person for doing a specific action. Every *mantra* starts with the monosyllable *oṁ*. It has a deity (*devatā*). In Sanskrit language, the name of the deity is given in the *mantra* in the dative case (*sampradāna kāraka*), e.g., Rāma ⟶ Rāmāya, Rādhā ⟶ Rādhāyai, Hari ⟶ Haraye, Lakṣmī ⟶ Lakṣmyai. The *mantra* contains the word *namaḥ* or *svāhā*. Some examples of *mantra*s are given here: 1. *oṁ namaḥ śivāya*; 2. *oṁ namo nārāyaṇāya*; 3. *oṁ namo bhagavate vāsudevāya*. Some tāntric *mantra*s will be given in section III of this chapter. In a few tāntric *mantra*s, the name of the goddess is given in the vocative case, e.g. Kālike, Parameśvari.

LIKHITA-JAPA

The word *likhita* means "written." Daily in the morning and the evening or in the morning only, the devotee writes God's name 108 times on a plain paper or a paper decorated on the four borders. The written *japa* of a *mantra* can also be done. But a *mantra*, being longer, occupies greater space on the paper.

The written *japa* is more convenient for a person for whom one-pointed concentration (*ekāgratā*) in mental *japa* is not easy. However, it is to be admitted that written *japa* is more mechanical and less meditative than mental *japa*.

KĪRTANA

For the purpose of *japa* here, the word *kīrtana* means loud, rhythmic repetition of God's (Goddess') name, individually or in a group, generally with instrumental music. When individually done, a pair of cymbals may be used for generating the musical rhythm. Hand-clapping, with rhythm, is sometimes done in the absence of, or in addition to, musical instruments.

The *kīrtana* may be *nāma-kīrtana* or *mantra-kīrtana*. Community *kīrtana* has its own advantages. In addition to spiritual arousal, it promotes communal harmony. But, strictly from the *yoga* point of view, individual *kīrtana*, in a secluded place, with a pair of cymbals, is ideal. Such personal *kīrtana* is *vaikharī* (loud) in nature, but it should not be disturbingly loud unlike the mass *kīrtana*. The devotional psychological setting and the *tanmayatā* (the state of being absorbed in or surrendering to God) are the key conditions for a full success in *kīrtana*.

Devotion — the Key Factor in Bhakti-Yoga

In section I, we dealt with *japa* in *Yoga-Vedānta*. It has more leaning on *jñāna-yoga* (the *yoga* of knowledge), although *bhakti* (devotion) cannot be exclusive of any system of *japa*. In section II, we put more emphasis on *bhakti* in *japa*. Here we would elaborate some special features of *bhakti-yoga* and the role of *japa* in it.

The *Śrīmadbhāgavata Mahāpurāṇa* enlists nine types of actions of a true devotee.[106] These are:

1. listening to the names and qualities of God — *śravaṇaṁ*
2. loud singing of God's name (*kīrtana*) — *kīrtanaṁ*
3. remembering God's name — *smaraṇam*
4. serving God's feet (the feet of His picture or icon) — *pāda-sevanam*
5. worshipping Him — *arcanam*
6. venerating Him respectfully — *vandanam*
7. becoming His servant — *dāsyam*
8. enjoying his friendship — *sakhyam*
9. offering one's own self to God — *ātma-nivedanam*

The *Bhagavad-Gītā* has devoted a full chapter on *bhakti-yoga* (chapter XII) and has got it dispersed throughout the scripture. In this scripture, *karma-yoga* (the *yoga* of unattached action) has preceded *jñāna-yoga* (the *yoga* of the knowledge of *Brahman*), which, in turn, has preceded *bhakti-yoga* (the *yoga* of devotion). *Yoga* culminates in *bhakti* that opens the door to liberation (*mokṣa*).

Devotional offering. God has no need of anything. Everything is the manifestation of God. There is nothing which is not God's and which can be offered to Him. In spite of this fact, the devotee, out of love and respect, offers some foliage, some flower, some fruit and some water. God pleasingly accepts these offerings of the devotee.[107]

Dedication of all actions. Whatever action does the devotee do (any work he does, any food he eats, any sacrifice he does, any benevolent donation he makes and any austerity he performs), he first dedicates it to God.[108]

Mind linked up with God. The *bhakti-yogī* constantly links up his mind with God.[109] Non-attachment to worldly attainments and enjoyments is a desirable quality. But, in *bhakti-yoga*, the *yogī*'s mind is tenaciously attached to God. This spiritual attachment is unconnected with the worldly attachment and is highly recommended. If it is practised with steadfastness, firmness and without wavering, the *yogī* transcends the three *guṇas* (strings or strands — *sattva, rajas,* and *tamas*) and becomes *brahma-like*.[110]

Shelter in God. The *yogī*'s mental faculty (*manas, buddhi* and *prāṇa*) takes shelter in God.[111] If it is done in right earnest, with strong faith and deep reverence, the *yogī* is not perturbed at all even in the situation of gravest calamities, frightening dangers and tempestuous peril. He feels safe and secure. And he does get divine protection.

Spiritual traits and equanimity in mind. A person truly devoted to God does not harbour enmity towards any being, and does not cause harm to anyone.[112] He is friendly and compassionate to everybody.[113] In all situations, he is self-contented and self-controlled.[114] He becomes I-less and my-less.[115] He develops equanimity of mind and is unaffected by opposites such as good or bad, auspicious or inauspicious, happiness or unhappiness, praise or blame, friend or foe.[116] He is clean in his body, mind and speech; he does not expect any return from anybody for his actions towards them; he sincerely and efficiently discharges his duties; he does not take any partisan attitude and remains much above narrowism; he is not perturbed over all *karmas* already initiated in this life and remains unworried and untroubled; he is a calm-minded person in all situations.[117]

Complete surrender to God. In the apex state of *bhakti*, the devotee completely surrenders to God and accepts His verdict with humility and joy and without grumbling and mental resentment. Every entity in the world, living or non-living, rides the world-machine which is constantly in revolving motion, made to move by God through His *Māyā*. God sits in the heart of all beings. One can escape from this hapless revolving motion through the grace of God only and thereby can get supreme peace and eternal state of stay. This divine grace one can get by complete surrender to God.[118]

When one is in a perplexing situation in which he cannot properly decide and cannot distinguish good from bad, the best path he should follow is to completely surrender to God who becomes the guide. It is God only who liberates one from all sins in actions committed in such situations.[119]

The goal of bhakti-yoga. Every *bhakti-yogī* is in a state of duality (*dvaita*). An *advaita* (non-dualist) cannot pray to himself. Going from *dvaita* to *advaita* is a transitional process and a process of the evolution of the bound self to the final state of liberation which is the complete identification of the self and Self (*jīvātmā* and *Paramātmā*).

The traditional dualism and non-dualism of Indian philosophy are divisive, especially with reference to the final goal. The liberated self in dualism goes to God and permanently lives in peace in the proximity of God. Liberation, in non-dualism, is different, however. The self, after complete purification, being purged of all karmic *saṁskāra*s and *vāsanā*s, merges in the Self, in the analogy of any river-water merging in ocean-water, thus establishing complete identity and non-difference.

We accept both dualism and non-dualism as facts. So long as the self is bound (apparently and empirically) to impurities of actions and thoughts that generate *saṁskāra*s and *vāsanā*s, it is different from *Brahman*. Once the former is distilled and re-distilled and thus becomes devoid of impurities and is completely purified, it loses its separate identity and becomes *Brahman*. The devotional technique is a means to the final end. And *japa*, becoming one of the devotional techniques, is a potent tool, leading to the final liberation (*mokṣa*) of the non-dualistic type.

Even a sinner of the worst type, by *japa* with sincere devotion, can become a pious person and he also attains to salvation.[120] A true devotee of God definitely ascends the path to salvation and he never ends in failure. How does it happen? Is the doctrine of *karma* (*karma-vāda*) violated then? The answer to this question is "No." God gives *buddhi-yoga* to the devotee, whose *buddhi* (intellect) is clarified and purified. His *vāsanā-saṁskāra*s and non-*vāsanā-saṁskāra*s are purged of his *antaḥkaraṇa*. As a result, he is liberated.[121] In this self-purificatory process, the self, immediately prior to the final liberation, becomes *Brahman*-like,[122] and finally becomes *Brahman*. This whole process may be accomplished in one life or more than one lives.

Japa for bhukti and mukti. The word *bhukti* means "attaining something that is desired." The word *mukti* means "liberation from bondage or salvation (*mokṣa*)." *Japa* can be either *sakāma* (with a desire for worldly attainments) or *niṣkāma* (desireless). To be *mukta* (liberated) is also a desire, but it is not a worldly desire. It is considered as *niṣkāma*. *Bhakti* for the sake of *bhakti* only is *niṣkāma*. A devotee does *japa* or adopts any other devotional technique out of his sheer love and reverence for God. This is *niṣkāma japa*, *japa* without any attachment (*saṅga-varjita*).[123] Although *niṣkāma bhakti* is much superior to the *sakāma* one, the latter is not discredited, however. Life has both pleasure and pain; with some, the former predominating and, with some others, the latter. But, there is no life, completely free from pain. In order to escape from painful situations, calamities and distress, a theistic person has to pray to God for redemption. There is nothing wrong with it. It is wrong, if the so-called *bhakti* is mis-utilized for covetous accumulation of wealth and power, for sensual indulgence, for torturing and exploiting others, for violence and destruction and for any other purpose antithetical to all norms of morals and ethics. *Sakāma bhakti* becomes a necessity for most of us if and when the situation needs divine grace for the good of the individual, the family, the society, the earth and the universe. The *Gītā* unambiguously declares that God's grace does shower when the *bhakti* is genuine and sincere and the redemptive purpose ot the *bhakti* conforms to the divine *ṛta* (cosmic order and laws).[124]

Japa at the Terminal Stage of Life

The Hindu scriptures lay much emphasis on the *japa* of God's name at the last moments preceding death.[125] It is not easy and practicable to remember God's name at the time of death, if one is not a staunch devotee throughout the life and has not practised *japa* and *dhyāna* on God for most of the years of life.

The *Gītā* states that the *jīva*'s life, after death, will take a shape in accordance with the thought in the mind immediately before death.[126] If the last moment's thought is on God, the *jīva*, after death, is cleansed of all the imprinted *saṁskāra*s through the superposition of the divine thought. God's names, other than *oṁ* (which is monosyllabic), are usually multisyllabic. If the dying person remembers and utters *oṁ* at the time preceding death, he merges in *Brahman* or attains to a divine life in his next incarnation.[127] If he can remember multisyllabic names of God, he gets the same benefits too.

How do we explain these scriptural statements? What is the mode of action? For a satisfactory explanation, we may take the analogy of a tape-recorder. Some sound is already recorded in the magnetic tape. A subsequent recording of some other sound automatically erases the previous recording. The last moment's recording of *oṁ* or any other God's name may erase all the *vāsanā* and non-*vāsanā saṁskāras*.

If the complete erasure of the karmic imprints is not possible by the last moment's super-imprint, it may be a fact that, in the life to come, the uppermost, surface imprint on the *antaḥkaraṇa* may be playing a dominating role not to allow the deeper karmic seeds to germinate. By staying in ungerminated condition, they may naturally die like a plant's seed stored for an indefinitely long period.

Japa-Yoga in Tantra

Before we discuss the nature of *japa-yoga* in Tantra, it becomes necessary to clarify what Tantra is. The atmosphere of Tantra is quite foggy and confusingly opaque. The vulgar Tantra is superstitious and full of fraud. Tantra has many cults in the world. All of them are esoteric and most of them are unscientific.

The left-path (*vāma-mārgī* or *vāmācārī*) Tantra is sex-centred. It uses the 5-Ms (*pañca-makāra*), namely, *madya* (liquor), *māṁsa* (meat), *matsya* (fish), *mudrā* (parched or fried grain; coital posture; we accept the second meaning) and *maithuna* (coitus) in its daily rituals and circles (*cakra*s). Animals, birds and even human beings are sacrificed to propitiate the tutelary mother deities. It is fantastic and absurd to think of the Mother of the universe to eat the flesh and drink the blood of her created beings. The aboriginal savage did not know farming, was a hunter and was living on flesh and blood food only. It was natural for him to think of his deity to be fond of flesh and blood. In his primitive condition, nature was angry and ferocious for him. Hence his deity became angry and ferocious rather than kind, compassionate, benign and benevolent. The old, primitive psychology is still continuing in some communities and individuals. Without any ambiguity, we condemn the *vāmācārī* Tantra and the Tāntric cults that are in legion throughout the world now.

Deities in Tantra

It is very often believed that Tantra is a feminine cult and that only female deities are worshipped in Tantra. This is partly true, but not wholly. Both Śiva (God, the Auspicious and the Benevolent) and Śivā (Mother Goddess, the Consort of Lord Śiva) are worshipped in Tantra. Of course, the one and the only one Mother is worshipped in different forms, with different names. These names are: 1. Kālī, 2. Tārā, 3. Chinnamastā, 4. Bhuvaneśvarī, 5. Śrībagalā, 6. Dhūmāvatī, 7. Tripurasundarī, 8. Mātaṅgī, 9. Ṣoḍaśī, 10. Tripurabhairavī. In addition to these ten systems of Tantra, Durgā-Tantra and *Śrīvidyā* are two important Tantra schools. Mother Durgā is the combined Divine Power of Mother Sarasvatī, Mother Kālī and Mother Lakṣmī — the three consorts of the Hindu Trinity. She is the Caṇḍī and the Cāmuṇḍī. She is the totality of all the Divine Powers. Mother Lalitā is worshipped in *Śrīvidyā*. Although mother-worship has gained importance in Tantra, the worship of masculine deities has not been completely ignored. We have Śiva-Tantra, Gaṇeśa-Tantra, Viṣṇu-Tantra, Hanumāna-Tantra, etc.

The Right-path (Dakṣiṇācārī) Tantra

The *tāntrika*s who follow the right path (*dakṣiṇa mārga*) themselves are vegetarians. They do not take alcohol. They do not offer meat, fish and alcohol to their tutelary deities.

They maintain high ethical standards in sex life. They do not associate sex with spirituality. They shun violence and are against sacrificing animals and birds. They do not believe that the Mother of the universe wants to eat flesh, drink blood and alcohol and indulge in sex. Their Mother Deity is benevolent, compassionate, calm, serene and kind. The same Divine Mother may take an angry, ferocious role to subdue the wicked, the barbarous and the savage. But such a role is not common and it becomes necessary only when rare occasions arise.

The *dakṣiṇa-mārgī tāntrika* is a devotee of the Mother of the universe. He is also a *kuṇḍalinī-yogī*. *Kuṇḍalinī* is the universal Mother who dormantly rests in the *mūlādhāra cakra* of everybody in the form of serpentine coils. Through the *tāntrika yoga*, the *dakṣiṇa-mārgī tāntrika* arouses the Mother who ascends through the six *cakra*s, unites with the Divine Father (Śiva) in the seventh *cakra*, the *sahasrāra*, and again descends to rest in the *mūlādhāra*. The *dakṣiṇa-mārgī* Tantra is a special type of *bhakti-yoga*, with the emphasis on the devotion to the Mother.

The Śākta and the Tāntrika

Both the Śākta and the *tāntrika* are Mother-worshippers. The literal meaning of the word *Śakti* is "power." *Māyā* is the power of *Brahman* and *Īśvara* (God). When one *Īśvara* is conceived of the Trinity, namely, Brahmā (the Creator), Viṣṇu (the Nourisher and Sustainer) and Rudra (the Annihilator or Destroyer), their respective powers or Consorts are Sarasvatī, Lakṣmī and Gaurī or Kālī. Subsequently, the one and the only one Mother of the universe has been assigned different forms and names. Both the Śāktas and *tāntrika*s worship them.

The Hindu scriptures maintain that *Īśvara* acts as a Chairperson (*Adhyakṣa*)[128] and that He functions through His Power who is the real executive agent.[129] Both the Śāktas and the *tāntrikas* do worship *Parameśvara* (the great Lord) by worshipping *Parameśvarī* (the Supreme Mother), both *Parameśvara* and *Parameśvarī* being the two poles of one and the only one Reality.

We accept what has been stated here. Then the question pops up: What is the difference between a Śākta and a *tāntrika*? The main devotional activity of the Śākta is worshipping the Divine Mother through specific rituals and praying to Her for getting mercy. The *tāntrika* also does that. But, in addition, he practises many special techniques which distinguish him from the Śākta. The *tāntrika*'s distinguishing features are briefly given in the following paragraphs.

The Special Features of Tantra

First we have to understand the literal meanings of two words, namely, *tanu* and *tantra*. Both these words have been derived from the verb root √*tan*. The affix *un* is used for the first word and *ṣṭran* for the second word. *Tanu* means "the body." The word *tantra* means "a loom," "a thread," "the warp or threads extended lengthwise in a loom." The spiritual expansion of the body (*tanu-vistāra*) is involved in Tantra and this word is used in its etymological sense.

There are some salient steps in the rituals of the Tantra. They are briefly mentioned here.

Physical purification of the gross body. The gross body of the *tāntrika* is purified through six purificatory processes (*ṣaṭkarmas*) of the *haṭha-yoga*. These are: 1. *Neti* or cleansing the nasal passage. 2. *Dhauti* or cleansing the anterior alimentary canal from the mouth to the pyloric sphincter (oesophagus and stomach). 3. *Nauli* or massaging and strengthening the abdominal organs. 4. *Basti* or cleansing the colon and the rectum by the yogic enema. 5. *Kapālabhāti* or cleansing the sinuses in the frontal portion of the head. 6. *Trāṭaka* or fixed gazing at one point.

Spiritual sanctification of the body. A *tāntrika* sanctifies his body by *ācamana* (sipping water that has been made sacred by *mantra*), *tattva-śuddhi* (making the body-elements sacred by sipping water processed by *mantra*), *mārjana* (wiping impurities off the body and the mind by sprinkling *mantra*-processed water on the body), *bhūta-śuddhi* (sanctifying the body-elements by special *mantra*s), and such other techniques.

Vitalizing the body with Prāṇa. The body has a network of *nāḍī*s (subtle channels for the flow of *Prāṇa*), supplying each organ, each tissue and each cell. They originate from the bulb (*kanda*) of the *mūlādhāra cakra*. The three important *nāḍī*s that flow along the spine are the *suṣumṇā*, the *iḍā* and the *piṅgalā* (*fig*. 1.1). The *suṣumṇā* flows in the centre of the spine; the *iḍā* on the left side and the *piṅgalā* on the right side of the spine. The *tāntrika* collects *Prāṇa* from the cosmic source, ensures its free flow in the *nāḍī*s and stores this Prāṇic energy in the *cakra*s of the body. The *cakra*s, in addition to other specific functions, are storage batteries of Prāṇic energy and the transducers of this energy. It is not practicable to arouse *kuṇḍalinī* without a good practice of *prāṇāyāma*. And the arousal of *kuṇḍalinī* is the hub of Tantra.

In the process of doing *prāṇāyāma*, some *bandha*s (yogic locks) and *mudrā*s (yogic seals) are practised. Some special

Fig. 1.1: The courses of the *suṣumṇā*, the *iḍā* and the *piṅgalā*

bandhas and *mudrās* are also very useful for the arousal of *kuṇḍalinī*.

The subtle body (*liṅga* or *sūkṣma śarīra*) is a very complicated web with *cakras* and *nāḍīs*. It is a special type of woven fabric. A representative picture of the *nāḍīs* in a complicated network has been presented in *fig*. 1.2. The nomenclature of Tantra issues from this web-structure. The control of this web-structure and of the switching of its special components is the art and science of Tantra.

Deification of the body. *Nyāsa* is the exclusive speciality of the Tantra. It is the mental appropriation of assignment of various parts of the body to tutelary deities. In this connection, the meaning of the Sanskrit word *mātṛkā* is to

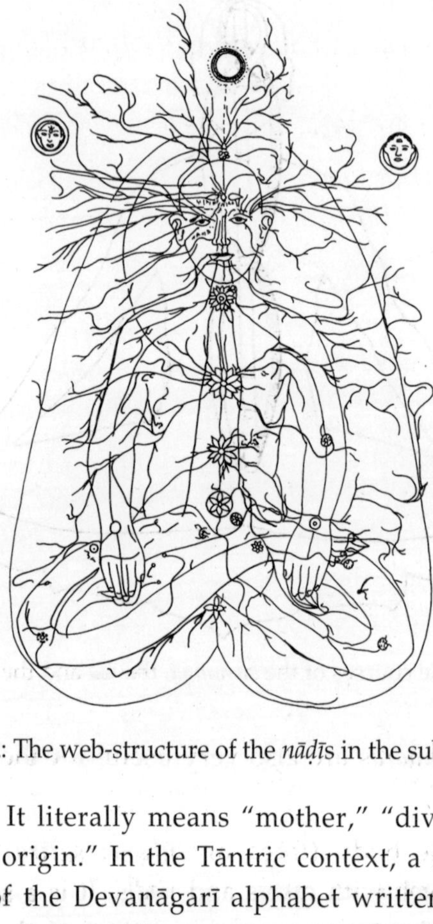

Fig. 1.2: The web-structure of the *nāḍī*s in the subtle body

be known. It literally means "mother," "divine mother," "source," "origin." In the Tāntric context, a *mātṛkā* is any character of the Devanāgarī alphabet written in *maṇḍala*s or *yantra*s (special Tāntric, geometric diagrams), or imprinted in the petals of the six *cakra*s, to which a divine power is ascribed. One of the principal applications of the audible pronunciations of the letters of the Sanskrit alphabet (*vaikharī-varṇamālā*) in Tantra-*sādhanā* is done in the *nyāsa*.

There are many varieties of *nyāsa*. Out of them, the external variety (*bahirmātṛkā-nyāsa*) and the internal variety (*antarmātṛkā-nyāsa*) are worth mentioning here. By *nyāsa*, each part of the body, gross or subtle, becomes a seat of a deity. Even the causal body (*kāraṇa śarīra*) is deified by the *nyāsa*. Thus, it is aptly said that one is to be deified first before one worships the deity[130] (*devo bhūtvā devaṁ yajeta*).

The arousal of kuṇḍalinī from her slumber. The Tantra has a concept of *piṇḍa-brahmāṇḍa*. The contextual meaning of *piṇḍa* here is "the body;" the word *brahmāṇḍa* means "the universe." Whatever exists in the *brahmāṇḍa* does exist in the *piṇḍa*, albeit in a miniature scale. This is the Tāntric concept. Lord Śiva sits in the thousand-petalled lotus (*sahasrāra*) in the crown of the head. It may be mentioned here that Śiva in the Śaiva philosophy and the Tantra is almost equivalent to *Brahman* in the Vedānta. The Tāntric Śiva is not the Rudra of the Hindu Trinity. Śiva's Power (*Śakti* or Consort), the *Mūla-Prakṛti* (the Primordial Nature who is the Mother of the manifested nature) stays in the *mūlādhārā cakra* in a coiled state and hence is known as *kuṇḍalinī* (the word *kuṇḍala* meaning a coil). Śiva is the Divine Father and Kuṇḍalinī is the Divine Mother of the universe. In each of the rest five *cakra*s in between the *mūlādhāra* and the *sahasrāra*, God and Goddess preside in different forms, with different names. *Fig*. 1.3 illustrates the seven *cakra*s in the body. For details, reference may be made to the book *Mind and Supermind*.[131]

In Tāntric scriptures, Śiva is known as *akula* and His *Śakti* (Mother Kuṇḍalinī) as *kula*. Kuṇḍalinī-Yoga is the most prominent special feature in the *kaula-mārga* (the path pertaining to *kula*). It may be mentioned here that Patañjali's *Yoga-Sūtram* nowhere mentions the word *kuṇḍalinī* and that the *Kriyā-Yoga*,[132] as defined by him, is not relevant to Kuṇḍalinī-Yoga. Some of the special features of the *kaula-mārga* are (1) *kumārīpūjanam*, (2) *pramadā-pūjanam*, (3) *cakrārcanam* and (4) *pañcamakārārcanam*. The original *kaula-mārga* was maintaining purity in its rituals. In course of time, it was corrupted and vulgarized. As an example, we will take the *pañca-makāra* and compare and

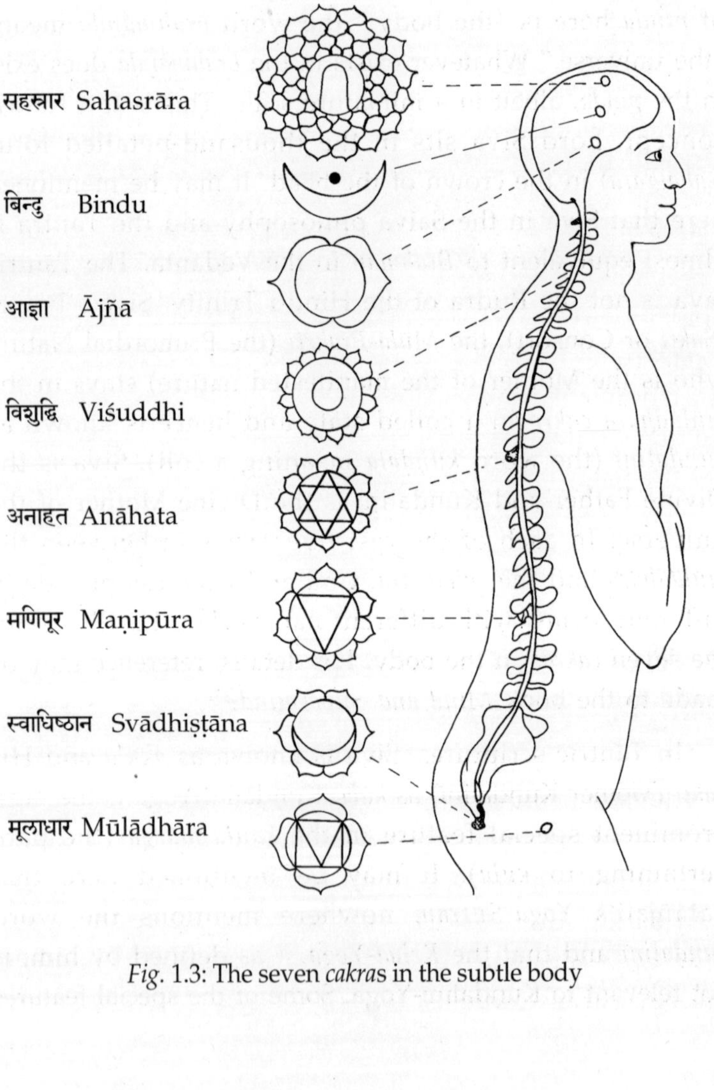

Fig. 1.3: The seven *cakras* in the subtle body

contrast the original and the later versions. The *Rudrayāmalam* is an authoritative Tāntric scripture on Kuṇḍalinī-Yoga. For the true meaning of the *pañca-makāra*, reference may be made to its relevant verses.[133]

Madyam (literally liquor or alcoholic drink) is stimulating nectar that dripples while performing the *khecarī-mudrā*.

Killing animals, birds and human beings and offering their flesh and blood to the deity is proscribed in the original *kaula-mārga*. To kill and sacrifice the animality (*paśutva*), present in the *sādhaka* himself, is prescribed. The *paśutva* generates *saṁskāra*s in the *antaḥkaraṇa* and these *saṁskāra*s out of the white and the black *karma*s are obstacles to *mokṣa* (liberation). Attachment (*āsakti*) to the physical body of flesh and blood and attachment to *vāsanā*s and non-*vāsanā-saṁskāra*s in the subtle and the causal bodies are to be sacrificed for spiritual attainment. The *sādhaka* is advised to kill the *paśutva* and throw away its meat (*māṁsam*).

The word *mīnaḥ* or *matsyaḥ* (fish) has also an occult (*sāndhya*) meaning. As fishes freely swim in streams of water, so should the *prāṇa* freely flow in the *nāḍī*s, namely, the *iḍā*, the *piṅgalā*, the *suṣumṇā* and the sundry branching *nāḍī*s. The *sādhaka* should practise *prāṇāyāma* and should have a control over the flow of *prāṇa* in the *iḍā*, *piṅgalā* and others.

Mudrā, in *pañca-makāra*, does not mean coital poses and postures (*maithuna-mudrā*s). It means the yogic *mudrā*s that function as temporary obstructions to the flow of *prāṇa* and also as switches to some subtle vital structures. Any *kuṇḍalinī sādhaka* must have a mastery over the performances of yogic *mudrā*s and *bandhas*. The *mudrā*s and *bandha*s do belong to the *Tantra-Yoga* and not to the *Pātañjala-Yoga*.

Next, we come to the fifth *makāra*, namely, *maithuna* (literally meaning the union of two). No one can gain proficiency in Tantra without being able to arouse Mother Kuṇḍalinī who ascends (*ārohaṇa*) through the central channel *suṣumṇā*, pierces the *cakras* sequentially, reaches the *sahasrāra*, unites with Lord Śiva, descends (*avarohaṇa*) on the reverse pathway and rests in the *mūlādhāra* again. The union of the Mother and the Father is *maithuna*. Without understanding the correct scriptural meaning of the word *maithuna*, many *vāma-mārgī tāntrika*s today indulge in coital pleasure with other women in the name of Tantra.

The *Rudrayāmalam* gives other meanings of *madyam* and *māṁsam*.[134] The *Śakti* (the Power of Śiva, Mother Kuṇdalinī) is the *madyam* (the alcoholic intoxicant or the stimulating elixir) and Lord Śiva is the *māṁsam* (flesh, the strength of muscles). In order to get success in *tantra-sādhanā*, the first prerequisite for one is to develop firm faith (*niṣṭhā*) and unwavering devotion for Śiva and *Śakti*.

The meanings of some words used by the original *kaula-mārga* have been totally distorted by the later *vāma-mārgī*s. The original *kumārī-pūjā* was the worship of Kumārī or Mother Durgā, performed by a ceremony at the great Durgā festival when a girl between ten and twelve years old is placed on a pedestal as the representative of the goddess, and fed with offerings made to the idol. On the other hand, the *vāmācārī*s did the *kumārī-pūjā* by worshipping the *yoni* of a sexually mature virgin girl and subsequently cohabitating with her.

The *kaula-mārgī*s do *pramadā-pūjā* by worshipping Mother Kālī in her posture and gesture of protruding her tongue and vigorously dancing delightfully on the chest of

Lord Śiva. The *vāma-mārgī* takes a young and wanton woman, does her *yoni-pūjā*, intoxicates him (including her) by taking the offered *māṁsa, matsya,* and *madya,* and subsequently cohabitates with her, she playing the role of the upper partner.

The *kaula-mārgī*s meditate on the seven *cakra*s and the deities who preside there. This is their *cakra-sādhanā* or *cakra-pūjā*. In the *vāmācāra*, a group of women lie on the ground with face upwards, without clothes, radially in a circle, with heads towards the centre. After the *yoni-pūjā*, the male *tāntrika*s do herd cohabitation in rotation.

In the last half of the twentieth century, there has been mushroom growth of tāntric institutions in countries outside India. There has been a tremendous increase in the number of foreign writers on Tantra. Most of them have no comprehension of the fact that Tantra is a highly developed spiritual science. They associate Tantra with Freudian psychology centring around sex-libido. In their attempt, they try to release the suppressed sex-libido by licentious sex-practices, both homo and hetero. They have vulgarized and barbarized Tantra with savage sexuality, without a trace of divinity. It is unfortunate that the present-day Tantra in India is *mostly* black magic, superstitious cult or total fraud and that the popularity of Tantra in the West is mainly due to sex-barbarism in *most* cases.

It is to be re-emphasized here that Tantra is a purely spiritual system in which the Mother of the universe (*Śakti*) and the Father of the universe (Śiva) are worshipped for *bhukti* (worldly living free from pain and suffering) and *mukti* (liberation of the spirit, *ātmā*). It has nothing to do with immoral sensuality and bestial pleasure.

Cakra-sādhanā. In addition to *kuṇḍalinī*-arousal, the *tāntrika* does *cakra-sādhanā*. For doing it, one has to be fully acquainted with the anatomy of the seven major *cakra*s (*mūlādhāra, svādhiṣṭhāna, maṇipūra, anāhata, viśuddhi, ājñā* and *sahasrāra*) and a few minor ones. The *cakra*s are located in the subtle body and may not be confused with gross structures such as the pineal, the pituitary, etc. Furthermore, each *cakra* is horizontally placed around the vertical axis of the spine. Some Yoga schools erroneously consider the *cakra*s to be vertical and dual, one in front and the other on the back. Some other Yoga schools speculate additional *cakra*s on the two hands and the two feet. This is pure speculation out of phantastic imagination.

Cakra-sādhanā belongs to *Tantra-Yoga* (not *Pātañjala Yoga*). This book does not need the details of the *cakra-sādhanā*. Only this much is said that, for *siddhi* in tāntric *mantra-japa*, both *kuṇḍalinī*-arousal and *cakra-sādhanā* are essential pre-requisites.

Puraścaraṇa. *Puraścaraṇa* is a preparatory or introductory rite before the actual *mantra-japa* or actual *pūjā* (ritual worshipping of a deity). Rites like *ācamana, tattvaśuddhi, prāṇāyāma, bandha*s, *mudrā*s, *mārjana, bhūtaśuddhi, nyāsa*, etc., are included in *puraścaraṇa*.

Pūjā. In Tantra, both *yantra-pūjā* and *mūrti-pūjā* are done. A *yantra* or a *maṇḍala* is a mystic, geometrical diagram specific for each deity. Spiritual powers are invoked and invited to be seated in different parts of the *yantra* and are worshipped there. *Āvaraṇa-pūjā* is also part of the *yantra-pūjā*. Spiritual powers seated in concentric spheres and the peripheral squares are worshipped in succession, starting from the centre and ending at the outermost structures.

The literal meaning of the word *āvaraṇa* is a cover, or a veil. In Tantra, the *yantra-pūjā* gains more importance than the *mūrti-pūjā*.

The word *mūrti* means an icon, an image, an idol, a form. It may be made of gold, silver, brass, stone, earth, etc. The deity may be invited to stay in the icon permanently to accept the worship by performing special rituals. Alternatively, the deity may be invited (*āvāhana*) to come and stay in the icon for one-time *pūjā* only. After the *pūjā* is over, the worshipper bids farewell to the deity (*visarjana*).

It has already been said that while doing the *japa* of a *mantra*, the meaning of the *mantra* is to be meditated upon. The same principle holds good for the *mūrti-pūjā*.[135] The statue of Mahatma Gandhi is not itself Mahatma Gandhi. Knowing it fully well, we still need a statue. God or Mother Goddess who is really formless and who is omnipotent, omniscient and omnipresent cannot be equated to an idol made by man out of materials such as any metal, alloy, wood, stone, etc. The worshipper's thought on the Divine Mother or Father, while sitting before the icon for worship, plays a crucial role here.

Mantra-japa. The tāntric *mantra-japa* follows the *mūrti-pūjā*, or in the absence of a *mūrti*, it follows the *yantra-pūjā*, preceded by the preliminary rites of *puraścaraṇa*. Each deity has a specific *mantra* or a number of specific *mantras*. Each *mantra* has its special *nyāsa*. No tāntric *mantra-japa* is done, unless it is preceded by its *nyāsa*.

If a *mantra-japa* is done, say, 100,000 times, *havana* (oblation in a fire-sacrifice) is to be done 10,000 times (one-tenth of *japa*), *tarpaṇa* (satiating the deity by presenting him/her libations of water) is to be done 1,000 times (one-tenth of *havana*), *mārjana* or *abhiṣeka* (purification by sprinkling or pouring water) is to be done 100 times (one-tenth of *tarpaṇa*) and feeding 10 spiritually realized and highly ethical persons, otherwise known as *brāhmaṇa-bhojana* is the final rite (one-tenth of *mārjana*).

For getting *mantra-siddhi* in Tantra, the total *puraścaraṇa*, starting from *ācamana* and ending with *brāhmaṇa-bhojana*, is to be completed. Of course, *puraścaraṇa*s may be repeated for years together in order to get Mother's grace, without which no *mantra-siddhi* is possible. The applications of the *mantra* through *japa* become more effective only after *mantra-siddhi* is attained. The applications are for *bhukti* (fulfilment of worldly desires and redemptions from miseries and misfortunes) and/or *mukti* (spiritual liberation).

Tāntric Mantras

The Vedic *mantra*s belong to the *Nigama* whereas the Tāntric *mantra*s to the *Āgama*. The word Tantra has already been etymologically expanded. It unfolds and dilates the meanings and the significance of the cosmos, gives techniques to control the cosmic events through *mantra-sādhanā* by which evils, misfortunes and sufferings can be averted and got rid of.[136] The word *mantra* has already been etymologically derived. It is an instrument of thought. By doing *japa* of the *mantra*, the *sādhaka* intensely thinks on its meaning. The *mantra* protects the person who meditates on it.[137] The words *mantra* and *āgama* are closely related if their meanings are considered. *Āgama* is that from which comes higher knowledge on techniques which can be adopted for the good of the universe.[138]

The word *mātṛkā*, in the Tāntric context, has already been explained. There are altogether 50 *mātṛkās*, staring from *a* and ending in *kṣa*. The *Mantra-mahodadhi* of Mahīdhara says that all *mantras* consist of *varṇas* (characters of the Sanskrit alphabet), that all *mantras* are rooted in Mother *Śakti*, that the *mātṛkās* are to be known as Mother *Śakti* and that *Śakti* is one pole of the bipolar Reality, the other pole being Śiva.[139]

The Tāntric tradition does not consider the *varṇas* (letters of the alphabet) as simple written symbols and their sounds as simple vibrations produced by the vocal organs. Mother Sarasvatī plays her *vīṇā* with three strings. The primal sound produced by her *vīṇā* is *oṁ* (*AUṀ*) which generates all other sounds. The whole universe of matter and energy is a manifestation of the vibrations (*spandana*) of the strings of the *vīṇā* of Mother Sarasvatī. This theory of vibration has been expounded by the *Yoginī-Hṛdaya Tantra*.[140] The Tantra regards the *mātṛkās* as the Primordial Power (*Ādyāśakti*), the Mother of the universe. *Mantras* are vitally important for the *tantra-sādhanā*.

Every tāntric *mantra* has its characteristic *nyāsa*, different from the general *nyāsa*. Before the *japa* of a tāntric *mantra*, its *nyāsa* must be performed. Unless the *nyāsa* precedes the *mantra-japa*, the *japa* is likely to hardly bear any fruit. Since Tantra scriptures are 64 in number, and the number of *mantras* are in millions or billions, the *nyāsa* of any particular *mantra* is not given here.

Tāntric *mantras* have *bījas* (seed-syllables). It is hard to find out the etymological meaning of any seed-syllable. However, they are the keys or the switches of the *mantras* which do not work if the *bīja*(s) is missing. The tāntric *mantra* is to be pronounced correctly and especially the *bīja*s are to be accurately uttered. Some *bījas* and their *devatā*s (deities) are given here.

bīja	*devatā, or tattva, or vācya*	*name of the bīja*
oṁ (AUṀ)	*Brahman, Īśvara*	*tāra, praṇava*
aiṁ	Sarasvatī	*vāgbīja*
hrīṁ	Gaurī,Śakti	*māyā-bīja, śakti-bīja*
śrīṁ	Lakṣmī, Kamalā	*lakṣmī-bīja*
krīṁ	Kālī	*kālī-bīja*
klīṁ	Ātmabhuḥ	*kāma-bīja*
gaṁ	Gaṇeśa	*gaṇapati-bīja*
glauṁ	Gaṇeśa	*bhū-bīja*
hauṁ, hrauṁ	Śiva	*rudra-bīja*
kṣrauṁ	Nṛsiṁha	*nṛsiṁha-bīja*
haṁ	Sadāśiva, *ākāśa*	*ākāśa-bīja, vyoma-bīja*
yaṁ	*vāyu*	*vāyu-bīja*
raṁ	*agni*	*vahni-bīja, agni-bīja*
vaṁ	*jala*	*amṛta-bīja, sudhā-bīja*
laṁ	*pṛthvī*	*kāma-bīja, bhū-bīja*
huṁ	*kavaca*	*krodha-bīja*
hūṁ	*kūrcam*	*varma-bīja*
saḥ	*haṁsaḥ*	*brahma-bīja*

In a typical *mantra*, *tāra* or *praṇava* (*oṁ*) is the first syllable. The name of the *devatā* (deity) is in the dative case-ending, placed either after the *praṇava* or in the end. The word *namaḥ* (meaning making an obeisance or paying obeisance) is used before or after the name of the *devatā*.

Instead of *namaḥ*, some *mantra*s contain *svāhā* (*vahnikāntā*), *vaṣaṭ*, *huṁ*, *vauṣaṭ* and *phaṭ*. *Svāhā* is mostly used while reverently offering something to God/Goddess.

In such cases, the dative case ending is used in the name of the *devatā* or the *aṅga* which is touched in the *nyāsa*.

A few *mantras* contain *svāhā*; but the name of the deity is used in the vocative case-ending (for example: *oṁ hrīṁ śrīṁ krīṁ parameśvari kālike hrīṁ śrīṁ krīṁ svāhā*).

It is generally believed that tāntric *mantras* are made use of in *sakāma japa* (*japa* done for the fulfilment of a desire), for material prosperity, for sensual pleasure and against enemies. This belief is not usually untrue. However, it is a fact that tāntric *japas* can be done and are being done by some *sādhakas* for spiritual transformation, for getting peace in life and for spiritual liberation. Tantra is an *ādhyātmika vidyā* (spiritual subject) and it should be used for every noble cause. It is unfortunate that the applications of Tantra have so far been made by many *tāntrikas* for ignoble, unholy and vulgar purposes.

The Mechanism of Action of Mantra-Japa

Without ifs and buts, we accept the fact that *mantra-japa* works. This is observational and experimental. Having accepted the fact, now we investigate into its mechanism of action.

The Mechanism of Action of the Praṇava-Japa and the Ajapā-Japa

In the *oṅkāra-japa*, we observe that *dhyāna-yoga*, *bhakti-yoga* and *jñāna-yoga* are mixed together. The whole process is a mixture of dualism and non-dualism, the latter following the former. In the *Vaiśvānara* and the *Taijasa* states, dualism of "I" and *Brahman* or "I" and God is distinct. Furthermore, pluralism is operative in these two states. The universe of manifoldness and diversity is experienced by the self either in the waking state or in the dream state. In the state of deep sleep, pluralism disappears, dualism fades and non-dualism dominates over dualism. None the less, dualism does not completely disappear. The awareness of "I" still persists in a thinly faint manner. In the fourth (*turīya*) state, pure non-dualism prevails, and in this state, there is complete identity of the *individual* self and the Universal Self. Here language fails in expression due to the absence of individuality in the *turīya*.

Bhakti-yoga has little relevance in non-dualism. A *bhakti-yogī* must be dualistic. His "I" (his self) prays to *Īśvara* or *Īśvarī* (God or Goddess) and surrenders to the latter. *Parameśvara* (God, the Supreme) or *Parameśvarī* (Goddess, the Supreme) is the *vācya* (one who is named or designated) and *oṅkāra* (*oṁ*) is the *vācaka* (the designating word). By simply repeating the utterance of *oṁ*, the devotee mentally prostrates at the feet of God (the Mother or the Father) and surrenders to Her or Him. The devotee's mind is fixed in God. He develops his concentration and one-pointedness (*ekāgratā*). He gets satisfaction. He develops his mental strength. He feels that he is not helpless and that he has a Protector, a Redeemer and a benevolent, compassionate friend, guide and saviour. His mind never experiences a vacuity surrounded by a whirlwind. He is always full, in supersaturation; he is calm, serene, firm and steady.

The *oṅkāra-japa*, in a mature state, becomes a *dhyāna*. One and only one idea of God alone flows in the mind in an unbroken state devoid of interruption. This is Patañjali's *dhyāna*. Thus, all the benefits of *dhyāna* one gets from the *oṅkāra-japa*.

The adept *dhyāna-yogī* who practises *oṅkāra-japa* suspends the *japa* in the concluding stage and remains in a thoughtless condition. This is the state of *samādhi*. The preceding state of *oṅkāra-japa* prepares the mind to easily enter into the *samādhi* state. Hence, the *sādhaka* gets the benefits of *samādhi* from his *oṅkāra-japa*.

Jñāna-yoga (the *yoga* of knowledge) is very often misinterpreted. Anybody who acquires vast informational knowledge and is an erudite scholar is not a *jñāna-yogī*. Anybody who has extensively and intensively studied religious scriptures, who can write books on God and who can eloquently deliver speech on God is not a *jñāna-yogī*. Who is a *jñāna-yogī* then? One who has acquired true knowledge on *Brahman*, who has realized *Brahman* and has merged in *Brahman*, albeit still living with the body, is a *jñāna-yogī*.

The Vedāntic *japa-yoga* has a *so 'ham* (He is I) *japa*. This is the *ajapā-japa* (a *japa* which is spontaneously done in perfect unison with the inhalation and the exhalation). Every living creature, human or non-human, unconsciously and spontaneously does this *japa*. But, this does not become a yogic *japa*. A *yogī* consciously does it. He fine-tunes his slow and effortless inhalation while silently uttering *so* (*saḥ*), and slow as well as effortless exhalation while silently uttering *ham* (*aham*). Thus, in every respiration (inhalation and exhalation) he silently utters "He (God) is I." Not only does he utter, but also intensely thinks over the idea. It becomes a life-long *dhyāna* for him. Intermittently, the *japa-dhyāna* is suspended to merge in a *samādhi*. Such a *yogī* attains *Brahma*-realization, the realization that he is not different from *Brahman*. The culmination of *jñāna-yoga* is the identification of the self with the Supreme Self. A *jñāna-yogī* acquires *buddhi-yoga*. A *buddhi-yogī*'s actions become spiritual. He becomes free from I-centredness. In the mature state of his *jñāna-yoga*, he becomes I-less and my-less. His *vāsanā*s and non-*vāsanā-saṁskāra*s are erased from his *karmāśaya*. He lives with his present body due to *prārabdha-karma* only. He is released from bondage. He becomes a *jīvanmukta* (released, albeit still living).

A *yogī*, with life-long, constant practice of *oṅkāra-japa*, continues to repeat the *praṇava* till he leaves his body at the time of death. Such a *yogī* dies with no *karmāśaya* or with a *sāttvika karmāśaya* with the imprint of *oṁ* only. In the former case, he is not reborn after death. In the latter case, he is reborn as a saint to dedicate his next life to the welfare of the creation.

The Mechanism of Action of the Devotional Japa

Dualism is an inseparable feature of *bhakti-yoga*. The self in the individual prays to the Universal Self, the Almighty, the Benevolent, the Compassionate, the Redeemer.

In our philosophy, non-dualism is the fact. But dualism is not discarded, at least emotionally and psychologically, in the apparently bound states of the self. In the course of the lives of an individual, he passes through dualism and reaches the ultimate goal of non-dualism. In our concept of *mokṣa* (liberation), the individual self, on liberation, loses its individuality, its separateness and becomes *Brahman*. Although, for empirical purpose, we accept and practise dualism as a ladder to ascend and reach our goal of non-dualism, there is no place of dualism at all in our concept of *mokṣa*.

Dualistic *japa* may be *niṣkāma* (without any desire for worldly fulfilment) or *sakāma* (with a desire for worldly fulfilment). The *niṣkāma japa* has two varieties, namely, devotion to God for the sake of devotion only and devotion for deliverance, redemption. The *sakāma japa* is done for getting rescued from worldly miseries, sufferings and disasters such as poverty, unemployment, diseases, impending death, natural or man-made calamities, etc. It is also done for getting success, more wealth, better position, more fame and all sorts of materialistic progress and prosperity.

Irrespective of the fact of the purpose of the *japa*, *sakāma* or *niṣkāma*, if done devoutly, the mind becomes undisturbed, calm and tranquil. A disturbed and worried mind adversely affects the organs of the body. A peaceful and calm mind keeps the diseases away. Moreover, bliss (*ānanda*), which is precious in life, saturates the mind and the body of the devotee. He also feels safe and secure. He does not helplessly move in a purposeless, random way in the midst of a whirlwind. He has a firm conviction that God, the Saviour, would protect and save him. This firm faith helps him fight the peril and adversity.

The *sakāma* devotee, if a true and staunch believer in God, unconditionally does *japa*. He becomes happy if his desire is fulfilled. He does not become unhappy if his *japa* does not bear desired fruits and his suffering is not relieved. He accepts the verdict of God without questioning. *Japa* does not and cannot compel God to always take action in favour of an individual. The universal welfare is taken care of sometimes even by sacrificing the interest of a devotee. And what is a calamity for an ignorant devotee may not be calamity at all.

The doctrine of *karma* (*karmavāda*) controls the lives of human beings. We earn a fate by virtue of our *karma* done in different lives. God whimsically does not decree a fate to anybody. Each one initiates a life for the fruition of some *karma* out of the karmic impressions accumulated in our *karmāśaya* of the subtle and the causal bodies. This *karma* with which this life initiates is the *prārabdha karma*. *Ordinarily*, this *prārabdha karma* is not altered and one has to undergo it in this life. One may be pious and saintly. One may be a sinner and a criminal. Each one has to get one's *karma-phala* (the fruits of the *prārabdha karma*) in this life, some of them being good and some others being bad. Some theorists of the *karmavāda* are rigidly deterministic. They hold that *karmavāda* fuctions mechanically and rigidly, obeying the law of cause and effect, and that God does not interfere with His Law under all circumstances.

We are reluctant to accept this rigid interpretation of the doctrine of *karma*. *Bhakti-yoga* loses its relevance if this rigid mechanics of *karmavāda* is accepted. Furthermore, we may say that religions are redundant if the rigid law of cause and effect is strictly adhered to.

In our opinion, God shows compassion to a devotee if the latter is sincere and staunch in his devotion. God judges the merit of each case. Does the devotee deserve compassion? How bad was his *karma* in his past lives? If divine compassion violates the Cosmic Law and the present devotee was a sinner of the first degree in his past lives, *japa* or any devotional ritual does not bear any tangible fruits. A heinous crime does deserve a stringent punishment. However, if the case is deserving, as judged by God, His compassion showers on the devotee. The punishment is either waived or reduced. And, for progress and prosperity, divine help paves the way for the devotee to walk smoothly for attaining the goal. Even for the worst sinner, *japa* is never vain and fruitless. If *japa* does not alleviate the suffering in this life, it does bear favourable fruit in the lives to come. It accelerates spiritual evolution. Forgiveness is a noble quality of good persons in the world. What is our concept of God if we think that He never forgives?

One earns a fate based on one's *karma* in one's past lives. The sufferings in this life are penances (*prāyaścittas*) for the past bad *karmas*. Such penances would subtract the bad *karmas* from the cumulative ledger in the *karmāśaya* (*sañcita karma*). It is to be emphasized here that God does not decree a good or a bad fate to anybody and that the person's *karma* in different births is responsible for what he is and what he will be.[141]

In the *Bhagavad-Gītā*, Lord Śrīkṛṣṇa assures Arjuna that his devotee is never annihilated.[142] A person who may be the worst sinner is transformed into an honest and pious man by sincere and unwavering devotion.[143] He has to repent, and repentance must be accompanied by the discontinuance of sinful acts. Without getting out of the mud and washing the feet, and without a strong determination not to enter into the mud again, one cannot be clean by devotion alone.

If we accept *karmavāda* and simultaneously accept the non-involvement of God in the fates of individuals, we have to explain the mechanism of action of *bhakti* in general, and *japa-yoga* in particular, in the alleviation of suffering of a devotee. Here we may be cautious against restricting our life to one incarnation only. The process of spiritual progress must spread through multiple incarnations. By virtue of *bhakti*, the devotee dusts off the dirt from his mirror of *buddhi* (a subtle organ of intellect in the *antaḥkaraṇa*).[144] His *buddhi* gains transparency. His ignorance is removed. Spiritual wisdom dawns on him. His actions become unattached to the fruits thereof. He becomes free from dualities and opposites. He develops equanimity of mind. The term *buddhi-yoga* is applied to all these attributes and actions.[145]

What has been described in the foregoing paragraph seems to be a natural (*svabhāvataḥ*), automatic mechanism operated by the usual law of cause and effect. Is it a natural process only? Does not God play any role in this process? The answer is: It is both. In this context, reference may be made to the book *Mind and Supermind*.[146] *Brahman* is the Fundamental, Pure Consciousness. Every created entity, living or non-living, gains induced consciousness. The *buddhi* of a person, reflected by the light of the Pure Consciousness, is rendered conscious. God (*Īśvara*) is not inert, inactive and indifferent. He gives *buddhi-yoga* to his devotee for ascending the rungs of the ladder of spirituality.[147]

The climax of the *bhakti-yoga* terminates in quashing the usual logic, the empirical science of cause and effect and all norms of rationality. Logic, rationality and morality are empirical subjects which cannot be applied to God, since He has no needs of His own and He functions through His Power for the welfare of His creation rather than for Him. The *Bhagavad-Gītā* culminates in the following advice of Lord Kṛṣṇa to Arjuna:

> Let your mind be united with me. Be devoted to me. Offer yourself to me. Prostrate thyself before me. "Thou shalt come to me." This is my true promise to thee. Thou art dear to me. Abandoning all conflicts and perplexities of do's and don't's, take shelter in me alone. I shall release thee from all sins. Be not worried and grieved.[148]

Brahman is an ocean of Pure Consciousness. The Power or *Śakti* of *Brahman* or *Īśvara*, first of all, creates the cosmic mind or supermind which is known as the *virāḍ* in the Vedas and the *mahat* in the Sāṅkhya. The individual mind, in an intense state of devotion and one-pointed state of *mantra-japa*, links up with the supermind which, in turn, connects the devotee with the ocean of Pure Consciousness or *Īśvara*. The Supreme Person (*Paramātmā*) does not reside elsewhere. He is all-pervading and omnipresent. He resides inside and outside the body of the devotee. But the union is accomplished in the intense state of meditation and devotion (*dhyāna* and *bhakti*).

When *dhyāna* and *bhakti* are mature, the *yogī* sees everything in God and God in everything.[149] At this state, he is a completely transformed person. His thoughts, actions and speeches cannot be anything other than divine. The *bhakti-yogī*, on gaining the Supreme Lord, realizes that there is no better gain whatsoever; being established in Him, he is not shaken even by the heaviest sorrow.[150]

The Mechanism of Action of the Tāntric Japa

In general, any particular *tāntrika* has an *iṣṭa-devatā* (a chosen tutelary deity; a favourite god or goddess; one particularly worshipped). The *iṣṭa-deva* is a male deity and the *iṣṭa-devī* is a female deity. Tantra and *bhakti-yoga* are inextricably woven. Hence all that has already been said for the dualistic *bhakti-yoga* on the mechanism of action can be applied to Tantra.

Tāntric worships are mostly *sakāma* (for the fulfilment of some worldly desire). Thus, it is said that Tantra is for *bhukti* (worldly benefits: getting more of material possession, power, success, sensual gratification, victory over enemies, cure of diseases, postponement of death and escape from calamities, etc.). Tantra can also be used for *mukti* (liberation from birth, old age, diseases, death and cycles of reincarnation, finally taking shelter at the feet of God or becoming God). Most *tāntrika*s hardly use Tantra for *mukti*. But it can be used and is being used by some highly enlightened *tāntrika*s purely for *mukti* alone.

In the course of performing tāntric rituals in the *puraścaraṇa* (the introductory phase of the worship), the *sādhaka* becomes a *kāliśī* (one whose all body-organs, tissues and cells get deified). He places the deity in each part of his body. He himself becomes the deity. In the state of heightened deification, it becomes really a fact that the deity worships the deity. At this state, dualism vanishes and non-dualism prevails.

All the lower six *cakra*s of the deified *tantra-sādhaka* are fully charged. The petals of the *cakra*s vibrate when the corresponding *mātṛkā* in a *mantra* is pronounced. The *Prāṇa* (the primal unified force and energy) stored in the *cakra*s, which act as transducers, gets converted into electromagnetic energy which, in turn, can be transformed into any other form of energy. A *sādhaka* cannot get *mantra-*

siddhi unless and until he can manipulate and fully control his six *cakra*s.

It is not easy at all to control and manipulate the *cakra*s without the arousal, ascent and descent of Mother Kuṇḍalinī. The passage of Mother Kuṇḍalinī through the *suṣumṇā* (passage through the *iḍā* or the *piṅgalā* is hazardous and dangerous) energises and activates the *bīja*s (seeds) and petals (*dala*s) of the *cakra*s. Without the periodical union of Śiva and Śakti of the composite bipolar reality, the full potency of a tāntric *mantra* is not a feasible proposition. Judging these hard facts, it can be said, without prejudice to the mushroom growth of *kuṇḍalinī yogī*s in the modern age, that one has to be skeptic in distinguishing a genuine *tantra-sādhaka* from a multitude of fake and fraudulent ones.

The *tāntrika* uses external *yantra*s or *maṇḍala*s in his worship. As a matter of fact, the *cakra*s inside his body are subtle *yantra*s or *maṇḍala*s. No *tantra* is very effective without the use of the internal *yantra*s and/or an external *yantra*. The *yantra* is the electronic circuit in the system of Tantra. Deities (*devatā*s) are placed at different points of the external *yantra* (deities permanently sit on the *cakra*s). They are worshipped according to specific rituals. *Yantra*s, deified in this way, act as switches to trigger tāntric actions.

Mind-waves are different from brain-waves. The former are subtler, with smaller wavelengths and higher frequency. Through uttering a *mantra*, either silently or verbally, mind-waves are generated and transmitted. They can be transmitted to all directions. But a tāntric *sādhaka* very often needs to focus them on a specified target. He can do it by training his subtle internal organs (*antaḥkaraṇa*) through special techniques. Once the mind-waves are focused on a target, living or non-living, they start affecting the target to produce the desired effect. The common saying "mind over matter" becomes operative through this mechanism. The organs of the target body can be healed. The organs of the target body can be diseased. A non-living body can also be affected in the way the *sādhaka* desires.

The mind-waves can be obstructed by intervening material bodies. A *tāntrika* cannot normally transmit his mind-waves from India to the USA or to any such distant place to affect a target. The curvature of the earth functions as an obstacle.

In Tantra, there is a way to get over this difficulty in the transmission of mind-waves to far-off places. In this context, reference may be made to the eight *siddhis*, given in *Pātañjala Yoga*.[151] Out of these, *mahimā* is a *siddhi* by which the *yogī* enlarges his body in any direction and any dimension. For the long distance transmission of mind-waves, the *tāntrika* enlarges his subtle body vertically to the *antarikṣa* (higher space) so that his *sahasrāra* is placed at a higher altitude to function as a satellite.

Inter-planetary and inter-galactic transmission by Tantra is also possible if the *tāntrika* is a *siddha* person. For this purpose, the mind-waves are to be converted into quanta and vice versa and the *tantra-yogī* has to be accomplished in *aṇimā siddhi* (by which the body or any material object including waves and particles is reduced in size). At this micro-level, the dual state of waves and particles of the mind-waves of the *yogī* passes through any obstruction in the analogy of neutrinos.

The transmission of mind-waves through tāntric *mantras* to affect matter and/or mind in the desired way is one type of tāntric mechanics which does not need the mediation of Mother Goddess. There is a second branch of tāntric mechanics, functioning without the mediation of Mother Goddess, and this is known as tāntric *ṣaṭkarma* (six ritual actions). These are: 1. *śānti-karma*; 2. *vaśīkaraṇa*; 3. *vidveṣaṇa*; 4. *stambhana*; 5. *uccāṭana*; and 6. *māraṇa*.[152]

The word *śānti* means "peace." *Śānti-karma* is the tāntric ritual for *mantra-japa* for restoring peace, getting cure from diseases, avoiding and dispelling calamities and propitiating unfavourable planetary gods (*graha-devatā*s). Among the six *karma*s, this is the only one that a benevolent *tāntrika* should do. The rest five are more or less malevolent and should be avoided for their offensive use.

Vaśīkaraṇa is the act of subjugating or bewitching a person by charms and incantations. There are two other sub-*karma*s that are included in *vaśīkaraṇa*. These are *ākarṣaṇa* and *sammohana*. To bring about attraction between two persons is *ākarṣaṇa*. *Sammohana* is deluding, infatuating or stupefying a person.

Every individual person has his or her own liberty. Goodwill or love between two persons should depend upon their freedom of will and consent. It is unethical, rather a criminal action, to apply Tantra for *vaśīkaraṇa*, *ākarṣaṇa* and *sammohana*, except in some special circumstances.

In some special cases, however, the *vaśīkaraṇa* group of the *karma*s may be applied to help a person to whom injustice has been done and who is really suffering for no fault of his or hers. But for such an application, the *tāntrika* should investigate into the case, find out the truth, and if found deserving, may apply the *karma* for ameliorating the suffering of a person. Under no circumstances, should the *tāntrika*'s personal interest and mercenary gain be involved in this tāntric *karma*. Here we cite an example for the clarification of the issue. A person is involved in extra-marital sex relation. He hates his wife, tortures her and attempts to kill her. This is a befitting case for a benevolent *tāntrika* to apply *vaśīkaraṇa* or *ākarṣaṇa* or *sammohana*.

Vidveṣaṇa means "causing to hate," "rendering hostile." Without qualification, it involves violence (*hiṁsā*), and it is a criminal action. No good *tāntrika* who wants to live a moral, spiritual life should practise it. However, its practice is ethical if done judiciously. The example already cited is a befitting case for consideration. The *tāntrika* may, by *vidveṣaṇa*, create a situation in which disliking and hatred may develop between the husband and his extra-marital, immoral beloved.

Stambhana is making a person rigid or immovable like a pillar. It is paralysing the whole body or part of the body of the target person. *Uccāṭana* is making a person violently excitable, talking loudly, incoherently and disconnectedly by the derangement of his mind. *Stambhana* and *uccāṭana* also involve violence and crime, committed by the *tāntrika*. These are morally prohibitive and legally criminal. They must not find a place in spirituality. However, a *tāntrika*, spiritually highly evolved and maintaining a very high standard of morality, may apply these two techniques, especially *stambhana*, against a person who is undoubtedly a menance to the world community or a very large section of humanity. In such cases, the *tāntrika* is to see that he is not personally inimical to the target person, that his self-interests are not involved in it, and that he applies these techniques *purely* for the benefit of the world, especially when humanity faces the gravest danger and disaster from the target person.

Māraṇa is killing the target person. *Unconditionally*, it is prohibited for the *human tāntrikas*. The hell waits for a human *tāntrika* if he applies this technique even for the most demoniac target person. *Māraṇa* is murder. Any murderous action cannot be part of spirituality. Nobody has the right to take law into his own hands. And anyone who takes God's law into one's own hands is the worst sinner who cannot escape from divine punishment.

That being so, the provision of *māraṇa* in Tantra seems to be redundant and meaningless. Why did the *tāntrika ṛṣis* reveal this technique? It is not meaningless in all circumstances. Occasions, albeit rare, do occur, when the application of this technique becomes unavoidable for protecting the world from the attacks of demons. It is the *jīvanmukta* who has the right to decide if and when this tāntric technique of *māraṇa* becomes unavoidably necessary for application. If the *tāntrika* is *really* a *jīvanmukta*, he may exercise his option to apply this last tāntric technology for the cosmic welfare or the welfare of a vast section of the society.

The Psychological and the Physiological Mechanism of the Action of Japa

In addition to the mechanisms of action of various types of *japa*, so far described, *japa* also exerts effects, through other mechanisms, on the psyche and the *soma*. The mind can be favourably affected by *japa*. The body too can be favourably affected by *japa*. The mechanisms will be briefly described here.

We hold the view that the mind is different from the brain and that the latter is an apparatus of the former. Further, we hold that the mind is material, albeit too subtle to be detected by our usual six sense-organs. All the elements of *dhyāna* are in-built in *japa*. As *dhyāna* has calming (*praśānta*) effect on the mind, so also has *japa* a similar effect. Both *dhyāna* and *japa* free the mind from mental distractions and disturbances and bring about pin-pointedness (*ekāgratā*). They improve mental concentration and working efficiency. Of the two, *japa* is easier than *dhyāna*, although the latter is more efficacious from yogic point of view.

Japa favourably affects the mind which, in turn, exerts favourable influence on the cerebrum of the brain of the gross body and also on the lower six *cakra*s in the subtle body. The prefrontal area (psychic centre) of the frontal lobe of the cerebrum is located below the spot between the two eyebrows. All the cerebral centres have access to the psychic centre through nerve fibres. Stressful stimuli received through the exteroceptors or the interoceptors ultimately converge on the psychic centre, from where messages are transmitted to the hypothalamus. There are direct nerve connections between the frontal lobe and the hypothalamus. Most of these connections are two-way and bilateral. The hypothalamus functions through the autonomic nervous system and the neuroendocrine apparatus.

There are neural connections between the hypothalamus and the sympathetic nervous system. The hypothalamus, stimulated by the psychic centre, activates the sympathetic nerves, resulting in the liberation of excess of noradrenaline.

The adrenal medulla receives stressful stimuli through the neural pathway. Thus, having been stimulated neurally, it causes an initial secretion of adrenaline, with some amount of noradrenaline, into the blood. There is also a second mode of action of the adrenal medulla. The psychic centre stimulates the hypothalamus which causes the anterior pituitary to secrete more adrenocorticotrophic hormone (ACTH) which, in turn, stimulates the adrenal cortex to secrete more corticosteroids. In the presence of an excessive quantity of plasma corticosteroids, the secretion of adrenaline by the adrenal medulla becomes copious.

The anterior pituitary is called the master gland, since it regulates all the other endocrine glands of the body. The pituitary, a small oval endocrine gland, is situated at the base of the brain in most vertebrates, in a cavity of the sphenoid bone. Although situated inside the cranium at the base of the brain, it is not neurally controlled by the brain due to the lack of nerve-connections. In spite of this fact, mind controls the pituitary gland and the other endocrine glands of the body through the mediation of the pituitary gland. How is it accomplished in the absence of nerve-connections between the brain and the pituitary gland?

Humoral transmission, rather than neural transmission, operates between the hypothalamus and the pituitary. The hypothalamus produces neurohumors or releasing hormones to be directly added to the blood. A short, narrow stalk (infundibulum) connects the pituitary gland to the hypothalamus. The blood vessel flowing in the infundibulum carries the releasing factors of the hypothalamus to the pituitary. This is the pituitary portal system (the venous blood passing from the tissues to the heart through two capillary beds instead of one only). In this case, one capillary bed is in the hypothalamus and a second one in the pituitary.

Through the portal circulation, the hypothalamus transports releasing and inhibiting hormones to the pituitary. These hormones of the hypothalamus influence the secretion and release of hormones formed in the anterior pituitary.

The pituitary, thus being influenced, secretes more or less specific anterior pituitary hormones that control the secretion of hormones of other endocrine glands in the body. Such glands are the thyroids, the adrenal cortex, the pancreatic islets, the ovaries, the female breasts and the testes.

The psychic influence on the parasympathetic nervous system has not yet been described. A peaceful and calm mind influences the cerebral cortex favourably. It maintains a balance of the neurohumors to do the right job. Neurohumors are constantly produced and constantly destroyed. Any psychic trauma initially results in an enhanced liberation of acetylcholine in the cerebral cortex. This chemical causes excitation in the cortical synapses and in the post-ganglionic endings of cholinergic nerve-fibres. In normal conditions, the accumulation of acetylcholine in the synaptic clefts is not allowed. It is rapidly broken down by cholinesterage which is an enzyme formed in the synaptic clefts. In psychic trauma, the psychic stimulus to the formation of acetylcholine is very strong and/or repetitive. In such a situation, the formation of acetylcholine is faster and that of cholinesterage is slower. As a result, the excess of acetylcholine in the synapses cannot be destroyed. Thus is the accumulation of acetylcholine in the synaptic clefts. This is the initial biochemical condition that causes stress disorders.

In addition to acetylcholine, there are other neurohumors in the brain. Some of them are catecholamines (noradrenaline), serotonin and histamine. Each neurohumor is destroyed by its respective enzyme. Psychic trauma decreases the activity of these enzymes such as monoamine oxidase and histaminase. As a result, an excessive accumulation of the neurohumors occurs in the various centres of the brain. In addition, there occurs an accumulation of cyclic AMP.

It is the cerebral cortex that controls the subcortical centres in the brain. The mechanism of control is through the excitatory and inhibitory functions of the cerebral cortex. Following a psychic trauma, the accumulation of acetylcholine causes exhaustion of the inherent excitatory and inhibitory functions of the cerebral cortex. This happens especially with the exhaustion of the inhibitory function which becomes more critical. The subcortical centres of the brain receive some excitation with little inhibition. As a result, they become hyperactive. They excessively excite themselves and their linked systems — the neuroendocrine system and the autonomic nervous system. Both these systems ultimately excite all the organs and tissues of the body.

So far, we have discussed the neurohumoral system of the brain. Changes in the cerebral neurohumors bring about changes in those of the sympathetic and parasympathetic divisions of the autonomic nervous system. We may focus our attention on the secretions of the nerve-endings of the post-ganglionic fibres of the divisions. The parasympathetic system secretes acetylcholine whereas the sympathetic system secretes principally noradrenaline. These two systems function in an antagonistic manner. This antagonism is apparent, however. In spite of the apparent antagonism, both the divisions of the autonomic nervous system have evolved for a holistic purpose. The parasympathetic division is associated with relaxation and rest. The sympathetic division functions in emergency situations such as anger, excitement, fear, anxiety, tension, etc. Psychic trauma accelerates the activity of the sympathetic division which increases the secretion of catecholamines (adrenaline and noradrenaline). The catecholamines, secreted in excess for a prolonged period, are the main causal factors of psychosomatic diseases.

The physiological mechanisms of psychic stress in bringing about disorders in the neuroendocrine system and the autonomic nervous system have been briefly described in this section. Any trauma to the psyche causes the humoral disorders which, in turn, cause pathology in many organs and tissues of the body. For details of the operation of the psychosomatic diseases, and the preventive and curative effects of yogic meditation, reference may be made to the book *Meditation*.[153]

Japa, with intense concentration on the unitary idea of its meaning, is a form of *dhyāna*. Thus, the benefits of *dhyāna* and those of *japa* are similar. *Japa* is for mental relaxation and rest. It brings peace, calmness and tranquillity to the mind. Mental stress and trauma are avoided or drastically minimized even if events, normally causing agonizing experiences, occur temporarily or persistently. *Japa* makes the psyche healthy and the body too.

This last section of this chapter is secular. It provides scientific explanations, without any reference to metaphysics.

In a nutshell, this chapter deals with the theoretical background of the *japa-yoga*. The next chapter will present practical techniques for the practice of the *japa-yoga*.

References

1. *BG*, X.25: *yajñānāṁ japa-yajño 'smi.*
2. *PYD*, I.28: *tajjapastadarthabhāvanam.*
3. We use the word *mantra*, not for magical spells or charms and not for sacred incantations, but for "an instrument of thought." The word has been derived from the Sanskrit verb-root *man* which means "to think." One thinks by it (*manyate anena iti mantraḥ*). By the repeated utterance or even a single pronouncement of a *mantra*, thought-waves are generated by the mind. Brain-waves are different from mind-waves, however. Mind-waves are subtler than brain-waves. Sometimes, our use of the word *mantra* refers to "a sacred formula addressed to any individual deity" (for example, *oṁ namaḥ śivāya*: I pay obeisance to Lord Śiva).
4. *PYD*, I.23, *Īśvara-praṇidhānād vā.*
5. Kapila, the founder of Sāṅkhya, has no book available to us now. The *Sāṅkhya-Sūtram* and the *Sāṅkhya-kārikā* have been written by his disciples. The Sāṅkhya metaphysics accepts the single, insentient *mūla-prakṛti* or the *pradhāna*, and multiple, sentient *puruṣa*s or individual selves (*SPS*, I.149-59). The former is active and the latter inactive. Evolution takes place as a result of the conjunction of *prakṛti* and *puruṣa*, the former being transformed from an unmanifest state to a manifest state. The Sāṅkhya nowhere mentions the existence of the Supreme Self (*Puruṣottama*, *Parameśvara* or God) and does not need Him to explain its evolutionary cosmology. It rather clearly mentions the lack of proof of the existence of *Īśvara* (*SPS*, I.92; *Īśvarāsiddheḥ*; V.10-12). Its aphorism (*SPS*,

III.57: *īdṛśeśvarasiddhiḥ siddhā*) refers to the multiple *puruṣas* and not to any single Supreme *Puruṣa*.

Patañjali accepted the metaphysics of the Sāṅkhya with the addition of *Īśvara*. But his *Īśvara* is not God, the Creator. Among the multitude of *puruṣas*, Patañjali's *Īśvara* is a special one (*Puruṣa-viśeṣaḥ, PYD*, I.23-6). He is special, because, unlike the other *puruṣas*, he has no *kleśa, karma, vipāka* and *āśaya*. The *praṇava* or *oṁ* is the *vācaka* (a word by which one is named) of *Īśvara* who is the *vācya* (the named one). In this connection, Patañjali has written an aphorism (*PYD*, I.27: *tasya vācakaḥ praṇavaḥ*).

6. The Sanskrit word *praṇava* is derived like this: *pra* √*nava*. The prefex *pra* means "front," "for the first time," "before," "excessive," "special," "prominent." The affix *nava* (*nū* + *ghañ* or *nu* + *ghañ*) means "new," "to be new," "to be fresh," "to sound loudly, to roar or to thunder." Thus, *praṇava* means (1) the primeval *oṅkāra* vibration and (2) the primeval explosion. The first meaning supports the theory of vibration (*spanda-vāda*). The second meaning has a reference to the Bing Bang explosion. Both the meanings are not unrelated.

   The *praṇava* has a special meaning with reference to religious worship and prayer: *prakarṣeṇa nūyate stūyate 'neneti nauti stautīti vā praṇava-oṅkāraḥ*. By the *praṇava-oṅkāra*, one intensely meditates and prays.

7. *Praṇu, praṇava, udgītha* and *oṅkāra* are equivalent: *CU*, I.1.1-2; I.4.1; I.4.3-5; I.5.1; I.5.3; I.9.1-2; II.23.2-3.
8. The essence of the *Vedas* is *oṁ*: *CU*, I.1.2; I.4.3-4; II.23.2-3.
9. *Praṇu*: *CU*, I.4.5; *oṅkāra*; *CU*, II.23.2-3; *Udgītha*: *CU*, I.1.1; I.4.1; I.9.2.
10. The *oṁ* is to be worshipped or meditated upon: *CU*, I.1.1; I.4.1; I.9.2.
11. *CU*, I.4.5.
12. *CU*, I.5.1.
13. *CU*, I.1.1.
14. *CU*, I.5.3.

15. *CU*, I.9.1.
16. *CU*, I.9.2.
17. *BG*, VII.8.
18. *BG*, IX.17.
19. *MTU*, VI.21.
20. *MTU*, VI.4-5.
21. *MUU*, II.2.4.
22. *PU*, V.1-2; V.7.
23. *ŚU*, I.13-4.
24. *CUŚB*, I.1.1:

    tadihetiparaṁ prayuktamabhidhyāyakatvādyāvartitaṁ śabdasvarūpamātraṁ pratīyate. tathā cārcādivatparasyātmanaḥ pratīkaṁ sampadyate. evaṁ nāmatvena pratīkatvena ca paramātmopāsanasādhanaṁ śreṣṭhamiti sarvavedānteṣvavagatam. japakarmasvādhyāyayādyanteṣu ca bahuśaḥ prayogātprasiddhamasya śraiṣṭhyam.
25. *CUŚB*, I.12.1.
26. *PYD*, II. 32; *śaucasantoṣatapaḥsvādhyāyeśvarapraṇidhānāni niyamāḥ.*
27. See S. Radhakrishan's *The Principal Upaniṣads*, 1969, p. 357n: *vedānta-śatarudrīyapraṇavādijapaṁ buddhāḥ. sattva-śuddhi-karaṁ puṁsāṁ svādhyāyaṁ paricakṣate.*
28. *Ibid.*, *svādhyāyo mokṣaśāstrāṇām adhyayanaṁ praṇava-japo vā.*
29. *MAU*, 1.
30. *BG*, VII.8.
31. *BG*, XVII.23 (*oṁ tatsat*), XVII.24.
32. *BG*, IX.17.
33. *BS*, I.3.39: *kampanāt*; *MKG*, I.6; IV.72.

    For references to Mother Sarasvatī, see *Ṛ̥V*, I.3.11-2; VI.61.4; VI.61.8; X.17.7. The word *sarasvatī* is derived from the verb-root √*sṛ̥*, which means "to flow." The river of the universe flows from Mother Sarasvatī. She is the Cosmic Spring, the source of the universe. She plays her *vīṇā*, with three strings

— *sattva*, *rajas* and *tamas*. These strings vibrate to generate the primal *oṅkāra* vibrations. The innumerable notes produced out of these vibrations generate the diverse entities of the universe. Mother Sarasvatī did not stop playing her *vīṇā* subsequent to the primeval creation. She continues to play. According to the Hindu concept, creation, sustenance and dissolution or annihilation are continual processes throughout every world-cycle.

34. See N.C. Panda's *The Vibrating Universe*, 2000, pp. 355-96.

35. *MAU*, 2: *sarvaṁ hyetad brahma; ayamātmā brahma; so 'yamātmā catuṣpāt.*

36. *MAU*, 8: *so 'yamātmādhyakṣaram oṅkāro 'dhimātraṁ pādā mātrā mātrāśca pādā akāra ukāra makāra iti.*

37. *MAU*, 3.

38. *MAU*, 4.

39. *MAU*, 5.

40. *MAU*, 7.

41. *MAU*, 6.

42. *MKG*, on *MAU*, 6: *eka eva tridhā smṛtaḥ.*

43. *MAU*, 12.

44. *MKG* on *MAU*, 12: *bīja-nidrā-yutaḥ prājñaḥ sā ca turye na vidyate.*

45. *MAU*, 9.

46. *MAU*, 10.

47. *MAU*, 11.

48. *MAU*, 12.

49. Quoted in *Pātañjala Yoga Pradīpa*, p. 209:

    1. *Mantrāṇāṁ praṇavaḥ setuḥ.*

    2. *māṅgalyaṁ pāvakaṁ dharmyaṁ sarvakāmaprasādhanam. oṅkāraḥ paramaṁ brahma sarvamantreṣu nāyakam.*

50. *CU*, I.4.4.

51. *PYD*, I.27: *tasya vācakaḥ praṇavaḥ.*

52. *PYD*, I.23: *Īśvarapraṇidhānād vā*; I.24: *kleśakarmavipākāśayairaparāmṛṣṭaḥ puruṣaviśeṣa Īśvaraḥ.*
53. *PYD*, I.28: *tajjapastadarthabhāvanam.*
54. *PYD*, I.23.
55. *PYD*, I.28.
56. *MUU*, II.2.4: *praṇavo dhanuḥ, śaro hyātmā, brahma tallakṣyamucyate, apramattena veddhavyaṁ, śaravat tanmayo bhavet.*
57. *ŚU*, I.13-4.
58. *PYD*, II.1: *tapaḥ svādhvāyeśvarapraṇidhānāni kriyāyogaḥ.*
59. *PYD*, II.29: *yamaniyamāsanaprāṇāyāmapratyāhāradhāraṇādhyānasamādhayo 'ṣṭāvaṅgāni.*
60. *PYD*, II.54: *svaviṣayāsamprayoge cittasvarūpānukāra ivendriyāṇi pratyāhāraḥ.*
61. *PYD*, III.1: *deśabandhaścittasya dhāraṇā.*
62. *PYD*, III.2: *tatra pratyayaikatānatā dhyānam.*
63. *BG*, II.72.
64. *Parātriṁśikā-Vivaraṇa* by Abhinavagupta, p. 207; *Īśvara-Pratyabhijñā-Vimarṣiṇī*, I.5.14; *MKG*, I.6; *BS*, I.3.39; *ŚT*, I.7-13; *PŚTCM*, I.67-70.
65. *Ṛ V*, X.90.5; *BU*, I.2.1.
66. *Ṛ V*, I.22.6 (*apāṁ napāt*); I.23.23 (*āpaḥ*); I.83.2 (*āpaḥ*); I.161.9 (*āpaḥ*); II.35 (*apāṁ napāt*); VI.50.7; VII.47.1 (*āpaḥ*); X.9.1 & 9 (*āpaḥ*); X.17.10 (*āpaḥ*); X.30.12 (*āpaḥ*); X.43.7 (*āpaḥ*); X.82.5-6; X.121.7-8 (*āpaḥ*); X.129.2 (*ambha*); X.129.3 (*apraketaṁ salilam*); *AV*, I.4.1-4; I.5; I.6; IV.2.6-8; VI.51.2; VIII.7.3; XI.4; XVIII.4.35-40; XX.25.2; XX.27.7; *YV*, I.26; IV.2; VI.10; VIII.63; IX.3 & 20; XI.29; XI.50-2; XII.35; XIII.2-4; XIII.53; XVII.7; XIX.71; XX.22; XXVII.25-6; XXXIII.18; XXXVI.14; *ŚBrā*, VI.7.1.17. (*tasya āpaḥ eva pratiṣṭhā. apsu hi ime lokāḥ pratiṣṭhitāḥ*); *ŚBrā*, XI.1.6.1 ff (*āpo ha vai idam agre salilamevāsa. tāḥ akāmayanta "kathaṁ nu prajāyemahi" iti tāḥ aśrāmyaṁstāstapo 'tapyanta. tāsu tapastapyamānāsu hiraṇyamayam āṇḍaṁ sambabhūva*); *MS*, I.5.9-11 (*āpaḥ eva sasarjādau tāsu bījam avāsṛjat. tadaṇḍam*

abhavad haimaṁ sahasrāṁśusamaprabham. tasmin yajñe svayaṁ brahmā sarvalokapitāmahaḥ. āpo nāraḥ iti proktāḥ āpo vai narasunavaḥ. tāḥ yad aśyāyanaṁ pūrvaṁ tena nārāyaṇaḥ smṛtaḥ.); *BU*, I.2.1; V.5.1; *CU*, IV.10.4; *KTU*, II.1.6; Vāpu, I.6.1-11; *Mbhā*, XII.6805f (*prajā-visargaṁ vividhaṁ mānaso manasā 'sṛjat. saṁrakṣaṇārthaṁ bhūtānāṁ sṛṣṭaṁ prathamato jalam*).

67. *ŚT*, I.7.13; *PŚTCM*, I.67-70; *PST*, I.41-4.

68. *AV*, XI.4; *BS*, I.1.23; II.4.1; II.4.7-8; II.4.17; *BU*, I.2.6; II.1.20; III.9.9; *CU*, V.1.1; *MUU*, II.1.3; *PU*, VI.4.

69. *CU*, III.19.1 (*asad evedam agra āsīt, tat sad āsīt. tat samabhavat. lat sasṁvatsarasya mātrām aśayata. tan nirabhidyata. te āṇḍakapāle rajataṁ ca suvarṇaṁ ca abhavatām.*

70. *BS*, I.3.39; *CU*, I.9.1; III.13.5; III.18.1; VII.26.1; *TU*, II.1.1.

71. *ṚV*, I.72.4; I.89.9-10.

72. *PYD*, III.4: *trayamekatrasaṁyamaḥ.*

73. *PYD*, I.17: *vitarkavicārānandāsmitānugamātsamprajñātaḥ*

74. *PYD*, III.3: *tadevārthamātranirbhāsaṁ svarūpaśūnyamiva samādhiḥ.*

75. *PYDVB*, I.28: *svādhyāyād yogamāsīta yogātsvādhyāyamāmanet; svādhyāya-yogasampattyā paramātmā prakāśate.*

76. *ācārahīnaṁ na punanti vedāḥ.*

77. *PYD*, II.30: *ahiṁsāsatyāsteyabrahmacaryāparigrahā yamāḥ.*

78. *PYD*, II.35.

79. *PYD*, II.36.

80. *PYD*, II.37.

81. *PYD*, II.38.

82. *PYD*, II.39.

83. *PYD*, II.32: *śaucasantoṣatapaḥsvādhyāyeśvarapraṇidhānāni niyamāḥ.*

84. *PYD*, II.40-1.

85. *PYD*, II.42.

86. *BG*, II.15; II.38; II.48.
87. *BG*, II.45; V.3.
88. *BG*, II.50.
89. *BG*, II.49.
90. *BG*, II.55.
91. *BG*, II.72.
92. *BG*, II.56.
93. *BG*, II.70.
94. *PYD*, II.43.
95. *PYD*, II.44: *svādhyāyādiṣṭadevatāsamprayogaḥ*.
96. *PYD*, II.45: *samādhisiddhir Īśvarapraṇidhānāt*.
97. *VC*, 495:

    nārāyaṇo 'haṁ narakāntako 'haṁ purāntako 'haṁ puruṣo 'hamīśaḥ. akhaṇḍa-bodho 'hamaśeṣaśakṣī nirīśvaro 'haṁ nirahaṁ ca nirmamaḥ.

98. *Ṛ̥V*, VII.21.5; *śiśnadevāḥ*; X.99.3; *śiśnadevāḥ*.
99. *BG*, XII.1-5.
100. *Ṛ̥V*, I.164.46; II.1.4; II.1.6-7; VI.36.4; X.81.3; *YV*, XXXII.1; *AV*, II.2.1-2; XIII.4.1, 12, 16-18, 21.
101. *Ṛ̥V*, X.129.6.
102. *BG*, XI.15-31; XIII.13; *Ṛ̥V*, X.90; *BU*, III.7.1; *MUU*, II.1.4-10; *ŚU*, III.14 & 16; *BS*, I.2.23.
103. *Ṛ̥V*, X.129.7; *BG*, IX.10 (*mayādhyakṣeṇa prakṛtiḥ sūyate sacarācaram; hetunānena kaunteya jagadviparivartate.*); *ŚU*, VI.11 (*karmādhyakṣah*).
104. *BS*, I.4.3; *BSŚB*, I.4.3; II.1.14; *BGŚB*, XIII.19; *ŚUŚB*, I.3, *SL*, 1-2.
105. *Ṛ̥V*.I.13.9; II.3.8; VII.2.8; *YV*, XXVII.19; *AV*, V.27.9. The three Mothers, described in the Vedas, are (1) Iḍā (2) Sarasvatī, and (3) Bhāratī or Mahī.
106. *Bhā*, VII.5.23:

    śravaṇaṁ kīrtanaṁ viṣṇoḥ
    smaraṇaṁ pādasevanam;

arcanaṁ vandanaṁ dāsyaṁ
sakhyamātmanivedanam.

107. *BG*, IX.26.

108. *BG*, IX.27.

109. *BG*, VII.1; X.9-10; XII.1-2; XII.8; XII.14; XVIII.51; XVIII.58; XVIII.65.

110. *BG*, XIV.26.

111. *BG*, VII.1; XVIII.57-8.

112. *BG*, XI.55; XII.13 & 15.

113. *BG*, XII.13.

114. *BG*, XII.14.

115. *BG*, XII.13.

116. *BG*, XII.17-19.

117. *BG*, XII.15-19.

118. *BG*, XVIII.61-2.

119. *BG*, XVIII.66.

120. *BG*, IX.30-1.

121. *BG*, X.10-11; XII.8; XII.14; XVIII.51-8; XVIII.65.

122. *BG*, XIV.26.

123. *BG*, XI.55.

124. *BG*, IX.30-1; X.9-11; XVIII.62; XVIII.66.

125. *BG*, VII.30; VIII.5-8; VIII.10; VIII.13.

126. *BG*, VIII.6.

127. *BG*, VIII.13.

128. See ref. 103.

129. See ref. 104.

Although Śiva, the Father of the universe, is the inactive Chairperson, and Śakti, the Mother of the universe, is the Executive Agent, they are not two separate metaphysical Beings. They constitute an inseparable Being with bipolarity, as indicated by the following verse (*PŚTCM*, p.10):

na śivena vinā devī
na devyā ca vinā śivaḥ;
ubhayorantaraṁ nāsti
candracandrikayoriva.

130. S. Malaviya, tr., 1999, Part 2, p. xi: *devo bhūtvā devaṁ yajeta.*

131. N.C. Panda, 1996, pp. 245-60.

132. *PYD*, II.1; *tapaḥsvādhyāyeśvarapraṇidhānāni kriyāyogaḥ.*

133. S. Malaviya, 1999, XXVI.130-45. Also see the same book, Part 2, pp. xiv-xv.

134. *Ibid.*, XXVI.132: *surā śaktiḥ śivo māṁsaṁ tadbhakto bhairavaḥ svayam; tayoraikyasamutpanna ānando mokṣa-nirṇayaḥ.*

135. *na kāṣṭhe vidyate devo na pāṣāṇe na mṛṇmaye; bhāve hi vidyate devastasmād bhāvo hi kāraṇaṁ.*

136. S. Malaviya, 1997, p.x:

tanoti vipulānarthāṁ-
stattvamantrasamāśritān,
trāṇaṁ ca kurute puṁsāṁ
tena tantramiti smṛtam.

137. *Ibid.*, p. xi: *mananāt trāyate iti mantraḥ, mananatrāṇa-dharmaṇo mantraḥ.*

138. *Ibid.*, p. x: *āgacchati buddhimārohati yasmādabhyudayaniḥ-śreyasopāyaḥ sa āgamaḥ.*

139. *Ibid.*, p. xii: *sarve varṇātmakā mantrāste ca śaktyātmakāḥ priye. śaktistu mātṛkā jñeyā sā ca jñeyā śivātmikā.*

Ibid., p. xiv: *mantrā varṇātmakāḥ sarve, sarve varṇā śivātmikāḥ.*

140. S. Malaviya, 1999, Part 2, p. xi: *yoginīhṛdaye varṇitamasti:- yad yadā ādyāśaktirviśvamayarūpamādhātumicchati, tadā tasyāṁ spandanaṁ jāyate. tasya spandanasya sphuratāyā vā prathamaḥ pariṇāmaḥ śrīcakram asti. asmin cakre pañca-mahābhūtāditattvānāṁ pratīkarūpāstattadvarṇāḥ kalpitāḥ.*

141. *BG*, V.14-15.

142. *BG*, IX.31: *kaunteya pratijanīhi na me bhaktaḥ praṇaśyati.*

143. *BG*, IX.30-1.

144. *BG*, III.38-9.

145. *BG*, II.48-51.

146. N.C. Panda, 1996.

147. *BG*, X.10-11; XVIII.56-8.

148. *BG*, XVIII.65-6:

manmanā bhava madbhakto madyājī māṁ namaskuru.
māmevaiṣyasi satyaṁ te pratijāne priyo 'si me.
sarvadharmān parityajya māmekaṁ śaraṇaṁ vraja,
ahaṁ tvā sarvapāpebhyo mokṣayiṣyāmi mā śucaḥ.

149. *BG*, VI.30:

yo māṁ paśyati sarvatra sarvaṁ ca mayi paśyati;
tasyāhaṁ na praṇaśyāmi sa ca me na praṇaśyati.

150. *BG*, VI.22:

yaṁ labdhvā cāparaṁ lābhaṁ manyate nādhikaṁ tataḥ;
yasminsthito na duḥkhena guruṇāpi vicālyate.

151. *PYD*, III.45.

152. See *Mantra-Mahārṇavaḥ*, 1996, pp. 656-68; 685-86; 689-703. Also See *Mantra-Mahodadhi* of Mahīdhara, 1997, pp. 771-98.

153. N.C. Panda, 2003, *Meditation: Science and Practice.*

2

Practice of Japa-Yoga

THERE are varieties of *japa*. Each school of Yoga has its own variety. Moreover, *mantras* are many and especially each tāntric *mantra* has its own *puraścaraṇa* (introductory rituals) before the actual *japa*. This part will present some representative samples and cannot afford to be exhaustive.

Preliminary Preparations and Prerequisites for Mantra-Japa

Preparation

Mantra-japa may be formal or informal. No preparation is necessary for the latter type. It may be done in any place (even in lavatories and bathrooms), at any time and in any condition (in sitting, standing or lying condition, with *yogāsanas* or without, with or without counting, and with face towards any direction).

For the formal type of *mantra-japa*, some simple preparations are necessary. These are the following:

Cleanliness. A bath is recommended. Washing the face, the hands and the feet may be a substitute for a full bath.

Clothes. Hindus do not enter their worshipping place without wearing new or cleaned old clothes. The worshipping place may be a temple or a *deva-gṛha* (a private worshipping room in the residential building). Clothes used during defecation and dining are not suitable for worshipping. Urination is an exception, however. The clothes should be loose and must not be tight. The weather conditions and the temperature of the room should decide the nature of the clothing.

Time. Morning and evening are the ideal times for *japa*. For the modern, busy man, the evening hours may not be suitable. He may do *japa* in the *brāhma-muhūrta* (4:00 a.m. to 6:00 a.m.) after taking a bath (after the usual daily morning routine work). If he is a late-riser, he may do it after 6 o' clock in the morning before taking breakfast. The seers of ancient India were observing four *sandhyā*s (the junction between two six-hour periods of a day of 24 hours). These periods are 6:00 a.m., 12:00 noon, 6:00 p.m. and 12:00 midnight. Since the 12:00 midnight falls during the sleeping hours, modern saints and devotees generally avoid the midnight *sandhyā*. In ideal conditions, *japa* may be done at the four *sandhyā*s.

Place. The *ṭhākura-ghara* (*deva-gṛha*) is the ideal place for doing *japa*. If one has not a *ṭhākura-ghara* at home, one may reserve a room for *japa* and meditation. The mind becomes conditioned if the time and place do not vary from day-to-day. The room should be secluded, free from noise and disturbances. The environment should be aesthetic. There may or may not be icons in the room. (The *tāntrika* may need the icon of his chosen tutelary deity or *iṣṭa-devatā*). To have icons, pictures or symbols in front of the devotee is optional, depending upon the psychological and cultural need. After all, God is formless. The form is a symbol devised by man for his psychological needs. Once the form becomes classical and an archetype, it is tenaciously retained by the mind that tries to escape from an abstract state to a concrete one. The form is like the map of a country or the plastic model of a chemical like methane. Rather than the form,

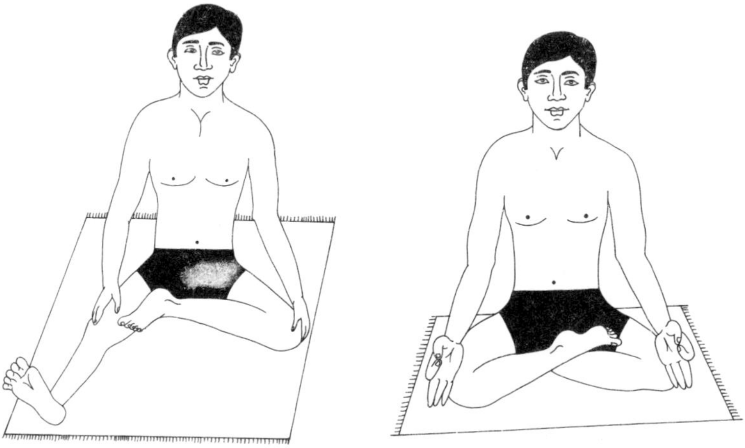

fig. 2.1: *Siddhāsana*

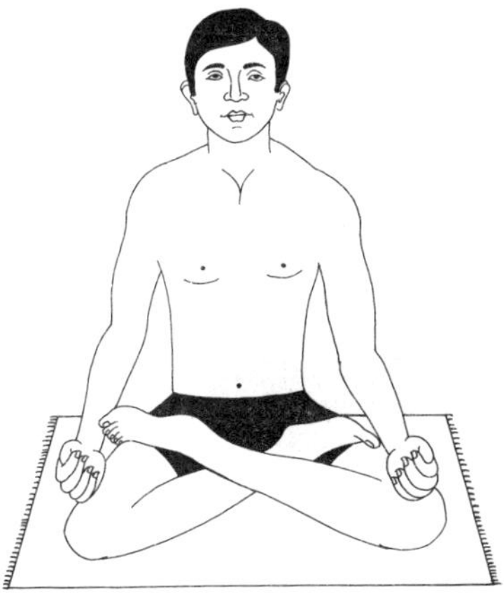

fig. 2.2: *Padmāsana*

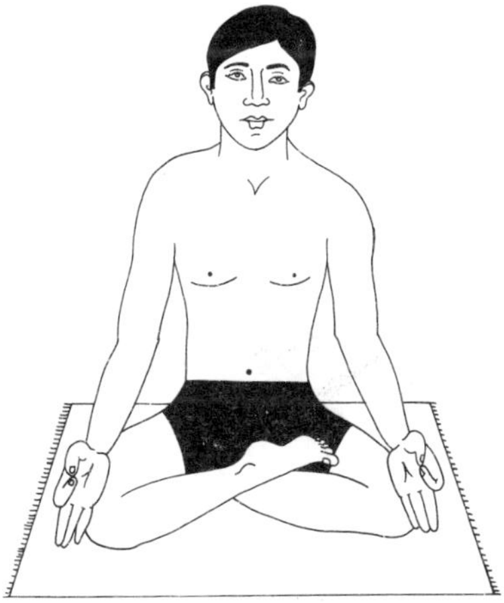

fig. 2.3: *Svastikāsana*

the idea (*bhāva*) is really important.[1] The Hindu devotee faces towards the east or the north, while doing formal meditation, *japa* or *pūjā* (worshipping).

Sitting posture. While doing *japa*, one may sit in *siddhāsana* (the accomplished pose, *fig*. 2.1), *padmāsana* (the lotus pose, *fig*. 2.2), *svastikāsana* (the auspicious pose, *fig*. 2.3), *vajrāsana* (the thunderbolt pose, *fig*. 2.4) or *sukhāsana* (the easy, comfortable pose, *fig*. 2.5). In *āsana*s other than *vajrāsana*, one may remain in *cin-mudrā* (*fig*. 2.6) or *jñāna-mudrā* (*fig*. 2.7), if one's right hand is not engaged in counting. If counting is done, the left hand only may remain in the said *mudrā*. For counting more than 10 *japa*s by *karamālā*, both the hands may remain busy, and, in that situation, the *japa* may be done without any *mudrā*. The *āsana*s may be performed on a hard floor on which a four-folded blanket may be placed. Special *āsana* cloths are also available for this purpose. If sitting on the floor is not

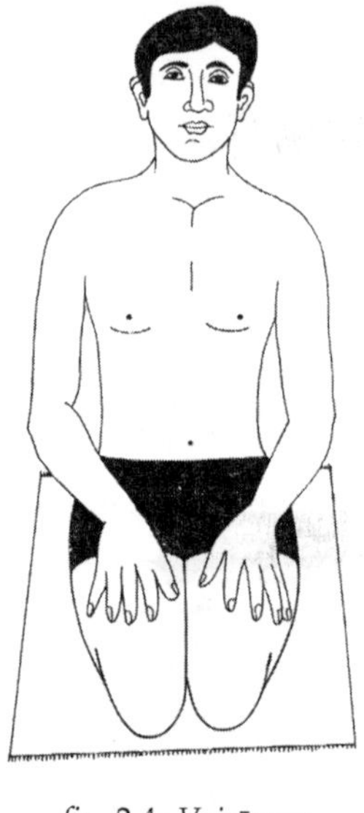

fig. 2.4: *Vajrāsana*

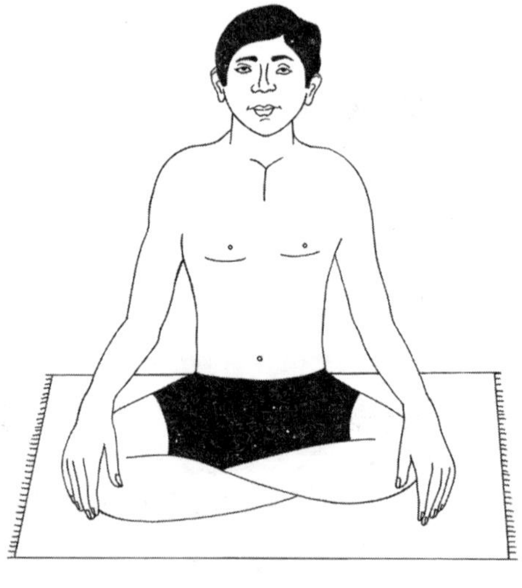

fig. 2.5: *Sukhāsana*

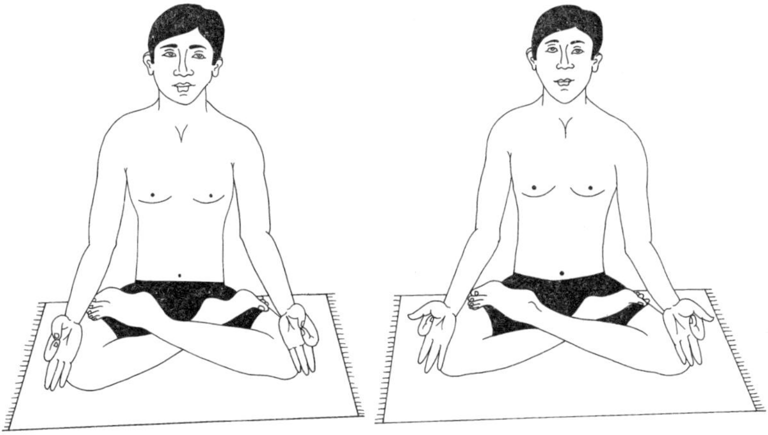

fig. 2.6: *Cin-mudrā*

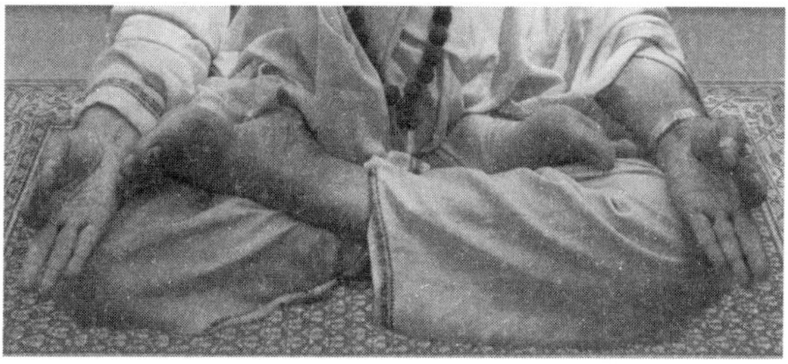

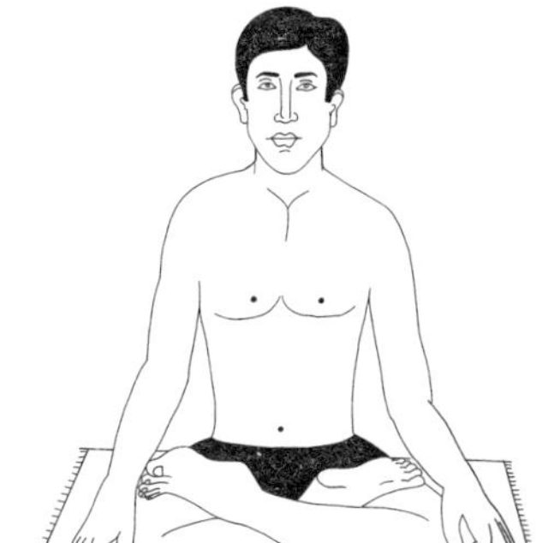

fig. 2.7: *Jñāna-mudrā*

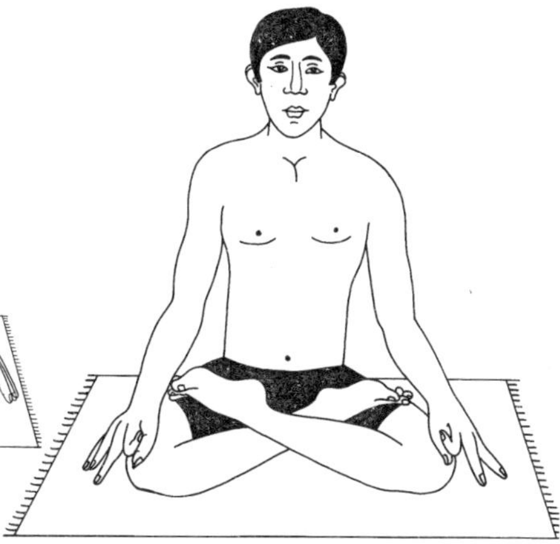

convenient, one may do *japa,* while sitting on a hard chair or a hard bed which is not foamy and soft. It may be emphasized here that the head, neck and torso should be on a straight line perpendicular to the ground level. While doing *japa,* all the muscles of the body should be relaxed and the mind should be free from tension.

Stomach and excretory organs. One may take a light snack, some fruit juice or milk or a cup of tea or coffee before doing *japa*. But, a full stomach is contraindicated. *Japa* may be done two hours after eating a full meal. In the morning, *japa* should preferably be done with empty stomach. Deep mental concentration, with much food in the stomach and the small intestine, reduces splanchnic blood circulation, enzyme secretion and the digestion of food. It would be decidedly an advantage if the colon, rectum and urinary bladder are evacuated before any *japa* session. However, *japa* may not be suspended if reflexes for defecation and micturition fail to function at the desired time.

Prerequisites

Japa is a spiritual activity and part of *yoga*. A *yogī* should be a vegetarian. He should avoid eating meat, fish, eggs and other types of foods that involve killing animals, increase blood cholesterol and stimulate the production of sex-hormones. He should live on cereals, pulses, lightly cooked green vegetables (without the addition of excess of fats and oils, spices and condiments and chillies), salads, fruits, milk, curd, cheese and such other foods. He should avoid over-eating and under-nourishment. One-half of his stomach should be filled with food, one-quarter with water and the rest of the stomach should be empty. Qualitatively and quantitatively, the *yogī*'s diet should not be conducive to obesity. Smoking tobacco, drinking alcohol and taking any intoxicant or drug are strictly forbidden for a *yogī*. If an individual, due to cultural food habits, cannot avoid non-vegetarian foods, he may at least avoid an excess. However, this concession is pragmatic and is not strictly yogic. There must not be any concession for a *yogī* with regard to avoidance of alcohol and drugs.

A person who does *puraścaraṇa-japa* should live on fruits and milk or *haviṣyānna* (rice cooked with more milk and less *ghī* and eaten only once a day at noon).

Observances of Yama and Niyama

The *yamas* and *niyamas* of *Pātañjala Yoga* have already been described in part one of this book. The *yamas* are proscriptive. They are: 1. Practise *ahiṁsā* or don't do violence. The practice of non-violence should be mental, vocal and physical. 2. Speak the truth (*satya*) or don't tell lies. 3. Practise *asteya* (non-stealing). Don't be a *stena* (a thief). Don't commit *steya* (theft and robbery). In this context, *steya* includes misappropriation of public property and government property too. 4. Practise *brahmacarya*. If you are a hermit or a recluse with full time dedication to spirituality, practise sex-abstinence. If you are a householder, don't indulge in sexual excess. Avoid sex abuse and premarital as well as extra-marital intercourse. 5. Practise *aparigraha* (non-accumulation of property). Don't accumulate wealth. Don't accept any bribe. Don't accept any kind or cash which you have not earned or which is not due to you. Don't accept gifts or donations from persons or organizations in case you have to show undue favour to them by virtue of your position or power. There are, of course, exceptions. You may accept gifts and financial assistance from your family members, friends and relatives.

The *niyamas* are prescriptive. They are also five in number. 1. Keep your mind, speech, body and physical environment clean. In other words, practise *śauca*. 2. Develop the property of *santoṣa* (contentment). Remain contented with whatever you get and in whatever circumstances you are when they accrue to you by your maximum efforts and right strivings. 3. Be ready to do *tapaḥ* for noble causes. The verb-root *tap* means "to make hot," "to heat," "to suffer pain." If physical discomfort and pain are unavoidably necessary to achieve a higher goal, one should offer oneself to do *tapas*. Hard, perspiring work for doing any good thing is *tapas*. Fasting, observances of *vratas* (religious vows, meritorious actions) and willing undertaking of penances as mental remedy for having committed sins are also examples of *tapas*. 4. Do *svādhyāya*. Study good scriptures, the knowledge of which can elevate yourself. Study scriptures that can give you *brahma-jñāna* (knowledge on *Brahman*). Study scriptures that can elevate you from the state of animality to that of humanity, of divinity and of *Brahman*-hood in succession. Mentally repeat the monosyllable *OṀ* to remain in communion with God. The *praṇava* is the quintessence of the Vedas and the Upaniṣads and that is the briefest and the best *svādhyāya*. 5. Practise *īśvara-praṇidhāna* or *brāhmī-sthiti* (stay in God). Be completely absorbed in God. Surrender yourself to Him. Dedicate your actions and everything of yours to Him.

A *japa-yogī* has to observe *yamas* and *niyamas* in order to get benefits from *japa*. The Hindu adage says: Even the

Vedas cannot purify a person whose conducts are bad.[2] The *nāma-japa* or the *mantra-japa* will give little benefits if the person does not spiritually transform himself. He has to develop unwavering faith in God. He sees God everywhere and sees everything in God. He has to shun sensual desires, anger, covetousness, delusion, pride and arrogance, and malice, envy and jealousy. Love, compassion and forgiveness are the qualities to be imbibed by him. Such a *japa-yogī* need not do any other form of *yoga* other than *japa*. He gets peace in this life and liberation after death by doing *japa* alone. Simply mechanical utterance of the name of God or a *mantra*, without shunning demoniac qualities and actions, and without spiritual self-tranformation, shall have little beneficial effect.

The Need of a Guru

This topic has importance in *yoga* in general and *japa-yoga* in particular. The *japa* of a *mantra* is done. In major instances, a *guru* initiates the disciple and gives him/her a *mantra*. This function is known as *mantra-dīkṣā*. The *guru* is a spiritual preceptor. Not only does he initiate the disciple by formally giving a *mantra*, but also he becomes his guide and philosopher in all matters of spiritual discipline. In the modern age of secularism, spirituality is not taught in schools, colleges and universities. There are practical problems of distinguishing religions from spirituality especially in multi-religious countries. In theocratic countries, more emphasis is given in teaching religious fundamentalism rather than spirituality. A *sadguru* (*sat* means "good") is one who teaches the disciple how to ascend the rungs of the spiritual ladder. He himself should be well-versed in scriptural studies. He lives a highly moral and spiritual life. He is an adept in *yoga* and other spiritual disciplines. He should have *śakti* (spiritual power) to transmit part of it to his disciple, a process being called *śaktipāta* (fall of *śakti* from the *guru* to enter into the disciple). If one is lucky to get a *sadguru,* one may be initiated by him. Otherwise it is better not to have a *guru* than to have one who is spiritually bankrupt or corrupted. Even if one is a *sadguru,* his duty is not over by initiating the disciple with a *mantra.* The *guru* continues to be the spiritual guide.

The *guru* should study the psychological aptitude of the disciple, should take the latter's opinion on his liking any particular deity, and then only should judiciously select a *mantra* for him. It has been a tradition to keep the *guru-mantra* strictly confidential. Each *mantra* contains the name of a deity. The disciple should not change the *guru-mantra* and his *iṣṭa-devatā* (tutelary deity). The disciple does the *japa* of this *mantra.* The *guru-mantra* is the best one for doing *japa.* Some *guru*s advise their disciples to do the *japa* of the *guru-mantra* only. They proscribe the *japa* of other *mantra*s. In our opinion, the *japa* of other *mantra*s may also be done if the disciple develops devotion and inclination sometimes for other names and forms of God/Goddess. For some *sakāma* (with worldly desires) *japa*s, it becomes necessary to select the appropriate deity and the appropriate *mantra.*

For learning the higher limbs of *yoga* and specialized techniques of *tantra,* it becomes indispensable to be instructed by a *guru.* For *japa-yoga,* however, we do not feel the indispensability of a *guru.* One may follow a good book on *japa-yoga,* written by some spiritual authority and can practise *japa-yoga* efficiently. There is no risk involved in it. The success depends on the sincerity, sustained efforts, *niṣṭhā* (devoted firmness and steadiness) and deep devotion to God.

Guru-Vāda

The word *vāda* means "doctrine." *Guru-vāda* is a classical tradition among the Hindus and now it has internationally spread. In this section, we shall scrutinize some positive and negative tenets of this system.

For a person, the parents are the first *gurus*. Secondly, the teachers who educate him are the *gurus*. The spiritual *guru* gives him training on spiritual matters, both theoretically and practically. Disciplines of specialized spiritual sciences cannot be correctly learnt without the guidance of competent *gurus*. Some of the disciplines are *yoga* and *tantra*. Lastly, a *sadguru* who has already attained *Brahma*-realization (*brahmānubhūti*), does efficiently guide the disciple in the path of spiritual ascension. The spiritual *guru* should be respected in the maximum way.

With regard to the *guru-vāda*, a debatable question pops up: Is the *guru* a substitute for God? Is he God himself? In this connection, we give a reference to a Sanskrit *śloka* (verse) which has served as the *summum bonum* of the *guru-vāda*. The English rendering of this *śloka* may be given as follows:

> The *guru* is Lord Brahmā, Lord Viṣṇu and Lord Maheśvara. He is directly the Supreme *Brahman*. Salutation to him, the revered *guru*. He has shown the sacred feet of God, the unbroken, continuous, homogeneous Being who pervades the spherical cosmos of the movable and the immovable, of the living and the non-living. Salutation to him, the revered *guru*.[3]

We agree to the suggestion that the *guru* is to be respected *as if* he is God. Please note our italicized words "as if." In our opinion, no *guru* of the past, the present and the future can be equated with God. The *guru* is a human being with many limitations, although he may be a superhuman. He is not omnipotent. He himself suffers from diseases and dies. He doesn't and cannot solve all problems of the society. Even if he is a *jīvanmukta* (released albeit living), he cannot create, sustain and annihilate the universe unless and until he is *videhamukta* (released after leaving the body). Here, it may further be noted that, in our opinion, a *videhamukta ātmā* merges in *Brahman* and that thereby he loses his separate identity. We believe that the said *śloka* has been composed by some *guru* in the past with the selfish intention of indoctrinating the disciples. And, till now, he has been successful in his attempt of indoctrination.

There are a number of religious organizations in which the members do not worship God and worship their respective *guru* only as God. Some of them worship the *guru* as God and *gurvī* (the wife or the spiritual partner of the *guru*) as Goddess. They reject the original Being and prefer newer editions. (Of course, they claim that they do not reject and that they substitute the original one with the recently incarnated one.) Our argument may be expressed algebraically: If *A*=*B*, *B*=*C* and *C*=*D*, and if *A* is the original, timeless, spaceless Being, unconnected with the human history and birth and death, it is logical to worship *A*, by which *B*, *C*, *D*, etc., are also worshipped.

According to the Hindu belief, with scriptural substantiation,[4] God is incarnated again and again to keep the society in order by subduing evils and re-establishing virtues. The Sanskrit word for God-incarnate is *avatāra*. We do not assert that the *avatāra-vāda* is not a fact. An *avatāra* is born to fulfil a mission. Born with a definite purpose, with required divine potency, he does fulfil the mission and correct the society. It would be self-contradictory to say that God who is omnipotent and the creator of the universe cannot create himself by taking a form and germinating in a womb. Notwith-standing these statements in favour of the *avatāra-vāda*, we qualify it by saying that even the *avatāra* is a *descent* from God. (The literal meaning of the word *avatāra* is "descent.")

The doctrine of *avatāra* has been and is being misused in Hinduism. Many religious *guru*s directly or indirectly claim that they are *avatāra*s. At a particular historical time and particular geographical area, *guru-avatāra*s are found to be many and they hardly fulfil any mission. We do not support this type of misused *avatāra-vāda*.

A number of Indian Yoga schools have branches throughout the world. Some of them do not utter the name of God. They teach their disciples to worship the original founder of the school as God or their *guru*-lineage as Gods. The *guru*-Gods, as they claim, are the protectors, saviours and redeemers of the devotees. They use the word "devotee" rather than the word "disciple."

Let us examine the veracity of this claim. According to the Advaita Vedānta, a released person's *ātmā* (self) becomes fully identified with *Brahman* after the death of his body. The *mokṣa* (liberation) concept of Advaita Vedānta does not uphold the separate existences of released selves. For this purpose, the *Gītā* uses the term *brahma-nirvāṇa*.[5] In the Dvaita Vedānta, however, the concept of liberation is different. It rejects the view that the *ātmā* merges in *Paramātmā* (God) on attaining liberation. The released self, in the system of dualism, does not lose its identity; it takes shelter at the feet of *Nārāyaṇa* (God) and permanently stays there in peace and bliss, without being reborn. The Dvaita Vedānta does not recognize an attributeless, functionless Being (*Brahman*). This school is averse to the idea that the *ātmā* is not essentially different from the *Paramātmā*. It steadfastly sticks to its view that the released *ātmā* stays as the servant (*dāsa*) of God and that it can never play the role of God.

The Yoga philosophy of Patañjali accepts the existence of innumerable *puruṣa*s (sentient spirits or *ātmā*s) that are birthless and deathless. Simultaneously, it accepts the existence of a special *puruṣa* (*puruṣaviśeṣa*) who is *Īśvara* (God). What are the specialities of *Īśvara*? Unlike the other *puruṣa*s, *Īśvara* is unconnected with *kleśa*s (afflictions), *karma* (the *karma-saṁskāra*s), *vipāka* (the fruition of *karma*s) and *āśaya* (*karmāśaya* or the reservoir of *karma*s). Thus, *Īśvara*, the *puruṣa-viśeṣa* is never in apparent bondage and, hence, he has no necessity of release. In contrast, the other *puruṣa*s, coming in association with *prakṛti* or *pradhāna*, are in apparent bondage and they need release (*kaivalya* in yogic terminology). But, a *puruṣa*, even after attaining *kaivalya*, cannot play the role of *Īśvara*. It stays in perfect peace in the highest realm, without further rebirth. The released *puruṣa* does not involve itself in the mundane affairs.

Coming back to the claim of some Yoga schools that their founder-guru or *guru*-lineage can function as protector, saviour and redeemer, such a claim does not stand the rigours of logical or scriptural scrutiny. If the *guru* is not liberated, he has to be reborn sometime or other. If he is liberated, he becomes *Brahman*, or permanently stays in the company of Viṣṇu/Nārāyaṇa (God) as his servant, or he stays in the *Satya-Loka* permanently as a blissful, isolated being. Then, where is the occasion of a *guru* to assume the role of God?

Ex hypothesi, let us tentatively accept the claim that *guru*s can play the role of God. Our common sense mundane experience says that a country cannot be properly ruled by many prime ministers and presidents, working simultaneously. How can the universe be ruled by many Gods? In order that the universe is a cosmos, it must be monotheistic; it must be ruled by one Being only. If the one Being becomes sub-Beings (*devatās*), the latter must be working under the one Being.[6]

In conclusion, we do say that there is a need for *guru*s and that a *guru* is certainly adorable. At the same time, we do not favour the *guru-vāda*, as outlined in the foregoing paragraphs. In order to do *japa*, it is not indispensable to have a *guru*. If one gets a *sadguru*, he is lucky. Nevertheless, he can do *japa* without a *guru*.

The Choice of a Mantra

The choice of a *mantra*, by a particular person and for that particular person, seems to be difficult. Some *guru*s insist that only the *guru-mantra* is to be used for the *japa*. We feel that it is not difficult to choose a *mantra* if the monotheistic metaphysics is properly comprehended. Reality is one and only one with, of course, its bipolarity. One pole is masculine and the second one is feminine. Any gender is not applicable to the attributeless, non-functional *Brahman*, which is conventionally neuter in gender. Its Power (*Śakti*) is *Māyā* which is feminine in gender. When it is associated with its Power which serves as the *upādhi* (limiting adjunct), it assumes properties and is called *Īśvara*. In the analogy of a neutron (with no charge) becoming a proton (with positive charge) and an electron (with negative charge), one and only one *Brahman*, without a second, is *Īśvara* (masculine) and *Īśvarī* (feminine). The former is inactive like a corpse, although the chairperson (*adhyakṣa*) of all cosmic activities. The latter is active as in the symbolic picture of Mother Kālī dancing on the chest of Father Śiva who lies like a corpse. God/Goddess is formless and nameless. We, human beings, visualize forms for God/ Goddess. Once we visualize different forms, we have to assign different names. With reference to the functioning of the universe, we associate God to different attributes (*guṇa*s — *sattva, rajas, tamas*). Hence is the Trinity (*trimūrti*) of Hinduism. Each member of the Trinity has a consort and so do we get the three Mothers (*tri-ambā*s) who are essentially one Mother only. If we have a good comprehension of this metaphysics, we do realize that all forms of God/Goddess refer to the one and the only one formless Being. And so are the names. If one realizes that all forms and all names refer to one Being only that is without forms and names, one solves and dissolves the problem. Once this realization comes, all *mantra*s are felt to be one only and no *mantra* is superior to the other.

Japa may be *niṣkāma* (without desires) or *sakāma* (with desires). The *niṣkāma japa* is not strictly *niṣkāma*. To be liberated is the *kāmanā* (desire) here. When the *kāmanā* is worldly, for getting wealth, power and promotion, for getting childern and family-prosperity, for getting cure from diseases, for getting protection from calamities and for sundry purposes, the associated *japa* is *sakāma*. The *guru-mantra* or any one of the other *mantra*s may be good enough for the *niṣkāma japa*. For the *sakāma japa*, however, there may or may not be a necessity for changing the *mantra*.

If you select the *mantra* for you, ponder over the issue for some time. Each *mantra* has a deity and contains the name of the deity. You decide which deity appeals to you the most. After you decide this, the selection of the *mantra* becomes easy. The deity of your chosen *mantra* becomes your *iṣṭa-devatā*. Be devoted to him/her all throughout your life. You are not expected to change your *iṣṭa-devatā*.

Even after chosing your tutelary god and the connected *mantra* which should be dear to you for most occasions, you may still do the *japa* of other *mantra*s connected with other deities when you feel to do so. It is not a sin to do that. Necessity also arises to change the *mantra* if the *kāmanā* differs. The *japa* of Lakṣmī-*mantra* is done for getting wealth; that of Sarasvatī-*mantra* is done for getting memory and knowledge; that of Kālī- or Durgā-*mantra* is done for getting protection from calamities; and that of Mahā-mr̥tyuñjaya-*mantra* is done for getting cure from diseases.

If you are indecisive and perplexed over choosing a *mantra*, select the monosyllable *mantra oṁ*. In our opinion, this is the best and easiest choice. Some *guru*s reserve this *mantra* for *saṁnyāsī*s only (spiritual persons who have renounced the world). We don't agree with them. They further say that it is for *mokṣa* (liberation) only. On this issue also, we differ from them. The *praṇava* (*oṁ*) is the *vācaka* (that which denotes or names) of *Brahman/Īśvara*. Any one can do *praṇava-japa* for *mokṣa* and also for fulfilling desires. He is to mentally re-orient himself in the realization of the actual meaning of *oṁ*. As we utter various words for God — Hari, Nārāyaṇa, Viṣṇu, Christ, God, Allah, for example, we utter the syllable *oṁ* for the same purpose. If the *japa* is *sakāma*, one has to make a *saṅkalpa* (an expression of the objective) just before the *japa* begins. The *praṇava* is an all-purpose *mantra*. Everybody can chant it. It is rather the tradition that no *mantra* gains strength unless it is preceded by the *praṇava*.

Number of Japa and Counting Technique

Some *japa*s may preferably be done without counting. The informal *japa*s, done in any place at any time and under all circumstances, are not counted. The *oṅkāra-japa* and the *ajapā-japa* are not counted.

Most *japa*s, done with ritualistic formality, are counted. The number of repetitions of the *japa* may be 10, 27 (28), 108, 1080, or *lākha*s (1 *lakṣa* or *lākh* is 0.1 million or 100,000).[7] With *karamālā*-counting, the *japa*-number is 28 instead of 27.

The *japa* may be done 108 times or multiples of 108 times. The number of multiples of 108 is variable depending upon the time available with an individual and his psychological need.

Puraścaraṇa-japa is the repetition of the *mantra akṣara lakṣa* times. The Sanskrit word *akṣara* means "syllable." To take an example, the Gāyatrī-*mantra* contains 24 syllables. The *puraścaraṇa-japa* of the Gāyatrī-*mantra* would be 24 *lakh*s (2.4 millions).

The *havana-japa* (the word *havana* means "fire sacrifice in which oblation of clarified butter or *ghī* is offered with a sacrificial ladle") customarily follows the *puraścaraṇa-japa*.

For each *havana*, the *mantra*, ending with *svāhā*, is chanted, and then the oblation is offered. The number of the *havana-japa* is one-tenth the number of the *puraścaraṇa-japa*.

The *tāntrika puraścaraṇa* comprises five components, namely, *mantra-japa*, *havana*, *tarpaṇa*, *mārjana* and *brāhmaṇa-bhojana*. These are performed in succession, each subsequent process in the sequence being one-tenth the number of the precedent one. *Tarpaṇa* is satiating gods by presenting them libation of water. While presenting each libation, a *mantra* is chanted. For example, the original *mantra* for Lord Śiva is: *oṁ namaḥ śivāya*. The *tarpaṇa mantra* would be *oṁ namaḥ śivāya, śivaṁ devaṁ tarpayāmi namaḥ*. *Mārjana* is one type of *abhiṣeka* (bathing the deity by sprinkling water). Each time, while sprinkling water with a tuft of *dūrbāṅkura* (tender *dūba* grass) or *aśvattha patra* (*pīpal* leaf), the *mārjana-mantra* is recited. The *mārjana-mantra*, for the said *śiva-mantra*, would be as follows: *oṁ namaḥ śivāya, śivaṁ devaṁ abhiṣiñcāmi*. In the last process of the *puraścaraṇa*, spiritual persons, with high morality (brāhmaṇas by attributes and actions, not necessarily by birth), are fed. Poor persons are also fed, with respect, and without contempt. This is *daridra-nārāyaṇa-sevā* (the service of the poor, regarded as gods). In *mantra-japa* where idols or pictures are not used for worship, *tarpaṇa* and *mārjana* are omitted. Sometimes, even in Vedic *japa* without images, *tarpaṇa* and *mārjana* are done. In such cases, these two *kriyā*s precede the *japa*. The water-libation (*tarpaṇa*) is done to propitiate God. If one takes bath in a river or a pond, one does *tarpaṇa* there by joining the two hands to make a palms-cup (*añjali*) and offering water which rolls down through the finger-tips. If one takes bath in a bathroom, one may do the *tarpaṇa* in the worshipping place by offering water with the right hand only in the said manner; but this is done before the image of the deity. The pre-*japa mārjana* is done to purify and sanctify the body and mind of the devotee by sprinkling sanctified water on his body. The *puraścaraṇa mārjana*, however, is done by sprinkling water on the image of the deity.

A *japa-mālā* (*mālā* means "rosary" or garland) may be used for counting. The beads of the rosary may be *rudrākṣa* (seeds of *Elaeocarpue ganitrus*), *tulasī* (the stem of the holy basil plant), red sandalwood, red coral or white quartz crystal (*sphaṭika*). The *rudrākṣa-mālā* is used for Śiva-*mantras* and also for Śākta-*mantras*. The *tulasī-mālā* is used for the *mantras* of Viṣṇu and Kṛṣṇa. The *pravāla* (red coral)-*mālā* is used for Lakṣmī-*mantras*. The red-sandalwood-*mālā* is used for the *mantra* of any female deity or Gaṇeśa. The *tāntrikas* use *sphaṭika-mālās*, in addition to *rudrākṣa, rakta-candan* (red sandalwood), and others.

Every *japa-mālā* has a *meru* (the central bead which is larger than the others). A rosary of 108 beads has really 108 + 1 beads, the extra one being the *meru*. If the rosary is conceived of as the circular dial of a clock, its 1 starts at the right-hand side of the *meru* and its 108 ends at the left-hand side. The counting of 108 *japas* is done clockwise. If *japa* is done 2 × 108 times, the second round is counted anticlockwise. If a third round is done, it is clockwise. It is to be noted that the *meru* is never crossed in counting multi-rounds of *japa*. This alternate system of counting clockwise and anticlockwise around the *meru*, remaining uncrossed, is illustrated in *fig*. 2.8.

Only the right hand should be used for counting the beads. The thumb, the middle finger and the ring finger of the right hand should touch the beads in sliding. The middle and the ring finger of the right hand provide a resting platform and the right thumb actively rolls the beads one after another. In the whole process of counting the beads, the index and the little fingers remain away from the rosary in an idle condition (illustrated in *fig*. 2.9).

While doing the *japa*, the rosary is not seen by the devotee himself and by anybody else. A specially made small cloth-bag (*gomukhī, japa-thalī* or *kothalī*), hanging from the neck, is used for concealing the rosary (*fig*. 2.10). In lieu of the *gomukhī*, the shoulder-cloth (*uttarīya*) may be used for this purpose. The two ends of one side of the *uttarīya* may be tied by a knot at the back of the neck. The right hand, holding the rosary, may be inserted into the folded cloth (*fig*. 2.11).

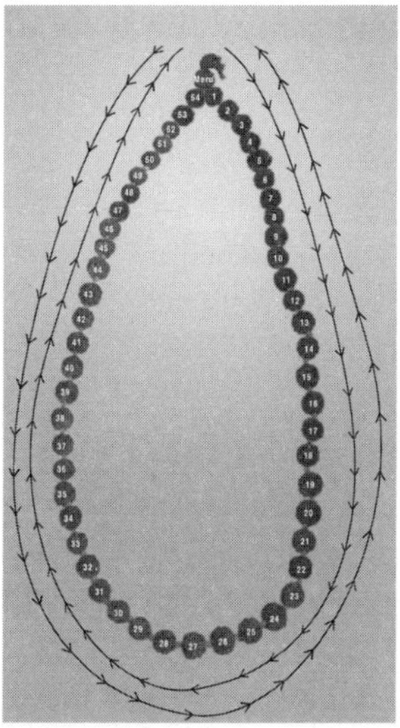

fig. 2.8: Clockwise and anticlockwise sliding of the rosary beads

fig. 2.9: The positions of the fingers and the thumb in rolling the rosary beads

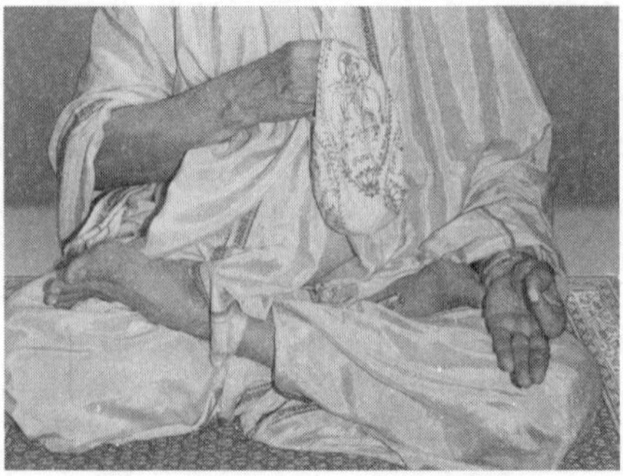

fig. 2.10: The rosary inside the hanging *gomukhī*

There are scriptural recommendations for holding the rosary at one of the three levels — the navel, the heart and the nosetip.[8] In the morning time, the rosary should be held at the level of the navel; at the noon, at the level of the heart; and in the evening, at the level of the nosetip. We, however, recommend one level only, the level of the heart at all times. In this regard, one point is to be emphasized. Under no circumstances, shall the rosary be held below the level of the navel.

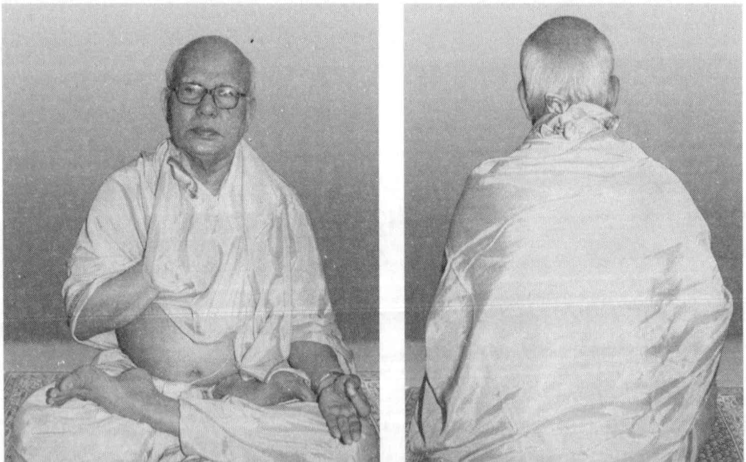

fig. 2.11: The use of the *uttarīya* while counting the rosary beads

So far, we have dealt with the rosary counting of *japa*. There is a second method of counting too. This is *karamālā* counting (*kara* means "hand" and *mālā* means "rosary"). In this method, the right hand serves the purpose of a rosary. There are two systems of *karamālā* counting, one for the *japa* of the male deities (*deva-japa*) and a second one for the *japa* of the female deities (*śakti-japa*). In both the systems, *japa* is not done on the thumb, the fingertips and the finger-nodes, and the *meru*s are also not crossed.[9] There should not be gaps in between the fingers which should be in touch with each other.[10] While counting the *japa*, the internodes (*parvan*s or *parva*s) of the fingers are to be touched with the tip of the right thumb.

For the *japa* of any *deva-mantra*, counting should be started with the middle internode (*madhya-parva*) of the ring-finger (*anāmikā*), should proceed clockwise and end with the base internode (*mūla-parva*) of the index finger (*tarjanī*).[11] The middle and the base internodes of the middle finger (*madhyamā*) are the *meru*s in this system. For counting eight *japa*s, starting is done with the base-internode of the ring-finger to end with the middle internode of the index finger. The *karamālā* of this system has been illustrated in *fig*. 2.12a & b.

For the *japa* of any *śakti-mantra*, counting starts with the middle internode of the ring-finger, moves clockwise, goes up to the base-internode of the middle-finger and then jumps to the base-internode of the index finger to stop there. In this case, the middle-internode and the top-internode of the index finger are the *meru*s.[12] To count eight *japa*s, starting is done with the base-internode of the ring-finger, to finally end with the base-internode of the middle-finger. The *karamālā* for the *śakti-mantra* has been illustrated in *fig*.2.13 a & b.

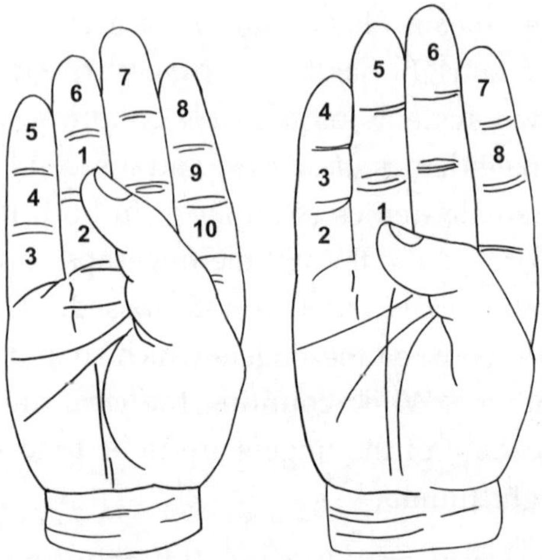

(a) Counting of ten (b) Counting of eight

fig. 2.12: *Karamālā* counting of a *deva-mantra*, with two *merus* in the middle finger

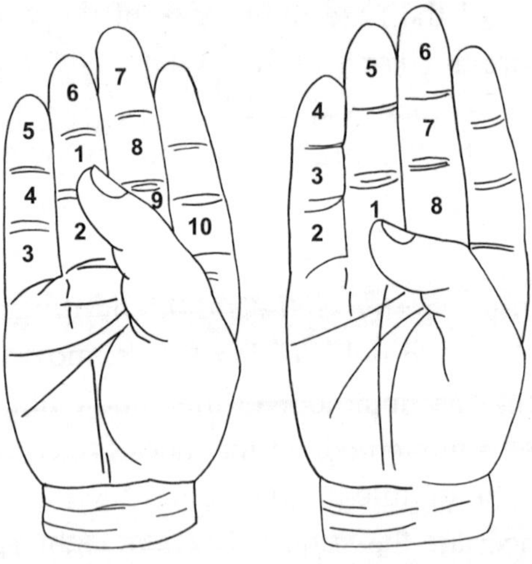

(a) Counting of ten (b) Counting of eight

fig. 2.13: *Karamālā* counting of a *śakti-mantra*, with two *merus* in the index finger

When we count ten *japa*s, one round of *karamālā* is enough. To count 28 *japa*s, three rounds are necessary, the first two rounds of ten *japa*s each and the final round of eight *japa*s. When we count 108 *japa*s, 11 rounds are necessary, the first ten rounds of ten *japa*s each and the final round of eight *japa*s. For keeping a record of the first ten rounds, the left hand is to be engaged in a parallel counting.

We have not yet dealt with the method of counting of the *puraścaraṇa-japa* which is in *lākh*s. If *karamālā* is used for this purpose, ten rounds of ten *japa*s each are taken account of by the left hand to make the total of 100 *japa*s. The units of hundreds are cumulatively recorded in a notebook. One hundred times hundred make one *lākh*. The *lākh*s are also recorded in the notebook. Counting finishes when the desired number of *lākh*s are completed.

Instead of the *karamālā*, smooth, rounded, small beads of glass or metal or stone or some hard seeds may be used for counting the *puraścaraṇa-japa*. Two containers are used, one with the desired number of beads and another empty one. Beads, while counting, are transferred, one by one, to the second container. The desired number of *japa* is attained when the first container is rendered empty.

Nowadays, small hand-counting-machines are available. One such machine can be accomodated inside the right hand. This type of counting machine is very suitable for *puraścaraṇa-japa*.

A question may be asked about the preference of the rosary or the *karamālā* for counting *japa*s. The minimum number of the Gāyatrī-*japa* is ten. This number may also be applicable to some other *mantra*s. If ten *japa*s are done, the *karamālā* is the choice. Even for 28 *japas*, the *karamālā* is also the choice.

For doing *japa* 108 times or multiples of 108 times, either the rosary or the *karamālā* may be used. For a beginner, a rosary is preferable, at least for his concentration on the *japa*. If more attention is paid to mechanics of counting, the real purpose of the *japa* is lost to some degree. For an adept in the *japa-yoga*, no definite recommendation is made. It is left to his convenience and choice. After all, counting is the means and not the end of *japa*.

Type of Japa Recommended

Three types of *japa*, namely, *vaikharī* (loud), *upāṁśu* (humming or whispering) and *mānasika* (mental or silent), have already been described in part I of this book. Their efficacies are in increasing order (*vaikharī* ⟶ good; *upāṁśu* ⟶ better; *mānasika* ⟶ best).

For a beginner, it is difficult to fix the concentration on the *bhāva* (idea) of the *japa*, if he silently repeats the *mantra*. The *vaikharī* type of *japa* is recommended for him until he has a good progress in practice. After three months of practice of the *vaikharī* variety, he may switch over to *upāṁśu* which may be practised for another three months. Finally, he may adopt the *mānasika japa* which is the best among the three varieties.

Even if a *yogī* is an adept, it is not necessary for him to stick to the *mānasika japa* always and under all circumstances. Sometimes he may develop the inclination to do the *japa* of a *mantra* loudly or hummingly. He may decide the type of the *japa*, depending on his mood, the purpose and the type of the *mantra*. He may like to purify the surrounding environment by the sound-vibrations of the *oṅkāra-(praṇava) japa* or the Gāyatrī-*japa*. For such a purpose, the *mantra* is to be chanted loudly. The same *oṅkāra-japa*, however, is to be done silently, in synchronization with the inhalation and the exhalation, in order to get relief from hypertension. For the purpose of liberation, the *oṅkāra-japa* should preferably be silent.

Many *tāntrika mantra*s are chanted loudly. Their *bīja*s (seed-syllables) and the *mantra*s themselves should be correctly pronounced. This is, however, not true for all *tāntrika mantra*s. For certain purposes, the *japa* of some *tāntrika mantra*s is done hummingly or silently.

Any syllable of a *mantra* is not to be swallowed or skipped over during utterance. The speed of the *mantra-japa* should be normal, neither too slow nor too fast. The rate should be steady.

As Patañjali has prescribed, the meaning of the *mantra* is to be meditated upon while doing the *japa*. He refers to the *praṇava-japa* only. But *japa-mantra*s are many, with variations in the deities and the textual meanings. In the *japa*-process, the *mantra* is to be placed in the *manas* (mind) and the *manas* is to be placed in the *mantra*, this being an interpenetration of the *manas* and the *mantra*.

With this, we finish the general features of *mantra-japa*. Now we shall describe the special features of some *mantra*s for the *japa*, and the special features of some varieties of *japa* too.

Some *mantra*s are more suitable for the *yoga* of knowledge (*jñāna-yoga*), some others for the *yoga* of devotion (*bhakti-yoga*). Some *mantra*s belong to highly specialized and technical disciplines like the Tantra. Some others are more popular and meant for the mass, like the *kīrtana* and *anuṣṭhāna*. We will start with the *mantra*s of Yoga-Vedānta.

The Practice of Mantra-Japa in Yoga-Vedānta

This section will deal with *mantra-japa* with special reference to *jñāna-yoga* (the *yoga* of knowledge) and *mokṣa-yoga* (the *yoga* for liberation). For all purposes, they are related and not two separate *yoga* systems. We will have three sub-sections, namely, *oṅkāra-japa, ajapā-japa* and Gāyatrī-*japa*. All the three related *mantra*s are Vedic and Vedāntic.

Oṅkāra Japa

Every entity of the universe, micro or macro, living or non-living, constantly repeats the *anāhata-nāda, oṁ*. This is true for the quarks, quanta, all micro-particles, particles, atoms, molecules, stars, planets, satellites, viruses, bacteria, amoebas, plants, animals and human beings. The Sanskrit word *anāhata* means "unbeaten" and *nāda* means "sound or tone." The lexicographical meaning of *anāhata-nāda* is "a sound produced otherwise than by beating." It is spontaneously produced without any external beating agency. It is auto-vibrational, very subtle, rhythmic and synchronous. Any person, in the deeper state of meditation, can listen to this feeble tone. It is really a test for the true, mature state of yogic meditation.

The *anāhata-nāda* is *praṇava* or *oṁ*. It is the first *nāda*, produced by the *vīṇā* (an Indian musical string instrument) of Mother Sarasvatī. From the vibration of her *vīṇā*, the monosyllable *oṁ nāda* is produced in innumerable musical notes which generate the universe. It is not a fact that the entities of the universe generate the sound *oṁ*. It is rather the fact that every entity of the universe is a manifestation of the sound *oṁ*. Mother Sarasvatī is the Consort or Power of Brahmā who creates the universe through the agency of his Consort. The Sanskrit word *saras* means "the flow of a fluid." From the *vīṇā* of Mother Sarasvatī flows the primeval vibration (*spandana*) *oṁ* in the form of innumerable musical notes. This *oṁ* is the *vāc* and hence she is known as Vāgdevī. She gives birth to the whole universe; she is known as Sāvitrī (the verb-root *sū* meaning "to beget, procreate, bring forth, bear, produce, yield)." She plays with her *vīṇā* and sings the primeval song; hence she is known as Gāyatrī (the verb-root *gai* meaning "to sing").

In the Vedic and Vedāntic cosmogony, the creation (or to use a better word, the manifestation) of the universe is not over in a single moment; it is rather continuous, although the process has a beginning with reference to a world-cycle. Mother Sarasvatī continues to play her *vīṇā*, and all the manifestation is a continuous process. The three strings of her *vīṇā*, on being vibrated, do not produce sound; they produce vibrations (*spandana* or *kampana*)[13] with wavelength and frequency in conformity with those of the sound *oṁ*. To hear a sound, the requisite conditions are some beating, a medium (such as air), a hearing organ and a hearing centre in the brain. These conditions were fulfilled much later in the evolutionary chronology. And even today these conditions are not ubiquitous in the entire universe. To sum up, the present *anāhata-dhvani* is not a relic of any primordial eruption, but is the product of the present vibrations of the strings of the *vīṇā* of Mother Sarasvatī.

In *oṅkāra-japa*, the subtle cosmic sound is made gross. The *japa* may be *vaikharī* (loud), *upāṁśu* (humming) or *mānasika* (mental and silent). In the *vaikharī* type, *oṁ* may be of short, medium, long or very long duration. On the basis of the pitch and duration, these four sub-types are many in number. The time taken in between *O* and *Ṁ* and the pitch produced make the differences. The pitch is the rate of highness or lowness of a tone and it is governed by the rate of vibrations producing the sound.

The *vaikharī oṅkāra-japa* purifies the environment and the body and mind of the *japa-yogī*. It stills the mind and corrects the functioning of the body organs, tissues and cells. It has a soothing effect on the brain.

Oṅkāra-japa is mainly *niṣkāma* (desireless). It is meant for *mokṣa* (the liberation of the self). But it is also done for reducing the mental tension and for getting peace. It can be used for the treatment of hypertension. This aspect will be discussed in the third chapter of this book.

Some *yoga-gurus* reserve *oṅkāra-japa* for *saṁnyāsīs* only. We do not find any justification for such a reservation. In our opinion, any householder can do this *japa* and can get benefit too. Being monosyllabic, it is the simplest *mantra*. It is the *mantra* which serves as the *ālambana* (support) in the beginning process of *dhyāna*. It is the best *mantra* for *brāhmī-sthiti* and *Īśvara-praṇidhāna* (stay in *Brahman* and *Īśvara*). It can be repeated at any time, at any place and under all circumstances. If this *japa* is practised throughout the life, one has every probability of doing it at the time preceding death. Thus, *mokṣa* is facilitated. A mental reorientation is necessary. By the *mantra oṁ*, we designate *Brahman* and *Īśvara*. If this fact is firmly ingrained in the mind, *oṅkāra-*

japa may be done for many purposes — *jñāna-yoga* and *bhakti-yoga, mukti* (liberation) or *bhukti* (desire-fulfilment). It may be noted that any *sakāma* (with desire) *japa* is to be preceded by a *saṅkalpa* (an introduction which expresses the objective and is addressed to God).

While doing the *oṅkāra-japa,* it is not necessary to keep the image of any deity in front, although there is nothing wrong if images are kept. The symbol *oṁ (fig.* 2.14) may be kept if one likes.

The *oṅkāra-japa* may be done in *siddhāsana, padmāsana, svastikāsana, vajrāsana, sukhāsana* or *śavāsana.* It may be done while sitting on a hard chair, standing, walking or lying. If *japa* is done in any *yogāsana* other than *vajrāsana* and *śavāsana,* both the hands may be in *cin-mudrā* or *jñāna-mudrā.* Counting is not necessary. The silent *oṅkāra-japa* may preferably be done in sychronization with the slow and steady inhalation and exhalation. If done so, the beneficial effects on the body and the mind will be maximum, and the cure of hypertension and many other physical as well as mental diseases is better facilitated. This type of *oṅkāra-japa* is a sort of *dhyāna* and it should be followed by a *samādhi* for getting the maximum benefits.

Ajapā-Japa

Every human being, within a day of 24 hours, repeats the *so 'ham* (He is I) *mantra* 21,600 times. This repetition continues daily throughout the life. While inhaling, he utters *so* (the *sandhi* form of *saḥ*), and, while exhaling, he utters *ham* (the *sandhi* form of *aham*). *Saḥ* means "He" and *aham* means "I." The first word stands for *Brahman* or *Īśvara* (God); the second word for the individual self. This is the concept of Śaṅkara's Advaita Vedānta. This *mantra* (*so 'ham*) is an important Vedāntic mantra which is constantly repeated by everybody. This *japa*, however, is unconscious and, hence, it is known as *ajapā* (spontaneously uttered and repeated).

fig. 2.14: The *oṅkāra* symbol

This *ajapā mantra* is to be repeated with conscious effort. Then only, does it become a *japa*, the *ajapā-japa*. It is a Vedāntic *japa* belonging to *jñāna-yoga* (the *yoga* of *Brahma*-knowledge) and *mokṣa-yoga* (the *yoga* for the liberation of the self). It is not meant for the fulfilment of any worldly desire and the protection from evils. Of course, if properly done, it does relieve hypertension, brings about mental stillness, wards off many psychosomatic diseases and improves physical, mental and spiritual health.

The *so 'ham japa* may be done at any time, in any place and under all circumstances. It may be done in *siddhāsana*, *padmāsana*, *svastikāsana*, *vajrāsana*, *sukhāsana* or *śavāsana*. If done in any *āsana* other than *vajrāsana* and *śavāsana*, the hands may be placed in *cin-mudrā* or *jñāna-mudrā*. The *japa* of this *mantra* may also be done while sitting on a hard chair, standing, walking and lying, without any *mudrā*s of the hands. No counting may be necessary. No icon or symbol is necessary, although the presence of any such thing is not proscribed.

It is recommended that the *so 'ham japa* is followed by *samādhi*. This especially holds good for doing the *japa* in *śavāsana*, in which the *japa* terminates in a prolonged state of thoughtlessness. *Śavāsana* relieves hypertension. If it begins with *oṅkāra-japa*, followed by *ajapā-japa* and ends in a prolonged relaxed state of thoughtlessness, the beneficial effects become synergistic. *Ajapā-japa* is always done by the *mānasika* (mental) method.

The Japa of the Gāyatrī-Mantra

THE GĀYATRĪ-MANTRA AND ITS INTERPRETATION

The Gāyatrī-*mantra* is Vedic.[14] Its seer is *ṛṣi* Viśvāmitra. Its metre (*chandaḥ*) is Gāyatrī. Hence it is known as the Gāyatrī or Sāvitrī-*mantra*. Its *devatā* (deity) is *Īśvara/Brahman*.

First, we may cite the original *mantra* in the Sanskrit language:

> ॐ भूर्भुवः स्वः तत्सवितुर्वरेण्यं भर्गो देवस्य धीमहि। धियो यो नः प्रचोदयात्॥
>
> *o. . . . . ṁ bhūr bhuvaḥ svaḥ tatsaviturvareṇyam bhargo devasya dhīmahi dhiyo yo naḥ pracodayāt.*

While chanting the *mantra*, attention may be paid to a few special features. *Oṁ* is chanted for a long duration and then a pause is given. The second pause is given after chanting the great *vyāhṛtis*, that is, after *svaḥ*. The third pause is given after *vareṇyam*. The fourth pause follows *dhīmahi*, and the fifth and the final one is after *pracodayāt*.

In the first part of the book, we have elaborated the concept of *oṁ*. It is the mystical monosyllable that stands for *Brahman* or *Īśvara* (God). Every *mantra* is preceded by this *oṁ*.

Here a clarification is necessary on the concept of *vyāhṛtis*. These are: *bhūḥ*, *bhuvaḥ*, *svaḥ*, *mahaḥ*, *janaḥ*, *tapaḥ* and *satya*. The first three are the *mahāvyāhṛtis* (*mahā* = great). Any Hindu worshipper initiates a prayer or a *mantra* by the *praṇava* (*oṁ*), followed by the three great *vyāhṛtis*. These are personified as the daughters of Sāvitrī, Gāyatrī or Sarasvatī. The seven *vyāhṛtis* are the mystical utterances of the names of the seven worlds. When Mother Sarasvatī played her *vīṇā* to generate the sacred monosyllable *oṁ*, its varying notes produced the seven *vyāhṛtis* to create the seven worlds.

Our concept of the seven worlds is different from the traditional one which conceives of seven worlds arranged spatially one over the other, the *bhūḥ* being the lowermost and the *satya* being the uppermost. Bereft of the gravitational pull of the earth on us, the concept of "below" and "above" is meaningless. If one lands on the moon, the earth is above one's head and the moon is below him. Similarly, are the other *dik*s (directions and dimensions) like right and left, length, breadth and depth or height, which are relative, mental concepts. Without the sun-rise and sun-set and without the existence of the pole star, we cannot think of east, west, north and south. To conceive of the spherical universe as seven worlds (*loka*s), geometrically arranged in seven horizontal strata and to name the hepta-worlds by dividing the perpendicular line serially does not seem to be scientific.

What are the *sapta-lokas* (seven worlds) then? According to our concept, all the seven *lokas* are coexistent everywhere in space (*ākāśa*), the materiality varying in coarseness and fineness, in grossness and subtlety. The first three *lokas*, namely, *bhūḥ, bhuvaḥ* and *svaḥ*, are materially gross (g) fine (f_1) and finer (f_2). The other four *lokas*, namely, *mahaḥ, janaḥ, tapaḥ* and *satya* are materially still subtler, serially graded, in increasing order of subtlety, as f_3, f_4, f_5 and f_6. The *satya-loka*, with f_6 materiality, is the subtlest world. In any geometrical locality in space (*ākāśa*), it is possible for a spiritual being to jump from one *LOKA* to the other, with change of dimensions, of course. The Supreme Puruṣa (*Puruṣottama* = God), the One and only One, presides over every *loka*.

When the Gāyatrī-*japa-yogī* chants the *vyāhṛtis* — *bhūḥ, bhuvaḥ, svaḥ*, he utters the name of the *Puruṣa* (God) who presides the concerned *loka*. Thus, in the present context, *bhūḥ* means *bhūrloka-puruṣa, bhuvaḥ* means *bhuvarloka-puruṣa* and *svaḥ* means *svarloka-puruṣa*.

Now we would give the meaning of the rest part of the Gāyatrī-*mantra*. The expression *tat savitur vareṇyam* may be taken as a statement. The word *savituḥ* means "of Savitā." The word *savitā* has been derived from the verb-root √*sū* (*sū* + *tṛc*), meaning "to procreate," "to bring forth," "to beget," "to produce." The word *savituḥ* means "of the one who procreates all" (*sarvasya prasavadātuḥ*). Many interpreters of the Gāyatrī-*mantra* of the Vedas take the meaning of *savitā* as the "sun." It is a fact that one of the meanings of *savitā* is the "sun," since all the planets of the sun have been separated from the original sun and that life on the earth cannot be supported without the sun. But the contextual meaning of *savitā* in the Gāyatrī-*mantra* is not the sun. Here the word refers to God (*Īśvara/Brahman*). Our solar system is an infinitesimally tiny point in the vast (how vast?) cosmos. And the Gāyatrī-*mantra* is cosmic in significance. The word *savitā* is in masculine gender and all the three genders are applicable to *Brahman*, although this latter word itself is neuter.

The word *tat* means "that." It is in neuter gender. It refers to *Brahman*. The *mantra* establishes the identity of *Īśvara* (God with attributes) and *Brahman* (God without attributes). The "that" (*Brahman*) of the Creator (*Īśvara* or *Sraṣṭā*) of the universe is adorable (*vareṇyam*). The subject part of the statement is *savituḥ tat* and the predicate part is *vareṇyam* (in neuter gender too). The verb "is" remains understood. Many Vedic interpreters have meant *tat* as "his" (*taditi saṣṭhyarthe*: *tasya savituḥ*). We do not agree with their view. If what they say is correct, the sentence has no subject. In conclusion, we sum up by saying that the statement *tat savitur vareṇyam* means "we worship the *saguṇa* (with attributes) and the *nirguṇa* (without attributes) *Brahman*, one and the only one Supreme Being.

The next statement in the *mantra* is *bhargo devasya dhīmahi*. This sentence may be rendered into English like this: We meditate on the resplendence (*tejaḥ*), radiance, lustre, splendour or glory of God. The word *bharga*s (derived from the verb-root √*bhṛj*) means *teja*s. It is in neuter gender and has the same form in the singular nominative and singular accusative cases. Here this word has been used as an object of the subject "we" which is understood. The root (*dhātu*) of the verb *dhīmahi* is √*dhyai* which means "to meditate on."

The last sentence (rather clause) of the *mantra* is *dhiyo yo naḥ pracodayāt*. Its English rendering would be: Who inspires our intellect. Here *yaḥ* means "who" with reference to *devaḥ* (God). The word *naḥ* means "our." *Dhiyaḥ* is the plural form of *dhīḥ* in the accusative case. It is the object of the verb *pracodayāt*. It means *buddhiḥ* (intellect) in accusative plural form. The verb *pracodayāt* has the root *cud* (*pra-*√*cud*) which means "to drive on," "to urge," "to impel", "to inspire."

THE DEITY OF THE GĀYATRĪ MANTRA

The Vedic Gāyatrī-*mantra* has no reference to any female deity. Its metre (*chandas*) is Gāyatrī. Nowadays, many religious organizations wrongly associate this *mantra* with a *Devī* (female deity) known as Gāyatrī with certain form(s). They speculate the deity and her form out of sheer imagination. The Vedic Āryans were not image-worshippers. Image-worship among Hindus came much later in the Purāṇic age. One may at best *imagine* the form of Mother Sarasvatī. The formless One (*Parameśvara* with *Parameśvarī*), if worshipped in forms for the psychological needs and easy visualization, may be worshipped in forms which are sheer human imaginations. But such a classical form of Mother Sarasvatī is already in vogue and has been an archetype in the Hindu mind. What is the further need of the multiplication of more sundry forms then?

Mother Sarasvatī has been classically projected as the giver of knowledge (*vidyā-dātrī*), as the Mother of the Vedas

(*Veda-mātā*), and as the Goddess of speech (*vāgdevī*). She has been hardly portrayed as the Mother Creatrix. She, being the consort of Brahmā, God who creates, should have been regarded as the *sraṣṭrī* (Goddess who creates), since God (as Viṣṇu, Brahmā or Rudra) cannot function without the mediation of the respective *Śakti* (Power). The initial creation of each world-cycle is done by her. The continued creation of the evolving universe in each world-cycle is done by her. She is a *vīṇā*-player (*vīṇā-vādikā*).

The Mīmāṁsakas and the linguistic philosophers (philosophers of grammar) introduced a big dose of confusion in the Vedic and Vedāntic cosmogony. The word *śabda* means "sound;" it may mean "noise;" and it also means "word" (referring to language and speech, a word used in a sentence or *vākya* is a *pada* or part of speech). The former meaning, i.e. sound or noise, is physical and the latter is linguistic. Both the meanings have no relevance at all with reference to the primeval creation. The present universe is about 15 to 18 billion (1 billion = 10^9) years old whereas our earth is only 4.5 billion years old. Air was a very late evolute on the earth. It is still not ubiquitous in the universe. The physical sound (*śabda*) needs a medium such as air to travel. There was no air when the creation began. Secondly, the human species (*Homo sapiens*) was a late addition to the living species on the earth. The auditory organ (the ears) had to evolve in order to receive sound waves. Further, auditory centres in the temporal lobes of the brain had to evolve to perceive sound. Genes connected with language evolved in *Homo sapiens* some 100,000 (0.1 million) years ago (exobiology excluded). This could make a big difference between animals and human beings. All these conditions were not available at the time of the primeval creation. The attempt to associate *śabda* in the physical and the linguistic senses is utterly futile.

The Mīmāṁsā school of Indian philosophy holds the view that the relation between a word and its meaning is eternal and unborn. It further holds that the Vedic words are the eternal words of God.[15] Even in the Vedas, some words are used with different contextual meanings in different places. It is man who coins a word and gives meaning to it. Sometimes, he gives different meanings to a word in different contexts. In course of the progress of human civilizations, many new words are coined and used; some old words change their meanings; and some of them die and remain in oblivion. We are of the firm conviction that all scriptures, however sacred they may be, are man-made, and that no man-made scripture is incorrigible and inviolable. Thus, we reject the Mīmāṁsā view on this topic.

Two important Indian philosophers of grammar are Pāṇini and Bhartṛhari. Pāṇini lived sometime between 600 and 300 BCE. Bhartṛhari died about CE 650. For the philosophy of grammar, reference may be made to *Sarvadarśana-saṅgraha*[16] and the *Vākyapadīya*.[17] Bhartṛhari, in his *Vākyapadīya*, says: *Śabda-Brahma* is the Logos from which the universe originates. The word (*śabda*) is eternal for him. He equates the eternal word and *Brahman*. He gives a name, *sphoṭa*, to the eternal word. His *sphoṭa* is partless. In his *sphoṭa-vāda*, he posits the reality of *Brahman* and he says that the whole universe is a *vivarta*, not absolutely real, but a phenomenon of the *śabda-brahma*. For him, *sphoṭa* and *Brahman* are synonymous.

The Mīmāṁsakas do not accept the grammarian view of *sphoṭa*, although they accept the eternality of the Vedic words. Upavarṣa, a Mīmāṁsaka, opposes the *sphoṭa-vāda* of the grammarians by saying that there is no separate perception of the *sphoṭa* over and above that of the letters (*varṇa*s).[18] Śaṅkara opposes the grammarians' view of the *sphoṭa* and also the view of Upavarṣa.[19] We also reject the views of both Bhartṛhari and the Mīmāṁsakas. We have already said that we reject the eternality of words. Secondly, there is no justification to associate a supersensuous Being (*Brahman*) with words. The notion of *sphoṭa* is speculative and lacks any base. We are reluctant to accept the view that *Brahman* (the Reality) and words are the same.

Now a dilemma is to be solved. We reject the Mīmāṁsā view that the Vedic words are eternal. We reject the *śabda-brahma-vāda* and the connected *sphoṭa-vāda* of the grammarians. At the same time, we assert that the whole universe, with its seven *loka*s, is the manifestation of the primal sound *oṁ* produced as a result of the vibration of the three strings (*sattva, rajas* and *tamas*) of the *vīṇā* of Mother Sarasvatī. There are scriptural references to the effect that "the word (*oṁ*) preceded the creation" (*śabdapūrvā sṛṣṭiḥ*).[20] How do we get out of the web and this anomalous situation? Śaṅkara explains in a different way: As we make jars after conceiving the meaning of the "jar," so does the Creator first conceive the words, and then, according to the conceptions, he creates the universe.

We have our own interpretation. Out of the vibrations of the strings of the *vīṇā* of Mother Sarasvatī, *oṁ* was produced. This *oṁ* was not a sound (*śabda* or *dhvani*) as we understand the word "sound" today for the earth and the human beings. The wavelengths and frequencies of the primal vibration (*spandana*) correspond to those of *oṁ* as we hear today. The *oṁ* vibration produces *virāḍ*, the Cosmic Mind or Supermind. This is the initial empirical consciousness, otherwise known as *Buddhi* or the Cosmic Mind. The subsequent evolutes of *Buddhi* took two paths. One path is mental and the second one is material. Egoism (*ahaṅkāra*) and *manas* from egoism are on one path. (The evolution of the subtle sensory and motor organs or *indriyas* took place much later, in the late phase of the animal evolution.) The Cosmic Fluid (*āpaḥ*), the Cosmic Activator (*prāṇa*) and Space (*ākāśa*) are in the second path. We do not agree to the Sāṅkhya view of the evolution of the *pañca-bhūtas* (five states of matter) from the five *tanmātras*. In our opinion and in the opinion of the Upaniṣads, Space is the source of microparticles and particles (matter and energy). This is also confirmed by the findings of quantum mechanics. *Āpaḥ*, *prāṇa* and *ākāśa* are inter-convertible (*āpaḥ* ⇌ *prāṇa* ⇌ *ākāśa*). *Prāṇa* is the super-unified force and is the source of the four fundamental forces. All these three initial substances are continuous rather than corpuscular. They are all-pervasive. They are Vedic deities (*devatās*) that preside over the respective material substances — *āpaḥ* or *nāra* or *kaḥ*, *prāṇa*, *ākāśa* or *kha*. The innumerable notes of the *oṁ* vibrations produced by the *vīṇā* of Mother Sarasvatī travel as waves in all these three media. Of course, *prāṇa* is the best medium for the travel of the *kampana*.

Mother Sarasvatī is the *Veda-mātā* and *oṁ* is the source of the Vedas. This statement needs some explanation. The word *veda* has been derived from the verb-root √*vid*, meaning "to know." Hence, *veda* means "knowledge." It does not necessarily mean the *Veda-Saṁhitās*. As we have already said, *Virāḍ* or *Buddhi* or the Cosmic Mind is the first manifested evolute from the Unmanifest (*Avyakta* or *Mūla-Prakṛti* or the Mother of the universe). It is the initial empirical consciousness. It evolves, under the chairpersonship of God (*Īśvara*), to be manifested as the manifold universe. This explains that Mother Sarasvatī is the *Veda-mātā*, the Mother of Knowledge.

Here we stop the discussion on the metaphysics of Mother Sarasvatī or Gāyatrī or Sāvitrī. This much we emphasize that, in the text of the Gāyatrī-*mantra*, there is no mention of the name of any female deity, including the name of Mother Sarasvatī. It can be emphatically said that the deity of the Gāyatrī-*mantra* is *Īśvara/Brahman*. We build a tall edifice without a foundation. That is what has happened by tradition.

THE JAPA OF THE GĀYATRĪ-MANTRA IN THE VEDIC SYSTEM

The following points are to be noted for doing the *japa* of the Gāyatrī-*mantra* in the Vedic system:

1. For the informal *japa*, there are no restrictions. You may do *japa* at any time, in any place, in any condition (sitting on the floor or on a hard chair, standing, walking) and facing any direction. For the formal *japa*, however, some minimum traditions are to be observed.
2. Most of the general recommendations, already given for *japa*, are applicable for the formal Gāyatrī-*japa*.
3. The deity of this *mantra* is *Īśvara/Brahman*, without form. No idol/image/picture is necessary. However, you may keep the symbol *oṁ* (ॐ) in front, if you like.
4. The *japa* may be done in the *tri-sandhyā*s (morning, noon, evening) or *dvi-sandhyā*s (morning and evening).

5. The word *savitā* in the *mantra* is *Īśvara* (God). The sun is, in no way, connected with the *mantra*.
6. The formal *japa* of the *mantra* is done, while facing the east or the north in any of the recommended *āsanas*. If you have some health problem, especially in the legs or hips, you may sit on a hard chair or a stool. Many *gurus* prescribe to face the east in the morning (before sunrise), the north in the noon and the west (before sunset) in the evening. They also prescribe to worship the deity Gāyatrī in the morning, Sāvitrī in the noon and Sarasvatī in the evening. The deity of this *mantra* is *Īśvara/Brahman*, and, secondly, Gāyatrī, Sāvitrī and Sarasvatī are one and the same. Hence, we do not agree with such recommendation. They recommend that we stand in the morning and noon and sit in the evening sessions. They wrongly think that the sun is the deity of the *mantra*. We do not agree with them. We recommend that you do the formal *japa* in the sitting posture, facing the east or the north.
7. You may normally do the *japa* 10, 28 (27), 108 or 1080 times. The minimum number for the formal *japa* is 10. You may do 10, 28 or 108 *japas* by the *karamālā*. For 27, 108 or 1080 *japas*, you preferably use a rosary of 27 or 108 beads (with the additional *meru* or crown), as the case may be. The beads of the rosary may be *rudrākṣa* or *tulasī*.
8. Some *gurus* recommend that we hold the rosary at the level of the navel in the morning, the heart in the noon and the nosetip in the evening. We recommend the heart level for the *japa* of the Gāyatrī-*mantra* or

any other *mantra* in all the *sandhyās*. We urge that the rosary should not be held below the navel.

9. The speed of the *mantra-japa* should not be too fast or too slow. Each syllable should be distinctly pronounced. No syllable should be swallowed or skipped over.
10. Continue your *japa* without leaving your seat, without break and without doing other work and talking to others during the whole period of a *japa*-session.
11. If you are doing *puraścaraṇa-japa* of the Gāyatrī-*mantra*, you are to do the *japa* 24 *lākh* (2.4 million) times. Do the *japa* 3,000 or 4,000 times daily and complete the *japa* in the required number of days. You may decrease or increase the daily *japa* according to your convenience. But, preferably, maintain the same number everyday. Live on fruits and milk or *haviṣyānna* (rice, cooked with milk and a small quantity of *ghī*, eaten only once in the midday). Avoid sex during the whole period of *puraścaraṇa-japa*. Observe *mauna* (silence) during the whole period, or only one day a week, or some definite hours everyday. Fix your mind on *Brahman* (*brāhmī-sthiti*) even when you are not doing the *japa*.

After finishing the *puraścaraṇa-japa*, do *havana* (one-tenth the number of *japa*). The *havana* is to be followed by *brāhmaṇa-bhojana* (feeding *Brahma*-knowers who live a life of high morality) and *daridra-nārāyaṇa-sevā* (feeding poor people and giving clothes and money to them, thinking that God lives in them).

Now we sum up the procedure of the *japa* in a few steps as stated below:

1. Do *dhyāna* on God for about three minutes before doing the actual *japa*. Your *dhyāna* may precede a short prayer.
2. Do the *japa*. You decide the number of repetition. It should not be less than ten.
3. Your *japa*-session should conclude with a short *samādhi*.

BENEFITS FROM THE GĀYATRĪ JAPA

As the text of the *mantra* indicates, the Gāyatrī-*japa* is primarily done to atttain *Brahman*-hood (*brahma-nirvāṇa*). The devotee transforms himself, finally to become *Brahman*. He purifies his intellect (*buddhi*), removes ignorance from him, ascends the ladder of consciousness, gives up impurities (*malas*), distils and re-distils himself and finally becomes Pure Consciousness, Pure Existence and Pure Bliss. (His self becomes *Saccidānanda*.)

Through the Gāyatrī-*mantra-japa*, benefits do accrue to the body too. Physical, mental and spiritual health is attained. It is, however, stressed that the Gāyatrī-*mantra* is not primarily meant for fulfilling worldly desires and getting material prosperity.

The *tāntrika* use of the Gāyatrī-*mantra* does give *bhukti* (worldly benefits) and *mukti* (liberation). Its application for worldly benefits will be discussed in the third chapter of this book.

The Tantricization of the Gāyatrī Mantra

At present, most Gāyatrī-*sādhakas* have tantricized the Gāyatrī-*mantra*. We are not against it. We only urge them to develop a holistic comprehension. If that is done, there is nothing wrong with the *tāntrika* approach.

The image of Gāyatrī. We have already said that Sarasvatī, Gāyatrī and Sāvitrī are synonyms of one deity only, the Power of Brahmā, the Mother Creatrix. She is one of the three Mothers (*tri-ambā*s) — Kālī, Lakṣmī and Sarasvatī. God, being bipolar, is *Īśvara* with his *Śakti* (Power) *Mahāmāyā*. The universe has one Father and one Mother only. For differences in attributes and functions, we conceive of *trimūrti* (three forms), namely, Brahmā (the creator), Viṣṇu (the sustainer) and Rudra (the destroyer). Each of this Trinity has the respective *Śakti*, namely, Sarasvatī, Lakṣmī and Kālī. Thus, one Mother becomes three mothers for our empirical purpose. Viṣṇu and Lakṣmī have the attribute of *sattva*; Brahmā and Sarasvatī have the attribute of *rajas*; and Rudra and Kālī have the attribute of *tama*s. For our psychological needs, we make symbols. And so do we give forms to the formless Father and the formless Mother. We would prefer the classical image of Mother Sarasvatī (with a *vīṇā* in hand) for the Gāyatrī worship (*fig*. 2.15). But the tradition has travelled on another route. Some *guru*s prescribe three forms of Mother Gāyatrī, one for the morning worship, a second one for the noon, and a third one for the evening. We make a compromise. We accept an image of Gāyatrī, separate from that of Sarasvatī; but we accept one image only, the five-faced one (*fig*. 2.16). We pragmatically accept it, because essentially the Mother is formless. A picture or an idol of Mother Gāyatrī may be kept in front of the devotee for worship (*pūjā*) and the *mantra-japa*. The devotee faces the east or the north and the idol or the picture faces the west or the south, that is, face to face.

fig. 2.15 : The picture of mother Sarasvatī (Purāṇic)

fig. 2.16 : The picture of mother Gāyatrī (*tāntrika*)

Ācamana

The word *ācamana* means "purifying the body by chanting *mantra* and sipping water." We will present three varieties of *ācamana*, namely, the Vedic, the *smārta* (Purāṇic) and the tāntric. After chanting each *mantra*, a spoon of water is taken in the cup-shaped right palm and sipped.

The Vedic *ācamana* is done by chanting the following *mantras*:*

1. *oṁ amṛtopastaraṇamasi svāhā.*
2. *oṁ amṛtāpidhānamasi svāhā.*
3. *oṁ satyaṁ yaśaḥ śrīrmayī śrīḥ śrayatāṁ svāhā.*

The above three *mantras* are translated into English as follows:

> O immortal Lord, you are our support (substratum); you are our protector (cover); let honour, fame and wealth come to me by honest efforts. O God, make this water sacred.

The *mantras* of the Purāṇic *ācamana* are the following:

1. *oṁ keśavāya namaḥ svāhā.*
2. *oṁ nārāyaṇāya namaḥ svāhā.*
3. *oṁ mādhavāya namaḥ svāhā.*

> Salutation to Lord Keśava; salutation to Lord Nārāyaṇa; salutation to Lord Mādhava. (Keśava, Nārāyaṇa and Mādhava are different names of Viṣṇu or God.)

---

* In south India the *ācamana mantras* are:
1. *Acutāya namaḥ.*
2. *Anantāya namaḥ.*
3. *Govindāya namaḥ.*

Next wash the right hand after chanting the following *mantra*.

oṁ govindāya namaḥ.

Salutation to Lord Govinda (another name of Viṣṇu or God).

The tāntric *ācamana* is as follows:

1. *oṁ aiṁ ātmatattvaṁ śodhayāmi namaḥ svāhā.*
2. *oṁ hrīṁ vidyātattvaṁ śodhayāmi namaḥ svāhā.*
3. *oṁ klīṁ śivatattvaṁ śodhayāmi namaḥ svāhā.*
4. *oṁ aiṁ hrīṁ klīṁ śarvatattvaṁ śodhayāmi namaḥ svāhā.*

After sipping water four times, wash the right hand. These are *mantras* for the purification of the body, the mind, the self and everything of the devotee.

Prāṇāyāma

Following *ācamana*, do three rounds of *prāṇāyāma.*

Saṅkalpa

The word *saṅkalpa* means "a solemn vow or determination to perform any ritual observance, declaration of purpose." It may be *niṣkāma* (without worldly desires) or *sakāma* (with worldly desires). The simplified, abbreviated *saṅkalpas* are given below in Sanskrit language. However, *saṅkalpa* may be made in any language.

***Niṣkāma saṅkalpa**: adyehāham amuka-devaḥ (devī vā) mama ādhyātmikottarottaragatyarthaṁ, citta-śuddhyarthaṁ, mokṣaprāptyarthaṁ gāyatrī-mantra-japaṁ kariṣye. tadaṅgatvena ādau nyāsa-kriyāñca mudrā-pradarśanañca kariṣye.*

This day, here, I, Devadatta Deva or Devadattā Devī (Devadatta or Devadattā is a name *X*. Substitute *X* with your name), for the constant ascendance of my spirituality, the purification of my intellect and heart and my liberation, will do Gāyatrī-*mantra-japa*. As component part of it, first I will do *nyāsa* and show *mudrā*s (special gestures).

Sakāma saṅkalpa: *adyehāham amuka-devaḥ (devī vā) mama (mama yajamānasya yajamānāyāḥ vā) sakuṭumbasya saparivārasya kṣemasthairyāyurārogya-iśvaryābhivṛddhyarthamādhibhautikādhidaivikādhy-ātmikatrividhatāpaśamanārthaṁ dharmārthakāma-mokṣaphala-prāptyarthaṁ nityakalyāṇalābhāya (viśeṣa-manaskāmanāpūraṇārthaṁ vā) bhagavatī-/bhagavat-prītyartham amuka-devasya/amuka-devyāḥ pūjanaṁ/ mantra-japaṁ kariṣye. tadaṅgatvena ādau nyāsa-kriyāñca mudrā-pradarśanañca kariṣye.*

This day, here, I, Devadatta Deva/Devadattā Devī, for my/for my client's Devapriya-Deva's/ Devapriyā-Devī's (the names given here are *X*'s, substitute the *X*'s with the actual names) and my family's and dependents'/my client's family's and dependents' improvement of security, stability, long life, good health and wealth and power, for the allaying of our afflictions caused by physical nature, gods or spirits and our own self/selves, for the performance of our duties, earning money, the fulfilment of our worldly desires and our liberation, and for our daily prosperity (or for fulfilling a special mental desire/physical need), for propitiating God/ Mother Goddess, I will worship God . . . ./

Goddess . . . ./I will do the *mantra-japa* of God . . . ./Goddess . . . . As component part of it, first I will do *nyāsa* and *mudrā*s.

In the *saṅkalpa* given here, the unnecessary portions will be deleted and the appropriate names will be used.

Kara-Nyāsaḥ

The word *kara* means "hand" and *nyāsa* means "location." The deity is placed in different locations of the body and thereby the body of the devotee is deified and, in this process, his awareness is shifted from place to place. The *nyāsa-kriyā* is *tāntrika* in origin.

Do *kara-nyāsa*s, by both hands, by chanting the following *mantra*s:

1. *oṁ bhūḥ aṅguṣṭābhyāṁ namaḥ.*

   The tip of the index finger touches the root of the thumb and slides up to the tip of the thumb.

2. *oṁ bhuvaḥ tarjanībhyāṁ namaḥ.*

   The tip of the thumb touches the root of the index finger and slides up to the tip of the index finger.

3. *oṁ svaḥ madhyamābhyāṁ namaḥ.*

   The tip of the thumb touches the root of the middle finger and slides up to the tip of the middle finger.

4. *oṁ tatsaviturvareṇyam anāmikābhyāṁ namaḥ.*

   The tip of the thumb touches the base of the ring finger and slides up to the tip of the ring finger.

5. *oṁ bhargo devasya dhīmahi kaniṣṭhikābhyāṁ namaḥ.*

   The tip of the thumb touches the base of the little finger and slides up to the tip of the little finger.

6. *oṁ dhiyo yo naḥ pracodayāt karatalakarapṛṣṭhābhyāṁ namaḥ.*

   The palm of the right hand is placed crosswise on that of the left hand and then the process is similarly repeated with the backs of the hands.

Ṣaḍaṅga-Nyāsaḥ

The word *ṣaṭ* means "six" and *aṅga* means "limb," "organ" or "part of the body." The *mantra*s in connection with the *aṅga-nyāsa* are given below:

1. *oṁ bhūḥ hṛdayāya namaḥ.*

   By the five fingers of the right hand, touch the heart area.

2. *oṁ bhuvaḥ śirase svāhā.*

   By the five fingers of the right hand, touch the front part of the head.

3. *oṁ svaḥ śikhāyai vaṣaṭ.*

   By the right thumb, touch the crown of the head.

4. *oṁ tatsaviturvareṇyaṁ kavacāya huṁ.*

   Simultaneously, touch the right shoulder and left shoulder by the five fingers of the left hand and the right hand, respectively, the fore-arms being placed crosswise.

5. *oṁ bhargo devasya dhīmahi netratrayāya vauṣaṭ.*

   By the tips of the five fingers of the right hand, touch the two eyes and the eyebrow centre (*ājñā cakra*).

6. *oṁ dhiyo yo naḥ pracodayāt astrāya phaṭ.*

   Take the right hand over the head to the left side of the back and bring to the front of the chest through the right side; clap by striking the right index and middle fingers against the left palm.

Pre-Japa and Post-Japa Mudrās

The practice of 24 *mudrā*s and 8 *mudrā*s before and after the *japa* of the Gāyatrī-*mantra*, respectively, is recommended.[21] However, the *mudrā*-practice is optional. If done, in addition to the enhancement of the efficacy of the *mantra-japa*, physical and mental benefits are immense.

Short descriptions, with illustrations of the pre-*japa mudrā*s, are given here.

Sumukham: The tips of the five fingers of each hand meet the respective tips of the other hand, in a front to front position, with the wrists kept apart in a diverging position (*fig*. 2.17).

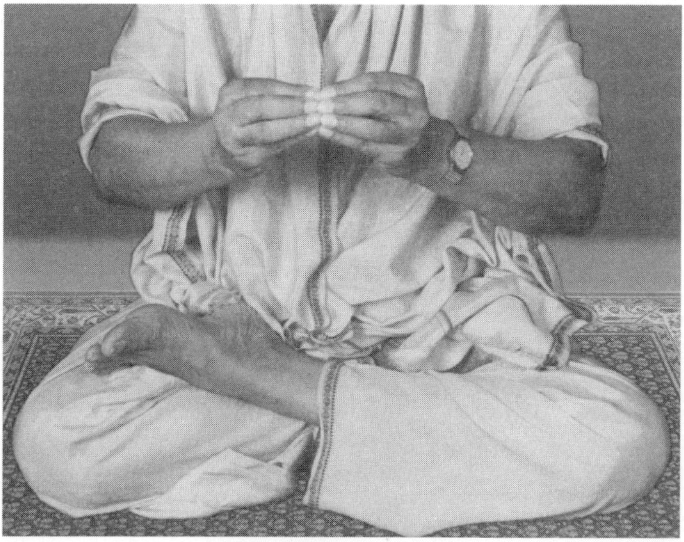

fig. 2.17: *Mudrā : sumukham*

Sampuṭam: The tips of the five fingers of each hand meet those of the other hand, with the palms bulged out, the bases of the palms in contact and the two wrists making an angle (*fig*. 2.18).

Vitatam: All the five fingers of each hand are close together. The fingers and palms of both the hands are kept in a vertical position, one hand facing the other, but without mutual contact (*fig*. 2.19).

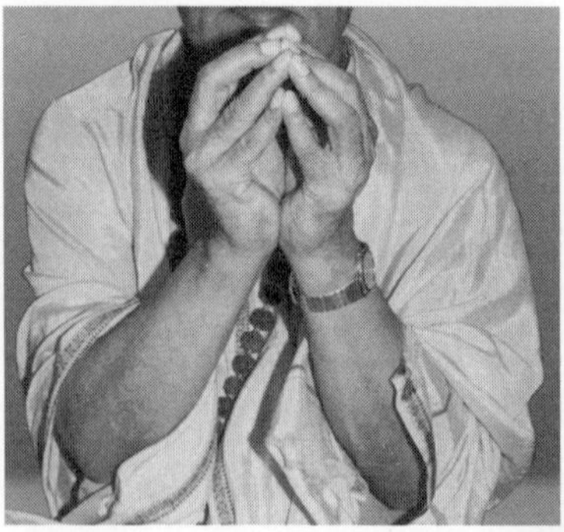

fig. 2.18: *Mudrā : sampuṭam*

fig. 2.18 (a): *Mudrā : sampuṭam* Vertical view

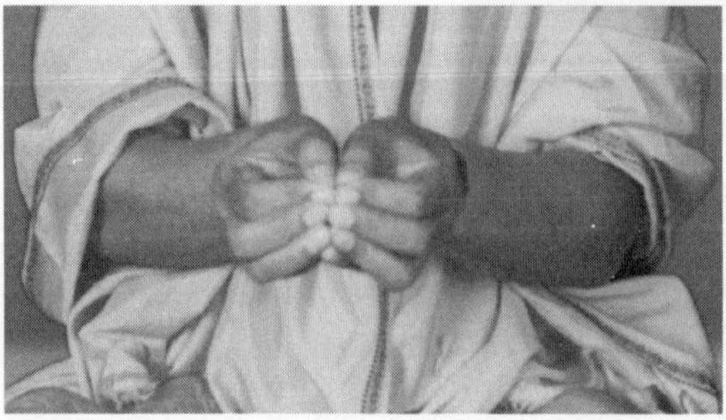

fig. 2.18 (b): *Mudrā : sampuṭam* Horizontal view

fig. 2.19: *Mudrā : vitatam*

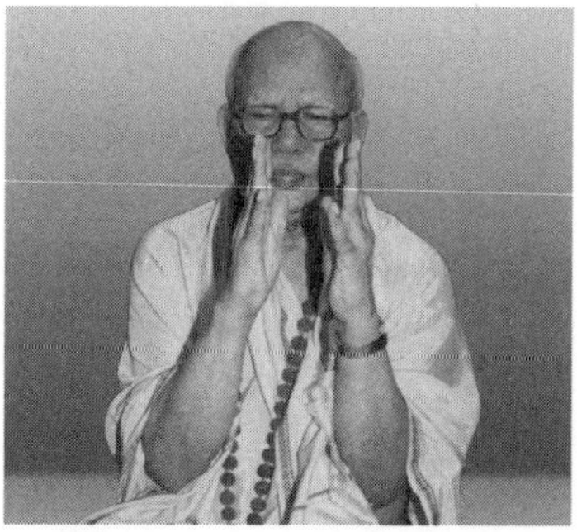

fig. 2.20: *Mudrā : vistṛtam*

Vistṛtam: It has some similarity with the *vitatam* with two differences. All the five fingers of each hand are slightly separated. The separation of the two hands is wider (*fig.* 2.20).

Dvimukham: The tips of the two little fingers and the two ring-fingers are joined, with the contact of the bases of the palms and the outward divergence of the other fingers and thumbs (*fig.* 2.21).

Trimukham: It is the same as the *dvimukham*, with the additional contact of the tips of the two middle fingers (*fig.* 2.22).

fig. 2.21: *Mudrā : dvimukham*

fig. 2.22: *Mudrā : trimukham*

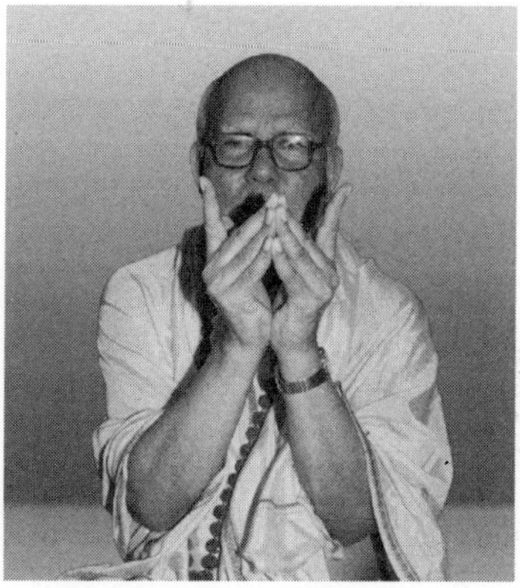

fig. 2.23: *Mudrā* : *caturmukham*

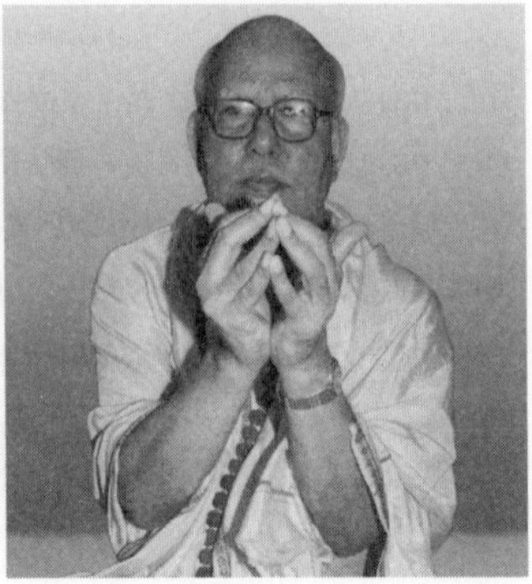

fig. 2.24: *Mudrā* : *pañcamukham*

Caturmukham: It is the same as the *trimukham*, with the additional contact of the tips of the two index fingers (*fig.* 2.23).

Pañcamukham: It is the same as the *caturmukham*, with the additional contact of the tips of the two thumbs (*fig.* 2.24).

Ṣaṇmukham: It is the same as the *pañcamukham*, with two differences: The little fingers are separate. The bases of the palms are wide apart, with the two wrists kept in a straight line and the palms facing downward (*fig.* 2.25).

Adhomukham: The two thumbs are kept separate and towards the body. The four fingers of each hand are kept

fig. 2.25: *Mudrā* : *ṣaṇmukham*

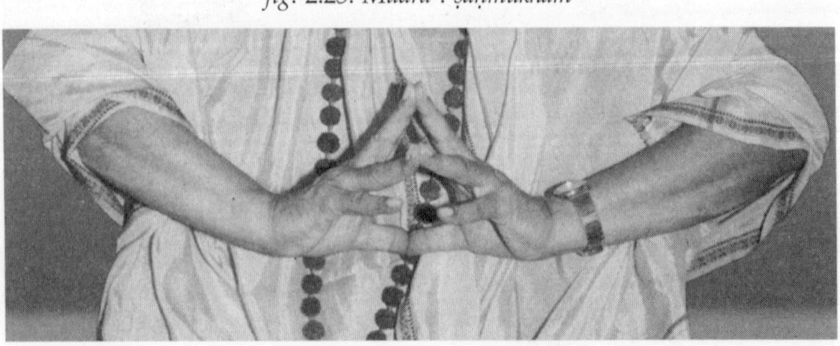

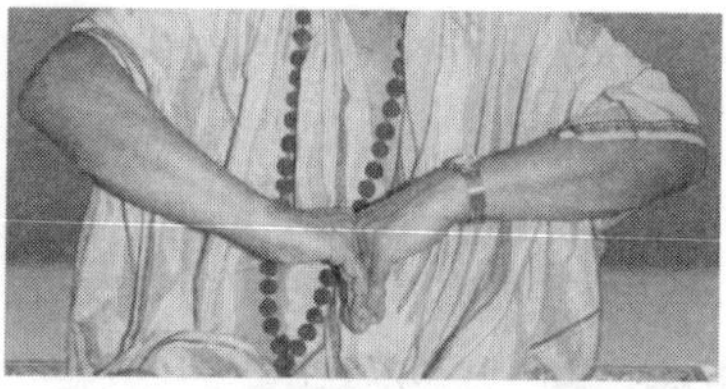

step-1

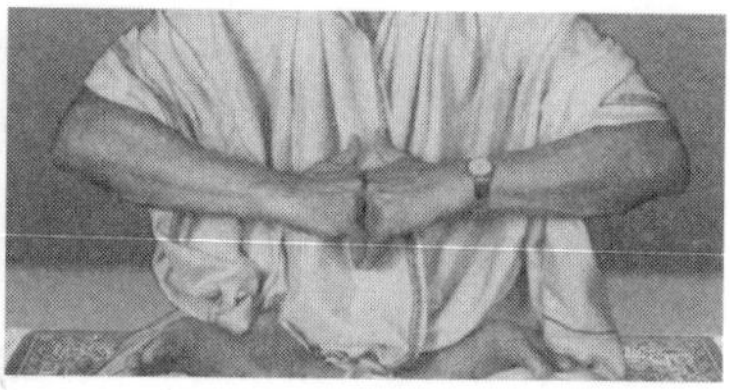

final pose

fig. 2.26: *Mudrā : adhomukham*

close together. The fingers of both the hands are kept in contact on the dorsal sides, with downward pointing. The two fore-arms are in a straight line (*fig.* 2.26).

Vyāpakāñjalim: Keep the five fingers of each hand close together, facing upwards. Keep both the hands in contact by the sides of the little fingers, with the expanded palms facing upwards and the fingertips away from the body (*fig.* 2.27).

Śakaṭam: Both the palms face downwards. The two thumbtips touch each other. The two index fingers are kept straight. The other three fingers are closed into fists (*fig.* 2.28).

Yamapāśam: The two index fingers are tied together, pointing upwards. The two thumbs are kept straight. The other three fingers are closed into a fist (*fig.* 2.29).

fig. 2.27: *Mudrā : vyāpakāñjalim*

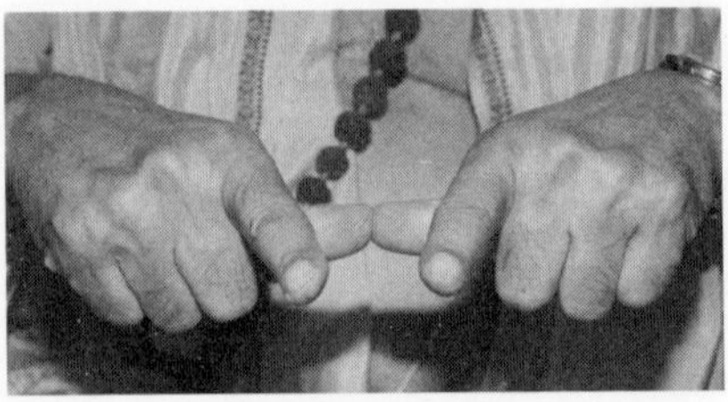

closer view

fig. 2.28: *Mudrā* : *śakaṭam*

Grathitam: All the fingers, including the thumbs, are interlocked, with the dorsal sides upwards. The hands are positioned in such a way that they make an angle (*fig*. 2.30), without the bases of the palms touching each other.

Unmukhonmukham: All the five fingers of each hand are kept close together. (a) Keep the four finger tips of the right hand on those of the left hand on a vertical line. (b) Repeat the same process by reversing the hands (*fig*. 2.31).

Pralambam: All the five fingers of both the hands are kept close together. Both the hands, without contact with each other, hang downwards vertically, with palms facing the body (*fig*. 2.32).

fig. 2.29: *Mudrā* : *yamapāśam*

closer view

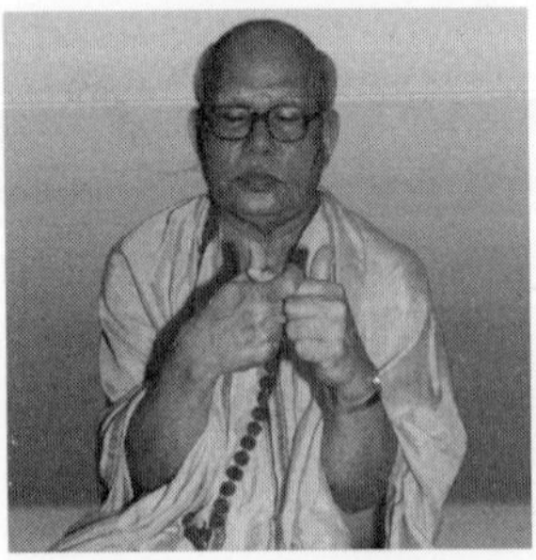

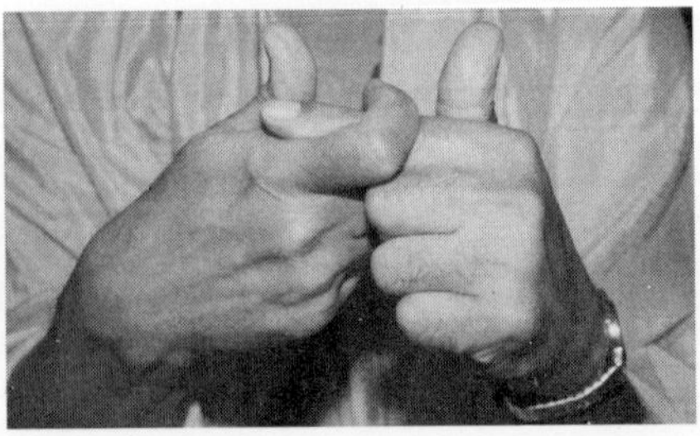

fig. 2.30: *Mudrā* : *grathitam*

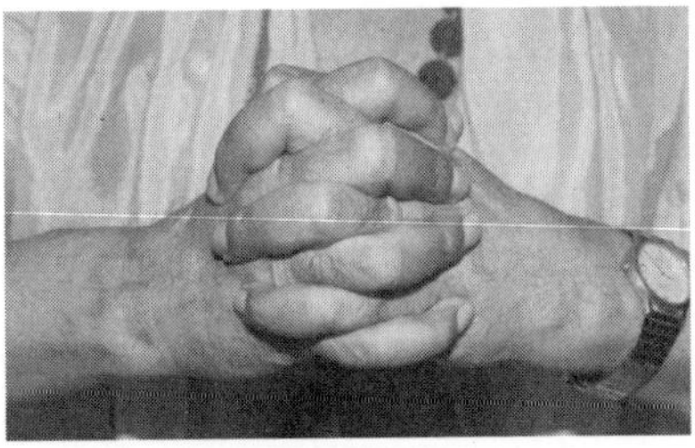

closer view

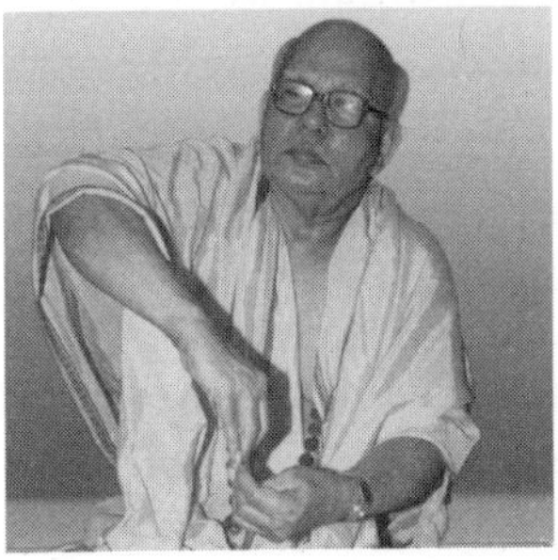

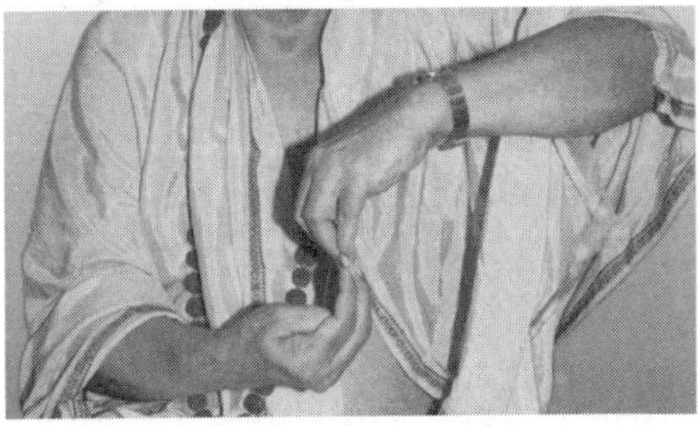

closer view

fig. 2.31: *Mudrā* : *unmukhonmukham*

fig. 2.32: *Mudrā* : *pralambam*

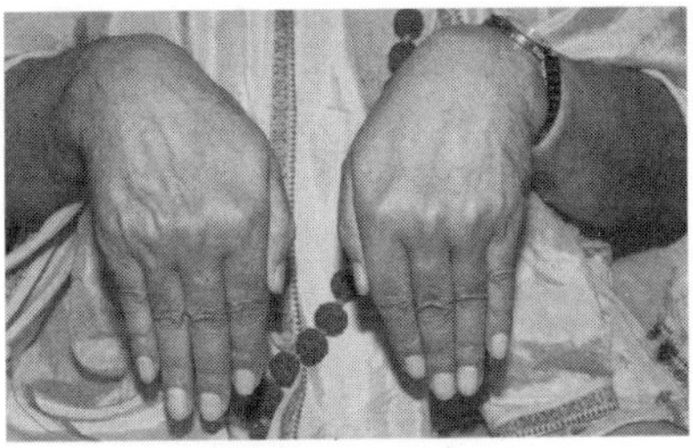

closer view

fig. 2.33: *Mudrā* : *muṣṭikam*

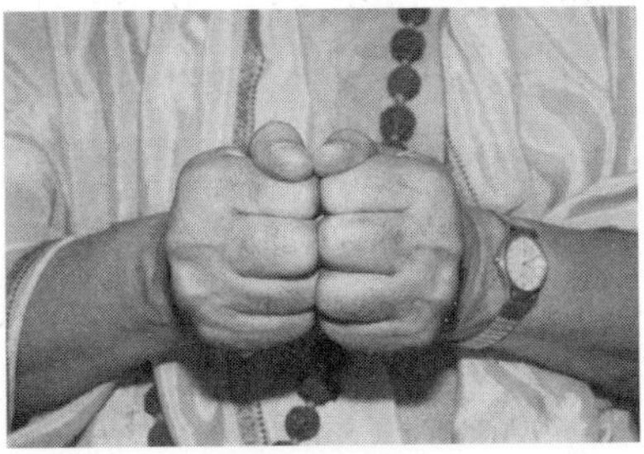

closer view

Muṣṭikam: The four fingers of each hand are closed into a fist, with the respective thumbtip placed on the knuckle of the respective index finger. The two fists are brought into contact with each other, with the backs of the hands facing sideways (*fig*. 2.33).

Matsyaḥ: The right hand is horizontally kept, with the palm facing downwards, the right thumb on the left side and the fingertips pointing forwards, the four fingers being close together. The left hand is superimposed on the right hand, with its back upwards and its thumb on the right side. Both the thumbs remain separate from the fingers and repeatedly move laterally and medially (*fig*. 2.34).

Kūrmaḥ: The right hand is kept with its palm upward. The middle, ring and little fingers of the left hand are folded and their dorsal sides are placed on the ventral side of the middle and ring fingers of the right hand. The tip of the right little finger touches that of the left index finger and the tip of the right index finger touches that of the left thumb (*fig*. 2.35).

Varāhakam: The right index finger and the left thumb are joined. All the other fingers of both the hands are closed into a fist (*fig*. 2.36).

Siṁhākrāntam: Both the hands are kept near the respective ears, with palms facing the front (*fig*. 2.37).

Mahākrāntam: The fingers of both the hands are placed near the respective ears, with palms towards the ears (*fig*. 2.38).

Mudgaram: The right hand is closed into a fist. The right elbow rests on the left plam, the right forearm being vertical (*fig*. 2.39).

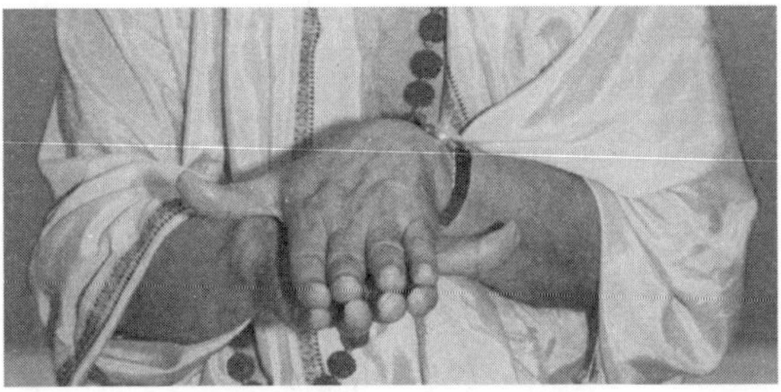

fig. 2.34: *Mudrā* : *matsyaḥ*

fig. 2.35: *Mudrā* : *kūrmaḥ*

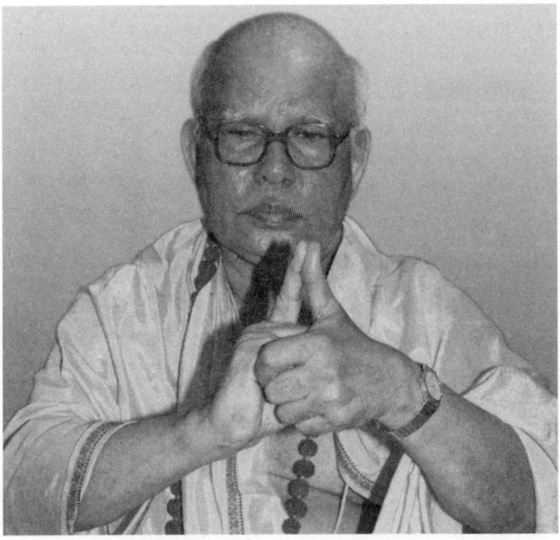

fig. 2.36: *Mudrā* : *varāhakam*

fig. 2.37: *Mudrā* : *siṁhākrāntam*

fig. 2.38: *Mudrā* : *mahākrāntam*

Pallavam: The right hand, with fingers straight and separated, is moved right and left in front of the face, the palm being towards the face (*fig*. 2.40).

The post-*japa mudrā*s are briefly described here with illustrations.

fig. 2.39: *Mudrā* : *mudgara*

fig. 2.40: *Mudrā* : *pallavam*

Surabhiḥ: The fingers are joined as follows:

(a) Left index finger with right middle finger.

(b) Left middle finger with right index finger.

(c) Left ring finger with right little finger.

(d) Left little finger with right ring finger.

The right fingers should be placed below the left fingers and the thumb sides of the palms should be close together (*fig*. 2.41)

Cetanā: The tips of the right index finger and the thumb are joined together and placed on the heart-centre. The tips of the left index finger and the left thumb are joined together and placed on the left knee, with the palm upwards (*fig*. 2.42).

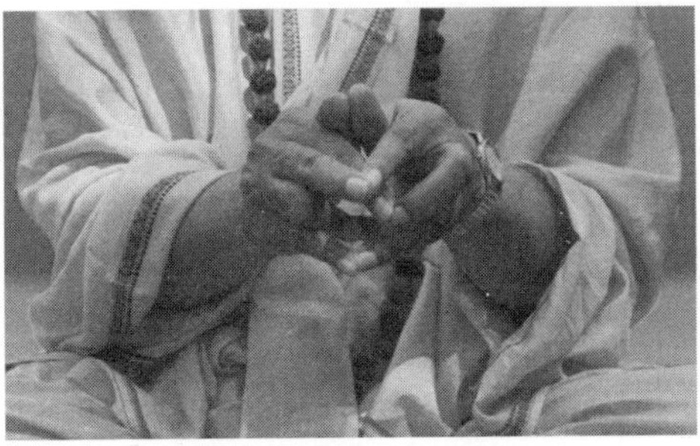

fig. 2.41: *Mudrā : surabhiḥ*

another pose

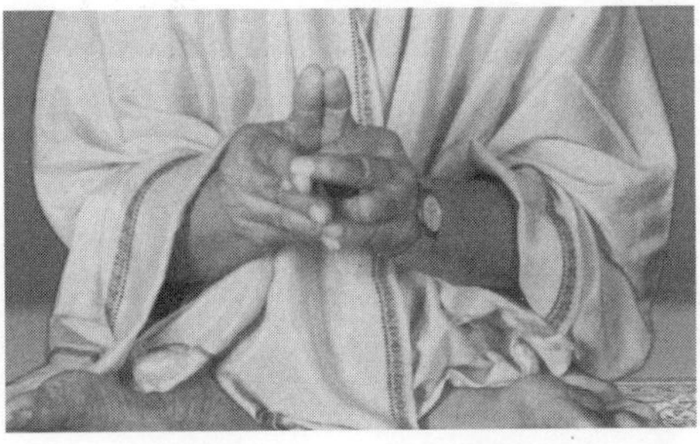

fig. 2.42: *Mudrā* : *cetanā*

Vairāgyam: The index finger and the thumb of each hand are joined at the tips and placed on the respective knees, with palms upwards (*fig*. 2.43). This *mudrā* is the same as the *jñāna-mudrā*.

Yoniḥ: In this *mudrā*, both the middle fingers should point upwards, with contact of the tips. Below the middle fingers, the index and the ring fingers should be joined as follows:

(a) Right ring finger on the left index finger.

(b) Left ring finger on the right index finger.

fig. 2.43: *Mudrā* : *vairāgyam*

fig. 2.44: *Mudrā* : *yoniḥ* another pose

By the upward pressure of both the index fingers, tightly hold all these four fingers below the two middle fingers (*fig.* 2.44). In this *mudrā*, the thumbs and the little fingers do not actively participate. The thumbs remain in contact with each other and the tips of the little fingers touch each other.

Śaṅkhaḥ: The left thumb is kept inside the right fist, with pressure at the root of the thumb. All the four fingers of the left hand twist across the back of the right hand so as to touch the right thumb by their tips. The same procedure is followed, with change of sides, by keeping the right thumb inside the left fist (*fig.* 2.45).

Paṅkajam: Both the hands are joined together, with the fingertips and the thumbtips pointing upwards. All the eight fingers are close together. Both the thumbs are close together, but separate from the fingers. The bases of the two palms at the wrist press each other. The *mudrā* looks like an open lotus flower (*fig.* 2.46).

Liṅgam: All the eight fingers of both the hands are interlocked, with the right thumb in an upright condition.

fig. 2.45: *Mudrā* : *śaṅkhaḥ*

fig. 2.46: *Mudrā* : *paṅkajam*

The left thumb presses the dorsal root of the right thumb. All the mounds of the right and the left hand press each other (*fig*. 2.47).

Nirvāṇam: The ventral right forearm is kept on the dorsal left forearm crosswise. Each hand is closed into a fist by the thumb and the fingers other than the index finger. The

fig. 2.47: *Mudrā* : *liṅgam*

fig. 2.48: *Mudrā* : *nirvāṇam*

hands are kept close to the chest and the neck, with each index finger in the proximity of the corresponding ear (*fig.* 2.48).

Worshipping Mother Gāyatrī before the Japa

We have prescribed *ācamana*, *nyāsa*s and *mudrā*s before doing the actual *japa*. Further, we have said that the practice of the *mudrā*s before and after the *japa* are not compulsory. But, those who tantricize the Gāyatrī-*sādhanā* do think that the *pūjā* should not be skipped over. For the details of the *pūjā*, some good book on *pūjā* may be referred to, or instructions may be had from the *guru*. We don't condemn the *pūjā*. But, we feel, for the daily *japa* of the Gāyatrī-*mantra*, one may better avoid it, for the sake of getting time in the modern busy life and eliminating too much complexity.

Japa of the Gāyatrī-Mantra

The procedure of any *mantra-japa* in general and of the *japa* of the Gāyatrī-*mantra* in particular has already been described. There is no need of repetition. Do *japa* at least 10 times in the morning and also in the evening. If time permits, (27) 28, 108, or 1080 *japa*s may be done in each *sandhyā*. The *puraścaraṇa-japa* of the Gāyatrī-*mantra* is done 24 *lākh* (2.4 million) times, covering a number of days.

Conclusoin of the Gāyatrī Sādhanā

Utter the following sentences after finishing the *mantra-japa*.

> *Anena sandhyopāsanākhyena karmaṇā śrīparameśvaraḥ** *prīyatāṁ na mama. oṁ tatsat śrībrahmārpaṇamastu. oṁ śāntiḥ śāntiḥ śāntiḥ.*

* In south India, the Vaiṣṇavites replace "Parameśvaraḥ" with "Mahāviṣṇu" or "Nārāyaṇa."

> O God, be pleased with my *sandhyā*-worship. It is not for my pleasure. Let my *japa* be offered to *Brahman*, the One which is the Reality. *Oṁ* peace; *oṁ* peace; *oṁ* peace.

Do *dhyāna*, ending in *samādhi*, for five minutes. This finishes the Gāyatrī-*sādhanā*.

The Practice of Mantra-Japa in Bhakti-Yoga

Mantra-japa, in general, is a kind of *bhakti-yoga* (the *yoga* of devotion). The *japa* which we have already described in relation to the Vedas, the Vedānta and the *Pātañjala Yoga* is, however, more related to *jñāna-yoga* (the *yoga* of *Brahma*-knowledge), although not totally bereft of *bhakti*. The *oṅkāra-japa* and the Gāyatrī-*japa* may come in both categories. But the *ajapā-japa* (*so 'ham*) is purely non-dualistic (*advaita*). Now we will cite some *nāma*s (names of God and/or Goddess) and some *mantra*s for purely devotional purposes.

Purāṇic Gāyatrī-Mantras

GAṆEŚA-*GĀYATRĪ*

1. *oṁ ekadantāya vidmahe.*
   vakratuṇḍāya dhīmahi.
   tanno dantī pracodayāt.

   ओ३म् एकदन्ताय विद्महे
   वक्रतुण्डाय धीमहि।
   तन्नो दन्ती प्रचोदयात्॥

2. *oṁ tatpuruṣāya vidmahe.*
   vakratuṇḍāya dhīmahi.
   tanno dantī pracodayāt.

ओ३म् तत्पुरुषाय विद्महे
वक्रतुण्डाय धीमहि।
तन्नो दन्ती प्रचोदयात्॥

BRAHMĀ-*GĀYATRĪ*

1. *oṁ vedātmane vidmahe.*
hiraṇyagarbhāya dhīmahi.
tanno brahmā pracodayāt.

ओ३म् वेदात्मने विद्महे
हिरण्यगर्भाय धीमहि।
तन्नो ब्रह्मा प्रचोदयात्॥

2. *oṁ caturmukhāya vidmahe.*
kamaṇḍaludharāya dhīmahi.
tanno brahmā pracodayāt.

ओ३म् चतुर्मुखाय विद्महे
कमण्डलुधराय धीमहि।
तन्नो ब्रह्मा प्रचोदयात्॥

3. *oṁ parameśvarāya vidmahe.*
paratattvāya dhīmahi.
tanno brahmā pracodayāt.

ओ३म् परमेश्वराय विद्महे
परतत्त्वाय धीमहि।
तन्नो ब्रह्मा प्रचोदयात्॥

VIṢṆU *GĀYATRĪ*

1. *oṁ nārāyaṇāya vidmahe.*
vāsudevāya dhīmahi.
tanno viṣṇuḥ pracodayāt.

ओ३म् नारायणाय विद्महे
वासुदेवाय धीमहि ।
तन्नो विष्णुः प्रचोदयात् ॥

NṚSIṀHA-*GĀYATRĪ*

1. *oṁ vajranakhāya vidmahe.*
tīkṣṇadaṁṣṭrāya dhīmahi.
tanno nṛsiṁhaḥ pracodayāt.

ओ३म् वज्रनखाय विद्महे
तीक्ष्णदंष्ट्राय धीमहि ।
तन्नो नृसिंहः प्रचोदयात् ॥

2. *oṁ nṛsiṁhāya vidmahe.*
vajranakhāya dhīmahi.
tannaḥ siṁhaḥ pracodayāt.

ओ३म् नृसिंहाय विद्महे
वज्रनखाय धीमहि ।
तन्नः सिंहः प्रचोदयात् ॥

KṚṢṆA-*GĀYATRĪ*

1. *oṁ devakī-nandanāya vidmahe.*
vāsudevāya dhīmahi.
tannaḥ kṛṣṇaḥ pracodayāt.

ओ३म् देवकीनन्दनाय विद्महे
वासुदेवाय धीमहि ।
तन्नः कृष्णः प्रचोदयात् ॥

2. *oṁ gopālāya vidmahe.*
gopījanavallabhāya dhīmahi.
tanno gopālaḥ procodayāt.

ओ३म् गोपालाय विद्महे
गोपीजनवल्लभाय धीमहि ।
तन्नो गोपालः प्रचोदयात् ॥

RĀMA-*GĀYATRĪ*

1. *oṁ dāśarathaye vidmahe.*
mahādurgāyai dhīmahi.
tanno rāmaḥ pracodayāt.

ओ३म् दाशरथये विद्महे
महादुर्गायै धीमहि ।
तन्नो रामः प्रचोदयात् ॥

RUDRA-*GĀYATRĪ*

1. *oṁ tatpuruṣāya vidmahe.*
mahādevāya dhīmahi.
tanno rudraḥ pracodayāt.

ओ३म् तत्पुरुषाय विद्महे
महादेवाय धीमहि ।
तन्नो रुद्रः प्रचोदयात् ॥

2. *oṁ tatpuruṣāya vidmahe.*
sahasrākṣāya dhīmahi.
tanno rudraḥ pracodayāt.

ओ३म् तत्पुरुषाय विद्महे
सहस्राक्षाय धीमहि ।
तन्नो रुद्रः प्रचोदयात् ॥

SŪRYA-*GĀYATRĪ*

1. *oṁ bhāskarāya vidmahe.*
mahādyutikarāya dhīmahi.

tanna ādityaḥ pracodayāt.

ओ३म् भास्कराय विद्महे
महाद्युतिकराय धीमहि।
तन्न आदित्यः प्रचोदयात्॥

2. *oṁ bhāskarāya vidmahe.*
sahasrakiraṇāya dhīmahi.
tanno bhānuḥ pracodayāt.

ओ३म् भास्कराय विद्महे
सहस्रकिरणाय धीमहि।
तन्नो भानुः प्रचोदयात्॥

3. *oṁ prabhākarāya vidmahe.*
divākarāya dhīmahi.
tannaḥ sūryaḥ pracodayāt.

ओ३म् प्रभाकराय विद्महे
दिवाकराय धीमहि।
तन्नः सूर्यः प्रचोदयात्॥

HANUMAT-*GĀYATRĪ*

1. *oṁ āñjaneyāya vidmahe.*
vāyuputrāya dhīmahi.
tanno hanumān pracodayāt.

ओ३म् आञ्जनेयाय विद्महे
वायुपुत्राय धीमहि।
तन्नो हनुमान् प्रचोदयात्॥

DURGĀ-*GĀYATRĪ*

1. *oṁ mahādevyai ca vidmahe.*
durgāyai ca dhīmahi.

tanno devī pracodayāt.

ओ३म् महादेव्यै च विद्महे
दुर्गायै च धीमहि।
तन्नो देवी प्रचोदयात्॥

2. *oṁ kātyāyanyai vidmahe.*
   kanyākumāryai dhīmahi.
   tanno durgā pracodayāt.

   ओ३म् कात्यायन्यै विद्महे
   कन्याकुमार्यै धीमहि।
   तन्नो दुर्गा प्रचोदयात्॥

3. *oṁ mahāśūlinyai vidmahe.*
   mahādurgāyai dhīmahi.
   tanno bhagavatī pracodayāt.

   ओ३म् महाशूलिन्यै विद्महे
   महादुर्गायै धीमहि।
   तन्नो भगवती प्रचोदयात्॥

LAKṢMĪ-*GĀYATRĪ*

1. *oṁ mahādevyai ca vidmahe.*
   viṣṇupatnyai ca dhīmahi.
   tanno lakṣmīḥ pracodayāt.

   ओ३म् महादेव्यै च विद्महे
   विष्णुपत्न्यै च धीमहि।
   तन्नो लक्ष्मीः प्रचोदयात्॥

2. *oṁ mahālakṣmyai ca vidmahe.*
   sarvaśaktyai ca dhīmahi.
   tanno devī pracodayāt.

ओ३म् महालक्ष्म्यै च विद्महे
सर्वशक्तयै च धीमहि।
तन्नो देवी प्रचोदयात्॥

KĀLĪ-*GĀYATRĪ*

1. *oṁ mahākālyai ca vidmahe.*
śmaśānavāsinyai ca dhīmahi.
tannaḥ kālī pracodayāt.

ओ३म् महाकाल्यै च विद्महे
श्मशानवासिन्यै च धीमहि।
तन्नः काली प्रचोदयात्॥

2. *oṁ ādyāyai ca vidmahe.*
parameśvaryaica dhīmahi.
tannaḥ kālī pracodayāt.

ओ३म् आद्यायै च विद्महे
परमेश्वर्यै च धीमहि।
तन्नः काली प्रचोदयात्॥

3. *oṁ kālikāyai ca vidmahe.*
śmaśānavāsinyai ca dhīmahi.
tanno 'ghorā pracodayāt.

ओ३म् कालिकायै च विद्महे
श्मशानवासिन्यै च धीमहि।
तन्नोऽघोरा प्रचोदयात्॥

SARASVATĪ-*GĀYATRĪ*

1. *oṁ vāgdevyai ca vidmahe.*
kāmarājāya dhīmahi.
tanno devī pracodayāt.

ओ३म् वाग्देव्यै च विद्महे
कामराजाय धीमहि।
तन्नो देवी प्रचोदयात्॥

ŚAKTI-*GĀYATRĪ*

1. *oṁ sarvasammohinyai ca vidmahe.*
viśvajananyai ca dhīmahi.
tannaḥ śaktiḥ pracodayāt.

ओ३म् सर्वसंमोहिन्यै च विद्महे
विश्वजनन्यै च धीमहि।
तन्नः शक्तिः प्रचोदयात्॥

Nāma-Japa

The word *nāma* means "name." The word *nāmī* means "one who is named." For the devotee, *nāma* and *nāmī* are the same. Any name of God or Mother Goddess may be used for *japa*. Some names are suggested below:

1. *hariḥ oṁ*
2. *hariḥ oṁ tat sat*
3. Rām (Rāma)
4. Kṛṣṇa
5. Sītārāma
6. Rādheśyāma
7. Rādhekṛṣṇa
8. *oṁ śrīrāmaḥ śaraṇaṁ mama*
9. *oṁ śrīkṛṣṇaḥ śaraṇaṁ mama*

Some *Mantras* for *Japa*

Some devotional *mantras* are given below. The list is not exhaustive, but a representative sample only.

1. ***oṁ gaṇeśāya namaḥ.***

   ॐ गणेशाय नमः

2. ***oṁ gaṇapataye namaḥ.***

   ॐ गणपतये नमः

   Gaṇeśa or Gaṇapati is the deity (*devatā*) of these two *mantras*. Its meaning is "Salutation to Lord Gaṇeśa."

3. ***oṁ namo nārāyaṇāya.***

   ॐ नमो नारायणाय

   Lord Nārāyaṇa is the *devatā* of this *mantra*. It comprises eight syllables (*aṣṭākṣara*). Its meaning is: "Salutation to God Nārāyaṇa or Viṣṇu."

4. ***oṁ namaḥ śivāya.***

   ॐ नमः शिवाय

   Lord Śiva or Śaṅkara or Rudra is the *devatā* of this *mantra*. It comprises five syllables (*pañcākṣara*), *oṁ* being omitted in counting. Its meaning is: "Salutation to God Śiva."

5. ***oṁ namo bhagavate rudrāya.***

   ॐ नमो भगवते रुद्राय

   Lord Rudra is the *devatā* of this *mantra*. It comprises ten syllables (*daśākṣara*), *oṁ* being included. Its meaning is: "Salutation to God Rudra."

6. ***oṁ namo bhagavate vāsudevāya.***

   ॐ नमो भगवते वासुदेवाय

   Lord Vāsudeva or Śrīkṛṣṇa is the *devatā* of this *mantra*. It comprises 12 syllables (*dvādaśākṣara*). Its meaning is: "Salutation to God Vāsudeva."

7(a). ***oṁ śrīkṛṣṇāya govindāya gopījana-vallabhāya namaḥ.***

ॐ श्रीकृष्णाय गोविन्दाय गोपीजनवल्लभाय नमः

Lord Śrīkṛṣṇa is the *devatā* of this *mantra*. Its meaning is: "Salutation to Lord Śrīkṛṣṇa or Govinda, the lover of the *gopīs*."

7(b). ***oṁ klīṁ kṛṣṇāya govindāya gopījana-vallabhāya svāhā.***

ॐ क्लीं कृष्णाय गोविन्दाय गोपीजनवल्लभाय स्वाहा

This *mantra* is really a *tāntrika* one. It comprises 18 syllables (excluding the first *Oṁ*).

8. ***oṁ śrīkṛṣṇāya namaḥ.***

ॐ श्रीकृष्णाय नमः

Lord Śrīkṛṣṇa is the *devatā* of this *mantra*. Its meaning is: "Salutation to Lord Śrīkṛṣṇa."

9. ***oṁ śrīrāmāya namaḥ.***

ॐ श्रीरामाय नमः

Lord Śrīrāma is the *devatā* of this *mantra*. Its meaning is: "Salutation to Lord Śrīrāma."

10. ***oṁ śrīrāma, jaya rāma, jaya jaya rāma.***

ॐ श्रीराम जय राम जय जय राम

Lord Rāma is the *devatā* of this *mantra*. Its meaning is: "Salutation to Lord Rāma whose name gets victory over evil."

11. ***oṁ śrīsītārāmacandrābhyāṁ namaḥ.***

ॐ श्रीसीतारामचन्द्राभ्यां नमः

Lord Rāma and Mother Sītā are the deities of this *mantra*. Its meaning is: "Salutation to Mother Sītā and Lord Rāma."

12. ***hare rāma hare rāma, rāma rāma hare hare,***
hare kṛṣṇa hare kṛṣṇa, kṛṣṇa kṛṣṇa hare hare.

हरे राम हरे राम राम राम हरे हरे।
हरे कृष्ण हरे कृष्ण कृष्ण कृष्ण हरे हरे॥

It is called the *mahāmantra* (great *mantra*). Its deities are Rāma and Kṛṣṇa who are incarnations of God Viṣṇu (Hari). It is really a *nāma-mantra*. God's names are repeated.

13. ***oṁ śrīhanumate namaḥ.***

ॐ श्रीहनुमते नमः

Hanumān, the devotee of Rāma, is the *devatā* of this *mantra*. Its meaning is: "Salutation to Śrī Hanumān."

14. ***oṁ śrīmahālakṣmyai namaḥ.***

ॐ श्रीमहालक्ष्म्यै नमः

Mother Mahālakṣmī is the deity of this *mantra*. Its meaning is: "Salutation to Mother Mahālakṣmī."

15. ***oṁ śrīsarasvatyai namaḥ.***

ॐ श्रीसरस्वत्यै नमः

Mother Sarasvatī is the deity of this *mantra*. Its meaning is: "Salutation to Mother Sarasvatī."

16. ***oṁ śrīkālikāyai namaḥ.***

ॐ श्रीकालिकायै नमः

Mother Kālī is the deity of this *mantra*. Its meaning is: "Salutation to Mother Kālī."

17. ***oṁ śrīdurgāyai namaḥ.***

ॐ श्रीदुर्गायै नमः

Mother Durgā is the deity of this *mantra*. Its meaning is: "Salutation to Mother Durgā."

The Practice of Mantra-Japa in Tantra

In Tantra, the *japa* of any *mantra* is generally practised after doing the appropriate *nyāsa*. Each *mantra* has its own *nyāsa* system. All the details of the *nyāsa*s and *pūjā*s that generally precede the *japa* are not described here. However, for some *japa*s, the *pūjā* follows the *nyāsa* in an abbreviated form, without material-offering, but with mental offering. This is known as *mānasa pūjā* (the word *mānasa*, meaning "mental").

Mānasa Pūjā of Mother Durgā

Mother Durgā is the collective form of the three Mothers — Lakṣmī, Sarasvatī, Kālī. Her *mānasa pūjā* is given below.

1. *oṁ laṁ pṛthivyātmakaṁ gandhaṁ parikalpayāmi.*
   oṁ bhūr bhuvaḥ svaḥ.
   oṁ hrīṁ duṁ durgāyai namaḥ.
   mānasa-gandhaṁ samarpayāmi.

2. *oṁ ham ākāśātmakaṁ puṣpaṁ parikalpayāmi.*
   oṁ bhūr bhuvaḥ svaḥ.
   oṁ hrīṁ duṁ durgāyai namaḥ.
   mānasa-puṣpaṁ samarpayāmi.

3. *oṁ yaṁ vāyvātmakaṁ dhūpaṁ parikalpayāmi.*
   oṁ bhūr bhuvaḥ svaḥ.
   om hrīṁ duṁ durgāyai namaḥ.
   mānasa-dhūpamāghrāpayāmi.

4. *oṁ raṁ vahnyātmakaṁ dīpaṁ parikalpayāmi.*
   oṁ bhūr bhuvaḥ svaḥ.
   oṁ hrīṁ duṁ durgāyai namaḥ.
   mānasa-dīpaṁ darśayāmi.

5. *oṁ vaṁ amṛtātmakaṁ naivedyaṁ parikalpayāmi.*
oṁ bhūr bhuvaḥ svaḥ.
oṁ hrīṁ duṁ durgāyai namaḥ.
mānasa-naivedyaṁ nivedayāmi.

6. *oṁ saṁ sarvātmakān śeṣopacārān parikalpayāmi.*
oṁ bhūr bhuvaḥ svaḥ.
oṁ hrīṁ duṁ durgāyai namaḥ.
mānasa-śeṣopacārān samarpayāmi.

For any other deity, the same *mānasa-pūjā* is applicable, with the single alteration that the *nāma-mantra* is changed appropriately. For example, in worshipping God Śiva, the *nāma-mantra* is *oṁ namaḥ śivāya* instead of *oṁ hriṁ duṁ durgāyai namaḥ.*

For the first five *mantra*s, five *bīja*s (seeds), namely, *laṁ, haṁ, yaṁ, raṁ,* and *vaṁ*, have been used. They are the *bīja*s of the *mūlādhāra*, the *viśuddhi*, the *anāhata*, the *maṇipūra* and the *svādhiṣṭhāna cakra*s, respectively. They are the *cakra*s that represent *pṛthvī* (solidity and smell), *ākāśa* (the subtlest state of matter), *vāyu* (gaseousness), *agni* or *vahni* (fire) and *jalam* (water), respectively. The word *parikalpayāmi* means "I am conceiving." The *mahā-vyāhṛti*s (great utterances) *bhūḥ, bhuvaḥ* and *svaḥ* are chanted before the *nāma-mantra* in *pūjā*s. The word *gandha, puṣpa, dhūpa, dīpa* and *naivedya* mean "sandalwood-paste, flower, incense, lamp and food for offering," respectively. The sixth step in the *pūjā* is an additional one for the offering of the rest of the rituals not mentioned.

Some Tāntric Mantras for Japa

GAṆEŚA MANTRA

1. *gaṁ.*
2. *glauṁ.*
3. *oṁ gaṁ gaṇapataye namaḥ.*
4. *oṁ gaṁ gaṇeśāya namaḥ.*

DURGĀ MANTRA

1. *oṁ hrīṁ duṁ durgāyai namaḥ.*

LAKṢMĪ MANTRA

1. *śrīṁ.*
2. *oṁ śrīṁ mahālakṣmyai namaḥ.*
3. *oṁ śrīṁ hrīṁ śrīṁ mahālakṣmyai namaḥ.*
4. *oṁ śrīṁ hrīṁ śrīṁ kamale kamalālaye prasīda prasīda. śrīṁ hrīṁ śrīṁ mahālakṣmyai namaḥ.*

SARASVATĪ MANTRA

1. *aiṁ*
2. *oṁ aiṁ sarasvatyai namaḥ.*
3. *oṁ aiṁ hrīṁ aiṁ sarasvatyai namaḥ.*

KĀLĪ MANTRA

1. *krīṁ.*
2. *krīṁ hūṁ hrīṁ.*
3. *krīṁ hūṁ hrīṁ huṁ phaṭ.*
4. *krīṁ kālike svāhā.*
5. *krīṁ hūṁ hrīṁ phaṭ svāhā.*
6. *hrīṁ śrīṁ krīṁ.*

DAKṢIṆA-KĀLĪ MANTRA

1. *krīṁ krīṁ krīṁ hūṁ hūṁ hrīṁ hrīṁ dakṣiṇe kālike krīṁ krīṁ krīṁ hūṁ hūm hrīṁ hrīṁ svāhā.*
2. *oṁ hrīṁ śrīṁ krīṁ parameśvari kālike hrīṁ śrīṁ krīṁ svāhā.*

GAURĪ MANTRA

oṁ hrīṁ śrīṁ klīṁ mahāgauryai namaḥ.

PARAMEŚVARĪ MANTRA

oṁ hrīṁ śrīṁ krīṁ parameśvari svāhā.

The *devatā* of this *mantra* is Gaurī, Kālī, Lakṣmī, Sarasvatī, combinedly known as Durgā. Gaurī and Kālī are one and the same except for their colour and form. The former is white-complexioned and the latter is black. Their forms are also different. Gaurī and Kālī are the different names of Lord Śiva's consort.

CĀMUṆḌĀ MANTRA

oṁ aiṁ hrīṁ klīṁ cāmuṇḍāyai vicce.
oṁ glauṁ huṁ klīṁ jūṁ saḥ.
jvālaya jvālaya jvala jvala prajvala prajvala.
aiṁ hrīṁ klīṁ cāmuṇḍāyai vicce.
jvala haṁ saṁ laṁ kṣaṁ phaṭ svāhā.

Mother Cāmuṇḍā, Caṇḍī, Saptaśatī and Durgā are not different.

NAVĀRṆA MANTRA

oṁ aiṁ hrīṁ klīṁ cāmuṇḍayai vicce.

This *mantra* comprises nine syllables (excluding the first *oṁ*) and hence is known as the *navārṇa mantra*. The deity is Mother Cāmuṇḍā.

fig. 2.49: Śrīdurgā-navārṇa-mantra-yantra

(a) *Durgā-yantra*

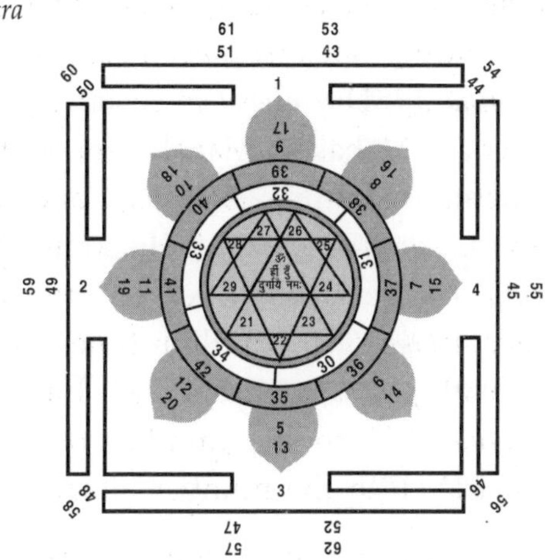

(b) *Navārṇa-yantra*

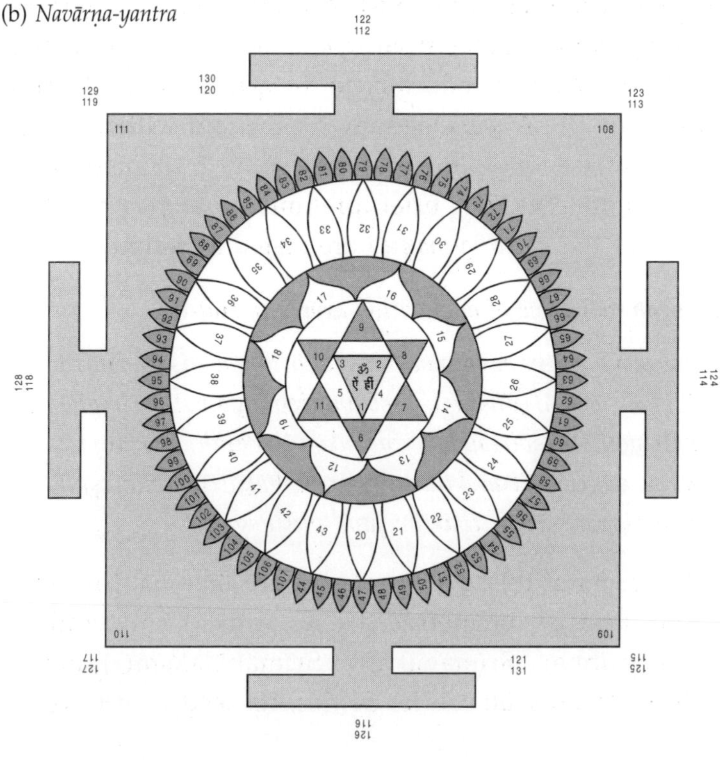

The details of the Cāmuṇḍā-*sādhanā* are not given here. The *nyāsa* of this *mantra* comprises 11 types with three additional, concluding ones (*ṣaḍaṅga-nyāsa, mantra-varṇa-nyāsa, vyāpaka-nyāsa*). The *nyāsa* is serially followed by *dhyāna* of Mothers — Mahākālī, Mahālakṣmī, Mahāsarasvatī, *mānasa-pūjā* (mental worship), *pīṭha-pūjā* and *yantra-pūjā*. The Durgā-*navārṇa-mantra-yantram* is illustrated in *fig*. 2.49. The *yantra-pūjā* is serially followed by *mantra-japa* (*puraścaraṇa-japa* 4 *lākh* or 0.4 million times), *havana* with *ghṛtāhuti* along with *pāyasānna, tarpaṇa* (1/10th the number of *homa*), *mārjana* (1/10th the number of *tarpaṇa*) and *brāhmaṇa-bhojana* (1/10th the number of *mārjana*).

In this book, our purpose is limited. It is not meant to make the reader an accomplished *tāntrika*. For the purpose of getting more benefits from *japa* alone, we are presenting a brief procedure, introductory to the actual *japa* (108 times, 28 times or 10 times). One may do the *japa* without these introductory steps, and may get some (not negligible, however) benefits. The brief, preliminary steps preceding the *japa* of the *navārṇa-mantra* are stated as follows:

Viniyogaḥ (objective of application expressly stated)

> *oṁ asya śrīnavārṇamantrasya brahma-viṣṇu-rudra-ṛṣayaḥ, gāyatryuṣṇiganuṣṭubhaśchandāṁsi, śrīmahā-kālī-mahālakṣmī-mahāsarasvatyo devatāḥ, aiṁ bījaṁ, hrīṁ śaktiḥ, klīṁ kīlakaṁ, śrīmahākālī-mahālakṣmī-mahāsarasvatī-prītyarthe jape viniyogaḥ.*
>
> The seers of this *navārṇa-mantra* are Brahmā, Viṣṇu and Rudra; its metres are Gāyatrī, Uṣṇik and Anuṣṭubha; Śrīmahākālī, Śrīmahālakṣmī and Śrīmahāsarasvatī are its deities; its seed is *aiṁ*; its

power is *hrīṁ*; its deeper cohesive strength is *klīṁ*. I engage myself in the *japa* of this *mantra* for propitiating Mothers Mahākālī, Mahālakṣmī and Mahāsarasvatī.

Ṛṣyādinyāsaḥ* (the nyāsa *of the seers and others)

1. *brahma-viṣṇu-rudra-ṛṣibhyo namaḥ — śirasi.*
2. *mahākālī-mahālakṣmī-mahāsarasvatī-devatābhyo namaḥ — hṛdi.*
3. *aiṁ bījāya namaḥ — guhye.*
4. *hrīṁ śaktaye namaḥ — pādayoḥ.*
5. *klīṁ kīlakāya namaḥ — nābhau.*

I make an obeisance to seers Brahmā, Viṣṇu and Rudra; I place them in my head. (Touch the head with the five fingers of your right hand.)

I make an obeisance to metres — Gāyatrī, Uṣṇik, Anuṣṭup; I place them on my face. (Touch your face with the five fingers of your right hand.)

I make an obeisance to Mahākālī, Mahālakṣmī, Mahāsarasvatī; I place them in my heart. (Touch your heart region with the five fingers of your right hand.)

I make an obeisance to the seed of the *mantra, aiṁ*; I place it in my private organs. (Touch your clothed private region with the five fingers of your right hand.)

I make an obeisance to the power of the *mantra, hrīṁ*. I place it on my feet. (Touch your feet with the five fingers of your right hand.)

I make an obeisance to the inner cohesive force (*kīlaka*) of the *mantra, klīṁ*. I place it on my navel. (Touch your navel with the five fingers of your right hand.)

Kara-nyāsaḥ (the nyāsa of the hands)

First purify your hands by chanting the *mantra* "*oṁ aiṁ hrīṁ klīṁ cāmuṇḍāyai vicce*" and imitate a gesture of washing your hands with soap and water. Use both the hands for *nyāsa*. For each thumb, the tip of the respective index finger touches the root of the thumb and glides up to its tip. For each of the four fingers of each hand, the tip of the respective thumb touches the root of the finger and glides up to the tip of the finger. When the *nyāsa* is done for the palms (*karatala*) and the back of the hands (*karapṛṣṭha*), they are placed across (not along) the hands, the right hand being placed on the left hand. The Sanskrit words for the thumb, index finger, middle finger, ring finger and little finger are *aṅguṣṭha, tarjanī, madhyamā, anāmikā* and *kaniṣṭhikā*, respectively.

Chant the following *mantra*s for the *kara-nyāsa*.

1. For the thumbs: *oṁ aiṁ aṅguṣṭābhyāṁ namaḥ*.
2. For the index fingers: *oṁ hrīṁ tarjanībhyāṁ namaḥ*.
3. For the middle fingers: *oṁ klīṁ madhyamābhyāṁ namaḥ*.
4. For the ring fingers: *oṁ cāmuṇḍāyai anāmikābhyāṁ namaḥ*.
5. For the little fingers: *oṁ vicce kaniṣṭhikābhyāṁ namaḥ*.
6. For the palms and backs of the hands: *oṁ aiṁ hrīṁ klīṁ cāmuṇḍāyai vicce karatalakarapṛṣṭhābhyāṁ namaḥ*.

Ṣaḍaṅga-nyāsaḥ

The procedure of *ṣaḍaṅga-nyāsa*, in connection with the Gāyatrī-*japa*, has already been stated. No further explanation is necessary here. It is being applied to the *navākṣara-mantra* in the following way.

1. *oṁ aiṁ hṛdayāya namaḥ.*
2. *oṁ hrīṁ śirase svāhā.*
3. *oṁ klīṁ śikhāyai vaṣaṭ.*
4. *oṁ cāmuṇḍāyai kavacāya huṁ.*
5. *oṁ vicce netratrayāya vauṣaṭ.*
6. *om aiṁ hrīṁ klīṁ cāmuṇḍāyai vicce astrāya phaṭ.*

Mantra-Varṇa-Nyāsaḥ or Akṣara-Nyāsaḥ (the nyāsa of the syllables of the mantra)

Chant the following *mantras* and, for each, touch the indicated part of the body with the fingers of the right hand.

1. *oṁ aiṁ namaḥ — brahmarandhre śikhāyāṁ vā* (the top of the head).
2. *om hrīṁ namaḥ — dakṣiṇa-netre* (right eye).
3. *oṁ klīṁ namaḥ — vāma-netre* (left eye).
4. *oṁ cāṁ namaḥ — dakṣiṇa-karṇe* (right ear).
5. *oṁ muṁ namaḥ — vāma-karṇe* (left ear).
6. *oṁ ḍāṁ namaḥ — dakṣiṇa-nāsāpuṭe* (right nostril).
7. *oṁ yaiṁ namaḥ — vāmanāsāpuṭe* (left nostril).
8. *oṁ viṁ namaḥ — mukhe* (face).
9. *oṁ cceṁ namaḥ — guhye pāyau vā* (genitals).

Vyāpaka-Nyāsaḥ (nyāsa of the whole body)

oṁ aiṁ hrīṁ klīṁ cāmuṇḍāyai vicce pādādibrahmarandhrāntam ityaṣṭavāraṁ nyaset.

Chant the whole *mantra* (*oṁ aiṁ hrīṁ klīṁ cāmuṇḍāyi vicce*) eight times, and each time touch all the parts of the body (front, back, right side and left side, twice each, bottom to top and top to bottom) from the feet to the apex with all the ten fingers of both hands.

This is the brief *nyāsa*. For the details, any good book on Tantra may be consulted.

The *nyāsa* is followed by the *dhyāna* of the *trirūpā* Mothers (three forms — Mahākālī, Mahālakṣmī, Mahāsarasvatī). After the *dhyāna*, the *mānasa-pūjā* (mental worship) of the three Mothers is done. The next ritual is the *pīṭha-pūjā* of the nine *devī*s (*nava-śakti*) in the *sarvatobhadramaṇḍala*. These *śakti*s are: Jayā, Vijayā, Ajitā, Aparājitā, Nityā, Vilāsinī, Dogdhrī, Aghorā, Maṅgalā. The *pīṭha-pūjā* is followed by *yantra-pūjā* (*āvaraṇa-pūjā*). The *navārṇa-mantra* has a specific *yantra*. In the *pūjā* of this *yantra*, the *yantra-pūjā* is done through eight *āvaraṇa*s, serially one after another. After the completion of these rituals, the *japa* of the *navārṇa-mantra* is done.

Japa

According to the tradition, the number of *puraścaraṇa-japa* of the *navārṇa-mantra* is 9 *lākh*s (0.9 million). The minimum number of the *japa* may be 4 *lākh*s.

When the *puraścaraṇa* is over, *homa* is done with *ghṛtāhuti* (oblation with clarified butter). *Pāyasānna* (rice cooked with milk to a semifluid consistency) should be offered to the sacrificial fire each time when the *ghṛtāhuti* is made. The number of oblations is one-tenth that of the *japa*. *Homa* is followed by *tarpaṇa*, *mārjana* and *brāhmaṇa-bhojana* in a serial sequence, each succeeding sequence being one-tenth the number of the preceding one.

We do not expect our readers to be full-fledged *tāntrikas*. Hence we recommend to do the *japa* after the brief *nyāsa* only. The number of the *japa* may be 108, 28 (27 with a rosary and 28 with *karamālā*) or 10. If the devotee has time, he may do the *japa* multiples of 108 times.

MAHĀ-MṚTYUÑJAYA-MANTRA

Before a discussion on the *mahā-mṛtyuñjaya-mantra*, we introduce its nucleus, the *tryambaka-mantra*.

Tryambaka-Mantra

The *mṛtyuñjaya-mantra* is Vedic.[22] Its *devatā* is Śiva. The *mantra* is stated as follows.

> *oṁ tryambakaṁ yajāmahe sugandhiṁ puṣṭivardhanam.*
> *urvārukamiva bandhanān-mṛtyormukṣīya mā 'mṛtāt.*
>
> O Lord of the three Mothers of the universe, we worship you. Give us a wholesome environment which is free from pollution and which would promote our physical, mental and spiritual health. Nourish us with good nutrients. As the seeds from the ripe fruit of the cucumber species, *Cucumis usitatissimus*, are released, release us from bondage and death, but not from immortality.

Most interpreters of this *mantra* think that the *devatā* of this *mantra* is Rudra of the Hindu Trinity (*trimūrti* = Viṣṇu, Brahmā and Rudra). It is, however, not a fact. The *trimūrti* concept is Purāṇic and not Vedic. The Vedas do unambiguously mention the concept of the three Mothers.[23] The word *tryambaka* does not etymologically mean "three-eyed," the word *tri* meaning "three" and *ambā* meaning "mother." The word Śiva means "Auspicious" and stands for God, the Supreme Lord, who does good to the universe.

Mahā-Mṛtyuñjaya-Mantra

Śukrācārya, the *tāntrika guru* has taken the Vedic *tryambaka-mantra* and hemispherically enveloped it with *tāntrika bīja*s and Vedic *mahā-vyāhṛti*s (great utterances) to convert it into a more potent *mantra* known as the *mahā-mṛtyuñjaya-mantra*. This process of hemispherical enveloping is known as *sampuṭīkaraṇa*. Sometimes, the *sampuṭa bīja*s (seed-syllables) ae unaltered in sequence. Some other times, their sequence is reversed. Here we quote three varieties of the *mantra*.

1. ***Mṛtyuñjaya-mantra.*** It is 48-syllabled, with the *tryambaka* inside. It covers the *vyāhṛtitrayam* (*bhūḥ, bhuvaḥ, svaḥ*) in reverse order. The *svarūpa* (own form) of the *mantra* is like this:

   oṁ bhūḥ oṁ bhuvaḥ oṁ svaḥ.
   oṁ tryambakaṁ yajāmahe, sugandhiṁ puṣṭivardhanam.
   urvārukamiva bandhanānmṛtyormukṣīya mā 'mṛtāt.
   oṁ svaḥ oṁ bhuvaḥ oṁ bhūḥ oṁ.

   ॐ भूः ॐ भुवः ॐ स्वः
   ॐ त्र्यम्बकं यजामहे। सुगन्धिं पुष्टिवर्धनम्।
   उर्वारुकमिव बन्धनान्मृत्योर्मुक्षीय माऽमृतात्।
   ॐ स्वः ॐ भुवः ॐ भूः ॐ॥

2. ***Mṛta-sañjīvanī-mantra.*** It is 52-syllabled. It is enveloped by the *tāram* (*oṁ*), the *tribījam* (*hauṁ, jūṁ, saḥ*) and the three *vyāhṛti*s (*bhuḥ, bhuvaḥ* and *svaḥ*).

The *prasāda-bīja* is *hauṁ* and the *mṛtyuhara-bīja*s are *jūṁ* and *saḥ*. The *svarūpa* of the *mantra* is like this:

oṁ hauṁ jūṁ saḥ
oṁ bhūr bhuvaḥ svaḥ
oṁ tryambakaṁ yajāmahe, sugandhiṁ puṣṭivardhanam.
urvārukamiva bandhanānmṛtyormukṣīya mā 'mṛtāt.
oṁ svaḥ bhuvaḥ bhūḥ
oṁ saḥ jūṁ hauṁ oṁ.

ॐ हौं जूं सः
ॐ भूर्भुवः स्वः
ॐ त्र्यंबकं यजामहे। सुगन्धिं पुष्टिवर्धनम्।
उर्वारुकमिव बन्धनान्मृत्योर्मुक्षीय माऽमृतात्
ॐ स्वः भुवः भूः
ॐ सः जूं हौं ॐ॥

3. ***Mahā-mṛtyuñjaya-mantra.*** It is 62-syllabled. Out of these three *mantras*, it is the most favoured one by Śukra. We recommend it to our readers. The *svarūpa* of this *mantra* is like this:

oṁ hauṁ oṁ jūṁ oṁ saḥ
oṁ bhūḥ oṁ bhuvaḥ oṁ svaḥ
oṁ tryambakaṁ yajāmahe, sugandhiṁ puṣṭivardhanam.
urvārukamiva bandhanānmṛtyormukṣīya mā 'mṛtāt.
oṁ svaḥ oṁ bhuvaḥ oṁ bhūḥ
oṁ saḥ oṁ jūṁ oṁ hauṁ
oṁ svāhā.

ॐ हौं ॐ जूं ॐ सः
ॐ भूः ॐ भुवः ॐ स्वः
ॐ त्र्यम्बकं यजामहे
सुगन्धिं पुष्टिवर्धनम्।
उर्वारुकमिव बन्धनान्मृत्योर्मुक्षीय माऽमृतात्॥
ॐ स्वः ॐ भुवः ॐ भूः
ॐ सः ॐ जूँ ॐ हौं
ॐ स्वाहा॥

TRYAKṢARA-MṚTYUÑJAYA-MANTRA

The *mṛtyuñjaya-mantra* of three syllables is *oṁ hauṁ jūṁ saḥ* (ॐ हौं जूँ सः), the counting of the syllables being done by the exclusion of the *praṇava*.

DVĀDAŚĀKṢARA-MṚTYUÑJAYA-MANTRA

This is a *mṛtyuñjaya-mantra* with 12 syllables. The *svarūpa* of this *mantra* is like this: *oṁ jūṁ saḥ pālaya pālaya saḥ jūṁ oṁ*. The three *bījas* (seed-syllables — *oṁ*, *jūṁ* and *saḥ*) are reversed in their sequence in the end.

MAHĀ-MṚTYUÑJAYA-MANTRA-JAPA-SĀDHANĀ

1. ***Saṅkalpa.*** Do the saṅkalpa through which you express the purpose of your japa-sādhanā.

2. ***oṁ śrīgurave namaḥ.*** I make an obeisance to my *guru*.

3. ***oṁ gaṇapataye namaḥ.*** I make an obeisance to Śrī Gaṇeśa.

4. ***oṁ iṣṭadevatāyai namaḥ.*** I make an obeisance to my tutelary deity. Suppose your *iṣṭadevatā* is Mother Durgā; you may say: *oṁ hrīṁ duṁ durgāyai namaḥ.*

5. ***Viniyogaḥ***

oṁ asya śrīmahāmṛtyuñjayamantrasya vāmadeva-

kaholavasiṣṭhā ṛṣayaḥ paṅktirgāyatryanuṣṭupśchandāṁsi sadāśivamahāmṛtyuñjayarudro devatāḥ, śrīṁ bījam, hrīṁ śaktiḥ mahāmṛtyuñjaya-prītaye jape viniyogaḥ.

6. *Nyāsaḥ*

I. *Ṛṣyādinyāsaḥ*

(a) *oṁ vāmadevakaholavasiṣṭharṣibhyo namaḥ, śīrasi.* Chant the *mantra* and touch your head with all the fingers of your right hand.

(b) *oṁ paṅktirgāyatryanuṣṭupchandobhyo namaḥ, mukhe.* Touch your face.

(c) *oṁ sadāśivamahāmṛtyuñjaya-rudra-devatābhyo namaḥ, hṛdi.* Touch your heart region.

(d) *oṁ śrīṁ bījāya namaḥ, guhye.* Touch your genitals covered with clothes.

(e) *oṁ hrīṁ śaktaye namaḥ, pādayoḥ.* Touch your feet.

II. *Ṣaḍaṅga-Nyāsaḥ*

(a) *oṁ hauṁ oṁ jūṁ oṁ saḥ oṁ bhūḥ oṁ bhuvaḥ oṁ svaḥ tryambakam oṁ namo bhagavate rudrāya śūlapāṇaye svāhā hṛdayāya namaḥ.* Touch the heart region.

(b) *oṁ hauṁ oṁ jūṁ oṁ saḥ oṁ bhūḥ oṁ bhuvaḥ oṁ svaḥ yajāmahe oṁ namo bhagavate rudrāya amṛtamūrtaye māṁ jīvaya śirase svāhā.* Touch your head.

(c) *oṁ hauṁ oṁ jūṁ oṁ saḥ oṁ bhūḥ oṁ bhuvaḥ oṁ svaḥ sugandhiṁ puṣṭivardhanam oṁ namo bhagavate rudrāya candraśirase jaṭine svāhā śikhāyai vaṣaṭ.* Touch the crown of the head.

(d) *oṁ hauṁ oṁ jūṁ oṁ saḥ oṁ bhūḥ oṁ bhuvaḥ oṁ svaḥ urvārukamiva bandhanāt oṁ namo bhagavate rudrāya tripurāntakāya hāṁ hīṁ kavacāya huṁ*. The gesture has already been described.

(e) *oṁ hauṁ oṁ jūṁ oṁ saḥ oṁ bhūḥ oṁ bhuvaḥ oṁ svaḥ mṛtyormukṣīya oṁ namo bhagavate rudrāya trilocanāya ṛgyajuḥsāmamantrāya netratrayāya vauṣaṭ*. Touch your eyes and the spot between the eyebrows.

(f) *oṁ hauṁ oṁ jūṁ oṁ saḥ oṁ bhūḥ oṁ bhuvaḥ oṁ svaḥ mā 'mṛtāt oṁ namo bhagavate rudrāya agnitrayāya jvala jvala māṁ rakṣa rakṣa oṁ aghorāstrāya astrāya phaṭ*.

The gesture has already been described.

III. *Varṇa-nyāsaḥ*

1. *oṁ hauṁ oṁ jūm oṁ saḥ oṁ bhūḥ oṁ bhuvaḥ oṁ svaḥ tryaṁ namaḥ, pūrvamukhe*. (Look at the east.)
2. *oṁ hauṁ . . . . oṁ svaḥ mbaṁ namaḥ, paścimamukhe*. (Look at the west.)
3. *oṁ hauṁ . . . . oṁ svaḥ kaṁ namaḥ, dakṣiṇamukhe*. (Look at the south.)
4. *oṁ hauṁ . . . . oṁ svaḥ yaṁ namaḥ, uttaramukhe*. (Look at the north.)
5. *oṁ hauṁ . . . . oṁ svaḥ jāṁ namaḥ, urasi*. (With your right-hand fingers, touch your chest.)
6. *oṁ hauṁ . . . . oṁ svaḥ maṁ namaḥ, kaṇṭhe*. (Touch your throat.)

7. *oṁ hauṁ . . . . oṁ svaḥ heṁ namaḥ, mukhe.* (Touch your face.)
8. *oṁ hauṁ . . . . oṁ svaḥ suṁ namaḥ, nābhau.* (Touch your navel.)
9. *oṁ hauṁ . . . . oṁ svaḥ gaṁ namaḥ, hṛdi.* (Touch your heart region.)
10. *oṁ hauṁ . . . . oṁ svaḥ ndhiṁ namaḥ, pṛṣṭhe.* (Touch your back.)
11. *oṁ hauṁ . . . . oṁ svaḥ puṁ namaḥ, kukṣau.* (Touch your belly.)
12. *oṁ hauṁ . . . . oṁ svaḥ ṣṭiṁ namaḥ, liṅge.* (Touch your covered genitals.)
13. *oṁ hauṁ . . . . oṁ svaḥ vaṁ namaḥ, gude.* (Touch your covered anus.)
14. *oṁ hauṁ . . . . oṁ svaḥ rdhaṁ namaḥ, dakṣiṇorumūle.* (Touch your right hip.)
15. *oṁ hauṁ . . . . oṁ svaḥ naṁ namaḥ, vāmorumūle.* (Touch your left hip.)
16. *oṁ hauṁ . . . . oṁ svaḥ uṁ namaḥ, dakṣiṇorumadhye.* (Touch your right thigh.)
17. *oṁ hauṁ . . . . oṁ svaḥ rvāṁ namaḥ, vāmorumadhye.* (Touch your left thigh.)
18. *oṁ hauṁ . . . . oṁ svaḥ ruṁ namaḥ, dakṣiṇajānuni.* (Touch your right knee.)
19. *oṁ hauṁ . . . . oṁ svaḥ kaṁ namaḥ, vāmajānuni.* (Touch your left knee.)
20. *oṁ hauṁ . . . . oṁ svaḥ miṁ namaḥ, dakṣiṇa-jānuvṛtte.* (Touch your right patella.)
21. *oṁ hauṁ . . . . oṁ svaḥ vaṁ namaḥ, vāma-jānu-vṛtte.* (Touch your left patella.)

22. *oṁ hauṁ . . . . oṁ svaḥ baṁ namaḥ, dakṣiṇastane.* (Touch your right breast.)
23. *oṁ hauṁ . . . . oṁ svaḥ ndhaṁ namaḥ, vāmastane.* (Touch your left breast.)
24. *oṁ hauṁ . . . . oṁ svaḥ nāṁ namaḥ, dakṣiṇapārśve.* (Touch the right side of your body.)
25. *oṁ hauṁ . . . . oṁ svaḥ mr̥ṁ namaḥ, vāmapārśve.* (Touch the left side of your body.)
26. *oṁ hauṁ . . . . oṁ svaḥ tyoṁ namaḥ, dakṣiṇapāde.* (Touch your right foot.)
27. *oṁ hauṁ . . . . oṁ svaḥ rmuṁ namaḥ, vāmapāde.* (Touch your left foot.)
28. *oṁ hauṁ . . . . oṁ svaḥ kṣīṁ namaḥ, dakṣiṇakare.* (Touch your right hand.)
29. *oṁ hauṁ . . . . . . oṁ svaḥ yaṁ namaḥ, vāmakare.* (Touch your left hand.)
30. *oṁ hauṁ . . . . oṁ svaḥ māṁ namaḥ, dakṣiṇanāsāpuṭe.* (Touch your right nostril.)
31. *oṁ hauṁ . . . . oṁ svaḥ mr̥ṁ namaḥ, vāmanāsāpuṭe.* (Touch your left nostril.)
32. *oṁ hauṁ . . . . . . oṁ svaḥ tāṁ namaḥ, mūrdhni.* (Touch the crown of your head.)

There are still some more *nyāsa*s. But we are omitting them.

7. *Dhyānam*: Have a mental picture of the image of Lord Śaṅkara. Meditate on him.

8. *The Pūjā of the Pīṭha-Devatās and the Pīṭha Śaktis*: For this purpose, the appropriate *maṇḍala* is required.

9. *Āvaraṇa-Pūjā*: For this purpose, the appropriate *yantra* is required. The *āvaraṇa*s are eleven in number.

10. *Rudra-Gāyatrī and Prayer*

Gāyatrī: oṁ tatpuruṣāya vidmahe; mahādevāya dhīmahi; tanno rudraḥ pracodayāt.

Prayer: oṁ mṛtyuñjaya mahārudra trāhi māṁ śaraṇāgatam. janmamṛtyujarārogaiḥ pīḍitaṁ karma-bandhanaiḥ,

stāvakastvadgataprāṇastvaccitto 'haṁ sadā mṛḍa. iti vijñāpya deveśaṁ japenmṛtyuñjayaṁ param.

11. *Japa:* *The puraścaraṇa-japa* of the *mahāmṛtyuñjaya-mantra* is one *lākh* (100,000). While doing the *japa*, five *mudrā*s (gestures) are to be shown in succession in multiple rounds. The *mudrā*s are described here.

Muṣṭi-mudrā — Make a fist of the right hand. Hold it with the right thumb upwards (*fig.* 2.50). Press the rights Mars' trough with the right fingertips.

Śakti-mudrā — Close each hand into a fist, with each

fig. 2.50: *Muṣṭi-mudrā*

fig. 2.51: *Śakti-mudrā*

thumb pointing upwards. Press the Mars' trough of each palm with the respective fingertips. Keep the right-hand fist on the left-hand one. Raise both the fists, kept one over the other, so that the right hand touches the upper part of the forehead (*fig*. 2.51).

Mṛga-mudrā or *sāraṅga-mudrā* — Join the tips of the right-hand thumb, ring finger and middle finger. Hold the forearm and the hand in a vertical position, with the little and the index finger pointing upwards (*fig*. 2.52).

Liṅga-mudrā — Tightly clasp the fingers of both the hands, the right thumb being upright, and the left thumb circling around the base of the right thumb with its tips on the back of the middle internode of the left index finger. For the illustration of the *liṅga-mudrā*, see *fig*. 2.47.

Pañcamukha-mudrā — The forearms and the wrists are ventrally kept in juxtaposition in a vertical position. The tips of the four fingers of each hand touch those of the other hand. The two thumbs are kept in contact with each other from their lateral sides (*fig*. 2.53).

fig. 2.52: *Mṛga* or *sāraṅga-mudrā*

fig. 2.53: *Pañcānana-mudrā*

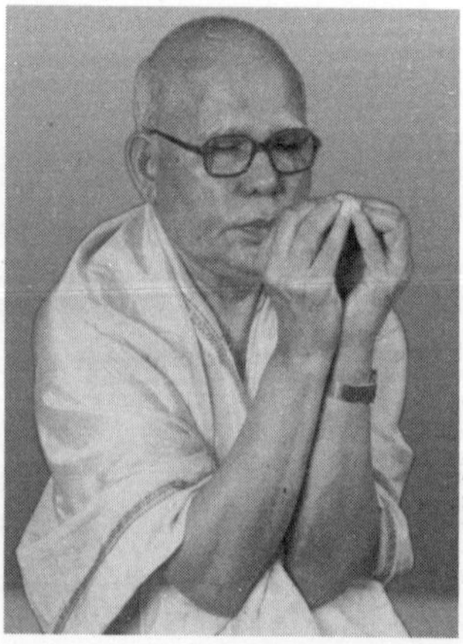

Caution — The blood-pressure of hypertensive patients is likely to shoot up by the *japa* of the *mahāmṛtyuñjaya-mantra*. Specially the *liṅga-mudrā* does not allow any increase in the blood-pressure. It has rather a lowering effect.

12. *Post-Japa Rituals*: As usual in *tāntrika puraścaraṇa-japa*, the post-*japa* rituals are *homa, tarpaṇa, mārjana* and *brāhmaṇa-bhojana*, each succeeding one is one-tenth the number of the preceding one. The same procedure is followed for the *mahāmṛtyuñjaya-mantra-sādhanā.*

A Special Note: We do not expect the common devotee to follow the details of the *tāntrika* procedure, which has not been exhaustively dealt with in this book. We recommend our readers to adopt the following simple steps:

1. Meditate on Lord Śiva and pray to him for about five minutes.
2. Daily do the *japa* 108, 54, 27(28) or 10 times, according to your convenience.
3. Conclude your *japa* with a short session of meditation and prayer. Practise *liṅga-mudrā* while you meditate or pray.
4. *Mudrā*s cannot be practised when your right hand is busy with the rosary or the *karamālā*-counting. If you do *japa* without counting or with rough counting by the time of the watch, it would be better if you don't miss the *mudrā*s, especially the *liṅga-mudrā*.
5. If you have a serious health problem, someone else for you may do the formal *puraścaraṇa-japa-sādhanā*.

Kīrtana

Kīrtana is *nāma-japa* or *mantra-japa*, done loudly either individually or in a group, with or without instrumental music. When done individually, a pair of cymbals may be enough to produce a musical atmosphere. There is a difference between *vaikharī-japa* and *kīrtana*. The *mantra* is chanted in association with some musical notes in *kīrtana*, even if when done without musical instruments. While doing *kīrtana*, the devotee is fully absorbed in the idea of God/Goddess. Then only does it become a *japa-yoga*. Here we recommend a number of *mantra*s for the *kīrtana*.

VEDIC AND VEDĀNTIC KĪRTANA

1. *Praṇava-kīrtana.* Only *oṁ* is repeated musically. The continuation of the vowel *o* varies in duration, creating a gap between *o* and *ṁ*. The varieties of the *kīrtana* are stated below:

(a) *o* . . . . *ṁ*

(b) *o* . . . . *ṁ, o* . . . . *ṁ*

(c) *o* . . . . *ṁ, o* . . . . *ṁ, o* . . . . *ṁ*

(d) *o* . . . . *ṁ, o* . . . . *ṁ*
o . . . . *ṁ, o* . . . . *ṁ*

(e) *o* . . . . *ṁ, o* . . . . *ṁ*
o . . . . *ṁ, o* . . . . *ṁ, o* . . . . *ṁ*

(f) *o* . . . . *ṁ, o* . . . . *ṁ, o* . . . . *ṁ*
o . . . . *ṁ, o* . . . . *ṁ, o* . . . . *ṁ*

(g) *o* . . . . *ṁ, o* . . . . *ṁ, o.* . . . . *ṁ*
o . . . . *ṁ, o* . . . . *ṁ, o* . . . . *ṁ,*
o . . . . *ṁ*

2. *Non-dualistic Vedāntic kīrtana*. Three varieties are given here.

(a) *so 'haṁ so 'ham*
so 'haṁ so 'ham

so 'haṁ so 'ham
so 'haṁ so 'ham

(b) *śivo 'haṁ śivo 'ham*
śivo 'haṁ śivo 'ham
śivo 'haṁ śivo 'ham
śivo 'haṁ śivo 'ham

(c) *so 'haṁ so 'ham*
śivo 'haṁ śivo 'ham
so 'haṁ so 'ham
śivo 'haṁ śivo 'ham

KĪRTANA OF BHAKTI-YOGA

In this type of *kīrtana*, the devotee has a feeling of duality — I and God/Goddess. She/he surrenders to God/Goddess and craves for His/Her mercy. The *mantra* is repeated musically and synchronously.

(a) ***Gaṇeśa-kīrtana***. The *mantra* is: *oṁ gaṁ gaṇeśāya namaḥ*.
(b) ***Durgā-kīrtana***. The *mantra* is: *oṁ hrīṁ duṁ durgāyai namaḥ*.
(c) ***Śiva-kīrtana***. The *mantra* is: *o . . . . ṁ namaḥ śivāya*.

Any one or all of the following varieties of Śiva-*kīrtana* may also be done.

(i) *namāmi śivaṁ śaṅkaram*
namāmi jagadīśvaram
namāmi ḍambarudharam
namāmi tāṇḍavakāram

namāmi candraśekharam

namāmi bhuvaneśvaram.

(ii) *śivaṁ namāmi, śivāṁ namāmi*

śivaṁ namāmi, śivāṁ namāmi.

(iii) *śivaṁ namā . . . . mi*

śivāṁ namā . . . . mi.

(iv) *śivaṁ namāmi . . . .,*

śivāṁ namāmi . . . .

(v) *oṁ śivāṁ namāmi,*

oṁ śivāṁ namāmi.

(d) ***Kālī-kīrtana***. The monosyllabic Kālī-*mantra* is repeated in this *kīrtana*:

krīṁ krīṁ krīm,

krīṁ krīṁ krīm.

(e) ***Sarasvatī-kīrtana***. The *bīja* (seed-syllable) of Mother Sarasvatī is *aiṁ*. Two varieties of the *kīrtana* are given here.

(i) *oṁ aiṁ sara . . . . . svatyai namaḥ,*

oṁ aiṁ sara . . . . . svatyai namaḥ.

(ii) *oṁ aiṁ sara . . . . . svatyai namaḥ,*

oṁ aiṁ sāvi . . . . . tryai namaḥ,

oṁ aiṁ gāya . . . . . tryai namaḥ.

(f) ***Nārāyaṇa-kīrtana***. The following *mantra* is musically repeated.

oṁ namo nārā . . . . . yaṇāya

oṁ namo nārā . . . . . yaṇāya.

(g) ***Lakṣmī-kīrtana***. The *bīja* of Mother Lakṣmī is *śrīṁ*. In the *kīrtana*, the following *mantra* is repeated.

oṁ śrīṁ hrīṁ śrīṁ, mahālakṣmyai namaḥ
oṁ śrīṁ hrīṁ śrīṁ, mahālakṣmyai namaḥ.

(h) ***Mahā-mantra-kīrtana/mahā-nāma-kīrtana***. The following *mantra* is popularly known as *mahā-mantra*. We feel that no *mantra* is better than the other. We would prefer to name it *mahā-nāma* for the Hindus of the Purāṇic tradition. This *nāma-kīrtana* is stated here.

hare rāma hare rāma, rāma rāma hare hare.
hare kṛṣṇa hare kṛṣṇa, kṛṣṇa kṛṣṇa hare hare.

(i) ***Hari-kīrtana***. One name of Viṣṇu is Hari. What it connotes is the same as "God" in English. He takes away (*haraṇa*) the sorrows and sufferings of human beings. The *mantra* contains the *praṇava oṁ*. The word *tat* means "that," and *sat* means "the Supreme Reality," "the Truth," "that which exists," "the Supreme Existence." The *kīrtana* is stated here.

hariḥ oṁ tat sat,
hariḥ oṁ tat sat,
hariḥ oṁ, hariḥ oṁ,
hariḥ oṁ tat sat.

The yogic *dhyāna* is silently done whereas the yogic *kīrtana* is loudly done. Notwithstanding this difference, *kīrtana* is nevertheless a type of yogic *dhyāna*. At the time of doing *kīrtana*, the *yogī*'s mind is firmly anchored to the idea of divinity only, without a trace of distraction. If thus done, *kīrtana* becomes a form of *dhyāna* and, hence, a component of *yoga*.

Anuṣṭhāna

The etymological meaning of the word *anuṣṭhāna* is "performance," "religious practice in conformity with scriptural prescription." *Anuṣṭhāna* is the practice of some religious austerity (*tapaḥ*), with special reference to *japa* or *svādhyāya*. Although an *anuṣṭhāna* may be practised for one day only, it is usually recommended for a protracted period — a week, a fortnight, a month, forty-eight days, ninety-six days, three months, six months or one year. The duration depends upon the ability of the *anuṣṭhātā* (one who performs the *anuṣṭhāna*) and his aptitude. The rigours of the austerity should vary on the basis of the place, the climate and the health condition of the *sādhaka*. The *anuṣṭhāna* should not follow any rigid rules of rituals at the health-risk of the performer. Rigorous mental discipline is more important than mere physical mortification in all *anuṣṭhāna*s.

During the whole period of an *anuṣṭhāna*, the *sādhaka* lives on milk or milk and fruits or *haviṣyānna* (rice cooked with a little *ghī*, more milk and just enough sugar to a semi-solid consistency). *Brahmacarya* (sex-abstinence or celibacy) is to be strictly practised during this period. The *sādhaka* should not involve himself in any worldly activities during an *anuṣṭhāna*. Complete or partial silence (*mauna*) is recommended. The mind should be constantly fixed on God. *Yama*s and *niyama*s are to be strictly followed.

An *anuṣṭhāna* may be done for *mokṣa* (emancipation of the self from cycles of births and deaths; release from bondage) or for fulfilling some worldly desires. In both cases, one has a desire. But, the former is known as *niṣkāma* (without desire) and the latter as *sakāma* (with desire). *Niṣkāma anuṣṭhāna* is preferable, although the other one is not condemned. However, *anuṣṭhāna*, done to cause harm to somebody, is unconditionally condemned.

For *sakāma anuṣṭhāna*, the specific desire for fulfilment decides the nature of the deity which, in turn, decides the *iṣṭa-mantra* to be selected. The number of *japa* for an *anuṣṭhāna* should preferably be *akṣara-lākh* times (100,000 for each syllable of the *mantra*). The number may be multiples of the *akṣara-lākh*, if one desires. But, in no case it shall be less than one *lākh*.

One may do *japa-anuṣṭhāna* or *svādhyāya-anuṣṭhāna*. In the latter case, scriptures like the Vedas, the *Mahābhārata*, the *Rāmāyaṇa*, the *Bhāgavata* or the *Bhagavad-Gītā*, are studied during the whole period of the *anuṣṭhāna*. There may be a necessity of studying the scripture a number of times. The austerities to be practised for *svādhyāya-anuṣṭhāna* are the same as those for *japa-anuṣṭhāna*.

The *sādhaka* does not neglect his physical needs such as eating, toilet, bath and sleeping during the period of an *anuṣṭhāna*. He should pray to the deity regularly.

Ladies may fix the duration of the *anuṣṭhāna* for less than a month. During the menstrual period, they would avoid these rites.

An *anuṣṭhāna* is started at the *brāhma-muhūrta* of a day. In an *anuṣṭhāna* of any type, *japa* or *svādhyāya*, the concluding rites are the *havana*, water-libation (*tarpaṇa*), water-sprinkling (*mārjana*) and *brāhmaṇa-bhojana* (feeding highly spiritual persons) and/or *daridra-nārāyaṇa-sevā* (feeding poor, needy persons with respect for them as if they are gods). The number of *āhuti*s (oblations) in the *havana* should be one-tenth the number of *japa* and at least 108 in the case of *svādhyāya*. The number of each succeeding rite is one-tenth the number of the preceding one. In *tāntrika sādhanā*, *mārjana* is usually done by sprinkling water on the statue or the *yantra* of the deity. In an *anuṣṭhāna*, where no idol or *yantra* is worshipped, *mārjana* is done by sprinkling water on the body of the *sādhaka* himself. Sometimes, *tarpaṇa* and *mārjana* are omitted and the number of feeding persons is not strictly maintained.

Many *gurus*, in their books, seem to have mixed up *anuṣṭhāna* and *puraścaraṇa*. The etymological meaning of the word *puraścaraṇa* is "preparatory to" or "a preparatory or introductory rite" (the word *puras* meaning "in front," "in advance," "forward"). Originally, it meant "the introductory rites preparatory to a *pūjā*. In due course of usage, the two words *anuṣṭhāna* and *puraścaraṇa* have been almost synonymous. In this book, we have followed the tradition against our conviction. One point is, however, to be noted that *puraścaraṇa* is generally used for *mantra-japa* and hardly for *svādhyāya*.

Japa-Yoga for all Religions

This book is not meant for Hindus only. Any person of any religion may practise *japa-yoga*, as outlined here. By accepting the spirit (not letters) of what has been given, one may adapt one's *japa-yoga*, *mutatis mutandis*, by substituting *mantras* and rites in usage in one's own religion. We are not conversant with the *mantras* and rites of other religions. We do not like to present them wrongly. That's why is the omission. If one understands the principles of *japa-yoga*, it would not be difficult to modify the procedure by suitable changes.

The Application of the Practices

This second part of this book has been devoted to the practice of *japa-yoga*. The applications of this *yoga* for different purposes for getting benefits have not been dealt with in this part. The third and the concluding part of this book is designed for the description of the applications.

References

1. See ref. 135 in Part I.
2. See ref. 76 in Part I.
3. *gururbrahmā gururviṣṇurgururdevo maheśvaraḥ,*
   guruḥ sākṣātparaṁ brahma tasmai śrīgurave namaḥ.
   akhaṇḍamaṇḍalākāraṁ vyāptaṁ yena carācaram,
   tatpadaṁ darśitaṁ yena tasmai śrīgurave namaḥ.
4. *BG*, IV.7-8:
   yadā yadā hi dharmasya glānirbhavati bhārata,
   abhyutthānamadharmasya tadātmānaṁ sṛjāmyaham.
   paritrāṇāya sādhūnāṁ vināśāya ca duṣkṛtāṁ,
   dharma-saṁsthāpanārthāya sambhavāmi yuge yuge.
5. *BG*, II.72; V.24-26.
6. *ṚV*, X.129.6:
   ko addhā veda ka iha pra vocat,
   kuta ājātā kuta iyam visṛṣṭiḥ,
   arvāgdevā asya visarjanenā
   athā ko veda yata ābabhūva.
7. M.V. Jyotishacharya, 1988, p. 18:
   aṣṭottaraśataṁ nityamaṣṭāviṁśatireva vā,
   vidhinā daśakaṁ vāpi trikāleṣu japed buddhaḥ.
8. Ibid., p. 17:
   prātarnābhau karaṁ kṛtvā madhyāhne hṛdi saṁsthitam,
   sāyaṁ japecca nāsāgre hyetajjapavidhiḥ smṛtaḥ,
9. S.B. Mishra, and L.B. Mishra, sam. 2054, p. 46:

aṅgulyagre ca yajjaptaṁ yajjaptaṁ merulaṅghanāt.
parvasandhiṣu yajjaptaṁ tatsarvaṁ niṣphalaṁ bhavet.

10. S.A.T. Acharya, 1998, p. 55:
aṅgulīrṇa viyujyeta kiñcidākuñcite tale,
aṅgulīnāṁ viyogācca chidre ca sravate japaḥ.

11. Ibid., pp. 55-56.

12. Ibid., p. 56.

13. See J. Singh, 1991; N.C. Panda, 2000; and *BS*, I.3.39.

14. *ṚV*, III.62.10; *YV*, III.35; XXII.9; XXX.2; XXXVI.3.

15. *MSJ*, I.1.5.

16. See *Sarva-Darśana-Saṅgraha* of Madhvācārya (1997 reprint, pp. 237-55). The following sentence has much relevance: *sphoṭākhyo niravayavo nityaśabdo brahmaiveti.*

17. See Bhartṛhari's *Vākyapadīya*, I.1:
anādinidhanaṁ brahma śabdatattvaṁ yadakṣaram.
vivartate 'rthabhāvena prakriyā jagato yataḥ.
Also see *Vākyapadīya*, ed. by S.S. Avasthi, 1990.
Bhartṛhari's *śabda-brahma-vāda* is contradicted by the Vedānta (*MTU*, VI.22; *BG*, VI.44).

18. Quoted by Śaṅkara, *BSŚB*, I.3.28: *varṇā eva tu śabdaḥ.*

19. *BSŚB*, I.3.28.

20. Ibid.

21. *DBhā*, XI.17.99-101.

22. *ṚV*, VII.59.12: *YV*, III.60.

23. *ṚV*, I.13.9; II.3.8; VII.2.8; *YV*, XXVII.19; *AV*, V.27.9.
The *Ṛgveda* (*ṚV*, I.3.11-12; VI.61.4 & 8; X.17.7) describes Mother Sarasvatī as *praṇo*, *codayitrī* and *dhiyaḥ*.

3

Applications of the Mantras of Yoga-Vedānta

In this section, we will deal with three *mantras* only, namely, the monosyllabic *oṁ*, the *ajapā-japa so 'haṁ* (He is I) and the Gāyatrī-*japa*. The first one, otherwise known as *praṇava,* is Vedic, Vedāntic and *Yogic*. The second one is Vedāntic, exclusively belonging to the non-dualistic (*advaita*) school. The third one is Vedic.

It has already been stated in Part II of this book that *japa* may be formal or informal. The informal *japa* may be done at any time, in any posture (sitting in yogic *āsanas*, sitting on hard chairs or beds, lying, standing and walking except on busy roads) and in any place (*devālaya, ṭhākura-ghara,* living rooms, bedrooms, bathrooms and even in lavatories).

In *niṣkāma-japa,* no *saṅkalpa* is necessary. At best, a short prayer or meditation may precede and follow. In *sakāma-japa,* a *saṅkalpa* is to precede the *japa*. It is an expression of the resolve of the devotee and the resolve must contain the purpose of the *japa,* briefly and precisely stating the desire to be fulfilled. The *saṅkalpa* may be done in any language, either verbally or silently.

The main formalities to be followed for a formal *japa* have already been outlined in the preceding part of this book. They will not be repeated here. Emphasis will be laid on the applications of some representative *mantra*s in this concluding part of this book.

Oṁ, the Easiest and the Best Mantra for Everybody

The monosyllabic *praṇava* (*oṁ*) is the easiest and the best *mantra* for everybody. It is a prerequisite for the *japa-sādhaka* to fully understand the meaning of *oṁ*. *Brahman* or *Īśvara* (God) is designated by this monosyllable. When one utters *oṁ*, one utters the name of God.

GOD-REALIZATION

The *oṅkāra-japa* may be done for the realization of God (*brahmopalabdhi* or *Īśvaropalabdhi*). One may make it a habit to do *oṅkāra-japa* everyday throughout the life. The silent variety of the *japa* is the best. It may be done in any of the meditational poses (*siddhāsana*, *padmāsana*, *svastikāsana*, *vajrāsana* or *sukhāsana*). Persons, having some problems in the legs, may do it while sitting on a hard chair or a hard bed. In addition, we recommend *śavāsana* (*fig*. 3.1) for doing the *oṅkāra-japa*. We rather feel that the *śavāsana* is the best posture, for some purposes at least, for doing *oṅkāra-japa*. In order to get the best benefit from *oṅkāra-japa*, it must be done in synchrony with the slow and steady inhalation and exhalation, silently uttering *oṁ* while inhaling and again *oṁ* while exhaling. The *japa* must finally merge in *samādhi*, a fully thoughtless condition. If thus done, the *japa* is converted into *dhyāna* and *samādhi*. We do not recommend counting for the *oṅkāra-japa*.

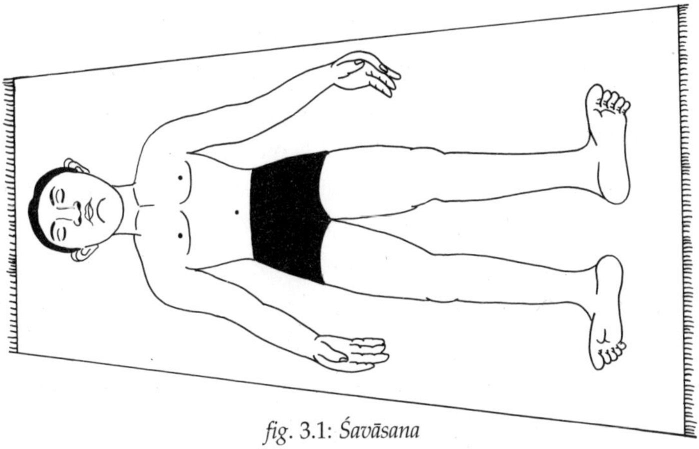

fig. 3.1: *Śavāsana*

Reference may be made to our book *Meditation*,[1] in which we have recommended *oṅkāra-japa* as an *ālambana* (support), preliminary to the state of attaining a thoughtless condition. There have been *japa, dhāraṇā, dhyāna* and *samādhi* blended together.

A constant practice of *oṅkāra-japa* throughout the life, with reflection on its meaning, renders the life divine, culminating in liberation (*mokṣa*). How does it do it? It is a blend of both *jñāna-yoga* and *bhakti-yoga*. If arduously and ardently done with *niṣṭhā* (firmness and steadfastness), the mind is linked and yoked to God. Such a person becomes self-transformed. He is purged of the impurities of his *citta* (mind-stuff). His thought, speech and action become humane and later divine. He develops inclination to *nivṛtti-mārga* (the path of self-abnegation and renunciation of worldly pleasure and attachment) and disinclination for *pravṛtti-mārga* (the path of propensities for worldly pleasure and attachment). He becomes theophilic. He distils and redistils himself, becoming purer and purer. The evil *karma-saṁskāras*, already printed in his *karmāśaya* through many past lives and the present life, are erased and, in their place, noble, pious *saṁskāra*s are substituted. In due course, the pious *saṁskāra*s are also erased and the *karmāśaya* becomes a blank slate, without scribblings, writings and prints. Such a person may become a *jīvanmukta* (released albeit living with a body). Subsequent to the death of this body, he gets *videha-mukti* (release after leaving the body — gross, subtle and causal). He merges in *Brahman* and becomes *Brahman*. This is known as *brahma-nirvāṇa*. If liberation is not achieved by the *oṅkāra-japa* and the concomitant processes in one single life, it shall be achieved through a few births. The spiritual progress may be gradual, but steadily upward. In the language of the *Gītā*, a *yogī* who engages himself in the good of the world never goes down.[2]

OṄKĀRA-JAPA IN KARMA-YOGA

Karma-yoga is the *yoga* of detached action,[3] done for the sake of duty only,[4] without considering the fruits of action, the pleasure and pain, the gain and loss, the success and failure and the victory and defeat.[5] It is not possible to convert action into *karma-yogī* action unless and until one's self is linked to the Great Self. One has to perform actions, while being united with God.[6]

This type of *karma-yoga* is mixed with *bhakti-yoga* (the *yoga* of devotion) and, when mature, is transformed into *jñāna-yoga* (the *yoga* of *Brahma*-knowledge and realization). After attaining to this state, the *yogī* perceives the presence of God and of only God everywhere. For him, his self is not different from the Great Self (*Brahman*). He sees his self everywhere. He sees everything and everybody in his self.[7] He sees God everywhere and sees all in God.[8] Lord Śrīkr̥ṣṇa says: "Such a *yogī* who perceives and worships me alone, present in beings, stays in me. He is liberated from all types of bondage."[9] His actions, at this stage of yogic attainment, cannot be anything else but perfectly divine and ethical. When he sees his self everywhere and sees everything in his self, without any difference at all, the foundation of his ethics rests on the fact that whatever is pleasant for him is pleasant for others and that whatever is painful for him is painful for others.[10]

A *yogī* can attain to this state by various types and techniques of *yoga*. Some of the types and techniques are not easy for all. But, *oṅkāra-japa* is an easy means to achieve what has been described in the foregoing paragraphs. Nevertheless, it is not very easy as it has been said. The *japa* must not be mechanical. The mind must be constantly yoked to God. Devotion, mixed with real *brahma-jñāna*, must be genuine and sincere. Actions must be in unison with the cherished ideals. The *yogī* must make active efforts for self-transformation. Then only will the Divine Power push the *yogī* from below and/or pull him from above.

OṄKĀRA-JAPA FOR MENTAL PEACE AND TRANQUILLITY

It is the intrinsic nature of mind to be unsteady and to always move without being concentrated at a particular point and on a particular topic.[11] For some individuals, it is almost impossible to concentrate. Mind can be yoked and pin-pointed concentration can be had by the practice of *yoga*. *Japa-yoga* and especially silent *oṅkāra-japa* in synchronization with the slow and steady inhalation and exhalation are the means to achieve the end. The *oṅkāra-japa* is relatively an easier means. It is possible to control the mind by practice (*abhyāsa*) and dispassionateness or aversion (freedom from all worldly desires or *vairāgya*).[12] In order to accelerate the process, it would be better for one to be *nirāśī*[13] (one who does not expect anything from others) and to adopt *aparigraha*[14] (one who does not accumulate property).

Passion (*rāga*, vehement desire, intense desire for worldly possession, power and sensual pleasure), expectation from others (*āśā*) and the propensity for the accumulation of more wealth (*parigraha*) are three important positively causal factors for the flickering of the mind. There are many negative factors too. Some of them are: poverty, unemployment, office-problems, business-problems, frustration, bereavement, accidents, diseases, natural calamities, family-disharmony, enmity, etc.

Some of the causal factors of mental peacelessness and inequilibrium are self-made and some others are external impositions. One should try to correct oneself to control or eradicate the former group of factors. The latter group is not under one's control. None the less, some of them like frustration, family discord and enmity can be corrected or ameliorated by self-efforts. To be over-ambitious and be frustrated in case of failure is really a fault of one's own. To be ambitious in consonance with one's ability is not a fault. But, to mentally collapse when expectations are not fulfilled is certainly a maladjustment.

In any case of disturbance of mental peace, one should surrender to God and pray to him. In addition, yogic *dhyāna* and *japa* should be practised.

The postures for *japa* have already been prescribed. Any of those formal or informal postures may be adopted according to one's convenience and aptitude. For getting maximum effect for steadying the mind and restoring peace, we prescribe *śavāsana* in which silent *oṅkāra-japa* should be done. It is to be specially noted that the *japa* should synchronize with the slow and steady inhalation and exhalation and that no counting is necessary. The *japa* should conclude with *samādhi* in the same *śavāsana*. This concluding phase is a state of complete thoughtlessness.

OṄKĀRA-JAPA FOR CORRECTING PSYCHIATRIC PROBLEMS

It is a common, popular belief that all psychiatric patients are mad. It is, however, far from truth. Quantitatively speaking, majority of the psychiatric patients are not mad. Further, it may be said that a good number of psychiatric patients are not conscious of the fact that they have some psychiatric or psychological problems and that they do not go to the doctor for treatment.

The causes of mental problems are diverse. Some of them are hostile, unfavourable environmental factors. Bad nurture in the early stage of life may also be one of the many environmental factors. The DNA-constitution, inherited from the parents, may be incriminatory. This is otherwise known as the genetic factor. Hereditary predisposition or suscepibility and directly hereditary incrimination are two varieties of the genetic causes of diseases. Most of the hereditary mental diseases are due to the faulty secretion of neurohumors by the brain cells. Some specific neurohumor may be secreted in higher or lower concentration. In both cases, hyper-secretion or hypo-secretion, the sequel is brain-pathology. Some cases are due to faulty embryological development of the brain-tissue.

Modern Western psychology is comparatively recent in origin. It does not recognize the mind as an entity, separate from the brain. It has no concept of the rebirth of the self (The Vedāntic self is different from the Greek psyche or soul and the Biblical soul.). Hence, the Indian concepts of *karmāśaya, saṁskāras* and *vāsanās* and the allied Indian Depth Psychology are alien to the West. As a fact, they are also alien to most of the Indian psychologists. We would like our readers to refer to our book *Mind and Supermind*[15] to be acquainted with the Indian Depth Psychology, in which the Unconscious is built up through many births.

The *vāsanā-saṁskāras* and the non-*vāsanā-saṁskāras* printed in the *karmāśaya* exert potent influences on the mental behaviour of a person. In addition to environment and heredity, some *saṁskāras* play important roles in the causation of abnormal psychology.

With our present science and technology (barring future development of genetic engineering), we can hardly do anything to change our bad genes. We cannot undo what has been done to our childhood nurture. Very often we cannot do much to alter our present environment to our advantage. We can do little to handle our past *saṁskāras*. Are we helpless then? No, we are not. Wherever a psychiatrist patient is not fully out of his control, he is cooperative and he is willing to help himself, he has every chance to heal himself by yogic therapy. And *oṅkāra-japa* is one potent technique to cure psychic diseases. Some patients may need drugs prescribed by a competent doctor. Even in such cases, *oṅkāra-japa* may be a complementary therapy. Patients, with milder clinical symptoms, may not use medicines at all.

The patient may select any posture suitable to him out of the ones we have recommended for *oṅkāra-japa*. For getting maximum benefits, we would, however, prescribe silent *oṅkāra-japa* in *śavāsana* in synchronization with the slow and steady inhalations and exhalations. No counting of the *japa* is necessary. The *japa* must terminate in *samādhi,* a state of complete thoughtlessness. Although we do not exactly know the mechanism of action, we know this much that this *japa* can correct the excess or the deficiency of neurohormones of the brain and can re-establish their balance. Further, we know that the *japa* can burn the seeds of the *karma-saṁskāra*s and erase them from the tape of the unconscious mind. The *yoga-nidrā* technique may also be supplemented to the *oṅkāra-japa*. For *yoga-nidrā*, the reader may like to refer to our book *Yoga-Nidrā (Yogic Trance): Theory, Practice and Applications.*[16]

OṄKĀRA-JAPA FOR CURING PSYCHOSOMATIC DISEASES

A number of diseases are psychosomatic. Peptic ulcer, chronic colitis due to sustained anxiety, eczema due to psychic trauma, migraine, thyrotoxicosis, asthma, hypertension and arthritis may be cited as examples. In addition to other aetiological factors, including hereditary ones, sustained tension, mental trauma, anxiety and agonizing experiences may cause such diseases in different organs and tissues of the body. Sometimes even serious ailments like ischaemic heart disease, cardiac arrhythmias, angina pectoris and myocardial infarction and various types of malignant growth in many organs may be caused by sustained agony and anguish.

The word "psyche" means "mind" and "soma" means "body." Any serious disturbance in the mind, conscious or unconscious, causes the manifestation of some disease in the physical body, and hence is the nomenclature of the term "psychosomatic." The physiopathology of the psychosomatic diseases has been dealt with in our books *Meditation* and *Yoga-Nidrā* which have already been referred to.

The root of a psychosomatic disease is in the mind and its branches, leaves and flowers are seen in the body. *Yoga* tries to uproot the disease by setting the mind in order.

The therapy of psychosomatic diseases can be done by *oṅkāra-japa*. The following steps may be taken:

1. Sit in a posture recommended for *oṅkāra-japa*. Lying in *śavāsana* is better than sitting for this purpose.
2. Do a *saṅkalpa* and express the purpose of the *japa* in it. Use any language for the *saṅkalpa*.
3. Silently do *oṅkāra-japa*, one *oṁ* while inhaling and another *oṁ* while exhaling. Inhale and exhale slowly and steadily. Don't count the *japa*, which may be done about 10-15 minutes.
4. Do *dhāraṇā*, *dhyāna* and *samādhi* (combinedly known as *saṁyama*) on the site of the disease (on the organ affected). Do the silent *oṅkāra-japa* in the *dhyāna*, with *dhāraṇā* on the site of the disease, and intensely contemplate on the healing of the disease by a thought like this: "O God, cure this disease." *Oṁ* stands for God and the idea for "Cure this disease" is subsequent to *oṁ*. Hence, a short pause is allowed between two adjacent *oṁ*s. Introduce *saṅkalpāyana* between the *dhyāna* and the *samādhi*. During *saṅkalpāyana*, the *oṅkāra-japa* is suspended and the *saṅkalpa* is repeated for a few minutes. The *saṅkalpa* may be affirmative or imperative, limited to one short simple sentence, or at best two. For example, the *saṅkalpa* for peptic ulcer may be like this: "My gastric glands secrete just enough acid, not more, not less. The ulcer in the stomach/duodenum, rapidly heal up." Alternatively, this *saṅkalpa* may be like this:

"The acid secretion in my stomach is normal. My ulcer has healed up." After the *saṅkalpāyana*, stay in *samādhi* for 5-10 minutes.

5. Repeat the whole process twice a day, in the morning and the evening until your disease is cured.

This *japa* therapy may be done along with any medical therapy, which is not contraindicated. The diet prescribed by the physician should be strictly followed. The patient and the doctor should excercise their discretion for the continuation or the discontinuation of medicines.

OṄKĀRA-JAPA IN THE TREATMENT OF HYPERTENSION

Essential hypertension whose aetiology is not yet clearly known has been included in the group of psychosomatic diseases. Its *japa*-therapy is, however, much simpler. *Oṅkāra-japa* and/or *ajapā-japa* (*so 'haṁ*) should be done to bring hypertension under control. Both the *japa*s should silently be done in *śavāsana*, with closed eyes. No counting is necessary. *Saṅkalpa* and *saṅkalpāyana* are also dispensed with. When both *japa*s are done, they should be done *in tandem*, *oṅkāra* first, followed by *ajapā-japa*. In the former case, silent *oṁ* is to be repeated during inhalation and exhalation which should be slow and steady. In the latter case, the silent *japa* of *so* (*saḥ*) during inhalation and *haṁ* (*aham*) during exhalation should be done. The *japa* is to be followed by *samādhi*, a state of thoughtlessness, while still in *śavāsana*. Preferably three sessions (morning, noon and evening) or at least two sessions (morning and evening) of the *japa* are recommended.

Periodical and regular check-up of blood pressure is advised. Medicinal therapy by a competent doctor is indispensable. The doctor may increase or decrease the dose, depending upon the progress of the *japa*-therapy. Hypertension, once started, generally continues to be a life-long disease. *Oṅkāra-japa* and *ajapā-japa* may or may not cure the disease permanently. But, undoubtedly, the *japa* of both the *mantra*s, outlined here, reduces high blood pressure appreciably.

ONKĀRA-JAPA FOCUSED ON DISEASED ORGANS

Some endocrine glands may not function normally. It may be the case with the pituitary, the pineal, the thyroid, the islets of Langerhans in the pancreas, the Leydig cells in the testes and the ovarian follicles. Some organs may be pathological due to faulty metabolism. The examples may be urolithiasis (stone in the kidney) and cholelithiasis (stone in the gall-bladder). It may be a joint-pain due to over-production of uric acid in the disease condition called "gout."

Many types of micro-organisms (viruses, bacteria, protozoa, fungi) attack specific organs in which pathological lesions are produced. Such diseases, caused by microbial infection, are called infectious diseases. Bronchopneumonia, viral hepatitis, nephritis, cystitis, gastro-enteritis, amoebiasis, sinusitis, dermatitis, metritis, tuberculosis, leprosy, AIDS are some examples of infectious diseases.

In some disease problems, healing is delayed. The repair of a bone-fracture is one such problem. The regeneration of the liver tissue, following hepatitis, may be a second example. The delayed regeneration of the peripheral nerves, following a stroke in the brain, resulting in partial paralysis, may be another example. The delayed repair of the lung-tissue, following an attack of pneumonia or tuberculosis, may pose a problem. The delayed involution of the gravid uterus, after a child-birth, to its normal position and size may be another problem. Such cases and many more may be cured by the *japa*-therapy.

Sometimes the biochemical activity of some organ or tissue is excessive or less than normal to cause serious pathological disorders. The brain cells may be involved in hyper- or hypo-secretion of neurohumors. The endocrine glands may do the same thing. An excessive quantity of cholesterol may be synthesized by the body-cells, finally resulting in atherosclerosis in the branches of the carotid artery in the cardiac musculature or the arterioles in the brain. An excess of catecholamines (adrenaline and noradrenaline) may increase the blood pressure and derange the cardiac health. An excess of corticosteroids secreted by the adrenal cortex may expose the individual to serious health hazards and may weaken the immune system.

The DNA-molecule (gene) present in each cell of the body may undergo mutation in some particular cell. This mutation generally involves some change in the base structure. A cell with a changed gene becomes rebellious, gets out of the holistic pact and multiplies and grows at the cost of the body. Such a growth is a tumour (when benign) or a cancer (when malignant). Malignant cells migrate to other parts of the body and grow there. This process is known as metastasis.

In the foregoing paragraphs we took some typical classes of pathogenesis. Now we give the methodology of the *oṅkāra-japa*-therapy. The therapy is common to all the mentioned classes, although the *modus operandi* varies from class to class of the diseases.

The method of the *oṅkāra-japa* is the same as already given for the treatment of psychosomatic diseases. The posture recommended is *śavāsana*. A *saṅkalpa*, befitting to the disease, initiates the *japa* process. The *japa* is silent and counting is not necessary. It should not be forgotten that the *japa* is synchronous with the inhalation and the exhalation which are slow and steady. After this initial phase of *japa*, there is a second phase of *japa* blended with *dhāraṇā* on the site of the disease and *dhyāna* for the cure of the disease. The *dhāraṇā* is done with eyes closed. This second phase of *japa* has already been described. Now the *japa* is suspended, to be followed by *saṅkalpāyana*. This is an auto-suggestion, a command to the diseased organ and the allied healing and immune systems. This *saṅkalpāyana* is to be repeated for a few minutes. *Samādhi*, a state of complete thoughtlessness, for a period of 5-10 minutes, follows the *saṅkalpāyana*. This concludes the process, which is to be repeated two to three times a day. The period of *oṅkāra-japa*-therapy depends upon the nature of the disease and the speed of recovery. It is advisable to continue the *japa*-therapy up to two months after the cure.

The *oṅkāra-japa*-therapy may be done in association with medical and/or surgical therapy by competent doctors.

Someone may be interested to know the mechanism of action. The theistic mechanism is just mentioned here without elaboration. God showers blessings on the devotee if He likes. And everything else happens naturally through physical, chemical, biochemical, physiological and immunological means. This interpretation is religious and spiritual and has nothing to do with science. Its claiṁ cannot be objectively proved; neither can it be disproved by any means.

How mind influences matter in the body has been briefly described in Part I of this book. What has been stated is purely scientific. We hold that brain and mind are separate. The former is a gross organ of the gross body. The latter is a subtle organ of the subtle and the causal bodies. The brain is the apparatus of the mind. Through the *oṅkāra-japa*, the mind influences all parts of the cerebral cortex in the brain. The prefrontal area, part of the frontal lobe, located a couple of centimetres below the spot between the eyebrows, is the psychic centre (PC). The PC gets information from any part of the cerebral cortex through neural pathways and can send its directive to the hypothalamus through neural pathway. The hypothalamus acts through two routes. One is a neural route by which the autonomic nervous system (sympathetic and parasympathetic) is activated. The second one is a chemical route through which some chemicals synthesized by the hypothalamus reach the pituitary gland through a special blood circulation called the pituitary portal circulation. Thereby the pituitary is asked to increase or decrease the secretion of its own hormones which are also chemicals. These hormones are transported through the bloodstream to reach the target-endocrines — the thyroid, parathyroid, adrenal cortex, testes and ovaries. The pituitary is the master gland in the body that controls all the other endocrine glands through a two-way mechanism. The adrenal medulla gets information through the neural route too to increase or decrease its secretion of adrenaline.

The autonomic nervous system has its two sub-systems — sympathetic and parasympathetic. Both these sub-systems are apparently antagonistic. But, they work in harmony and in coordination in a holistic way for the welfare of the whole organism. We do not consciously regulate our vital organs and other visceral organs of our body. They are controlled by our autonomic nervous system without our awareness.

Each human body or even animal body has an immune system which is the defence department. The immune system is not confined to a particular organ or a particular location. It is a diffuse system distributed in various organs such as the bone-marrow, the thymus, the lymph glands, the spleen, etc. The leucocytes (white blood-corpuscles) are made in the bone-marrow and transported in blood to different parts of the body. The immune system fights against any invading micro-organism by its cellular and humoral mechanisms. Its special cells are its soldiers. Its antibodies are its agents for a chemical warfare. Without the immune system, the body can hardly live for a couple of weeks. The hidden agent in the body cannot be observed by our naked eye and even through an electron microscope, or any other instrumentation. But it is this agent only that is always vigilant for the defence and the protection of the body. It is this agent that commands the defence department to take prompt action. The *japa*-therapy somehow (we do not exactly know) mobilizes the immune system of our body.

Any damage done to any organ physically or chemically, by microbial invasion and resultant inflammation or through other means is repaired actively and intelligently without our awareness. It may be the fracture of a bone. It may be a pulmonary infection by a bacteria. It may be an infection of the liver by a virus. The damaged tissue must be repaired. The repair is done *naturally*. But the exact meaning of *naturally* in the present context is not known to us. We are satisfied by the use of some words. This repair process is accelerated by the *japa*-therapy.

The gene-change explanation of oncogenesis has already been stated. The *japa*-therapy acts as a prophylactic to prevent the onset of genetic mutation in our body. Thus, the danger of cancer is averted. The *japa*-therapy can also be used as a curative. The cancer-cells are devoured and destroyed by our body-soldiers. The cancerous tissue regresses if the *japa*-therapy is done with firm conviction.

When the cancerous growth is advanced and metastatic growths appear in different parts of the body, the situation may be out of control and *japa*-therapy may not give the desired effects.

Even when surgery has been done to remove the cancerous growth and chemotherapy has been resorted to, *japa*-therapy may be a potent tool to fight the disease of cancer and aid the doctor's treatment.

In the treatment of cardiac diseases and even after a bypass surgery, the *japa*-therapy is recommended as a complementary healing technique and as a preventive of recurrence.

OṄKĀRA-JAPA FOR THE FULFILMENT OF A WORLDLY DESIRE

Some *guru*s advise their disciples to do *japa* for devotion only and for salvation. They denounce *sakāma* (with worldly desire) *japa*. On this issue, our views are different. Devotees are of four types, namely, highly enlightened (*jñānī*) persons, persons ascending the rungs of the ladder leading to full *Brahma*-knowledge (*jijñāsu*), persons who want more wealth, more power, more social prestige (*arthārthī*) and persons struck with calamity, fallen into misfortune and afflicted with physical and mental sufferings (*ārta*).[17] Among the devotees of God, about 90 per cent of them are *arthārthī* and *ārta*. They ordinarily don't bother about God unless they have a need for the fulfilment of their desires. This, being true for God, is truer for a *guru*. Moreover, there is nothing wrong in praying to God when one is in distress. To whom else would one approach when one suffers and is tortured? Of course, God helps those sufferers who are genuine devotees and deserve divine mercy. Even sometimes, a genuine devotee does not get relief if the suffering serves some greater cosmic cause, or it is in accordance with the divine laws, not *ordinarily* violated by God. For the mortal human being, howsoever wise he may be, inscrutable is the decision of God. It is the duty of a true devotee to gladly accept the verdict of God, favourable or unfavourable, without murmuring.

We do recommend *sakāma oṅkāra-japa* (in addition to *niṣkāma*) if and when an *urgent* need arises. *Japa* done for hankering after worldly possession, power, prestige and prominence, for accumulation of more and more wealth by exploiting others and depriving others of their rightful needs, for torturing others and getting sadistic pleasure out of it, for committing crimes and for sensual gratification is undoubtedly heinous and cannot be supported under any circumstance. If one does *japa* for such purposes, one violates the fundamental concept of God who is truth (*satya*), benevolent (*śiva*), beautiful (*sundara*), all-intelligent (*sarvajña*), and the one and only one Cosmic Justice.

Before doing the *oṅkāra-japa* for getting redress and redemption, for avoiding an impending calamity and for escaping from an already befallen misfortune, an appropriate *saṅkalpa* is made. In emergency situations, the *japa* is done both formally and informally, irrespective of time and place.

The *japa* is silent and without counting. In order to have greater concentration, the eyes are better closed. One should have a clear conception of the monosyllable *oṁ* which is the name of God, a syllable that denotes (*vācaka*) God. When the *japa* is formal in a sitting posture or in *śavāsana*, one may conclude the *japa* with a short session of *samādhi* (a state of complete thoughtlessness). If the *japa* is done in synchronization with the slow and steady inhalation and exhalation, the distressed devotee gets physical and mental relief.

OṄKĀRA-KĪRTANA

The *kīrtana* of the monosyllable *oṁ* is done loudly. It is better done with musical rhythm. A pair of cymbals may be used. In the absence of the cymbals, the two palms of the hands may clap rhythmically.

There are seven varieties of the *oṅkāra-kīrtana*. The first variety is known as mono-*caraṇic* (with a single step). The *o* continues a long time till lastly the *ṁ* is pronounced. This mono-*caraṇa* is repeated throughout the *japa* session.

The second variety is bi-*caraṇic* (with two steps). Each step is shorter than the mono-step, with a short pause in between the two steps.

The third variety has three steps; the fourth variety has four steps; the fifth one has five steps; the sixth one has six steps; and the seventh one has seven steps. In each case, there is a short pause in between two adjacent steps.

The varieties are indicated below:

I. *o* . . . . *ṁ*.

II. *o* . . . . *ṁ* . . . . *o* . . . . *ṁ*.

III. *o. . . . . .ṁ . . . . .o. . . . . .ṁ . . . . . . o . . . . ṁ.*

IV. *o. . . .ṁ . . . . o. . . .ṁ . . . . .o. . . ṁ . . . . . . o . . . . . ṁ.*

V. *o. . . . ṁ. . . . o. . . . ṁ. . . . .o. . . . ṁ. . . . . o. . . ṁ. . . . . o . . .ṁ.*

VI. *o. . . ṁ. . . o. . . ṁ. . . o. . . ṁ; . . . o. . . ṁ. . . o. . .ṁ. . .o. . . ṁ.*

VII. *o. . .ṁ. . . .o. .ṁ. . . . o. . ṁ. . . . o. .ṁ; . . . o. . ṁ. o. . . .ṁ. . o. .ṁ.*

In a single *japa* session, one variety may be repeated or more than one variety may be repeated. All the seven varieties may also be repeated in a sequence in a single session of the *japa*.

In *kīrtana, tanmayatā* (a mental state of being fully absorbed into the idea of the Being whose name is uttered) is an essential characteristic. If sincerely done in right earnest, *kīrtana* gives mental peace and tranquillity and removes worries from mind.

Ajapā-Japa

The *oṅkāra-japa* consists of one syllable only, whereas the *ajapā-japa* comprises two syllables. Two words have been conjugated to an abbreviated form (*saḥ* + *ahaṁ* = *so 'haṁ*). The word *saḥ* means "He," referring to God (*Brahman*). The word *ahaṁ* means "I." This *mantra* belongs to the non-dualistic (*Advaita*) Vedānta. It is a *mantra* of *jñāna-yoga*, not of *bhakti-yoga*. We, of course, believe that there is not a single *jñāna-yogī* who is not a *bhakti-yogī* at some phase of his life.

The *so 'haṁ mantra* is repeated while sitting in any of the meditational postures (*siddhāsana, padmāsana, svastikāsana, vajrāsana* or *sukhāsana*). The *śavāsana* is also suitable and, for certain purposes, is the best. A person may do the *so'haṁ japa* while sitting on a hard chair or a hard bed and while standing and walking also. The *japa* is silently done. The syllable *so* is mentally uttered while inhaling and *haṁ* while exhaling. Both the inhalations and exhalations should be slow and steady. While contemplating on the meaning of *so 'haṁ* during the *japa*, one should also be conscious of the incoming and the outgoing breath. The duration of a *japa* session may be 10 to 15 minutes or more, depending upon the availability of time. Two to three sessions a day may be enough. No counting of the *japa* may be done.

Sometimes it is recommended to do *oṅkāra* and *so 'haṁ japas in tandem* while lying in *śavāsana*. The *oṅkāra-japa* is done first and next the *so 'haṁ japa*. After the *so 'haṁ japa*, the *sādhaka* goes to the *samādhi* state of complete thoughtlessness.

What benefits does one get from the *so 'haṁ japa*? If done regularly throughout the life, one gets *Brahma*-realization (*brahmopalabdhi*). He gets *citta-śuddhi*. His *manas* and *buddhi* are cleansed. Bad *saṁskāras* printed in the *karmāśaya* of the *antaḥkaraṇa* are uprooted first. Along with this *citta-śuddhi*, one's actions become divine and one is completely transformed gradually from animality to humanity, from humanity to divinity and from divinity to *Brahman*hood. Lastly the good *saṁskāras* are also erased. The *sādhaka* becomes a *jīvanmukta* (released while still living), waiting for *videha-mukti* with the death of the body. By the *so 'haṁ japa*, in one life or more than one lives, the self merges in the Great Self, a process known as *brahma-nirvāṇa*. This is the advaitic (non-dualistic) liberation.

The *so 'haṁ japa* is not done for the fulfilment of any desire. In other words, it is not *sakāma*. In addition to its principal effect, that is, progress on the path of liberation, it imparts peace, tranquillity and steadiness to mind. It improves concentration and memory. It re-establishes humoral balance in the body and strengthens the immune system.

Persons suffering from mental disturbance, worries, tension and even serious psychiatric problems are benefitted by regularly practising *so 'haṁ japa*. Hypertensive patients, by regularly practising this *japa*, can keep their blood pressure under control. At least, the dose of hypertensive drugs is minimized. Although it has been said that *so 'haṁ japa* is not *sakāma*, it can be made *sakāma* for such purposes. The steps to follow are given here.

1. Do *ujjayī prāṇāyāma* for about 5 minutes. It may be done in any posture — in some meditative *āsana*, in sitting on a hard chair or a hard bed and in *śavāsana*. It may also be done immediately after a meal. Silently utter *so* while inhaling and *haṁ* while exhaling. Both the inhalation and the exhalation should be done through both the nostrils and they should be deep and slow.
2. After the *prāṇāyāma*, do the *saṅkalapa* in which you are to express (silently, of course) the purpose of your *japa*. If you want to reduce your hypertension, express it in your *saṅkalpa*.
3. You may not change your posture, or you may if you like. We would recommend you *śavāsana* for this *japa* in order to derive maximum benefits. In the *japa*, mentally utter *so* while inhaling and *haṁ* while

exhaling. This time, the inhalation and the exhalation should not be deep, but should be slow and steady. No counting is necessary. Do this *japa* for about 10 to 15 minutes in each session. Three sessions a day — morning, noon and evening — are necessary. You may skip the noon session if you do not get time.

4. End your session with *samādhi* in *śavāsana* for about 5 minutes. Remain in a state of complete thoughtlessness while you are in *samādhi.*

Your psychic problem may be due to the deficiency or the excess of any brain-chemical (neurohumor secreted by your brain-cells). This *japa* will restore the neurohumoral concentration to normalcy. If you are not in a condition to control yourself and do concentration needed for this *japa,* take medicine prescribed by a competent doctor for a period and at a dose to be decided by your doctor. You may take medicine and do the *japa* concurrently.

So 'haṁ Kīrtana

The *so 'haṁ-kīrtana* is done loudly (not too loudly), preferably with a pair of cymbals in the hands. Mild hand-clapping in musical rhythm may be done in the absence of cymbals. The *kīrtana*-rhythm may be as follows:

1. *so . . . haṁmm*
   so . . . haṁmm
   so . . . haṁmm
   so . . . haṁmm
2. *so . . . haṁ. . . . so . . . haṁ;*
   so . . . haṁ. . . . so . . . haṁ.

The *kīrtana* may be done by the conjunction of two *mantras*, namely, *so 'haṁ* and *śivo 'haṁ*. The expression *śivo 'haṁ* means "I am Śiva (God, the Benevolent)." The tuning of this *kīrtana* will be as follows:

so . . . haṁ. . . . so . . . haṁ;
śivo . . . haṁ. . . . śivo . . . haṁ.

Gāyatrī-Japa

NIṢKĀMA GĀYATRĪ-JAPA

The *Gāyatrī-mantra* is Vedic. Its original form has already been cited in Part II of this book. It is not a tāntric *mantra*. Its metre (*chanda*) is Gāyatrī. Its deity (*devatā*) is God, the Creator (*Parameśvara*) and *Brahman*, the Absolute Reality. The deity is not the sun or the sun-god, as claimed by some. Any tāntric female deity is not concerned with it. We may take Gāyatrī or Sāvitrī or Sarasvatī, the consort of Brahmā, the Creator, as the deity. But it is contextually appropriate to take *Parameśvara* (the Supreme Lord) as the deity of this *mantra*.

The *japa* of the *Gāyatrī-mantra* is primarily meant for attaining to *Brahman*hood, the non-dualistic liberation. It is a prayer for *citta-śuddhi* (the purification of the *buddhi* which is likened to a mirror); it is to be dusted off; the thick layer of *tamas* or ignorance on it is to be washed and wiped so that the opaqueness is removed and transparency is restored; it is to be got rid of *rajas* or passion. It is a prayer for getting *buddhi-yoga*. In the process of the continuous purification of the *citta*, finally the *sattva* also dwindles away and the *sādhaka* becomes free from the three *guṇas*. He becomes pure *Brahman*. In this process of spiritual ascendancy, the *sādhaka* himself undergoes a phase of metamorphosis. His physique, actions and mental traits are gradually transformed. The caterpillar becomes a butterfly.

SAKĀMA GĀYATRĪ-JAPA

The *japa* of the *Gāyatrī-mantra* may be done for the fulfilment of a desire. For this purpose, a *saṅkalpa* is to precede the *japa*. The deity of this *mantra* may be thought to be *Parameśvara* (the Supreme Lord or God). Alternatively, the deity may be taken as the three Mothers — Sarasvatī, Lakṣmī and Kālī, combinedly the Great Mother, *Parameśvarī* (the Consort or Power of God). The *japa* must be done devoutly. If you have no faith (strong and unwavering) in the Father and the Mother of the universe, you better don't do the *japa*. You should also realize that a prayer is not a demand which must be complied with by God. Pray to Him for getting His mercy. God's verdict cannot be questioned.

After the *mantra-japa* is over, take a deep breath through both nostrils. During the period of breath-retention (*kumbhaka*), in one or two sentences, pray to Father or Mother for the fulfilment of your desire. Then exhale through both the nostrils.

If you have prayed to God, with folded hands, say: *oṁ śrīparamātmane namaḥ* (Obeisance to God, the Supreme). If you have prayed to Mother Goddess, conclude the session with the following prayer:

namaste devi gāyatri
sāvitri tripadākṣare.
ajare amare mātas
trāhi māṁ bhavasāgarāt.

Salutations to Goddess Gāyatrī or Sāvitrī, with trisyllabic name, the undecaying (non-ageing), the immortal. O Mother, protect me from the sea of metempsychosis.

Gāyatrī-japa for the improvement of memory — Do the *japa* of the *Gāyatrī-mantra* with the addition of *aiṁ* at the end.

Gāyatrī-japa for the removal of poverty — Do the *japa* of the *Gāyatrī-mantra* with the addition of *śrīṁ* at the end. If you cannot do the *japa* for this purpose everyday, at least do it on every Thursday.

Gāyatrī-japa for curing sterility — First, get yourself checked by a specialist doctor for any infection in your oviduct, uterus, vagina, etc., for any blockage in your fallopian tube, for any abnormality in the functioning of your ovaries and for any hormonal imbalance. For male sterility, the sperm-count in the semen, the abnormality of the sperms, if any, and any pathology in the male reproductive organs are to be checked by a specialist doctor. In some individuals, the medical report may be normal and still infertity or sterility may persist. This type of sterility is especially suitable for the *japa*-therapy. The *japa* of the *Gāyatrī-mantra* may be done with the addition of *vaṁ* at the end.

Gāyatrī-japa for avoiding accidents — If one is prone to frequent accidents, one may try to avoid them by the *japa* of the *Gāyatrī-mantra* by the addition of *krīṁ* at the end.

Gāyatrī-japa for getting rid of fear — To get rid of fear, do the *japa* of the *Gāyatrī-mantra* with the addition of *hauṁ hūṁ phaṭ svāhā* at the end.

Gāyatrī-japa for strengthening the immune system and for improving the auditory functions — Do the *japa* of the *Gāyatrī-mantra* with the addition of *haṁ* at the end.

Gāyatrī-japa for better cardiac and pulmonary health — Do the *Gāyatrī-japa* with the addition of *yaṁ* at the end.

Gāyatrī-japa for better digestion, better eye sight and better health of the legs — Do the *japa* of the *Gāyatrī-mantra* with the addition of *raṁ* at the end.

Gāyatrī-japa for the better health of the reproductive organs — Do the *japa* of the *Gāyatrī-mantra* with the addition of *vaṁ* at the end.

Gāyatrī-japa for the better health of the excretory organs — Do the *japa* of the *Gāyatrī-mantra* with the addition of *laṁ* at the end.

Gāyatrī homa for the general welfare of the individual, family and society — Chant the *Gāyatrī-mantra* with the addition of *svāhā* at the end. Immediately after *svāhā*, offer the oblation of *ghṛta* (melted, dehydrated, clarified butter) to the sacrificial fire. Repeat the *mantra* and oblation 10, 27 (28), 54 or 108 times in a single session of *homa*. It may be mentioned here that the *japa* of the *Gāyatrī-mantra* is always counted, irrespective of it being *sakāma* or *niṣkāma*.

Gāyatrī-japa for arousing kuṇḍalinī — Before you do the *kuṇḍalinī sādhanā*, be acquainted with the seven *cakras*, their locations, petals, *maṇḍalas* and the colours of the petals and the *maṇḍalas*. Details have been given in our book *Mind and Supermind*.[18] For ready reference, a sketchy illustration of the *cakras* has been given in *fig*.1.3. In ascending order, the *cakras* are: the *mūlādhāra*, the *svādhiṣṭhāna*, the *maṇipūra*, the *anāhata*, the *viśuddhi*, the *ājñā* and the *sahasrāra*. Their *bījas* (seed-syllables) are *laṁ*, *vaṁ*, *raṁ*, *yaṁ*, *haṁ*, *oṁ* and *oṁ*, respectively. We have already given the three *mahā-vyāhṛtis* (*bhūḥ*, *bhuvaḥ*, *svaḥ*) in the *Gāyatrī-mantra* in the second part of this book. There are four additional *vyāhṛtis*, namely, *mahaḥ*, *janaḥ*, *tapaḥ* and *satyam*. These are not the seven worlds located spatially one over the other. Each world is present here and everywhere. They gradually increase in subtlety from *bhūḥ* to *satyam*, or in other words, they gradually increase in grossness from *satyam* to *bhūḥ*. The change of dimensions is necessary to leave one world and enter into another. One cannot enter into the *svarloka* from the *bhūrloka* unless one becomes massless. With this much background information, we present the following steps to do *Gāyatrī-japa* for the arousal, ascent and descent of Mother Kuṇḍalinī.

1. Sit in *siddhāsana* or *padmāsana* with erect torso, neck and head.
2. Close your eyes and relax your body and mind.
3. Inhale through both the nostrils. Retain your breath. During this retention-period (*kumbhaka*), do *dhāraṇā* and *dhyāna* (mental visualization) on the *mūlādhāra cakra*. Silently and mentally chant *oṁ bhūḥ*. Exhale through both the nostrils. Visualize the ascent of *kuṇḍalinī* from the *mūlādhāra* to the *svādhiṣṭhāna*.
4. For the *svādhiṣṭhāna*, repeat the process as in (3), except the silent chanting of *oṁ bhuvaḥ*. Visualize the ascent of *kuṇḍalinī* from the *svādhiṣṭhāna* to the *maṇipūra*.
5. For the *maṇipūra*, repeat the process as in (4), except the silent chanting of *oṁ svaḥ*. Visualize the ascent of *kuṇḍalinī* from the *maṇipūra* to the *anāhata*.
6. For the *anāhata*, repeat the process as in (5), except the silent chanting of *oṁ mahaḥ*. Visualize the ascent of *kuṇḍalinī* from the *anāhata* to the *viśuddhi*.

7. For the *viśuddhi*, repeat the process as in (6), except the silent chanting of *oṁ janaḥ*. Visualize the ascent of *kuṇḍalinī* from the *viśuddhi* to the *ājñā*.
8. For the *ājñā*, repeat the process as in (7), except the silent chanting of *oṁ tapaḥ*. Visualize the ascent of *kuṇḍalinī* from the *ājñā* to the *sahasrāra*.
9. For the *sahasrāra*, take a deep inhalation (*pūraka*) to be followed by *kumbhaka*. During the *kumbhaka*, silently chant *oṁ satyaṁ tatsaviturvareṇyam, bhargo devasya dhīmahi, dhiyo yo naḥ pracodayāt*. Then completely exhale (*recaka*). After the exhalation, remain in *samādhi* for 3-5 minutes.
10. Now feel that Mother Kuṇḍalinī is descending from the *sahasrāra* to the *mūlādhāra*, stepwise through *cakras*, finally to rest in her coiled form (three and a half coils) in her original location. Chant *oṁ, haṁ, yaṁ, raṁ, vaṁ* and *laṁ*, while she reaches the *ājñā, viśuddhi, anāhata, maṇipūra, svādhiṣṭhāna* and *mūlādhāra*, respectively.
11. Sit in *samādhi* for a while. Take a deep breath through both nostrils. During the *kumbhaka*, silently chant *viśvasya kalyāṇamastu. oṁ śāntiḥ śāntiḥ śāntiḥ* (let everything good happen to the universe, peace, peace, peace).

Mantras of Bhakti-Yoga

In Part III of this book, we were so far dealing with only three *mantras* which are Vedic and Vedāntic. They were more relevant to *jñāna-yoga*. Now we switch over to *mantras* of *bhakti-yoga*. These *mantras* are traditionally Purāṇic. Some representative *mantras* have been enlisted in Part II of this book. Their applications are briefly outlined here.

The *japa* of the Purāṇic *mantras* may be *sakāma* or *niṣkāma*. The latter is preferred, but the former is not condemned by us.

Devotion should be for the sake of devotion only. The *nāma-japa* or the *mantra-japa* of a deity should be purely devotional, out of love and respect for him or her. The *japa* is a medium for surrendering the life of the devotee to the deity.

No *mantra* is superior to the other. No deity is superior to the other, since all of them are essentially one and one only. By convention and tradition in India, the *guru-mantra* is given the top priority. Again, by tradition, the *iṣṭa-devatā* (chosen tutelary deity) is worshipped first and his/her *nāma-mantra* is the most sacred for a devotee.

When we do *japa* for fulfilling a worldly desire, the appropriate deity and the appropriate *mantra* is to be selected. For the removal of obstacles, Lord Gaṇeśa is the appropriate deity. For getting wealth, Mother Lakṣmī is the chosen deity. For liberation and salvation, Lord Nārāyaṇa is the choice. For getting a long, disease-free life, being saved from imminent death and being protected from the attack of evil spirits, Lord Śiva is the deity of choice. For avoiding accidents and death and getting protection from calamities, disasters, misfortunes and dangers, Mother Kālī is the special deity. For getting knowledge and wisdom, Mother Sarasvatī is to be worshipped. Mother Durgā is the unification of the three Mothers, namely, Lakṣmī, Sarasvatī and Kālī. She functions for all the three Mothers when she is devoutly addressed to.

For a *sakāma-japa*, adopt the following steps:

1. Do the *saṅkalpa*. Express the objective of your *japa* through the *saṅkalpa*.

2. Do the *japa* of the *nāma-mantra* of Lord Gaṇeśa.
3. Do the *japa* of the *mantra* given by your *guru*. Your *guru-mantra* should contain the name of your *iṣṭa-devatā*. There is something wrong if it doesn't. In that case, do the *japa* of the *mantra* of your *iṣṭa-devatā*, in addition. Skip over this step if you have not been initiated by a *guru*.
4. Do *mānasa pañcopacāra pūjā* (*pūjā* by mental offering of five articles) to the deity whose *mantra* you are going to use for your *japa*. This *mānasa-pūjā* has already been given in Part II of this book.
5. Do *japa* by counting, either by *karamālā* or by rosary-beads. *Japa* may be done 10, 27(28), 54, 108, 1080 or 0.1 million times. When *karamālā* is used, the *japa* is done 28 times; when rosary is used, the *japa* is done 27 times. If full-scale *puraścaraṇa-japa* is practised, the number of syllables in the *mantra*, multiplied by 0.1 million, should ordinarily be the number of the *japa*.

After the *japa*, sit in *dhyāna* or *samādhi* for about three minutes. Pray to the deity. Prostrate at his/her feet. This finishes the *japa* session.

One may be doing the *sakāma-japa* for the cure of a disease. In that case, while doing the *japa*, *dhāraṇā* is to be done on the affected organ or part of the body and *dhyāna* on the meaning of the *mantra* and the idea of getting cure, the two ideas being fused together into one only.

In both the *sakāma* and the *niṣkāma-japa* of devotional *mantra*s, the mind is stilled, mental peace is attained, anxieties and worries are removed and a sense of being protected by the Almighty Lord is obtained. In the cases of diseases, the body tries to fight the disease and heal the damage in a more efficient way. The immune system becomes more alert and fortified. Benefits of *japa* are clearly perceptible. Academic controversy may arise if these benefits are due to faith alone or due to divine intervention. We dissolve this controversy in two ways. If the effects are secular and are explained by mere faith, pragmatism does not dismiss the effects, irrespective of the explanation. Secondly, *japa* is irrelevant to an atheist who does not believe in God. There is no question of faith in him. And hence benefits are not likely to accrue to him.

Tāntrika Mantras

Some *tāntrika mantra*s have already been given in Part II of this book. Their *nyāsa* techniques and *puraścaraṇa* methods have also been briefly described. No further repetition is necessary here. Some special features of importance are being mentioned with special reference to applications.

Sampuṭīkaraṇa of a Tāntrik Mantra

The Sanskrit word *sampuṭa* means a hemispherical bowl. In Tantra, *sampuṭīkaraṇa* means enveloping or covering a nucleus *mantra* with *bīja*s (seed-syllables). Sometimes, the sequences of the *bīja*s, used before and after the nucleus *mantra*, are the same, as in the *dakṣiṇa* Kālī *mantra*, already given in Part II. Some other times, the subsequent *bīja*s are in the reverse order of the precedent *bīja*s. Such an example is provided by the *Mahāmṛtyuñjaya-mantra* of Śukrācārya. Here we are presenting a third type of *sampuṭīkaraṇa*. A *tāntrika mantra* is enveloped by a *nāma-mantra*.

1. *oṁ hrīṁ duṁ durgāyai namaḥ.*
   oṁ namo devyai mahādevyai

śivāyai satataṁ namaḥ,
namaḥ prakṛtyai bhadrāyai
niyatāḥ praṇatāḥ sma tām.
oṁ hrīṁ duṁ durgāyai namaḥ.

Salutations to Mother Durgā. My constant obeisance to Mother Goddess, the Great Goddess, the Consort of Lord Śiva. Obeisance to the Primordial Nature, to the Cosmic Mother who is Gentle and Benign. Our dutiful salutations to her. Salutations to Mother Durgā.

2. *oṁ hrīṁ duṁ durgāyai namaḥ.*
oṁ jayantī maṅgalā kālī
bhadrakālī kapālinī,
durgā kṣamā śivā dhātrī
svāhā svadhā namo 'stu te.
oṁ hrīṁ duṁ durgāyai namaḥ.

Salutations to Mother Durgā. O Mother, with your various names such as Jayantī, Maṅgalā, Kālī, Bhadrakālī, Kapālinī, Durgā, Kṣamā, Śivā, Dhātrī, Svāhā and Svadhā, my salutations to thee. Salutations to Mother Durgā.

3. *oṁ hrīṁ duṁ durgāyai namaḥ.*
oṁ sarvamaṅgalama(mā)ṅgalye
śive sarvārthasādhike,
śaraṇye tryambake gauri
nārāyaṇi namo 'stu te.
oṁ hrīṁ duṁ durgāyai namaḥ.

Salutations to Mother Durgā. O Mother, the doer of everything good to everybody, the benevolent and benign, the fulfiller of all desires of everybody, the one who is the Shelter, the three Mothers in One, the Consort of Lord Śiva, the Consort of Lord Nārāyaṇa, salutations to thee. Salutations to Mother Durgā.

4. *oṁ hrīṁ duṁ durgāyai namaḥ.*
oṁ śaraṇāgatadīnārta-
paritrāṇaparāyaṇe,
sarvasyārtihare devi
nārāyaṇi namo 'stu te.
oṁ hrīṁ duṁ durgāyai namaḥ.

Salutations to Mother Durgā. O Mother who protects the suffering and inflicted devotees seeking shelter at your feet, who removes all afflictions and grief, O Goddess Nārāyaṇī, my salutations to thee. Salutations to Mother Durgā.

The japa of *mantra* 1 is done for the sake of devotion to Mother; of *mantra* 2 for getting rid of a general calamity, natural calamity, for changing the course of Nature for social well-being and also for personal protection; of *mantra* 3 for the welfare of a person or a family; and of *mantra* 4 for the protection of a person or a family from any serious, impending danger and misfortune. A *saṅkalpa* is to precede the *japa*. In between the *saṅkalpa* and the *japa*, a five-step mental *pūjā* is preferably done. The *pañcopacāra mānasa pūjā* of Mother Durgā has already been given in Part II. The *mantra-japa* is to be counted.

The *japa* of the Durgā-*mantra* is preferably done while performing the *mātṛ(māyā)-mudrā*. Especially for patients suffering from hypertension, this *mudrā* is unavoidable since *tāntrika bīja*s are likely to shoot up the blood-pressure. Even otherwise, this *mudrā* switches on the appropriate places in the *cakra*s to link up with Mother in the *mūlādhāra*.

To perform this *mudrā*, interlock the fingers and thumbs of both the hands (*fig*. 3.2). Press hard so that the fingertips and thumb-tips put pressure on the backs of the palms (*karapṛṣṭha*) and the opposite mounds on the two palms (*karatala*) hard-press each other. In this *mudrā*, the clefts in between fingers and thumbs at their bases are also hard-pressed. Place the hands in the *mudrā* in front of the neck below the chin, with the two forearms making an inverted V from the wrists to the elbows and the two upper arms touching the chest.

The Japa of a Vedic cum Tāntric Mantra

The 62-syllabled *mahā-mṛtyuñjaya-mantra* of Śukrācārya is a Vedic-*cum*-Tāntric *mantra*. It has already been cited in Part II of this book. The *japa* of this *mantra* is efficacious for lengthening life, delaying or postponing death and getting

fig. 3.2: *Mātṛ-mudrā*

cure of diseases. It strengthens the immune system and thereby helps the body fight microbial infections. It corrects metabolic disorders, establishes humoral and hormonal balance and normalizes physiological functions.

The *bījas* of this *mantra* are likely to shoot up the blood-pressure especially when the *japa* is done loudly. The flow of *Prāṇa* in the *nāḍīs* is accelerated and this is the cause of the temporary increase of blood-pressure. There are five *mudrās* to be performed while doing the *japa* of this *mantra*. All these five *mudrās* have been described in Part II of this book. The *liṅga-mudrā* is the most important one among these five. It not only reduces the blood-pressure, but also triggers off many sensitive points in the *cakras* of the subtle body. In addition to its special functions, it plays the roles of the *mātṛ-mudrā*. The *mātṛ-mudrā* and the *liṅga-mudrā* activate the immune system, keep the body healthy and give long life.

If the devotee cannot do *nyāsa* and the other introductory rituals necessary for a formal *puraścaraṇa-japa* of the *mahā-mṛtyuñjaya-mantra*, he may briefly adopt the following steps:

1. Do the *saṅkalpa*. Express the objectives of the *mantra-japa* through your *saṅkalpa*. Any language (not necessarily Sanskrit) may be used for the *saṅkalpa*.
2. Do the *pañcopacāra mānasa pūjā*. These five steps are the following:

   (a) *oṁ laṁ pṛthivyātmakaṁ gandhaṁ parikalpayāmi.*
   ॐ लं पृथिव्यात्मकं गन्धं परिकल्पयामि।

   Do *dhāraṇā* and *dhyāna* on the *mūlādhāra cakra*.

Utter the *bīja-mantra laṁ*. Imagine the odour of the sandalwood paste.

oṁ bhūrbhuvaḥ svaḥ.

oṁ namaḥ śivāya.

mānasa-gandhaṁ samarpayāmi.

Salutations to Lord Śiva. I am mentally offering the sandalwood paste.

(b) *oṁ haṁ ākāśātmakaṁ puṣpaṁ parikalpayāmi.*

ॐ हं आकाशात्मकं पुष्पं परिकल्पयामि।

Do *dhāranā* and *dhyāna* on the *viśuddhi cakra*. Utter the *bīja-mantra haṁ*. Imagine a flower, preferably blue in colour.

oṁ bhūrbhuvaḥ svaḥ.

oṁ namaḥ śivāya.

mānasa-puṣpaṁ samarpayāmi.

Salutations to Lord Śiva. I am mentally offering a flower.

(c) *oṁ yaṁ vāyvātmakaṁ dhūpaṁ parikalpayāmi.*

ॐ यं वाय्वात्मकं धूपं परिकल्पयामि।

Do *dhāraṇā* and *dhyāna* on the *anāhata cakra*. Utter the *bīja-mantra yaṁ*. Imagine the burning incense producing a sweet smell.

oṁ bhūrbhuvaḥ svaḥ.

oṁ namaḥ śivāya.

mānasa-dhūpaṁ samarpayāmi.

Salutations to Lord Śiva. I am mentally offering the incense.

(d) *oṁ raṁ vahnyātmakaṁ dīpaṁ parikalpayāmi.*
ॐ रं वह्न्यात्मकं दीपं परिकल्पयामि।

Do *dhāraṇā* and *dhyāna* on the *maṇipūra cakra*. Utter the *bīja-mantra raṁ*. Imagine a burning lamp which dispels darkness by its bright light.

oṁ bhūrbhuvaḥ svaḥ.
oṁ namaḥ śivāya.
mānasa-dīpaṁ samarpayāmi.

Salutations to Lord Śiva. I am mentally offering a lamp.

(e) *oṁ vaṁ amṛtātmakaṁ naivedyaṁ parikalpayāmi.*
ॐ वं अमृतात्मकं नैवेद्यं परिकल्पयामि।

Do *dhāraṇā* and *dhyāna* on the *svādhiṣṭhāna cakra*. Utter the *bīja-mantra vaṁ*. Imagine cleanly prepared, nectar-like food.

oṁ bhūrbhuvaḥ svaḥ.
oṁ namaḥ śivāya.
mānasa-naivedyaṁ samarpayāmi.

Salutations to Lord Śiva. I am mentally offering food for the Lord.

(f) *oṁ saṁ sarvātmakān śeṣopacārān parikalpayāmi.*
ॐ सं सर्वात्मकान् शेषोपचारान् परिकल्पयामि।

Utter the *bīja-mantra saṁ*. Imagine all the rest of the offerings.

oṁ bhūrbhuvaḥ svaḥ.
oṁ namaḥ śivāya.
sarvān śeṣopacārān samarpayāmi.

Salutations to Lord Śiva. I am offering all the rest to be offered to the Lord.

3. Do the *japa* of the 62-syllabled *mahā-mṛtyuñjaya-mantra* while performing the five recommended *mudrā*s in sequence. Especially the *liṅga-mudrā* is important. Counting the *japa* is necessary. Especially for this counting, because of the two hands remaining busy with the *mudrā*s, a mini-counter is very useful. Press the lever of the counter after each *japa.*
4. After the termination of the *japa*, sit in *samādhi*, a state of complete thoughtlessness, for about five minutes.

Japa in Āsanas for the Cure of Joint and Spinal Problems

All sorts of *yoga*-therapy for the cure of joint and spinal problems will not be presented here. Only some of the *āsana*s and *mudrā*s, associated with *japa*, are being discussed and these are some representative samples only. Some of them have other beneficial effects too, over and above their effects on the joints and spine. These additional benefits will also be casually mentioned.

The principal joint-problems which are relevant to yogic therapy are (1) osteoarthrits or osteoarthrosis, (2) rheumatoid arthritis, and (3) gout.

Osteoarthritis is a degenerative, non-inflammatory disease of the articular cartilage. The late middle age is the age of onset. Weight-bearing joints, e.g. the hip and the knee, are affected. The joints of the cervical and lower lumbar spine are also affected. Only a single joint is often involved. In this disease, the rate of renewal of the articular cartilage is less than that of its breakdown, and hence the cartilage gradually becomes thinner. Eventually the bony articular surfaces come in contact and the bones begin to degenerate. This results in pain and restricted movement of the affected joint(s).

The osteoarthritis of the spine is relatively common in the elderly. As a result of degenerative changes, narrowing of intervertebral discs occurs and osteophytes may develop round the margins of joints of the vertebral column. This commonly occurs in the cervical region and this condition is known as cervical spondylosis. The damage to the nervous system, caused by it, may be compression of individual spinal nerves and may also be spinal cord injury.

The rheumatoid arthritis is a chronic, progressive, inflammatory, autoimmune disease. This disease first appears in people of any age, mainly 30 to 55 years. Occasionally children suffer from this disease too. The synovial membrane of the joint is affected. Small joints, e.g. the wrists and the finger joints of the hands and the ankles and the toe joints of the feet, are affected. It is often the case that many joints are simultaneously affected. The body produces antibodies to the synovial membrane that lines the synovial joints. These antibodies bind to the synovial membrane. As a result, the joints are chronically inflamed. Due to this chronic inflammation, the joints become stiff, painful and swollen. It is more common in females than males.

Gout is caused by the deposition of sodium urate crystals in joints and tendons, resulting in an acute inflammatory condition. Uric acid is a normal catabolic product of nucleic acids, i.e. DNA and RNA. Its concentration in the blood increases due to either overproduction or defective excretion by the kidneys. Only one joint is commonly involved (monoarthritis). The metatarsophalangeal joint of the big toe and the ankle, knee, wrist and elbow joints are the most commonly affected sites. Gout is more prevalent in males than females. There is hereditary predisposition to it.

Osteoporosis is not a disease of the joints. It is a disease of the bones. Bones constitute an organic matrix in which bone-salts (calcium phosphate) are deposited. The osteoblasts are the bone-forming cells. When the deposition does not keep pace with resorption (outgo is more than intake), the bone mass is reduced. The peak bone mass reaches around 35 years of age and then gradually declines in both sexes. The bones of an osteoporosis patient becomes porous like a honeycomb and hence is the nomenclature.

This disease is more frequent in females than males. Post-menopausal lowered oestrogen levels are associated with a period of accelerated bone loss in women. The surgical removal of the ovaries and the uterus accentuates the deficiency of oestrogens. Men, in advanced age, beyond 65 years of age, are susceptible to this disease due to their lowered androgen (testosterone) levels. Both oestrogens and androgens are anabolic steroids whereas glucocorticoids are antianabolic steroids. Exercise and dietary calcium intake are favourable factors for bone health. Exercise increases the flow of blood, carrying nutrients to the bone sites. Familial susceptibility to this disease has been observed.

Skeletal deformity, vertical compression of vertebrae, bone pain and fractures, especially of the hip (neck of femur), wrist and vertebrae are the common symptoms of osteoporosis.

The action of hormones on calcium metabolism may briefly be mentioned here. The concentrations of calcium and phosphorus in serum are inversely correlated; the increase of one decreases the other and vice versa.

Calcitonin is a hormone secreted by the thyroid. When its level is raised in the blood, it acts on the bones and the kidneys to reduce the level of blood calcium. It reduces and inhibits the reabsorption of calcium from bones. It also inhibits the reabsorption of calcium by the renal tubules. An increase in the blood calcium level is a stimulus to the release of calcitonin by the thyroid gland.

The four small parathyroid glands, embedded in the thyroid, secrete parathyroid hormone (PTH or parathormone). The secretion of this hormone is regulated by the blood level of calcium. A decrease in blood level of calcium increases the secretion of PTH and vice versa. How does PTH increase the blood calcium level? Its first action is indirect. It increases the amount of calcium absorbed from the small intestine and reabsorbed from the renal tubules. If this first action is inadequate, PTH stimulates the osteoclasts (the bone-destroying cells), resulting in the resorption of calcium from bones. The actions of calcitonin and PTH are opposite to each other; but they act in a complementary manner to maintain blood calcium levels within the normal range. This is necessary for muscle contraction, blood clotting and nerve-impulse-transmission.

Dry joints are due to the deficiency of synovial fluid. This is a common condition in elderly persons. The joints become stiff and movement is painful. The synovial membrane lines the joint cavities and surrounding tendons. It secretes a clear, sticky, oily synovial fluid of egg-white consistency. It acts as a lubricant to the joints. It provides nutrients for the structures within the joint cavity. Phagocytes, contained in it, remove microbes and cellular debris. It maintains joint stability. It prevents the ends of the bones from being separated in a joint. In some joints like the knee, little sacs of synovial fluid (bursae) act as cushions to prevent friction. The scanty secretion of the synovial fluid by the synovial membrane in some joints is a geriatric problem.

With this much introduction to the physiology and physiological anatomy of joints and bones, we now proceed to the prevention and treatment of the ailments by yogic techniques with which *japa* is associated. It may specially be mentioned that yogic preventive measures are more effective than curative measures. A patient, severely affected with arthritis, can hardly be able to move. The practice of yogic *āsana*s is difficult for him/her. Males beyond the age of 65 and females after their menopause and especially after hysterectomy and oophorectomy run the risk of bone-fracture due to the practice of some strenuous *āsana*s. Eye-patients, with retinal problems, are advised to give up some *āsana*s and some *prāṇāyāma*s. A *yoga-guru* should have sufficient knowledge of both *yoga* and medical science to judiciously advise the disciple on a schedule of yogic practices which are beneficial rather than harmful. All types of *haṭha-yoga* may not be beneficial for all types of persons with different problems; and some may be hazardous too.

The readers are advised to refer to our book *Yoga-Nidrā*[19] for their practice of *prāṇa-sañcālana-kriyā*. An elderly person, either female or male, can dispense with other exercises, yogic and non-yogic, by the practice of this *kriyā*. At best, walking may be supplemented to it. Sometimes, walking is also not possible for a patient suffering from a severe type of arthritis. In that case, this *kriyā*, with or without walking or exercise, may be practised. If it is possible, the following exercises may be supplemented to the *prāṇa-sañcālana-kriyā*.

Śayāna Vyāyāma (Exercise in Lying Position)

Lie on your back on a four-folded blanket spread on the floor. Lift your right leg from the ground while folding it at the knee. Bring the foot towards your right hip. Let your right heel softly strike the root of your right leg. Then extend your leg towards the front and straighten it to the original position. Repeat the procedure 25 times. Do the same thing with your left leg.

Next lift both of your forearms. Bring them back towards your shoulders, while folding the arms at the elbows. In this process, the fingers of your hands touch the respective shoulders. Then extend the forearms to the original straight positions and ground-level. Repeat this process 50 times.

Repeat this alternate leg and hand exercise 4 to 7 times.

If some step of the *prāṇa-sañcālana-kriyā* or the *śayāna vyāyāma* is very painful due to the severe nature of your arthritis, try to do it as less as possible. You may omit some steps too.

Bīja-Japa in Vīrāsana (Vīryāsana)

Sit in *vīrāsana* (*fig*. 3.3) with face towards the east or the north. For the *āsana*, adopt the following techniques:

1. Kneel on a four-folded blanket spread on the floor or sit on a hard bed. Keep the knees together. Spread the feet to rest them by the sides of the hips.
2. Rest the buttocks on the floor. See that the feet do

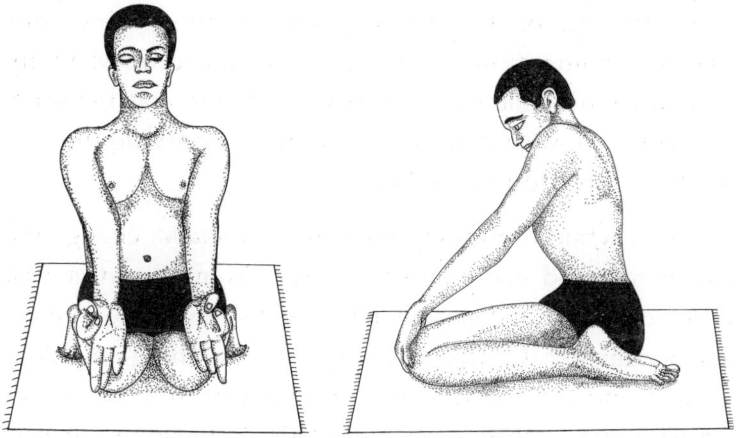

(a) with *cin-mudrā* (b) with palms facing downward, resting on the knees

fig. 3.3: *Vīrāsana*

not take the main load of the body. The inner side of each calf touches the outer side of its respective thigh. The toes point backwards and touch the floor.

3. Keep the wrists on the knees, with palms facing up, and with the tips of the index finger and the thumb of each hand touching each other (*cin-mudrā*). Keep the other fingers extended. Keep your torso, neck and head perpendicularly straight.

While sitting in *vīrāsana*, make a *saṅkalpa* to cure your osteo-arthrosis, rheumatoid arthritis, gout, dry joints (due to failure of the secretion of the synovial fluid), lumbago and sciatica.

Comb your hairs on the head with the fingernails of both hands. See that the skin of your head gets the sensation of scraping. This is necessary to arouse the centres of your cerebral cortex.

Do the *japa* of the *vahni-bīja* (*raṁ*), while closing your eyes, and doing *dhāraṇā* on your *maṇipūra-cakra*. Mentally utter *raṁ* with a slow and steady inhalation and the same *raṁ* with a slow and steady exhalation. Continue the *japa* for about three to five minutes.

Now, while continuing the same *cin-mudrā*, change the *japa* of *raṁ* and use instead *haṁ saḥ*. Mentally utter *haṁ* while you slowly and steadily inhale and *saḥ* while you slowly and steadily exhale. This *haṁ saḥ japa* is a shifting one. Your *dhāraṇā* and *dhyāna* (awareness of location and idea of getting a cure) continue to shift in the following sequence: right loin, right hip, right knee, right ankle, right toes, right toes, right ankle, right knee, right hip, right loin, left loin, left hip, left knee, left ankle, left toes, left toes, left ankle, left knee, left hip, left loin. For each locality, the *haṁ saḥ japa* should be repeated thrice before shifting to the next locus. A second or a third round of rotational *japa* may also be done.

Now lift your *cin-mudrā* and keep your palms facing down on your respective knees. With closed eyes, remain in *samādhi*, a state of complete thoughtlessness for about five minutes.

It may be noted that, like *vajrāsana*, *vīrāsana* can be practised immediately after food. It can be practised at other times too.

If *bīja-japa* in *vīrāsana* is practised regularly, the joint diseases, mentioned earlier, are cured or greatly relieved. It may take two to three months' practice to clearly detect the benefits.

Bīja-Japa in Makarāsana

Lie in *makarāsana* (*fig*. 3.4), with head towards the east or the north. For the *āsana*, adopt the following techniques:

Lie flat on the stomach, with legs stretched backwards. Use a four-folded blanket spread on the floor, or a hard bed instead. Keep the elbows on the ground and raise the head and the shoulders, by resting the mandibles on the palms of the hands. See that the wrist sides of your palms put pressure on the sides of your trachea. (Your thyroids and parathyroids and your throat area should feel the palm pressure.) Lower the chin towards the collar-bone for getting full pressure on the thyroids and parathyroids. Close your eyes while you are in this *āsana*.

Make a *saṅkalpa* to improve and balance the actions of your thyroid and parathyroid glands, to improve the calcium assimilation by your bones, to fortify your immune system and stall your auditory degeneration.

Do *dhāraṇā* and *dhyāna* on your *viśuddhi cakra* for a couple of minutes.

Do the *japa* of the *ākāśa-bīja haṁ* in synchronization with the slow and steady inhalation and exhalation. Continue the *japa* for about 15 minutes. Get up and relax.

The effects of the *japa* of the *ākāśa-bīja* (*haṁ*), while in *makarāsana*, are many. The functions of the thyroid and parathyroids are normalized, coordinated and balanced. As a result, osteoporosis and osteoarthrosis are cured or greatly controlled. In the latter disease, the articular cartilage degenerates. That degeneration is prevented probably by the restoration of the bone-health. The degeneration of the intervertebral discs is also prevented. Hence the spinal health

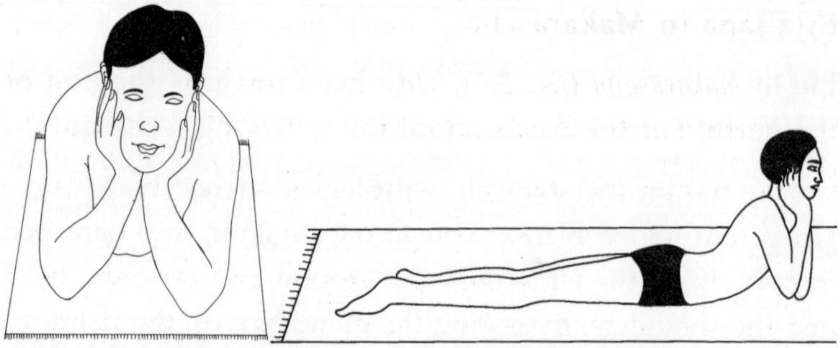

(a) Front view (b) Side view

fig. 3.4: Makarāsana

is restored. Diseases like lumbago, sciatica and spondylosis are cured.

In the treatment of osteoporosis, *makarāsana,* with the *japa* of *haṁ*, is not enough to get a full cure. In addition to this yogic therapy, the calcium-nutrition is to be improved. Milk which is rich in calcium and phosphorus should be a component of the daily diet. One may take curd if milk is incompatible with one's system. Calcium carbonate (or any other suitable form of calcium), at a daily dose of 0.5 to 1.0 gm of elemental Ca, may be taken as a mineral supplement to the diet. The supplement must contain vitamin D_3 too so as to facilitate the absorption of calcium from the intestine. Green vegetables should be the components of the diet. Leguminous vegetables are better sources of calcium. Cereals are poor sources. Direct exposure of the skin to sunlight for at least 15 minutes a day should be allowed.

The *nīlakaṇṭhī-mudrā*, associated with the *makarāsana* and the *japa* of *haṁ*, stimulates the *viśuddhi-cakra* which activates the immune system. As a result, the immune system corrects itself. Rheumatoid arthritis is an autoimmune problem. Hence this disease is tackled at its root level.

The degeneration of the auditory nerve is a geriatric problem with some persons. Their hearing capacity is partially or drastically reduced due to this reason. The *viśuddhi cakra* controls the subtle sensory organ of audition (*śravaṇendriya*). The *nīlakaṇṭhī-mudrā*, which is part of the *makarāsana*, and the *japa* of *haṁ*, the *bīja* of the *viśuddhi*, stimulate the *cakra* to halt or retard the auditory degeneration. Along with the yogic therapy, a specialist doctor should be consulted to treat any infection or other pathology of the ear. It is not claimed that *yoga*-therapy can dispense with the doctor altogether.

Japa in Ūrdhvamukhī Tāḍāsana

This posture is backward bending while standing on the toes. It is *kriyā*-12 in the *prāṇa-sañcālana-kriyā* recommended by us. Adopt the following technique for doing the *āsana*.

Stand by the side of a table or a wall. Get support of the table or the wall by a light touch with the fingers of both hands. Raise the posterior soles and heels to stand on the toes. Raise the head upwards and backwards as far as possible. See that the spine makes a concavity in the middle of the back, the abdomen bulges forward and the abdominal muscles (*rectus abdomini*) are stretched. This posture has been illustrated in *fig*. 3.5.

While standing in this posture, silently and mentally do the *japa* of the *mantra oṁ hauṁ oṁ jūm oṁ saḥ*. Do the *japa* several times. If you can stay in this posture for about three minutes, it is ideal. Otherwise, come to the original position, take a little pause and repeat. Never forget to precede this *kriyā* with a *saṅkalpa*.

The *japa* and the *āsana* improve the health of the total spine and all the joints of the legs.

Japa in Meru-Agra-Vakrāsana

fig. 3.5: *Ūrdhvamukhī tāḍāsana*

Sit in *sukhāsana*. Straighten the arms and place the palms on the floor about 25 cm behind the buttocks. Lift your torso so that it makes a maximum curvature with its convexity towards the front. Raise your face upwards and backwards as much as possible. In this process, both the knees, both the palms, the dorsal feet and the lower legs between the knees and the ankles touch the floor and transmit the body-weight to the ground (*fig*. 3.6).

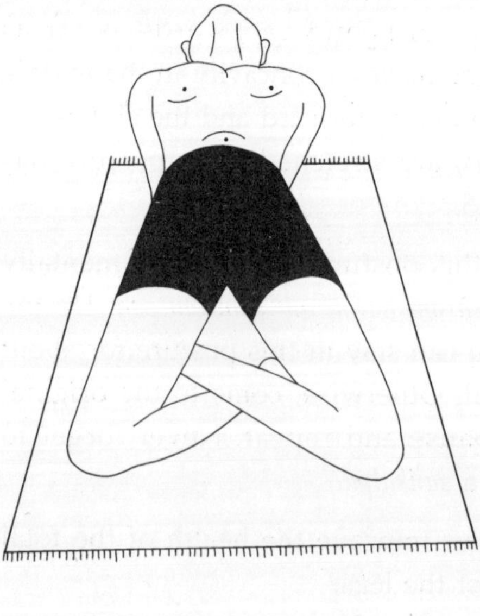

fig. 3.6: *Meru-agra-vakrāsana*

Make a *saṅkalpa*. Do the *japa* of the *mantra oṁ hauṁ oṁ jūm oṁ saḥ* and go on repeating the *japa*. You may stay in this posture and continue the *japa* for two to three minutes. Alternatively, you may repeat the process several times with short pauses in between two unitary processes.

The joint problems of the legs, the loins, the total spine and the hands are removed or ameliorated by this *japa* and *āsana*.

Japa in Meru-Pārśva-Vakrāsana

Adopt the following techniques for the *āsana*:

Sit in *sukhāsana*. Place the right palm on the external part of the root of the left thigh with a grip on it. Place the dorsal side of the left hand on the right lateral loin just above the right hip. Twist the head to the left and back. Stay in this posture for a while. Follow the same procedure for the right spinal twisting, with change of sides, of course. The posture has been illustrated in *fig*. 3.7 a & b.

Do a *saṅkalpa* before the *japa*. During each spinal twist, do the *japa* of the *mantra oṁ hauṁ oṁ jūm oṁ saḥ*. Go on changing the sides of the twists, about 25 twists for each side.

This yogic *kriyā* prevents and cures sciatica, lumbago, spondylosis and the degeneration of the intervertebral discs.

Japa in Bhujaṅgāsana

For maintaining the spine in a healthy condition, the regular practice of *bhujaṅgāsana* is very beneficial. Diseases like sciatica, lumbago, spondylosis and the degeneration of intervertebral discs are prevented or cured. The wrists, the joints of the hands, the hips, the ankles and the toe joints do

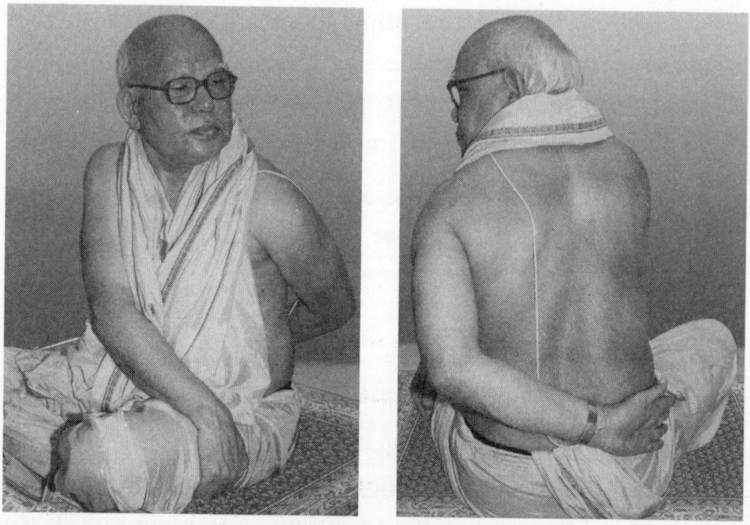

Front View (a) Left spinal twist Back View

fig. 3.7: *Meru-pārśva-vakrāsana*

(b) Right spinal twist

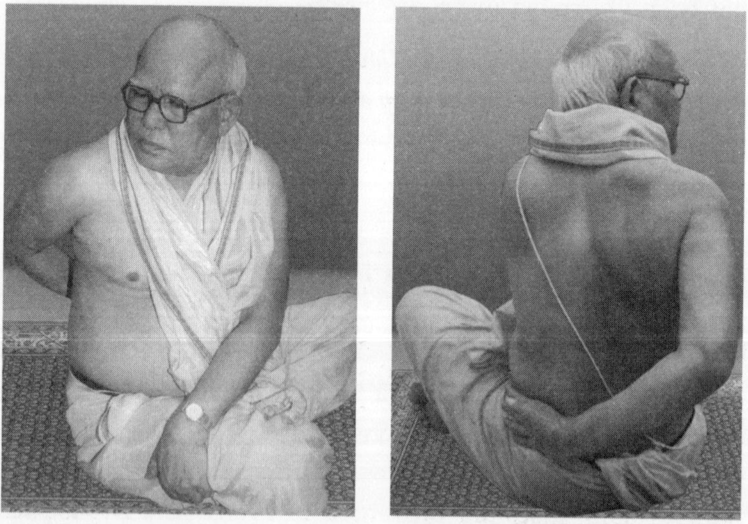

Front View Back View

also get some benefits. For the *āsana*, the following techniques may be adopted.

Lie on the floor, with face downwards, legs straight and feet extended back. Place the palms flat on the floor by the sides of the lower chest. Slowly raise the head and the shoulders off the ground. Cautiously bend the back and the head upwards and backwards as much as possible until the arms are straight at the elbows. Keep the navel as near to the ground as possible. The final posture is illustrated in *fig*. 3.8.

Make a *saṅkalpa*. Do the *japa* of the *mantra oṁ hauṁ oṁ jūm oṁ saḥ*. Silently and mentally repeat the *japa* as long as you can comfortably stay in the posture. If you like, you may come back to the original step, pause a while, resume the final posture and repeat the *japa*. You will decide the number of repetitions of the *āsana*, which may preferably be about 10.

Japa in Śalabhāsana

For very elderly persons and for persons with advanced osteoporosis, osteoarthrosis, rheumatoid arthritis and gout, it may be difficult to practise the regular *śalabhāsana*. This *āsana* is contraindicated for persons with retinal problems.

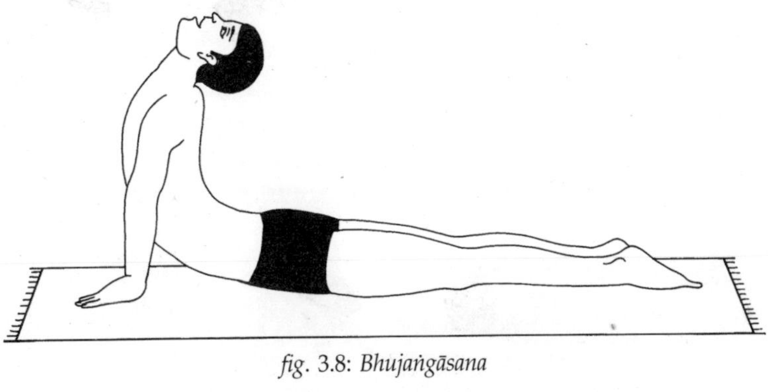

fig. 3.8: *Bhujaṅgāsana*

We recommend *ardha-śalabhāsana* for them. First, we describe the *ardha-śalabhāsana* and then the *śalabhāsana*.

Ardha-śalabhāsana. Lie flat, with face downward. Keep your arms straight so that the palms face upward and are placed under the roots of your respective thighs. Raise your right leg up to a maximum height, keep the leg at that height for a while (*fig*. 3.9) and bring it back to the ground-level. Repeat the procedure about 25 times. Follow the same procedure for the left leg. While the leg is raised and kept off the ground-level, do the *japa* of the *mantra oṁ hauṁ oṁ jūm oṁ saḥ*.

Śalabhāsana. Lie full length on the floor, with the face downward, the hands under the thighs, with palms facing upward. Use the palms as lever to raise the legs and the lower abdomen. Without bending the legs at the knees, raise the legs and the lower abdomen as high as possible (*fig*. 3.10).

fig. 3.9: *Ardha-śalabhāsana*

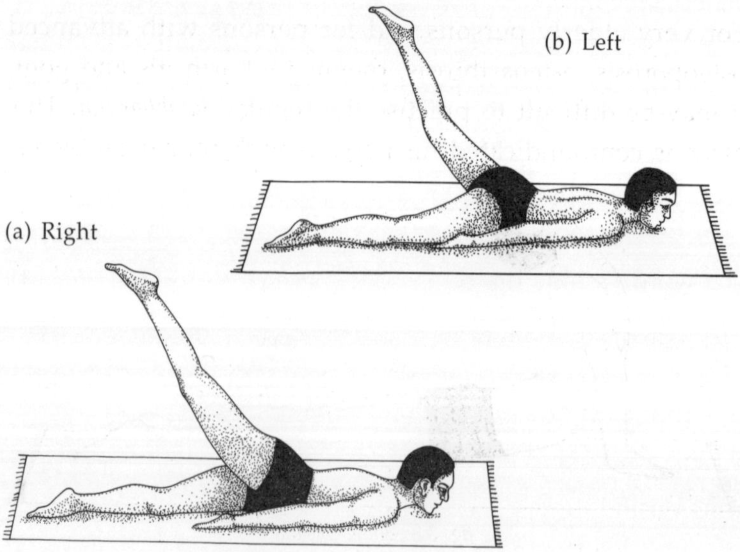

(b) Left

(a) Right

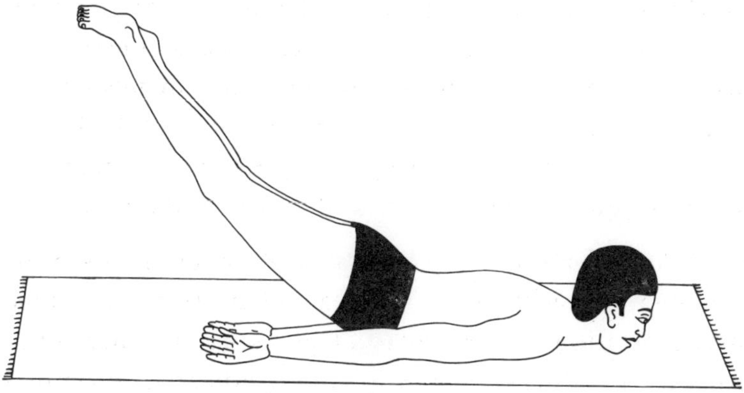

fig. 3.10: *Śalabhāsana*

Return to the starting position and repeat the process about five times. While your legs and lower abdomen are off the ground, do the *japa* of the *mantra oṁ hauṁ oṁ jūm oṁsaḥ*.

Śalabhāsana, half or full, corrects the ailments in the lumbar region of the spine and the hips. Osteoarthritis in the hips is likely to be prevented and cured. It is also very beneficial in sciatica and lumbago. If a person has severe osteoporosis, he may avoid the *śalabhāsana* until improvement is obtained by dietary calcium supplementation for a period of about six months. Osteoporosis patients are very susceptible to hip-fracture.

Japa in Paścimottānāsana

The word *paścima* literally means "west." But here it means "the back of the body." The back-muscles of the body are stretched in this pose and hence is the name.

Adopt the following steps to do the *paścimottānāsana*.

Sit on the floor, with legs stretched in front and the lower arms on the thighs. Slowly bend your trunk forward while your hands slide along the top of the legs. When you bend down, bend the head between the hands. Grasp the big toes with the respective thumbs and the index and middle fingers. Touch the knees with the forehead. Do not bend the legs at the knees. Remain in this final pose (*fig*. 3.11) for a comfortable length of time. Slowly return to the starting position.

You may not practise this *āsana* if you are in a serious condition of osteoporosis. Your painful arthritis of any type may not allow you to bend. This *āsana* and any other forward-bending *āsana* are contraindicated if spinal problems have already sat in. This yogic technique is a preventive and must not be a curative one for spinal and hip ailments. In a very advanced age, it may not be possible for you to touch the big toes. In that case, hold the distal parts of the legs, or the ankles, or the heels. Do a *saṅkalpa*. Do the *japa* of the *mantra oṁ hauṁ oṁ jūm oṁ saḥ* while you stay in the final stage of the posture. You may repeat the posture three to five times.

fig. 3.11: *Paścimottānāsana*

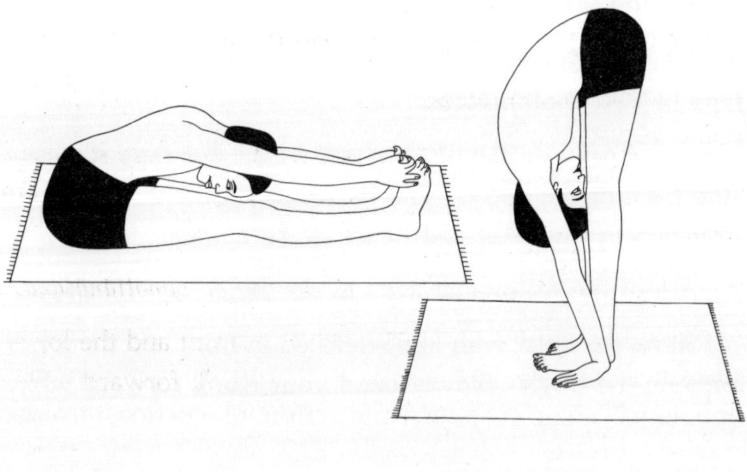

Japa with Mudrās for Specific Health Problems

Nyāsas, yantras or *maṇḍalas, bandhas, mudrās* and the *bījas* of *mantras* are the exclusive contributions of the Tantra. *Mudrās* are too many in number. Here we are presenting a very small sample of only those *mudrās* that exert beneficial effects on the prevention and cure of some diseases especially with reference to their applications in conjunction with *japas*.

Immuno-Fortification

The body succumbs to many infectious diseases due to easy exposure to invading micro-organisms and to a weak immune system. With improved hygienic conditions, the first factor can be overcome to a great extent, but cannot be totally eliminated. With better protective nutrition (quantitative and qualitative intake of proteins, dietary supply of vitamins and minerals, supply of adequate calories to the underfed and under-nourished), the second factor can be brought under control. It may be noted that antibodies are made up of proteins. The cellular and the humoral immune bodies produced by the immune system are the soldiers and the weaponry of the body. Under-nutrition and malnutrition render the immune system inefficient and weak due to the inadequate supply of raw materials. But, sometimes, the immune system of some individuals is intrinsically weak due to genetic factors. Some persons do contain some bad genes that interfere with normal immune production, or that produce immune bodies harmful to the body itself. Autoimmune reaction is a glaring example. It may also so happen that immuno-suppression takes place due to sustained worries and stress that bring about hormonal imbalance such as over-production of corticosteroids, noradrenaline and adrenaline. Corticosteroids are definitely immunosuppressive. Here lies the importance of *yoga* in immuno-promotion. Meditation does help restore the hormonal balance. The *viśuddhi-cakra* regulates the immune system. If properly manipulated, it activates the immune system to improve the efficiency of the latter. Here we describe some techniques of *yoga-tantra* (*japa* with *mudrā*s) to activate the immune system.

Any comfortable posture (yogic or non-yogic) on the floor or on a hard chair may be adopted. The eyes are to be closed. The body and the mind are to be relaxed. An appropriate *saṅkalpa* must precede the *japa*. If a series of *kriyā*s are practised, one after another, for the same purpose, only one *saṅkalpa*, at the beginning of the series, may serve the purpose.

1. ***Mātṛ(māyā)-mudrā with the japa of hrīṁ*** :— How to perform the *mātṛ-mudrā* has already been described. The hands, in this *mudrā*, are to be placed below the chin. The monosyllable *hrīṁ* is the *māyā-bīja*. The *japa* of this *bīja* is done along with this *mudrā* in synchronization with the slow and steady inhalation and exhalation. Silently utter *hrīṁ* while inhaling and again *hrīṁ* while exhaling. The practice is done for about three minutes at a time two times a day in empty stomach.
2. ***Liṅga-mudrā with the japa of hauṁ*** :— The *liṅga-mudrā* has already been described and illustrated. Place the hands in front of your face so that the tip of the erect right thumb is at the level of a point in between your eyes. While doing the *mudrā*, the silent *japa* of the *bīja hauṁ* is to be done, synchronous with the slow and steady inhalation and exhalation (*hauṁ* while inhaling and again *hauṁ* while exhaling). The

practice is done for about three minutes at a time two times a day in empty stomach.

3. ***Kāma-mudrā with the japa of klīṁ*** :— Interlock the two thumbs of the two hands, with the four fingers of the left hand pressing the back of the right hand and the four fingertips of the left hand pressing the moon-mound and the mercury-mound of the right palm. The four fingers of the right hand are straightened (*fig*. 3.12). Place the hands below the navel. Do the silent *japa* of the *kāma-bīja, klīṁ*, while performing this *mudrā*, in synchrony with the slow and steady inhalation and exhalation. Do the practice for about three minutes a time two times a day in empty stomach.
4. ***Śaṅkha-mudrā with the japa of vaṁ*** :— The *saṅkha-mudrā* has already been described and illustrated. For the present purpose the *mudrā* with the silent *japa* of *vaṁ*, synchronous with the slow and steady inhalation and exhalation, is to be done for each hand. The hands are to be placed near the heart. The practice is done for about three minutes at a time two times a day in empty stomach.

fig. 3.12: *Kāma-mudrā*

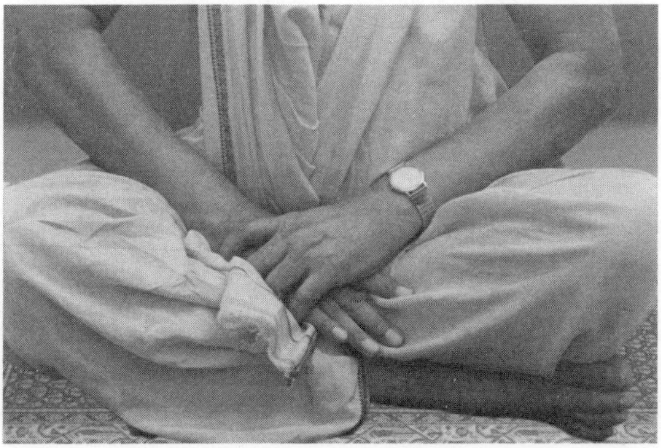

5. ***Kaṇṭha-mudrā with the japa of haṁ*** :— Make a fist of each hand with the thumb straight and fingertips pressing the respective middle part (Mar's trough) of the palm. Press the throat from both sides of the trachea by the backs of the middle and top internodes of the fingers beyond the knuckles. Press the notch between the two clavicles (collar bones) with your thumbtips. Now your throat between the mandibles and clavicles is pressed from both the sides (*fig*. 3.13) and your forearms make an inverted V, diverging towards the elbows, kept in contact with the front chest. While in this *mudrā*, silently do the *japa* of the *ākāśa-bīja, haṁ*, synchronous with the slow and steady inhalation and exhalation.
6. ***Japa with the nīlakaṇṭhī-mudrā*** :— It may substitute the *kaṇṭha-mudrā*, with the *japa* of *haṁ* remaining common. This is a *mudrā*, with the same inverted V-shape, with the difference that the two palms, placed between the mandibles and the clavicles, press the

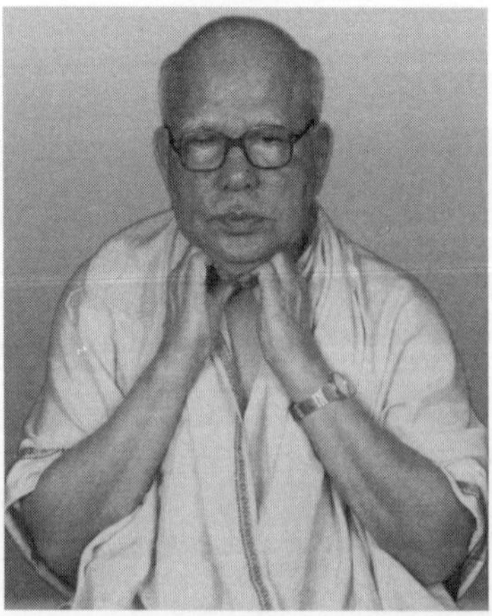
fig. 3.13: *Kaṇṭha-mudrā*

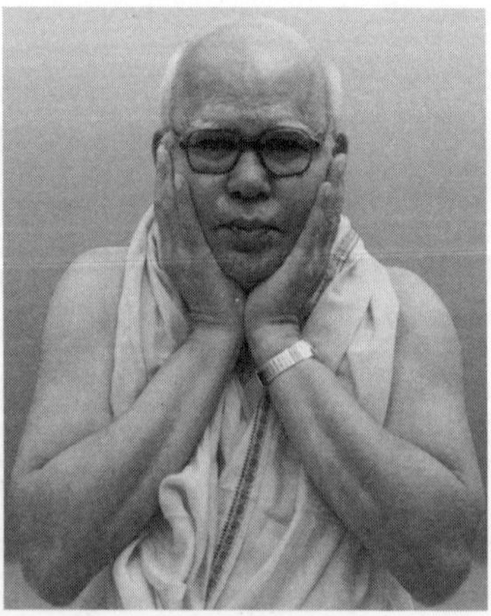
fig. 3.14: *Nīlakaṇṭhī-mudrā*

throat from both the sides, the thumbs supporting the mandibles and the fingers being placed on the outer sides of the face below the ears. The *nīlakaṇṭhī-mudrā* is illustrated in *fig.* 3.14. It is, however, to be noted that the *kaṇṭha-mudrā* can exert more pressure on the *viśuddhi cakra* than the *nīlakaṇṭhī-mudrā*, unless the latter is associated with *makarāsana*. Even in the same *āsana*, the pressure on the throat is more if the chin is pressed down towards the collarbone. For strengthening the immune system, it is advisable to do the *japa* while in the *makarāsana*.

7. ***Japa with the khecarī-mudrā*** :— All the *mudrā*s, prescribed here for immuno-fortification, may be done in conjunction with *khecarī-mudrā* for added benefits. Of course, it may be noted here that *khecarī-mudrā* is not practised in any lying posture. For the *khecarī-mudrā*, the tongue is retracted back so that its tip touches the roof of the pharynx.

   It may be uncomfortable for one to remain in *khecarī-mudrā* for a sufficiently long period. In that case, the *khecarī-mudrā* may intermittently be done while the other *mudrā* becomes continuous without breaks.

8. ***Japa with the ākāśī-mudrā and the khecarī-mudrā*** :— The *ākāśī-mudrā* is practised by folding the middle finger at the knuckle of each hand, softly pressing the ventral base of the thumb and the venus-mound (crest) by the fingertip and softly pressing the back of the middle internode of the middle finger by the thumbtip. The other fingers are straightened. The hands are placed on the respective knees with palms facing upwards. The *ākāśī-mudrā* is illustrated in *fig.* 3.15. The silent *japa* of the *ākāśa-bīja* (*haṁ*) is done,

fig. 3.15: *Ākāśī-mudrā*

while in *ākāśī-mudrā* and *khecarī-mudrā,* in synchronization with the slow and steady inhalation and exhalation.

It may casually be mentioned here that hearing problems due to senile degeneration of the auditory nerve may be improved by the silent *japa* of *haṁ* with *ākāśī-mudrā, kaṇṭha-mudrā* and *nīlakaṇṭhī-mudrā,* the last one in association with the *makarāsana*. The degenerative process may be slowed down or even halted. In addition to this yogic therapy, consultation with a specialist doctor is always advisable.

A *tāntrika* technique known as *haṅkāra-kriyā* is also beneficial in retarding the geriatric, degenerative process of the auditory nerve. Do the *vaikharī-japa* of the *ākāśa-bīja* (*haṁ*) for 3-5 times. While uttering *ha . . . . ṁ,* continue the *ha* sound for a long time with a high pitch. Immediately after the *haṅkāra-japa,* exert repeated sudden pressure on the internal ear by the *haṅkāra-kriyā*. Take a deep inhalation through the mouth. Close the mouth and tightly close both the nostrils (the right one by the tip of the thumb and the left one by the tip of the ring finger). In this state of closed mouth and closed nostrils, make an expiratory effort so that the internal air gushes into the auditory or Eustachian tube which connects the nasopharynx and the middle ear. The potential, latent auditory tube is thereby opened. The extra air-pressure in the middle ear is transmitted to the internal ear. The specialized cochlear hair-cells on the basilar membrane of the cochlea get a sudden vibratory shock. This exerts a stimulating effect on the auditory receptors and subsequently on the vestibulocochlear nerve (8th cranial nerve). Do this *haṅkāra-kriyā* 5-10 times a session, 2-3 sessions a day.

The *mudrā*s and *japa*s for the fortification of the immune system are invaluable aids in the prevention and treatment of acute and chronic diseases. Some persons are more susceptible to colds, sore throat, tonsilitis, asthma and such other chronic problems. Some others have some genes to cause problems like autoimmune reactions. Such patients are immensely benefitted by the techniques of *yoga-tantra*, described in this section.

Mudrā-Japa for Curing Sinus-Infection and Migraine

(A.) ***Japa with dhenu-mudrā*** :— To cure chronic sinusitis and migraine, adopt the following steps before doing the *mudrā-japa*:

Sit in any meditational *āsana*. You may sit on a hard chair or a hard bed if you cannot sit in any yogic posture. Sit in an erect condition. Close your eyes. Relax your body and mind.

Do a *saṅkalpa*, expressing the objective of your *yoga-kriyā*.

Show the *dhenu-mudrā*. While in the *mudrā*, do the *japa* of the *mantra oṁ jūṁ saḥ* for about 5 minutes. To perform the *dhenu-mudrā*, proceed with the following steps:

fig. 3.16: *Dhenu-mudrā*

Join the tips of the

1. right ring finger and left little finger,
2. right little finger and left ring finger,
3. right middle finger and left index finger,
4. right index finger and left middle finger, and
5. right and left thumbs.

Your finger-nails should be trimmed. The tips of the left fingers and thumb should feel the pointed pressure of the nails of the right fingers and thumb. The *dhenu-mudrā* has been illustrated in *fig*. 3.16.

(B.) ***Japa with sumukhī mudrā*** :— Next do the same *japa* with *sumukhī-mudrā*, already described and illustrated in Part II of this book. Bring the fingertips and thumbtips of both the hands from opposite lateral sides to meet the corresponding partners. Press so that the nail-pressures of one hand are felt by the tips of the other hand. Change the tips and nails after about 5 minutes. This total period of the *sumukhī-mudrā* may not be less than about 10 minutes.

(C.) ***Japa with grathitā mudrā***.:— This *mudrā* has already been illustrated in Part II of this book. Interlock the fingers and thumbs of both hands, with diverging wrists. Press the fingertips and thumbtips against the backs of the palms of the opposite hand. With closed eyes and relaxed body and mind, silently do the *japa* of the *mantra oṁ jūṁ saḥ* for about 3-5 minutes.

(D.) ***Japa with liṅga-mudrā*** :— This *mudrā* has already been described and illustrated in Part II of this book. The *bīja-mantra* for this *mudrā* is *hauṁ*. Silently do the *japa* of this *mantra* in synchronization with the slow and steady inhalation and exhalation. Relax and close the eyes while you do this *japa*. The duration of the *japa* is about 5 minutes. This *mudrā-japa* sets your immune system in order and activates it to maximize its efforts.

(E.) ***Japa in agrasparśī tāḍāsana*** :— Stand with both feet touching each other, toe to toe and heel to heel. For a support, *lightly* touch a wall or a table with the fingers of both hands. See that your hands take very little weight of your body. Raise the heels and stand on the tips of your toes and the mounds just behind your toes. While standing in this posture (*fig.* 3.17), do the *japa* of the *mantra, oṁ jūṁ saḥ*, for about 10 minutes.

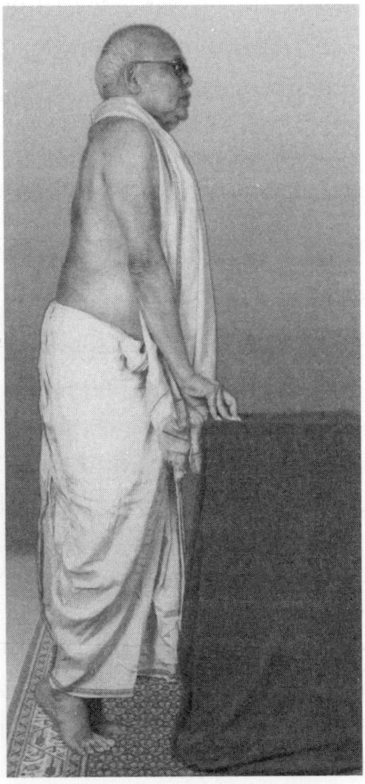

fig. 3.17: *Agrasparśī tāḍāsana*

(F.) ***Meditation on the bindu*** :— Do *dhāraṇā* and *dhyāna* on the *bindu* (*jyotirbindu*), located in between the *brahmarandhra* and the *ājñā cakra*, at an approximate level of the pineal gland. Please note that the *bindu* is located in the subtle body and has nothing to do with the gross body. While doing the *dhyāna*, try to listen to the *anāhata-nāda*. After about 10-15 minutes of *dhyāna*, merge in *samādhi* for about 5 minutes.

In addition to the *yoga-kriyā*, suggested in the foregoing paragraphs for the treatment of chronic sinusitis and migraine, the following *kriyā*s, if done, would give added benefits.

1. *Neti* (nasal cleansing).
2. *Sarala-nāsā-śodhana-kriyā*.
3. *Anuloma-viloma-prāṇāyāma* (*kumbhaka-rahita*).

Reference may be made to our book *Meditation: Science and Practice*[20] for these three *kriyā*s.

Mudrā-japa for Relief from Hypertension

If your hypertension is essential or of unknown cause (90 per cent hypertensive patients suffer from essential hypertension), you will be benefitted by yoga-therapy. If it is organic, such as renal diseases due to pathological lesions in the kidneys, or a tumour in the adrenal medulla, or some such disease, chances are bleak for getting benefits from *yoga*.

If you continue *yoga*, you may cure yourself and may not need medicines at all. You may need some hypotensive drugs at low doses in addition to the *yoga*-therapy. You have to consult your doctor regarding the medicine that suits you and the dose you need. There is no doubt at all that your hypertension will remain under control by *yoga* with or without medicinal therapy. Do the following *yoga-kriyā*s in succession.

Sit in *siddhāsana, padmāsana, svastikāsana* or *sukhāsana.* If you cannot sit on the floor, sit on a hard chair or a hard bed. Close your eyes. Relax your body and mind. Do a *saṅkalpa*.

1. Practise *mātṛ(māyā)-mudrā* for about three minutes. While you do the *mudrā,* silently do the *japa* of the *māyā-bīja* (*hrīṁ*) in synchrony with the slow and steady inhalation and exhalation.
2. Practise *liṅga-mudrā* and *japa* as in 1, except the difference in the *bīja,* which is *hauṁ.*
3. Practise *kāma-mudrā* and *japa* as in 1, except the difference in the *bīja,* which is *klīṁ* (the *kāma-bīja*).
4. Practise *śaṅkha-mudrā* and *japa* as in 1, except the difference in the *japa* which is *vaṁ* (*varuṇa-bīja*).
5. Now lie in *śavāsana* with eyes closed and body and mind relaxed. Silently do the *oṅkāra* (*oṁ*) *japa* in synchrony with the slow and steady inhalation and exhalation. Continue the *japa* for at least 5 minutes, and preferably about 10 minutes.
6. In the same *śavāsana,* change the *praṇava-japa.* Silently do the *so 'haṁ japa* (*so* while inhaling and *haṁ* while exhaling) for at least 5 minutes, and preferably about 10 minutes.
7. Lie in the same *śavāsana.* Discontinue the *japa.* Plunge into *samādhi,* a state of complete thoughtlessness, for a period of at least 5 minutes.

In addition to the *japa*s and *mudrā*s, recommended in the foregoing paragraphs, some special *āsana*s may be done, along with the *japa of bīja-mantras*, for the relief from hypertension. These have been listed separately for the sole reason that these *āsana*s have specific, beneficial effects on the flow of *prāṇa* in the central channel, the *suṣumṇā nāḍī*. The smooth flow of *prāṇa* in all the *nāḍī*s of the body and especially in the *suṣumṇā* can cure (at least relieve) essential hypertension. An assertive claim to get a full cure is not made because of other complicating factors such as geriatric hardening of the arteries, narrowing of the arterial lumen due to serious atherosclerosis, and others.

For producing hypotensive effects, we recommend *vajrāsana, vīryāsana, bhadrāsana* and *madhyabhedī-prāṇāsana* (variety 1 and 2). All these *āsana*s may be practised with empty or full stomach. As such, they induce the flow of *prāṇa* in the *suṣumṇā nāḍī* and, thus, produce some hypotensive effects. They may better be associated with the *ujjayī prāṇāyāma* and the *japa* of the appropriate *bīja-mantra*. Nose-tip-gazing (*nāsāgra-dṛṣṭi*) is also recommended while sitting in these postures and doing the *prāṇāyāma* and *japa*. The silent *oṁkāra-japa* is a recommendation common to all these *āsana*s for the reduction of hypertension. However, specific *bīja*s may also be mentally repeated — *ram* in the *vajrāsana*, *vam* in the *vīryāsana*, *lam* in the *bhadrāsana* and *oṁ* in the *madhyabhedī-prāṇāsana*. The *japa* of the *bīja* should be done in synchronization with the inhalation and exhalation which should be slow, deep and steady. For the purpose of reducing hypertension, *dhāraṇā* is done on the nose-tip, with closed eyes, rather than on the respective *cakra*s. If this series of *āsana*s is practised (One of them may be practised, if not all.), the concluding *āsana* should be *śavāsana*, as described earlier. The *vajrāsana* and the *vīryāsana* have already been illustrated in *fig*. 2.4 and 3.3, respectively. The *bhadrāsana* and the *madhyabhedī-prāṇāsana* are now being illustrated in *fig*. 3.18 and 3.19, respectively.

Mudrā-Japa for Relief from Heart Diseases

Genetic predisposition to cardiac ailments, adiposity (obesity) resulting from hereditary susceptibility, lack of exercises, intake of calorie-rich diet containing excess of saturated fat, and bad habits of smoking and alcoholism are some causes contributing to the development of heart diseases. Hypercholesterolaemia is an incriminating factor for the causation of ischaemic heart disease. Rat-race for materialistic gain of wealth, power, name and fame and sensual pleasure breeds mental tension which causes morbidity in the heart. A life full of anxiety, discontent and frustration makes the heart sick. Hormonally speaking, continued, higher concentration of catecholamines (adrenaline, noradrenaline) and corticosteroids is harmful to the heart. Uncontrolled hypertension for a very prolonged period tells upon cardiac health.

fig. 3.18: *Bhadrāsana*

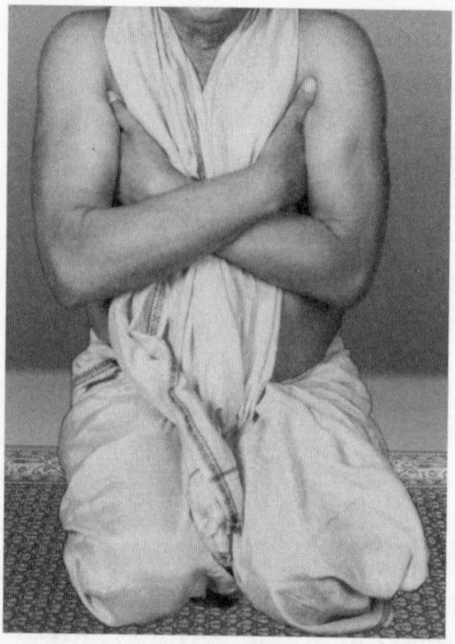

fig. 3.19: *Madhyabhedī-prāṇāsana*

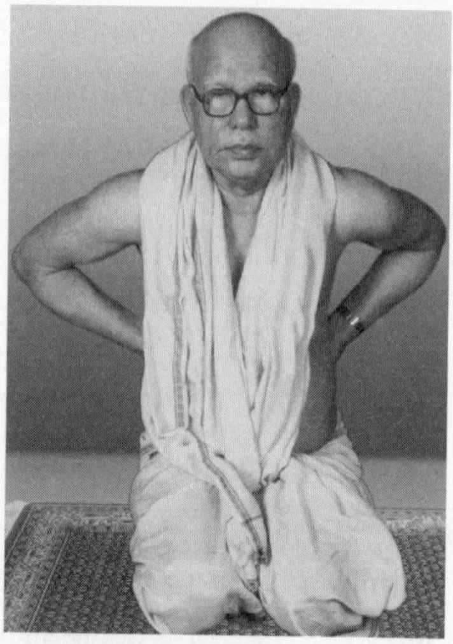

another pose

The broad spectrum of *yoga* is very conducive to cardiac health. Yoga, directly or indirectly, favourably influences the body and mind which, in turn, help the development and functioning of a healthy heart. Here we restrict our discussion to *mudrā* and *japa*. Adopt the following *yoga-kriyā* for better cardiac health.

Sit in any meditative *āsana* such as *siddhāsana, padmāsana, svastikāsana* or *sukhāsana*. If you cannot sit on the floor, you may sit on a hard chair or a hard bed. Close your eyes. Relax your body and mind.

Make a *saṅkalpa* for gaining better cardiac health.

Do *dhāraṇā* and *dhyāna* on the *anāhata cakra* at the central, lower part of the chest.

1. ***Prāṇa-mudrā*** :— Remain in *prāṇa-mudrā* by joining the tips of the little finger, ring finger and thumb of each hand. Keep the other fingers extended. Don't strain your hands and fingers. Keep your hands, with palms upwards

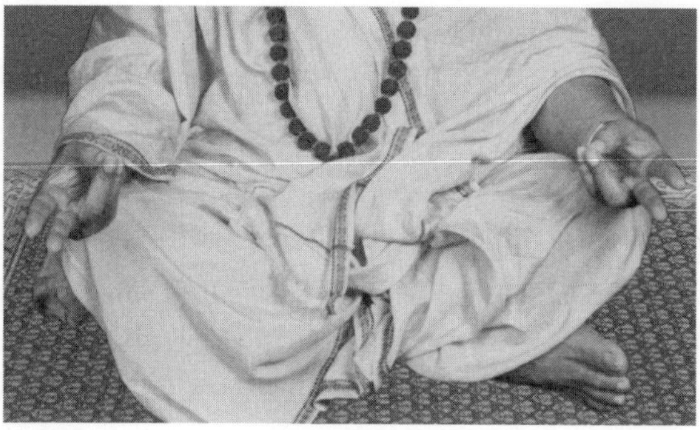

fig. 3.20: *Prāṇa-mudrā*

on the respective knee (*fig.* 3.20). Now do the mental *japa* of the *mantra, oṁ prāṇāya svāhā, oṁ* while inhaling and *prāṇāya svāhā* while exhaling. Your inhalations and exhalations should be slow and steady. Do the *japa* for about 20 minutes.

2. ***Vāyu-mudrā*** :— Without changing your *āsana,* change your *mudrā* and *mantra*. Perform the *vāyu-mudrā* (*fig.* 3.21). The index finger of each hand should be folded so that the tip of the index finger touches the base of the respective thumb. Mildly press the back of the middle internode of the index finger by the thumb. Keep your other fingers extended. Rest the hands, with palms upwards on the

fig. 3.21: *Vāyu-mudrā*

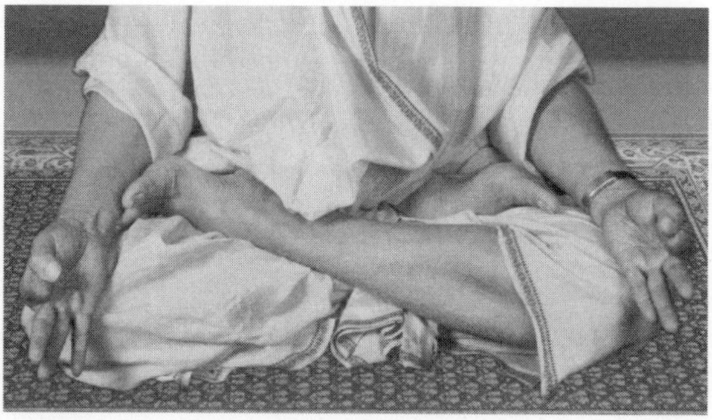

respective knee. Now do the *japa* of the *vāyu-bīja* (*yaṁ*) in synchrony with the slow and steady inhalation and exhalation. Do this *japa* for about 10 minutes, with *dhāraṇā* on the *anāhata cakra*.

3. ***Mātṛ-mudrā*** :— Do the *japa* of *hrīṁ* with the *mātṛ-mudrā* for about 5 minutes. Silently utter *hrīṁ* while inhaling and the same *hrīṁ* while exhaling. Both the inhalations and the exhalations should be slow and steady.

4. ***Hasta-ṭaṅka-mudrā*** :— To perform this *mudrā*, bring both the palms in juxtaposition horizontally in a front-to-back direction. All the four mounds or crests below the bases of the fingers should press each other. The fingers and the bases of the palms curve to the sides. Both the palms come in contact with each other at the sub-phalangeal crests only (*fig*. 3.22). While in this *mudrā*, do the *japa* of the *vāyu-bīja*, *yaṁ*. The *japa* may be done for about 3 minutes.

5. ***Pada-ṭaṅka-mudrā*** :— To perform this *mudrā*, stand in an upright position near a wall or a table with a light touch with the fingers of your hands for a support. Raise

fig. 3.22: *Hasta-ṭaṅka-mudrā*

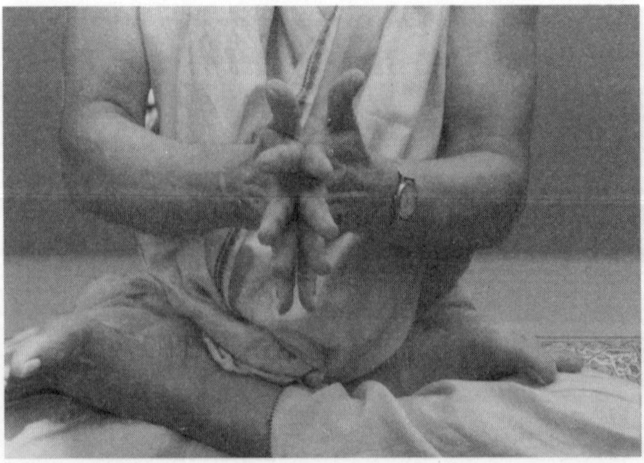

the toes and the heels so that you stand on the mounds just behind the bases of your toes (*fig.* 3.23). While you are in this *mudrā*, do the *japa* of *yaṁ* in synchronization with your slow and steady inhalation and exhalation. Do the *japa* for 2-3 minutes.

6. ***Piṇḍadā-mudrā*** :— This *mudrā* may be performed by folding the right leg at the knee, sitting on the right toes and all the mounds just behind them, while raising the rest part of the right sole, resting the right buttock against the back of the right heel. The left leg, from the knee to the toes, rests on the floor, with which the top of the left foot is in contact. The left heel should not touch the left buttock. The left palm, facing downwards, is kept across the right knee. On the back of the left hand is placed the right hand in *vāyu-mudrā*, with palm facing upward and the rest of the fingertips pointing to the front. This *mudrā* is illustrated in *fig.* 3.24. While in this *mudrā*, the *japa* of the *vāyu-bīja* (*yaṁ*) is done in synchrony with the slow and steady inhalation and exhalation. The *japa* may be done in the morning and evening for about three minutes each time.

fig. 3.23: *Pada-ṭaṅka-mudrā*

7. ***Praṇava-japa*** :— Next lie on the *śavāsana*. Close your eyes. Keep your body and mind relaxed. Do *dhāraṇā* on the *anāhata cakra*. Do the *praṇava-japa* (*oṁ*) in synchrony

fig. 3.24: *Piṇḍadā-mudrā*
front view

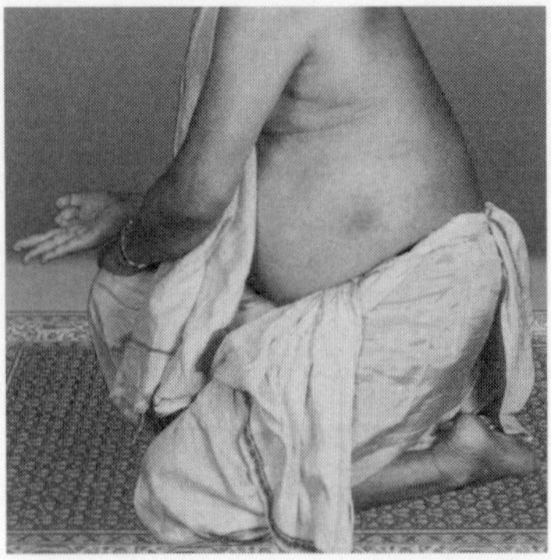

side view

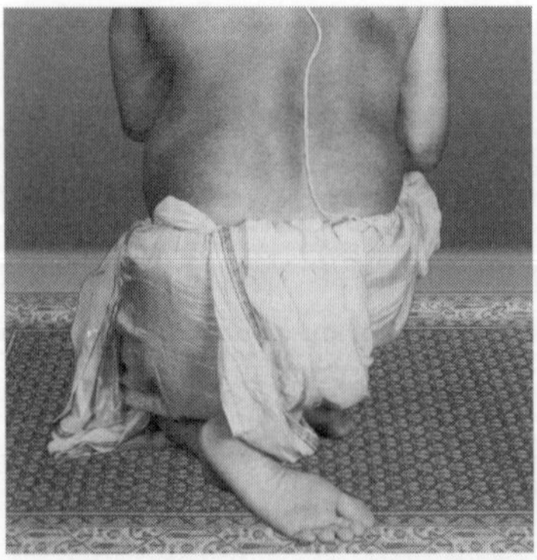

back view

with your slow and steady inhalations and exhalations. Continue this *japa* for about 10 minutes.

8. ***Ajapā-japa*** :— By following everything of step 7, only change the *mantra*. Do the *japa* of *so 'haṁ, so* while inhaling and *haṁ* while exhaling. Continue this *japa* for about 10 minutes.

9. ***Samādhi*** :— Finally plunge into *samādhi*, a state of complete thoughtlessness. Stay in *samādhi* for about 10 minutes.

If you have hypertension, do the *mudrā-japa* for controlling your hypertension too.

Mudrā-Japa to Control the Disease of Diabetes

The disease of diabetes is primarily due to the failure of the secretion of insulin by the beta-cells of Langerhans of the pancreas, situated in the duodenal loop, immediately after the stomach. Insulin is a hormone which is chemically a protein. It increases the permeability of the cell-membrane to glucose which, after entry into cells, is oxidized to supply energy. Genetic predisposition to diabetes has been observed in many families. Sedentary life, obesity, prolonged worries and tension increase the susceptibility to this disease. The juvenile diabetes may be due to viral infection of the beta cells of the pancreas.

The disease may be controlled by oral administration of hypoglycaemic drugs, that stimulate the beta cells to secrete insulin. In the case of total or near-total failure of the secretion of insulin, the hormone must be supplied parenterally in order to save the life of the patient. In addition to medicinal therapy, exercise and diet-control (lowering the calorie-content of the diet, avoiding sugar, saturated fat and cholesterol) are indispensable for getting the desired benefits.

Āsanas, *prāṇāyāma*, *bandha*s and *mudrā*s are very useful for the treatment of diabetes. We have described the applications of meditation and *yoga-nidrā* for the treatment of diabetes in our books — *Meditation*[21] and *Yoga-Nidrā*.[22] Here our discussion is limited to *japa*s with *mudrā*s for the control of diabetes.

Adopt any meditative posture already prescribed. If you have some physical problem, sit on a hard chair or a hard bed. Do *dhāraṇā* on the *maṇipūra cakra* at the region of the navel. If you have a good grasp of the anatomy of the pancreas, do *dhāraṇā* on the pancreas itself. Your *japa* should be preceded by a *saṅkalpa*. In your *dhyāna*, while doing the *japa*, you should concentrate on the idea of increasing the efficiency of insulin-secretion by your pancreas. The following are the *japa*s and the associated *mudrā*s.

Mātṛ-mudrā :— This *mudrā* has already been described. The *bīja-mantra* is *hrīṁ*. The *devatā* is Mother Gaurī or Durgā. Do the *japa* of this *bīja* in synchrony with the slow and steady inhalation and exhalation. The duration should not be less than three minutes. Preferably three sessions or at least two sessions a day are necessary.

Liṅga-mudrā :— This *mudrā* has already been described. The *bīja-mantra* is *hauṁ*. The *devatā* is Rudra-Śiva. The rest of the practice is as for the *mātṛ-mudrā*.

Śakti-mudrā :— This *mudrā* has already been described. Its *bīja-mantra* is *hauṁ*. The rest of the practice is as for the *mātṛ-mudrā*.

Muṣṭika-mudrā :— This *mudrā* has already been described. Keep the *mudrā* at the heart level, with the thumbs pointing upwards. Its *bīja-mantra* is *jūṁ saḥ*. Mentally utter *jūṁ* while inhaling and *saḥ* while exhaling. The *devatā* is Rudra-Śiva. See that your fingertips hard-press the Mars' trough in the middle of your palms.

Kuja-mudrā :— This has a similarity with the *muṣṭika-mudrā*. Make a fist of each hand, with the fingertips hard-pressing the Mars' trough and the thumbtip pressing the side of the knuckle of the index finger. Place the fists with palms facing upwards and the base internodes of the fingers of each hand pressing those of the other at the dorsal side (*fig*. 3.25). Keep the *mudrā* at the level of the navel, with the little fingers in contact with the abdomen. Close your eyes and relax. Do the *japa* of the *bījas*, *jūṁ saḥ*, *jūṁ* while inhaling and *saḥ* while exhaling. The inhalations and the exhalations must be slow and steady.

Sūrya-mudrā :— Practise this *mudrā* by both hands. Fold the ring finger so that its tip touches the palm. Gently press

fig. 3.25: *Kuja-mudrā*

the back of the middle internode of the ring finger with the respective thumbtip (*fig*. 3.26). Place each hand on the respective knee. The *bīja* for the *japa* is *raṁ*, done in synchrony with the slow and steady inhalation and exhalation.

Kulīra* (*pādāgni*)-*mudrā :— Practise this *mudrā* while sitting on a floor or a hard bed. Sit with the two legs folded at the knees and the two soles juxtaposed. Separate the soles and keep them apart at a distance of about 10 cm. Fold the four fingers of each hand at the knucles. Press the middle depressed part of each sole with the respective fingertips (*fig*. 3.27). Start from the front of the depression

fig. 3.26: *Sūrya-mudrā*

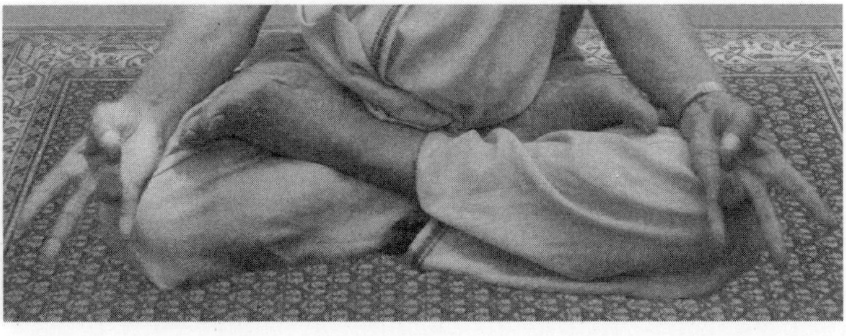

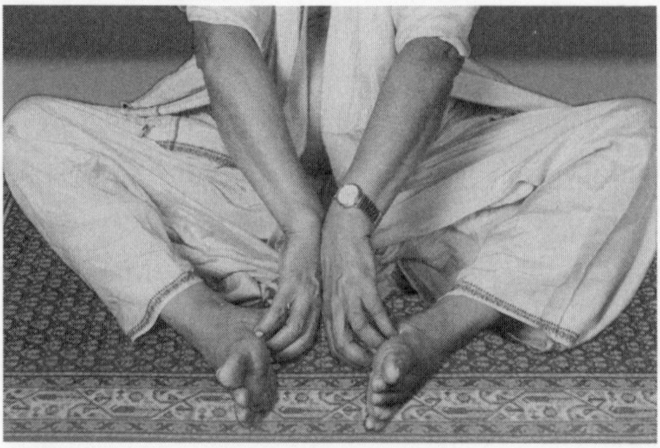

fig. 3.27: *Kulīra (pādāgni)-mudrā*

and go backwards to the back of the depression by four steps. In each step, do the *japa* of the *mantra*, *jūṁ saḥ* (*jūṁ* while inhaling and *saḥ* while exhaling) for about two minutes. Practise the whole *kriyā* with closed eyes, with *dhāraṇā* at the *maṇipūra* and *dhyāna* on the idea of the increased secretion of insulin by your pancreas.

Samāna-nābhi-mudrā :— The *samāna-mudrā* is performed by joining the tips of the four fingers and the thumb (*fig*. 3.28). When the *samāna-mudrā*s of both hands are placed together at the navel, with mild pressure on the

fig. 3.28: *Samāna-mudrā*

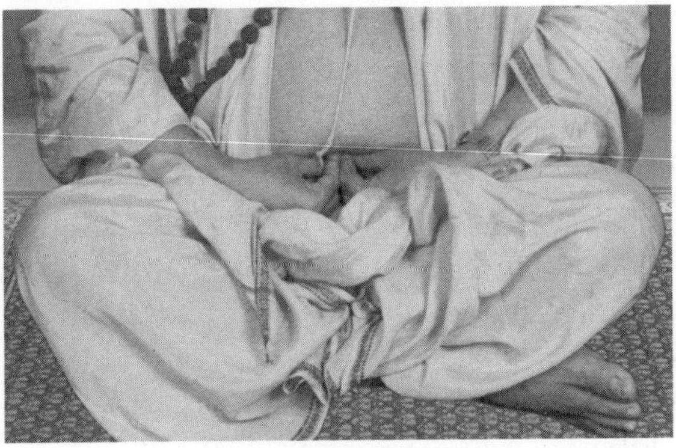

fig. 3.29: *Samāna-nābhi mudrā*

central abdomen, it becomes *samāna-nābhi-mudrā* (*fig.* 3.29). Persons suffering from hypertension should not apply too much pressure on the central abdomen. Most diabetics generally suffer from concomitant hypertension. While closing the eyes and doing this *mudrā*, one should do *dhāraṇā* on the *maṇipūra*, concentrate on the idea of the increased efficiency of the pancreas in insulin-secretion, and do the *japa* of the *vahni-bīja*, *raṁ*, in synchrony with the slow and steady inhalation and exhalation.

For the control of diabetes, seven *mudrā*s with *japa* have been prescribed here. In each case, the *japa* is to be followed by a short session of *samādhi*, if only one *mudrā* is practised. When more than one *mudrā* or all these *mudrā*s are practised one after the other, only one short session of *samādhi* is to conclude the *kriyā*.

The *mudrā-japa* may not produce tangible effects on the pancreas if all the beta cells have already been dead. Nevertheless, practise the *mudrā-japa*, with a change in the idea of the *dhyāna*. Do the *dhyāna* on the idea of the improved permeability of the cell-membranes of the body to the entry of glucose.

Sarvāṅga-saṁyama with mantra-japa :— Sit in *siddhāsana, padmāsana, svastikāsana* or *sukhāsana*. You may sit on a hard chair or a hard bed. Do the *japa* of the *navārṇa-mantra* (*oṁ aiṁ hrīṁ klīṁ cāmuṇḍāyai vicce*) while shifting your *dhāraṇā* from the head to the feet and from the feet to the head. The minimum number of shifting is eight — to and fro shifting in the front, the back and the two sides. The *dhāraṇā*-shifting may be multiples of eight. The *dhyāna* should be on the concentration of the idea of the increased permeability of the membranes of all cellls to the entry of glucose. Conclude the *kriyā* with a short *samādhi*.

Caution — Do the *yoga-kriyā* for the control of diabetes, over and above the treatment by a competent doctor. Check your blood periodically for the glucose level. The doctor will decide if medicinal treatment is not necessary, and if necessary, the dose to be adopted.

Mudrā-Japa for Relief from Hepatic Disorders

Alcoholics may damage their livers. The specialized hepatic cells are replaced by white connective tissue (collagen fibres) and, as a result, the liver may shrink to a hard mass. This is an irreparable condition and mostly fatal. If the disease is detected early and if alcohol is completely given up, the prognosis may not be very bad. Only in such a case, *yoga* may be helpful.

Hepatic sluggishness may also sometimes occur due to metabolic dysfunction. Fatty liver may be another problem. Liver-malfunctioning may be the incriminating factor. These cases are responsive to yogic therapy.

Viral hepatitis is a common problem. The liver is infected by a virus that has different strains. Hepatitis, due to the attack of virus B or C, is usually fatal, whereas the death-rate due to the attack of the virus A is low. There are other strains of the virus too. Water, contaminated with patients' excreta, is the usual medium of infection of virus A, whereas blood, seminal fluid, vaginal fluid, saliva, etc., containing virus B, coming in contact with the mucous membrane or entering directly into the blood stream, spread the infection of the B virus.

Two varieties of *mudrā-japa* are prescribed here for the treatment of liver-diseases.

Japa with bahupadī mudrā :— Sit in any one of the postures already recommended for the *mudrā-japa*. Do the *saṅkalpa*. Close your eyes. Press your navel with the tips of the two index fingers. Press the upper brim of your upper abdomen just below the level of the diaphragm with your thumbtips. Press your right and left sides of the abdominal region between the lower and the upper abdomen with the tips of the rest of the three fingers of the respective hands. The *bahupadī-mudrā* is illustrated in *fig*. 3.30. Do *dhāraṇā* on the *maṇipūra*. Do *dhyāna* on the idea of getting cure of the liver disease. Do the *japa* of the *mantra, oṁ jūṁ saḥ*. Do this

fig. 3.30: *Bahupadī-mudrā*

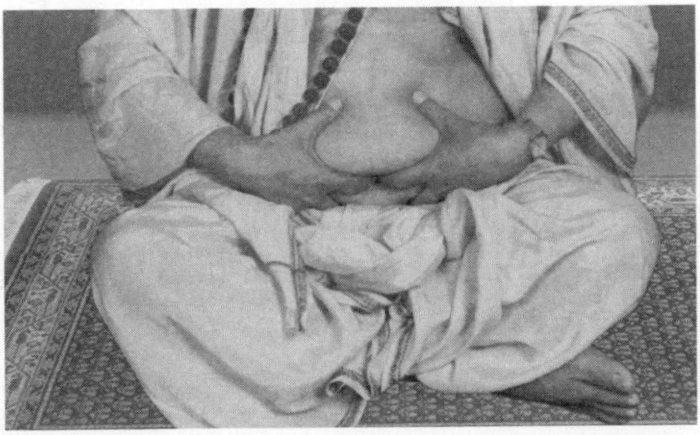

kriyā for at least five minutes a session and three sessions a day.

Japa with kara-pārśva-mudrā :— This is the same as *vyāpakāñjali-mudrā* with some modifications. It has two varieties, namely, (a) the fully-spread (*mukulita*) and (b) the half-open (*ardha-mukulita*)-*mudrā*. In both varieties, the palms are at the level of the neck and chin, and the two forearms make an inverted V, with the elbows pressing at the sides of the abdomen. In the former variety, the fully-spread palms touch each other, with pressure, at the sides of the little fingers, the Mercury crests and the lunar mounds. In the half-open variety, the pressure contact of the two palms is between the palmar sides of the little fingers and the sides of the two palms, straight with the little fingers. In the half-open variety, the corresponding fingertips touch each other without pressing, the pressure being exerted on the Mercurian-cum-lunar meridian only. In both the varieties, all the fingers and thumbs are closely in contact. Both the varieties of the *kara-pārśva-mudrā* have been illustrated in *fig*. 3.31. The *mantra* for the *japa* is *oṁ jūṁ saḥ*. The *japa* may be done for at least five minutes a session. Three sessions a day would be enough.

If hepatitis (inflammation of the liver) is due to infection by the attack of bacteria or viruses, *japa-mudrā*s that stimulate the immune system for the enhanced production and deployment of the soldiers and weaponry of the body are to be practised. They have already been described. The *mudrā- japa* for immuno-fortification is done with *dhāraṇā* on the *viśuddhi cakra* and *dhyāna* on the idea of triggering the immune system.

If hepatitis is a case of toxicosis, *varuṇa-mudrā* (*jala-*

mudrā) may additionally be practised for the flush of toxins from the body through the urine. The *varuṇa-mudrā* is practised by joining the tips of the ring finger and the thumb of each hand. The hands are to be placed on the respective knees, with the other fingers extended and palms upwards. The *mudrā* has been illustrated in *fig.* 3.32. While doing the *mudrā*, the *japa* of the *varuṇa-bīja* (the *bīja* of the *svādhiṣṭhāna cakra*), *vaṁ*, is to be done. The *japa* is done in synchrony with the slow and steady inhalation and exhalation. *Dhāraṇā* on the *svādhiṣṭhāna*, *dhyāna* on the idea of the flush of toxins through the urine and faeces and the *japa* of *vaṁ* must be done simultaneously. This *mudrā-japa* is very useful in dermatitis and gastro-enteritis too.

fig. 3.31: *Kara-pārśva-mudrā*

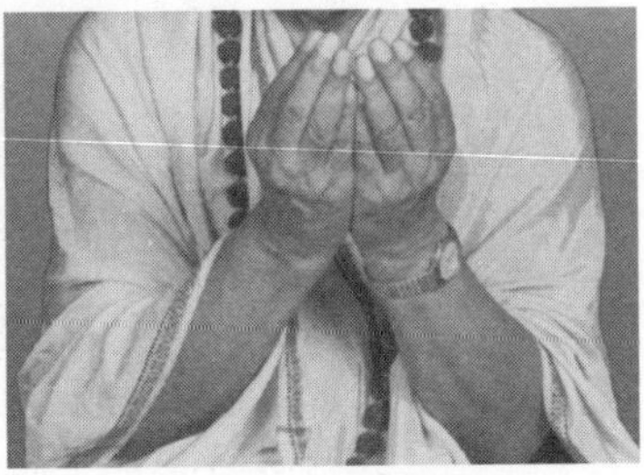

(a) *Mukulita*

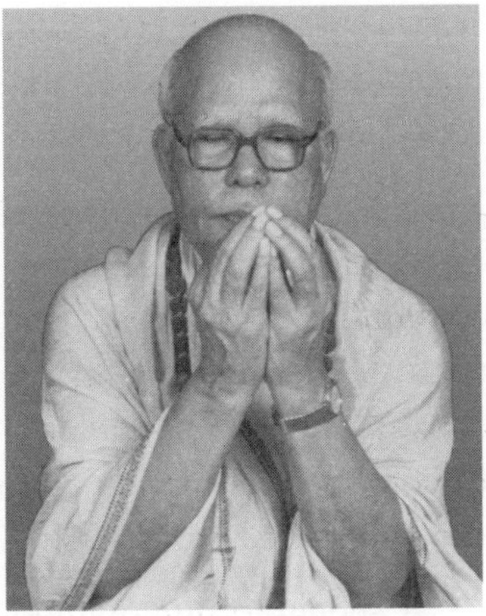

(b) *Ardha-mukulita*

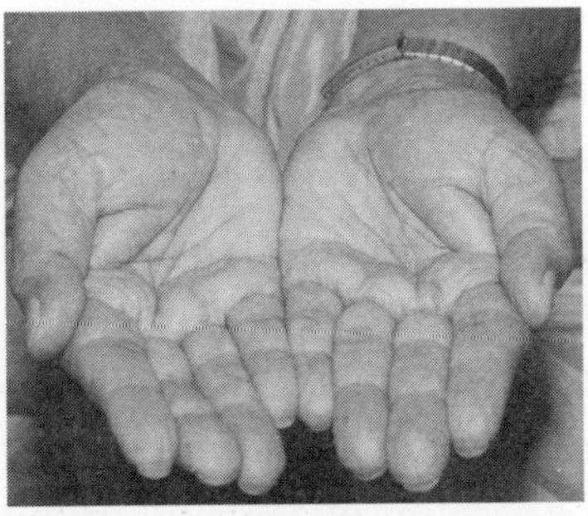

(c) *Vistārita*

Mudrā-japa for Relief from Chronic Constipation

Chronic constipation seems to be a minor ailment. But, if not

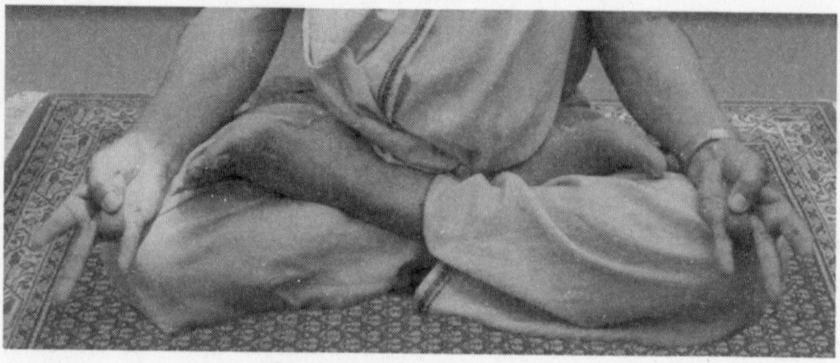

fig. 3.32: *Varuṇa-mudrā* (*Jala-mudrā*, *Āpo-mudrā*)

taken care of, it is a predisposing factor for a number of serious diseases. Hyperacidity, dyspepsia, appendicitis, piles and haemorrhoids are some of the sequelae to chronic constipation. Even cancer in the colon may result from this condition.

A diet, very refined in nature, poor in fibre, hardly containing vegetables, salads and fruits, is constipating in nature. A non-vegetarian diet is comparatively more constipating than vegetarian one. Hence, the first attempt to correct constipation should be to include fibre, fibrous vegetables and fruits in the diet.

A sedentary life, without physical work and exercise, is predisposed to constipation. Even if one's vocation and profession are likely to be sedentary in nature, one should find some time to do some exercises, morning walk and *yogāsana*s.

Ladies, after menopause or after ovariectomy, suffer from oestrogen-deficiency. Old males, in very advanced age (after 65 years of age), suffer from the deficiency of testosterone. The female and the male hormones are anabolic. They are necessary for mineralization (deposition of calcium phosphate) in the organic matrix of bones. Thus, in the deficiency of the sex-hormones, osteoporosis is developed. Hypocalcaemia (lowered concentration of calcium in the plasma) is a concomitant condition of osteoporosis. Calcium is necessary for activating smooth muscles. In calcium-deficiency, the intestinal motility and peristalsis are retarded, resulting in constipation. It is recommended that old persons should take some milk (preferably separated milk) daily and, if prescribed by the doctor, some calcium-tablets.

Here our focus is on the *japa* in some *āsana*s or with some *mudrā*s. It may be noted, however, that this yogic therapy is an aid to other therapies, already indicated.

The *japa* of the (*dharā-*) *pṛthvī-bīja* in *pavana-muktāsana*. First, three varieties of *pavana-muktāsana* are described. Take at least three glasses of warm water and then do *pavana-muktāsana* just before the usual time of defecation. Lie on your back on the floor on which a carpet or a four-folded blanket is spread. Fold your right leg at the knee and, with clasped hands, hold your leg just below the level of the knee. Press hard so that your right thigh puts pressure on the right side of your abdomen. While doing this, do *dhāraṇā* on your *mūlādhāra-cakra*, do *japa* of *laṁ* and *dhyāna* on the idea of the backward peristalsis of your colon and rectum. Repeat this procedure with your left leg. At the third stage, fold both the legs at the knees. This time, clasp both the legs below the knees with your hands, the right hand clasping your left wrist. The rest of the procedure remains the same. The *pavanamuktāsana*, half and full, has been illustrated in *fig*. 3.33.

***The japa* of *laṁ* with *pṛthvī-mudrā* and *aśvinī-mudrā* :—** The *pṛthvī-mudrā* is performed by joining the tips of the little finger and the thumb of each hand (*fig.* 3.34). The hands are placed on the respective knee, with the palms facing upward. All the other fingers remain in a straight condition. For the present purpose, the *japa* of the *dharā-bīja* (*laṁ*) is done, while performing both the *pṛthvī-*

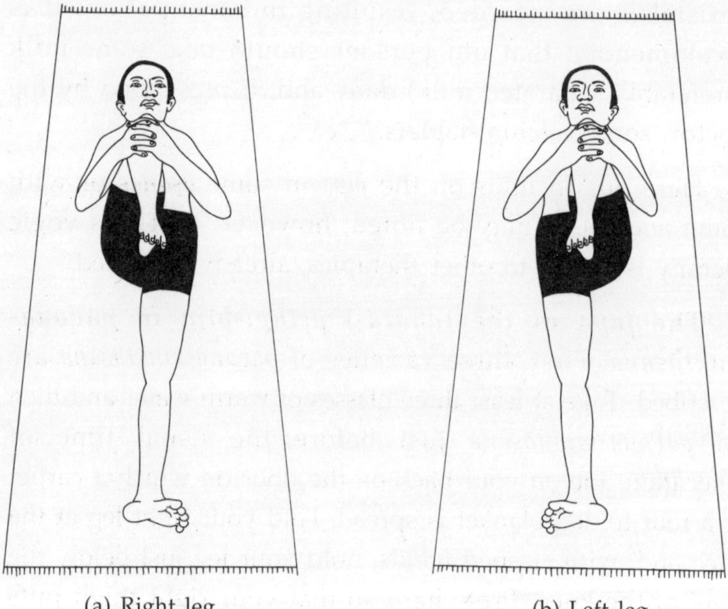

(a) Right leg (b) Left leg

fig. 3.33: *Pavana-muktāsana*

(a) Both legs

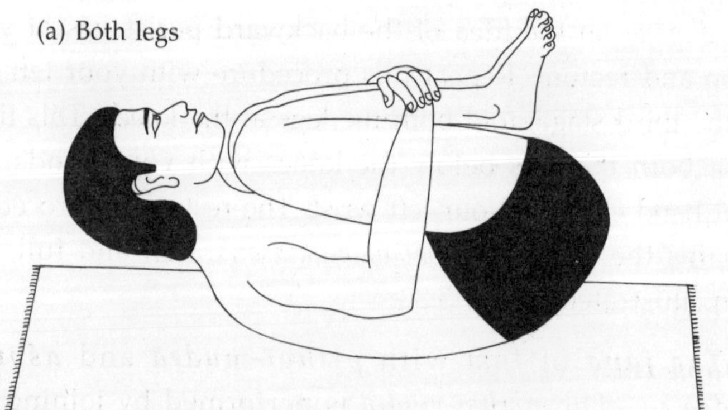

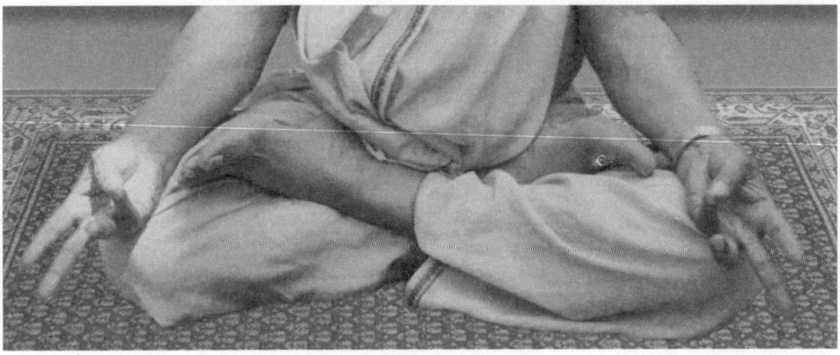

fig. 3.34: *Pṛthvī-mudrā*

mudrā and the *aśvinī-mudrā*. The word *aśva* means "a horse." For doing this *mudrā*, sit in *sukhāsana* and rhythmically contract and relax the muscles of your anal region and the two anal sphincters. The horse is imitated in doing this *mudrā* and hence is the name. While you contract and relax these muscles and the sphincters, mentally utter the *mantra laṁ*, and do *dhāraṇā* on the *mūlādhāra*. Repeat the *japa* for about 25 times.

The japa* of *vaṁ* with *mūla bandha :— The *mūla bandha* is practised in any of the meditative postures including the *sukhāsana*. After a deep inhalation, the muscles of the lower abdomen, from the anus to the navel, are pulled backwards and upwards, with full retention of breath. During this phase of this *kriyā*, do the *japa* of the *bīja vaṁ*, with *dhāraṇā* on the *svādhiṣṭhāna cakra*. When you feel to exhale, do that, and repeat the process several times. Your *dhyāna* should be on the idea of the expulsion of the faeces. You may also perform the *mūla bandha* without the initial *pūraka* and the subsequent *kumbhaka*. While in the *bandha*, you may inhale and exhale.

Japa* with the *apāna-mudrā :— Sit in *sukhāsana* (the comfortable pose) or on a hard chair or hard bed. Use both

fig. 3.35: *Apāna-mudrā*

hands separately for doing the *apāna-mudrā* by joining the tips of the ring finger, the middle finger and the thumb. Rest the hands on the respective knees. The *apāna-mudrā* is illustrated in *fig*. 3.35. The *mantra* for the *japa* is *oṁ apānāya svāhā*. Mentally utter this *mantra*, a long *oṁ* while inhaling and *apānāya svāhā* while exhaling. Do *dhāraṇā* on the *mūlādhāra* and *dhyāna* on the idea of the expulsion of the faeces.

Japa **with the** ***upastha-mudrā*** :— The *upastha-mudrā* is performed by loosely (without pressing) interlocking the

fig. 3.36: *Upastha-mudrā*

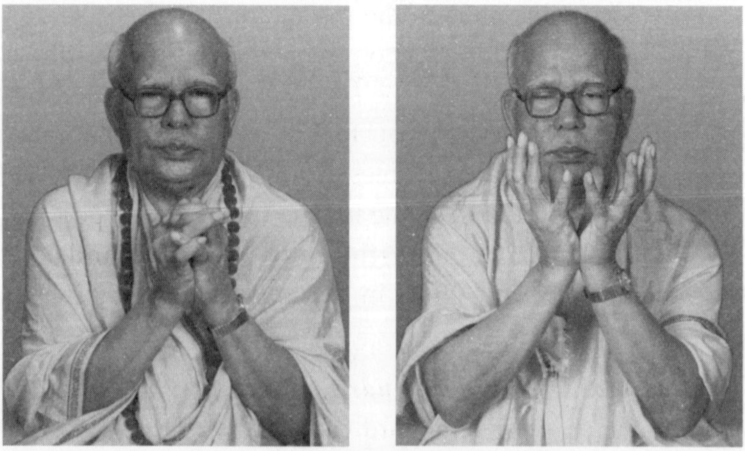

fingers of both hands at the knuckles, placing the thumbtips on the left index finger, making a hollow by both palms, joining the hind parts of the palms in front of the wrists with the mutual exertion of pressure on the Venus mound and the lunar mound and making an inverted V, with the convergence of the hands, the divergence of the elbows and the contact of the forearms with the sides of the abdomen. The *upastha-mudrā* is illustrated in *fig*. 3.36. This is a *mudrā* which is useful for the generative organs and also for the excretory organs. In the former case, the associated *cakra* is the *svādhiṣṭhāna* and the *bīja-mantra* for *japa* is *vaṁ*. In the latter case, the associated *cakra* is the *mūlādhāra* and the *bīja-mantra* is *laṁ*. For relief from constipation, the *japa* of *laṁ* is done with the *upastha-mudrā*, while doing *dhāraṇā* on the *mūlādhāra* and *dhyāna* on the idea of the expulsion of the faeces.

Japa with the ***dvināḍa-paṅkaja-mudrā*** — The *paṅkaja-mudrā* has already been described and illustrated in Part II of this book. In performing this *mudrā*, the ventral sides of the two forearms are kept in contact between the wrists and the elbows. Thus, it is *ekanāḍa* (with a single stalk only). This *mudrā* is positioned vertically, with the lotus-flower-like hands in front of the face. In contrast, the *dvināḍa-paṅkaja-mudrā* has two stalks, the two forearms diverging from the joined wrists towards the elbows. The tips of the little fingers and those of the thumbs are in mutual contact. All the other fingers are separate and infolded. The hands, with the fingers, present the resemblance of a semi-blossomed lotus-flower. The *mudrā* is positioned below the level of the nose, in front of the chin, neck and chest, with the elbows in contact with the sides of the upper abdomen. The hind parts of the palms up to the wrists should feel the

fig. 3.37: *Dvināḍa-paṅkaja-mudrā*

pressure, while doing this *mudrā* in *sukhāsana* (*fig*. 3.37). The *bīja-mantras* for the *japa* are *laṁ* and *vaṁ*, *laṁ* while inhaling and *vaṁ* while exhaling. The *japa* is silent and may last for about three minutes. The inhalations and exhalations are slow and steady. *Dhāraṇā* on the *mūlādhāra* and the *svādhiṣṭhāna* shifts, the former for *laṁ* and the latter for *vaṁ*. Concentration on the idea of excretion or generation is fixed, depending on the objective.

Japa with ***pārṣṇi-mudrā*** :— To perform this *mudrā*, stand by the side of a table or a wall with light touch on this support with all the fingers of both the hands. See that the hands transmit very little weight of your body. Raise the front parts of both soles and stand on the two heels only. Stand in this posture for about three minutes. While standing, do the *japa* of the *pṛthvī-bīja* (*laṁ*). The *japa* should be synchronous with the slow and steady inhalation and exhalation. The *mudrā* has been illustrated in *fig*. 3.38.

Japa-Therapy in Cancer

fig. 3.38: *Pārṣṇi-mudrā*

Cancer affects all organs and all tissues of the body. Any chronic irritation — physical, mechanical, chemical, or otherwise — may bring about a genetic change at the cellular level. Such agents are called mutagens. Due to their influence, the cellular DNA changes any of the four bases or the base sequence. A cell with changed DNA becomes alien to the body. It declares its own autonomy and sovereignty. It grows wildly. It migrates to different parts and establishes its colony. It works outside the holistic relatedness. Such uncontrolled growth becomes fatal to the body.

If the disease is detected at an early stage, or, in the worst case, not at a very late stage, surgical and medical treatment may be complemented with *japa* therapy. The following steps may be adopted:

1. Do the *saṅkalpa.*
2. Switch all your *cakra*s on by the following technique. Sit in any meditative posture or on a hard chair or a hard bed in erect position. If you are unable to sit, lie in *śavāsana*. Close your eyes. Relax. Mentally utter

the following *mantra* with shifting visualization (*calad-dhāraṇā*).

oṁ aiṁ hrīṁ śrīṁ krīṁ klīṁ duṁ durgāyai namaḥ.

When you utter *oṁ*, visualize the *sahasrāra* and *ājñā* in succession. When you utter *aiṁ, hrīṁ, śrīṁ, krīṁ* and *klīṁ*, visualize the *viśuddhi*, the *anāhata*, the *maṇipūra*, the *svādhiṣṭhāna* and the *mūlādhāra*, respectively. When you mentally utter a long *duṁ* with some force and a rushing ascent, visualize the uncoiling of Mother Kuṇḍalinī and her serial ascent from *cakra* to *cakra* until it reaches the *sahasrāra*. Make a short pause there and visualize the union of the Mother and the Father. When you silently utter *durgāyai namaḥ*, visualize the serial descent of the Mother who finally settles in the *mūlādhāra* in a coiled state. Repeat the *kriyā* three times.

3. Recharge your *cakra*s with the *bīja*s in the following way. Mentally utter the *bīja*s with shifting visualization.

   Descending: — 1. *oṁ, haṁ, yaṁ, raṁ, vaṁ, laṁ.*

   Ascending: — 2. *laṁ, vaṁ, raṁ, yaṁ, haṁ, oṁ.*

   Utter a long *oṁ* for the *sahasrāra* and the *ājñā, haṁ* for the *viśuddhi, yaṁ* for the *anāhata, raṁ* for the *maṇipūra, vaṁ* for the *svādhiṣṭhāna,* and *laṁ* for the *mūlādhāra*. Repeat the process several times, from the crown to the bottom and from the bottom to the crown.

4. Do *sarvāṅga nyāsa* by the *navārṇa mantra*: *oṁ aiṁ hrīṁ klīṁ cāmuṇḍāyai vicce*. Do the *nyāsa* two times for the front, two times for the back, two times for the right side and two times for the left side of the

body. Start from the top, go down to the feet and start from the feet, go up to the top. Touch the body with the tips of all your fingers including the thumbs of both hands.

5. Touch the superficial part of the body which is affected by the cancer with the ring finger and the thumb in *tattva-mudrā*. This *mudrā* is performed by joining the tips of the ring finger and the thumb of the right hand, the two tips touching the body (*fig.* 3.39). The palm, in *tattva-mudrā*, generally does not face upwards unlike the *varuṇa-mudrā*.

   While touching the cancerous part as described, mentally or whisperingly utter the *cāmuṇḍā-mantra* which is given below:

   oṁ aiṁ hrīṁ klīṁ cāmuṇḍāyai vicce.

   oṁ glauṁ huṁ klīṁ jūṁ saḥ.

   jvālaya jvālaya jvala jvala prajvala prajvala.

   aiṁ hrīṁ klīṁ cāmuṇḍāyai vicce.

   jvala haṁ saṁ laṁ kṣaṁ phaṭ svāhā.

fig. 3.39: *Tattva-mudrā*

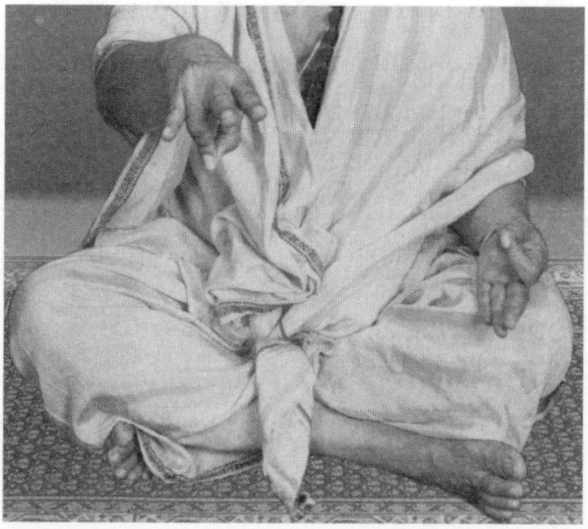

ॐ ऐं ह्रीं क्लीं चामुण्डायै विच्चे ॥
ॐ ग्लौं हुं क्लीं जूं सः
ज्वालय ज्वालय ज्वल ज्वल प्रज्वल प्रज्वल
ऐं ह्रीं क्लीं चामुण्डायै विच्चे
ज्वल हं सं लं क्षं फट् स्वाहा ॥

This *mantra* is to be recited as many times as you can and at any time you like, even without the preliminaries we have given here. When you recite this *mantra*, do the *dhāraṇā* on the cancer-site and the *dhyāna* on the idea that the soldiers of your immune system kill the cancer-cells, devour them and burn them.

6. Your immune system is to be fortified for killing the cancer-cells. For this purpose, practise the *mātṛ-mudrā*, the *liṅga-mudrā*, the *kāma-mudrā*, the *śaṅkha-mudrā* and the *kaṇṭha-mudrā*, preferably with the *khecarī-mudrā*. These *mudrā*s are to be practised twice or thrice a day. Enrich your diet with quality-proteins, vitamins and minerals.

In addition to doing these *mudrā*s, awaken your immune system to be conscious of the fact that the cancer-cells present in your body are potent enemies and that they must be eliminated. For this awakening, take energized water, processed as follows, thrice daily. You may process it and keep it for use for about a week's time. Three tea-spoonfuls of this water thrice a day would be enough.

Take a copper-vessel. Fill it with pure water. Potentiate this water with *mahā-mṛtyuñjaya-mantra* of Śukrācarya. While you recite the *mantra*, the water in the vessel is to be stirred by your right-hand fingers in *tattva-mudrā*. The *mantra* is to be recited 10, 27, 54 or 108 times. If you have less time, stick to the minimum number 10. The *mantra* is quoted here:

oṁ hauṁ oṁ jūṁ oṁ saḥ.
oṁ bhūḥ oṁ bhuvaḥ oṁ svaḥ.
oṁ tryambakaṁ yajāmahe,
sugandhiṁ puṣṭivardhanam,
urvārukamiva bandhanān-
mṛtyormukṣīya mā 'mṛtāt.
oṁ svaḥ oṁ bhuvaḥ oṁ bhūḥ
oṁ saḥ oṁ jūm oṁ hauṁ
oṁ svāhā.

This water, treated thus, is further processed by the following healing *mantra* (*ārogya-mantra*).

oṁ saṁ sāṁ siṁ sīṁ suṁ sūṁ seṁ saiṁ soṁ sauṁ saṁ saḥ.
vaṁ vāṁ viṁ vīṁ vuṁ vūṁ veṁ vaiṁ voṁ vauṁ vaṁ vaḥ.
haṁ saḥ. amṛtavarcase svāhā.

The water is processed by reciting this *mantra* 10 or 27 times.

The *devatā* of both the *mahā-mṛtyuñjaya-mantra* and the healing *mantra* is Rudra-Śiva. One who is an atheist may not try the *japa*-therapy at all. There is little likelihood for him to get any benefit from the *japa-yoga*.

Sos in Yoga-Tantra

In any situation of extreme distress for an individual, family, a social group, a State, the total humanity of the Earth (exobiology is also included for the future), or the total universe, the Tantra has prescribed *japa*s for avoiding imminent calamities or for getting relief from befallen calamities. Here we mention a few of them.

The Japa of Sampuṭa-Mantras

1. *oṁ hrīṁ duṁ durgāyai namaḥ.*
   oṁ jayantī maṅgalā kālī
   bhadrakālī kapālinī,
   durgā kṣamā śivā dhātrī
   svāhā svadhā namo 'stu te.
   oṁ hrīṁ duṁ durgāyai namaḥ.

2. *oṁ hrīṁ duṁ durgāyai namaḥ.*
   oṁ śaraṇāgatadīnārta-
   paritrāṇaparāyaṇe,
   sarvasyārtihare devi
   nārāyaṇi namo 'stu te.
   oṁ hrīṁ duṁ durgāyai namaḥ.

3. *oṁ hrīṁ śrīṁ krīṁ*
   parameśvari kālike
   hrīṁ śrīṁ krīṁ svāhā.

4. *krīṁ krīṁ krīṁ hūṁ hūṁ hrīṁ hrīṁ*
   dakṣiṇe kālike
   krīṁ krīṁ krīṁ hūṁ hūṁ hrīṁ hrīṁ svāhā.

Do the *japa* of any one of these *mantra*s any number of times without counting. Continue the *japa* intermittently at your convenience until things are in order and the situation is normalized. Surrender yourself to Mother Goddess and devoutly do the *japa*. Do not grumble if things do not happen as you wish. Only She knows what is good for you and for the entire cosmos. Remember that even your death may be good for you.

For the Durgā-*mantra*, perform the *mātr̥-mudrā* and for the Kālī-*mantra*, perform the *kleśahā-mudrā*. Adopt the following steps for the practice of the *kleśahā-mudrā*.

Interlock the thumbs of both hands. Place the right thumbtip by the side of the base of the left thumb in front of the left wrist. Fold the four fingertips of the left hand over the back of the right hand to touch the crests or mounds of Mercury and Venus. Keep the four fingers of the right hand straight under the palm of the left hand. This *mudrā*, so far described, is not different from the *kāma-mudrā* which is placed below the navel and with which the *japa* of *klīṁ* is done. The *kleśahā-mudrā* is placed on the forehead with the right-hand palm facing your front side (*fig*. 3.40). The *bīja krīṁ* is used with this *mudrā* for the *japa* of the Kālī-*mantras*.

The Japa of Some other Trāṇa (SOS)-Mantras

1. *krīṁ*. (*Devatā*: Kālī).
2. *oṁ hrīṁ śrīṁ krīṁ parameśvari svāhā*. (*Devatā*: Mother Goddess by any name and form.)

fig. 3.40: *Kleśahā-mudrā*

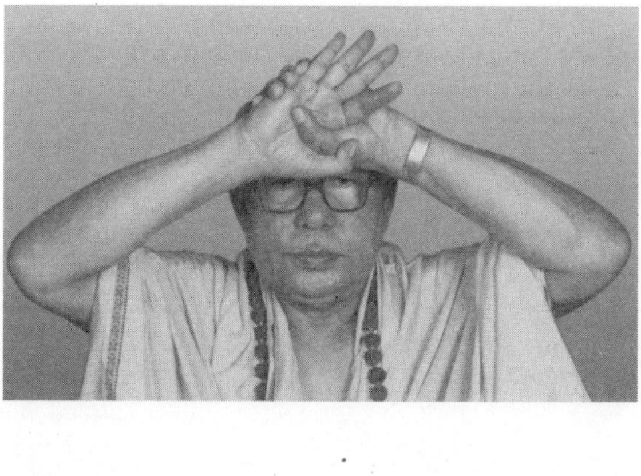

3. *oṁ vaṁ vaṁ vaṁ*
   namo rudrebhyaḥ
   kṣraṁ kṣrāṁ kṣrīṁ
   svāhā. (*Devatā*: Rudra-Śiva).
4. *oṁ kṣīṁ kṣīṁ kṣīṁ kṣīṁ kṣīṁ phaṭ*. (*Devatā*: Your *iṣṭa-devatā*.)
5. *oṁ aiṁ hrīṁ klīṁ cāmuṇḍāyai vicce*. (*Devatā*: Cāmuṇḍā, Caṇḍī, Mother Durgā.)
6. *oṁ aiṁ hrīṁ klīṁ cāmuṇḍāyai vicce.*
   oṁ glauṁ huṁ klīṁ jūṁ saḥ.
   jvālaya jvālaya jvala jvala prajvala prajvala
   aiṁ hrīṁ klīṁ cāmuṇḍāyai vicce.
   jvala haṁ saṁ laṁ kṣaṁ phaṭ svāhā.
   (*Devatā*: Cāmuṇḍā, Caṇḍī, Mother Durgā.)
7. *kṣraum*. (*Devatā*: Nṛsiṁha-Viṣṇu.)
8. *oṁ kṣraum oṁ*. (*Devatā*: Nṛsiṁha-Viṣṇu.)
9. *oṁ haṁ kṣaṁ haṁ saḥ svāhā*. (*Devatā*: Rudra-Śiva.)

For the *japa* of the Śiva-*mantra*, perform the *liṅga-mudrā*. For the Nṛsiṁha-*mantra*, perform the *nakha-vidīrṇa-mudrā* (*fig*. 3.41). For doing this *mudrā*, fold the four fingers of each

fig. 3.41: *Nakha-vidīrṇa-mudrā*

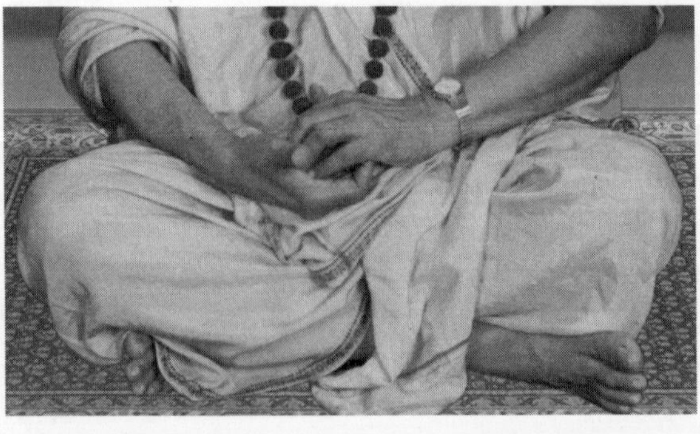

hand at the knuckles, place the four fingertips of the left hand on the Mars' trough of the right hand which should lie below the former, press the left-hand-Mars' trough with the four fingertips of the right hand, separate the two thumbs sideways from the fingers and position the *mudrā* horizontally at the level of the navel. Both the Mars' troughs should feel the piercing pressure.

For the *japa* of any of the *trāṇa-mantras*, do not bother about the formalities. Be yoked to God/Goddess, surrender to him/her unconditionally with unwavering faith and devotion and continue the *japa-kriyā* until your wrecked ship in the tempest is rescued or it sinks with you within it.

Japa for Mukti and Bhukti

The Sanskrit word *mukti* means "release," "liberation," "salvation," "escape from the cycles of metempsychosis." The word *bhukti* means "the enjoyment of the body and the world," "getting sensual pleasure," "sensual indulgence," "living a life, with some material facilities and fulfilment of desires, without pain, calamities, disasters and diseases." Tantra pleads for both *mukti* and *bhukti* whereas some other religious schools lay emphasis on *mukti* only. The latter schools teach to renounce the world and any pleasure in life and to neglect the body. We are in favour of *bhukti* and *mukti* and not of *mukti* only. Of course, our concept of *bhukti* is not equivalent to sensual indulgence or hankering after wealth and power, or neglecting spiritual pursuit. *Tyāga* (sacrifice) and *tapaḥ* (austerities) are components of our *bhukti* which makes attempts to get the basic necessities of life, to get worldly joy and bliss and to avert diseases and calamities that make life miserable and painful. Sāttvic pleasure is part of our *bhukti*.

The philosophy of non-dualism (Advaita Vedānta) has the maximum optimism. Accordingly, nobody is eternally damned. Everything and everybody have essential identity with *Brahman*, although temporarily alientated. The ultimate goal of each manifested entity is to reach the original source and, not to rest in *Brahman*, but to become *Brahman*. A birth or a life is a chance, an opportunity, a supplementary examination for self-purification, for a progress from the domain of darkness to that of light. Home-coming, sooner or later, even for the worst sinner, is a certain truth. Every life is a supplementary examination, and the final pass is a "must." Every suffering is a penance (*prāyaścitta*) which heats gold to remove its impurities. If this idea is fully comprehended and firmly grasped, one makes conscious effort for spiritual ascent to reach the final goal and at the same time one does not neglect this life and this world. If one tries to climb up a wall, one must not neglect the ladder.

Generally, books on *japa-yoga* deal with *mukti*, and most of them favour dualism rather than non-dualism. A very few persons associate *japa* with non-dualism. Our concept of *japa* is a departure from the general trend, however. We have made a blend of dualistic Vedānta, non-dualistic Vedānta, Yoga and Tantra. Non-dualism is the apex of our philosophy. Dualism constitutes the steps to lead to the apex. After reaching the goal, the differences between you and I, this and that, here and there, the past, present and future altogether vanish. But all does not vanish to become an absolute void, an absolute zero. All vanishes to become *tat* (that) which is *sat* (Absolute Existence), Absolute Consciousness and Absolute Bliss.

We do not fully accept the Yoga philosophy which is a modification of the Sāṅkhya, the modification being the recognition of *Īśvara* which is a *special puruṣa* (self) among the innumerable ones. We have a conviction that the Sāṅkhya and the Yoga do not accept a Creator God, the creation of the universe and the cyclic nature of the universe, comprising creation, sustenance and dissolution. They rather accept the eternality of the universe in which individual living beings are created due to the conjunction of the insentient *prakṛti* and an individual *puruṣa* (sentient self). Once the *puruṣa* is embodied and karmic *saṁskāra*s are generated, birth and death become cyclic until the complete separation (*kaivalya*) of these two *tattva*s (principles) is achieved. In spite of our non-acceptance of the Yoga metaphysics, we do accept the yogic techniques and fundamental yogic theories of Patañjali. We have tried to take maximum advantage of *Pātañjala Yoga Darśanam* in presenting our theory and practices of *japa-yoga*.

As we have already indicated, our basic philosophy is non-dualistic. We have made use of the Vedas and the Upaniṣads in our synthetic approach. We feel that the *Bhagavad-Gītā* is a very good source of yogic theories and practices. The *Gītā* is a marvellous and supreme piece of scripture that synthesizes many ancient Indian systems. We have made use of the holistic *yoga* of the *Gītā* in synthesizing our theory.

The Tantra is a Pandora's box which contains the most sublime and the most ignoble ideas and practices. Now it is almost impossible to weed out and purify it. We regard Tantra in high esteem; simultaneously we hate the *vāma-mārga* of the Tantra. In our opinion (which may be totally wrong), today's Tantra is mostly (we don't universalize) a bundle of fraud and savage, primitive practices in the East and bestial sexuality in the West. Tantra is purely a spiritual science which has been adulterated and polluted through the ages by the animality and barbarity of the sensual, wicked. Our *tantra* does not budge even a nanometre from the path of spirituality; it worships only one Mother of the universe and only one Father of the universe (Śakti and Śiva; Śivā and Śiva) in different forms and by different names. Our Tantra has many special methods and techniques to make this life worth living, to get the mercy of the Mother and the Father and to attain to liberation. We have made use of Tantra in our *japa-yoga*.

We hope, our holistic approach would benefit our readers if they try to practise *japa-yoga* in their life. *Sādhanā* is the only key to success in *yoga* and *tantra*.

References

1. N.C. Panda, 2003, *Meditation: Science and Practice*.
2. *BG*, VI.40-45, V.11.
3. *BG*, II.47-48, III.9; III.19; IV.23; V.10-11.
4. *BG*, III.19; IV.21; VI.1.
5. *BG*, II.38, II.48; IV.22; VI.1; VI.7-9.
6. *BG*, II.48, VI.6-7; VI.29; VIII.27.
7. *BG*, VI.29.
8. *BG*, VI.30.
9. *BG*, VI.31.
10. *BG*, VI.32.
11. *BG*, VI.26; VI.33-35.
12. *BG*, VI.35.
13. *BG*, III.30; IV.21; VI.10.

14. *BG*, IV.21; VI.10.
15. N.C. Panda, 1996, *Mind and Supermind*.
16. N.C. Panda, 2003, *Yoga-Nidrā* (*Yogic Trance*): *Theory, Practice and Applications*.
17. *BG*, VII.16.
18. N.C. Panda, 1996, *Mind and Supermind*, pp. 245-60.
19. N.C. Panda, 2003, *Yoga-Nidrā* (*Yogic Trance*): *Theory, Practice and Applications*.
20. N.C. Panda, 2003, *Meditation : Science and Practice*.
21. *Ibid*.
22. N.C. Panda, 2003, *Yoga-Nidrā*.

Glossary

abhiṣeka : 1. Anointing, inaugurating or consecrating by sprinkling water processed by a *mantra*. 2. Religious bathing, ablution. 3. Bathing a deity to whom worship is offered, while chanting a *mantra*.

abhyāsa : Practice.

ācamana : Sipping water that has been made sacred by a *mantra*.

adhomukham : Literally, "faced below." A kind of *mudrā* done before the Gāyatrī-*japa*.

adhyakṣa : Chairperson.

ādhyātmika : Spiritual.

Aditi : 1. The same as *Ākāśa* in the superheated state. 2. Devourer. 3. Boundlessness; immensity; inexhaustible abundance; unimpaired condition; creative power; indeterminate expanse; Mother of shining entities.

Advaita : 1. Non-dual. 2. A non-dualist.

advaita-vāda : The doctrine of non-dualism.

Ādyāśakti : The Primordial Power; the Mother of the universe.

Āgama : Tantra, the knowledge narrated by Lord Śiva to His *Śakti* (Pārvatī or Gaurī); the science directly given by the Lord, God.

agni : 1. The *tattva* of fire or heat in particular and energy in general. 2. Fire.

agni-bīja : The name of the *bīja raṁ*.

agnihotra : Sacrificing to Agni, God who presides in fire and all types of energy.

agra : Front.

agra-sparśī-tāḍāsana : A standing posture, while resting on the tips of the toes.

aham : I.

ahaṅkāra : Ego or egoism; the evolute of *buddhi*.

ahiṁsā : Non-violence in thought, speech and action.

āhuti : Offering; oblation with fire to the deities.

aiṁ : The seed-syllable of Mother Sarasvatī.

ajapā : The unconscious repetition of a *mantra*, without the movement of the lips; the spontaneous repetition of the *mantra so 'haṁ* (He is I); spontaneously uttered and repeated.

ājñā : 1. Command, order. 2. The eyebrow centre in the subtle body.

ākarṣaṇa : 1. Attraction. 2. The *tāntrika* ritual to bring about attraction between two persons.

Ākāśa : Space, the subtlest state of material existence; the subtlest one among the five states of the existence of matter and energy.

ākāśa-bīja : The name of the seed-syllable *haṁ*, the *bīja* of the *viśuddhi cakra*.

ākāśī-mudrā : A kind of gesture, done by the contact of the back of the middle finger and the tip of the thumb.

akṣara : 1. Syllable. 2. Undecaying and imperishable; *Brahman* and *Māyā*.

akula : The *tāntrika* meaning is "Divine Father" or "Śiva."

ālamba : Support.

ālambana : The same as *ālamba*.

amātra : Devoid of *mātrā*, any of the three elements of *AUṀ*, *A, U, Ṁ*.

ambā : Mother.

amṛta : Ambrosia.

amṛta-bīja : The name of the seed-syllable *vaṁ*, the *bīja* of the *svādhiṣṭhāna-cakra*.

anāhata : 1. Unbeaten. 2. The psychic centre in the subtle body at the level of the heart.

anāhata-dhvani : The unbeaten, subtle sound *oṁ*. See *anāhata-nāda*.

anāhata-nāda : The subtle *oṅkāra* sound, produced without being beaten, the sound of the *vīṇā* of Mother Sarasvatī, reflected by all entities of the micro- and the macro-universe.

anāmikā : Ring-finger.

Ānanda : Pure Bliss without the trace of joyfulness and sorrowfulness.

ānanda : 1. Bliss, delight. 2. Experience.

anāsakti : Non-attachment.

aṅga : Limb; organ; part of the body.

aṅguṣṭha : The thumb.

aṇimā : A *siddhi* by which a *yogī* can reduce himself to a micro-size so that he may pass through any obstruction.

añjali : The open hands placed side by side and slightly hollowed.

aṅkura : A sprout; a newly germinated shoot; a tender blade of leaf.

antaḥ/antar : Internal.

antaḥkaraṇa : The subtle, internal organ in which the karmic impressions are printed; its main components are: the *buddhi*, the *ahaṅkāra* and the *manas*.

antarikṣa : 1. The intermediate space between heaven and earth. 2. The intermediate state between *bhūḥ* and *bhuvaḥ* and between *bhuvaḥ* and *svaḥ*.

anuloma-viloma-prāṇāyāma : A kind of *prāṇāyāma* with breathing through alternate nostrils; (*anuloma* = in the direction of the hair; *pratiloma* = against the direction of the hair).

anuṣṭhāna : 1. Performance. 2. Religious practice in conformity with scriptural prescription. 3. The practice of religious austerity, with special reference to *japa*, *kīrtana* or *svādhyāya*.

anuṣṭup : The name of a Vedic metre.

Āpaḥ : The primordial cosmic fluid or plasma, evolved from *Mahat* or *Virāḍ*.

apāna-mudrā : A kind of yogic posture shown by joining the tips of the ring-finger, the middle finger and the thumb.

aparigraha : The non-accumulation of property; the non-acceptance of unearned cash or kind.

araṇi : The lower friction-stick; the lower piece of wood (taken from *Ficus religiosa*) used for kindling fire by attrition.

ardha : A half.

ardha-mukulita : Half-open.

ārogya : Cure; healing.

ārohaṇa : The act of ascending.

arpaṇa : Offering.

ārta : One struck with calamity, fallen into misfortune, or afflicted with physical or mental suffering.

arthārthī : One who hankers after more and more money, wealth, power and prestige.

arūpa : Formless.

āśā : 1. Hope. 2. Expectation of gain from others.

āsakti : Attachment.

āsana : 1. A yogic posture. 2. Something on which one sits.

āśaya : Reservoir.

asmitā : 1. The possession of the experience of "I am." 2. Egocentricity.

āśraya : Shelter.

aṣṭa : Eight.

aṣṭāṅga : Eight limbs.

asteya : Non-stealing.

astra : used in the dative case (*astrāya*) before the mystical syllable *phaṭ* in a *tāntrika mantra*, meaning "Let it work as a weapon, a missile."

aśva : Horse.

aśvattha : Pipal (*Ficus religiosa*).

aśvinī-mudrā : A kind of yogic gesture, in which the muscles of the anal sphincters contract and relax rhythmically, simulating what the horse does.

Ātmā : Self; the universal Self; *Īśvara* or *Brahman*; *Brahman* associated with *Māyā*.

ātmā : The individual self; *Brahman* associated with a created entity.

āvāhana : Invitation; calling.

āvaraṇa : A cover; a veil.

āvaraṇa-pūjā : The *yantra-pūjā*, in Tantra, in a definite sequence of layers in the mystic geometrical diagrams.

avarohaṇa : The act of descending.

avatāra : God-incarnate. The word *avataraṇa* means "to descend."

avidyā : Ignorance; lack of right knowledge.

Avyakta/avyakta : 1. Unmanifest; unmanifested. 2. The unmanifested Primordial Nature, the precursor state of the universe of matter and energy.

avyavahārya : Something that cannot be made use of; not empirical; not phenomenological.

bahiḥ/bahir : External.

bahupadī-mudrā : A kind of gesture in which the upper abdomen is pressed with the fingertips and thumbtips of both hands.

bandha : Any *tāntrika* technique for binding, bonding, obstructing or locking the flow of *Prāṇa*.

basti : 1. A *haṭha-yoga* technique for cleansing the colon and the rectum by the yogic enema. 2. Lower belly. 3. An enema.

bhagavān/bhagavat : God.

bhakti : Devotion.

bhakti-yoga : The yoga of devotion.

bhargaḥ/bhargas : Radiance, lustre, splendour. (Derived from the verb-root √*bhṛj*.)

bhāva : Idea; thought.

bhojana : Eating; a meal.

bhū : 1. The earth. 2. The *tattva* of the *mūlādhāra cakra*. 3. The solid state of matter.

bhū-bīja : 1. The name of the seed-syllable *laṁ*, the *bīja* of the *mūlādhāra*. 2. The name of the *bīja glauṁ*.

bhūḥ : 1. The world, present here and everywhere, which is gross and with four dimensions. 2. God who presides the *bhūḥ* world.

bhujaṅgāsana : The cobra-pose.

bhukti : Attaining something that is desired; the fulfilment of worldly desires.

bhūta : 1. Any of the five states of material existence — solids, liquids, gases, energy and *ākāśa* (space). 2. Any created entity, either living or non-living.

bhūta-śuddhi : Sanctifying the body-elements by special *mantras*.

bhuvaḥ : 1. The world, present here and everywhere, which is subtler than *bhūḥ*, with its specific dimensions. 2. God who presides the *bhuvarlokaḥ*.

bīja : 1. Seed. 2. A mystical seed-syllable in Tantra.

bījākṣara : A seed-syllable.

bindu : 1. A point. 2. Singularity. 3. A point in the subtle body, located half-way between the *brahmarandhra* and the *ājñā*, roughly at the level of the pineal gland.

Brahmā: One and only one God, with reference to His role in creating the universe initially and continually; one of the Hindu Trinity.

brahma-bīja : The name of the seed-syllable *saḥ*.

brahmā-bīja : The name of the seed-syllable *klīṁ*.

brahmacārī : One who practises *brahmacarya*.

brahmacarya : Sex-abstinence for a *saṁnyāsī*; regulated and ethical sex-life for a householder.

brahma-jñāna : Knowledge on *Brahman*.

brāhma-muhūrta : The time at 4:00 a.m. or 4:00 to 6:00 a.m. (*brāhma* = pertaining to *brahma*; *muhūrta* = moment).

Brahman : The formless, attributeless, actionless, unmodifiable, timeless, spaceless, immaterial Reality that is pure Existence, Consciousness and Bliss.

brāhmaṇa : A spiritually enlightened person with knowledge on *Brahman* and realization of *Brahman*.

brahmāṇḍa : 1. The universe; the cosmos; the *viśva* or all (the whole of the existing matter and energy). 2. A galaxy out of the innumerable ones.

brahma-nirvāṇa : The complete merging of the self in *Brahman*, with the concomitant loss of identity of the former and without its being converted into nothing.

brahmānubhūti : The experience of *Brahman*.

brahmarandhra : The apex orifice in the subtle body; the exit-opening in the *suṣumṇā* at the summit of the head.

brāhmī sthiti : The word *brāhmī* is in feminine gender and means "pertaining to *brahma*". The word *sthiti* means "stay" or "situation." The whole expression means "stay in *Brahman* or *Īśvara*."

brahmopalabdhi : The realization of *Brahman*.

Buddhi : Cosmic Intellect; Cosmic Mind; Supermind; *Mahat*; *Virāḍ*; the first evolute whose evolvent is *Māyā* or the *Mūla-Prakṛti*, the unmanifested Primordial Nature.

buddhi : *Buddhi* or the Cosmic Intellect encased in an individual body that serves as an *upādhi*; the individual intellect; a subtle organ for intellection in the *antaḥkaraṇa*.

buddhi-yoga : *Karma-yoga* with con-stant fixation of intellect on God and with an equanimity of mind in both success and failure.

cakra : 1. The wheel; the circle; the vortex; the disc; the discus. 2. Any one of the psychic centres in the subtle body.

cakra-pūjā : 1. The right-path *tāntrika*s' meditation on the *cakra*s and on the deities presiding therein. 2. The left-path *tāntrika*s' worshipping rituals (worshipping the vulva: *yoni-pūjā*), followed by herd or flock coitus in sequential shifts. Undressed women lie on the floor in a circle like spokes in a wheel, with heads towards the centre and faces upward. The *bhairava*s (male *tāntrika*s) do sex-play with the *bhairavī*s (female *tāntrika*s) in rotation.

cakrārcanam : See *cakra-pūjā* of the left-path *tāntrika*s.

cakra-sādhanā : Meditation on the *cakra*s individually and/or serially.

calad-dhāraṇā : *Dhāraṇā* in motion; shifting visualization.

Cāmuṇḍā/Cāmuṇḍī : Mother Durgā in her angry, over-active state.

Caṇḍī : Mother Durgā, with preponderance of *rajas*.

caraṇa : Step.

caturmukham : Literally "four-faced." A kind of *mudrā* done before the Gāyatrī-*japa*.

cetanā : Literally "consciousness." A kind of *mudrā* done after the Gāyatrī-*japa*.

chandaḥ : Any metre of a Vedic *mantra*.

cin-mudrā : The yogic seal made by the contact of the tips of the thumb and the index finger and placed on the knee, with the palms facing upward, for the promotion of consciousness.

Cit : Pure Consciousness.

citta : Mind-stuff; a yogic term for the thinking faculty.

citta-śuddhi : The purification of the *citta* or *buddhi*.

citta-vṛtti : The whirls of mind.

dakṣiṇa : 1. Right side. 2. South.

dakṣiṇācārī : A follower of the

right-path of the Tantra.

dakṣiṇa-mārga : The right path.

dakṣiṇa-mārgī : A follower of the right path of the Tantra.

dala : A petal of any *cakra* of the subtle body.

daridra-nārāyaṇa-sevā : The service to the poor, regarded as if they are gods.

daśa : Ten.

dāsa : Servant.

deva/devaḥ : 1. A god; a male deity. 2. One who is shining, lustrous, resplendent.

deva-gṛha : A private worshipping room in one's residential building.

devālaya : A worshipping place (*deva* = deity; *ālaya* = house); a temple.

devatā : 1. Deity. 2. Somebody who is resplendent.

Devī/devī : A female deity; feminine of *Deva/deva*.

dhāraṇā : A yogic process by which concentration is focused on a spot.

dhātu : Verb-root.

dhauti : A *haṭha-yoga* technique for cleansing the anterior alimentary canal (oesophagus and stomach).

dhenu-mudrā : A kind of tāntric gesture done with fingers.

dhīḥ : Intellect.

dhīmahi : We meditate on (the verb-root being √*dhyai*).

dhiyaḥ : The plural form of *dhīḥ* in the accusative case.

dhūpa : Incense.

dhvani : Sound.

dhyāna : Focusing the attention on a single idea that flows in the mind continuously without interruption.

dhyeya : The idea, thought or object meditated upon.

dik : Direction; dimension.

dīkṣā : The initiation of a disciple by a *guru* with a *mantra*.

dīpa : Lamp.

duṁ : The seed-syllable of Mother Durgā.

dūrbā : A species of grass (*Panicum dactylon*).

Durgā : The Mother Deity who is the combination of Kālī, Lakṣmī and Sarasvatī. The Mother of the universe who dispels calamities and misfortunes.

dvādaśa : Twelve.

dvaita : Dual.

dvaita-vāda : The doctrine of dualism.

dvi : Two.

dvimukham : Literally "two faced." A kind of *mudrā*, done before the Gāyatrī-*japa*.

dvināḍa-paṅkaja-mudrā : The gesture of a lotus with two stalks.

ekāgratā : One-pointedness in concentration.

ekākṣara : Monosyllable (*eka* = one; *akṣara* = syllable).

ekanāḍa : With a single stalk.

ekeśvara-vāda : The doctrine of monotheism.

gaṁ : The seed-syllable of Lord Gaṇeśa.

Gaṇapati : The Lord of all; Lord Gaṇeśa.

gaṇapati-bīja : The name of the seed-syllable *gaṁ*.

gandha : 1. Odour, smell. 2. Sandalwood-paste; its fragrance.

Gaṇeśa : The Lord of all. The icon of the deity is pot-bellied, with an elephant-head.

Gaurī : The Power or Consort of Rudra-Śiva.

gāyati : Sings.

Gāyatrī : 1. Mother Sarasvatī, the Consort of Brahmā; the Divine Mother who sings and plays her *vīṇā*, who produces the *oṅkāra* vibrations that generate the Supermind (*Virāḍ* or *Buddhi*) and the universe therefrom. This word has been derived from the verb-root, √*gai*, meaning "to sing." 2. A specific metre, containing 24 syllables of some Vedic *mantra*s.

ghī : A word derived from the Sanskrit word *ghṛta*, meaning "dehydrated and clarified butter."

ghṛta : The same as *ghī*.

glauṁ : The seed-syllable of Lord Gaṇeśa.

gomukhī : A specially made small cloth-bag, hung from the neck, used for concealing the rosary while counting *japa*.

gopī : The lady of the ancient Indian town, Gopa, where cow-husbandry was the vocation of the inhabitants.

Govinda : One of the names of Lord Viṣṇu.

graha : Planet.

grahaṇa : The subtle, mental, internal organs of perception.

grahītā : The perceiver or the self.

grāhya : Something which is perceivable.

grathitam/grathitā mudrā : A kind of gesture done before the Gāyatrī-japa.

gṛhastha : A householder.

guda : Anus.

guhya : To be covered or concealed or hidden or kept secret; concealable, private part of the body.

guṇa : 1. Strand or string. 2. Attribute, property or quality. 3. Any of the three strings — *sattva, rajas* or *tamas*.

guru : 1. Spiritual preceptor. 2. Teacher.

gurvī : 1. The wife of the *guru* (*guru-mātā*). 2. The spiritual partner of the *guru*. 3. A female spiritual preceptor.

haṁ : The seed-syllable of Lord Sadāśiva; the *bīja* of *ākāśa tattva;* the *bīja* of the *viśuddhi cakra*.

haṁ saḥ : 1. *Ahaṁ saḥ* (I am He; I am God; I am *Brahman*). 2. *Haṁsaḥ*, as one word, means "a goose or a swan."

Hanumat/Hanumān : 1. The word *hanu* means "cheek or jaw." The word *hanumān* literally means "one having (large) jaws." 2. Hanumān of the *Rāmāyaṇa* is the great devotee of Lord Rāma.

Hari : Derived from the verb-root √*hṛ*, meaning "to take away or remove evil, sin, sorrows and calamities;" one of the names of Lord Viṣṇu or Kṛṣṇa.

hasta-ṭaṅka-mudrā : (The word *hasta* means "hand" and *ṭaṅka* means "a hatchet" or "a stamped coin"). It is a kind of *mudrā*, in the shape of a hatchet, shown by the two hands.

haṭha-yoga : The word *haṭha* means "force," "forcibly," "rigorous." *haṭha-yoga* is a system of Yoga which prescribes rigorous discipline to yoke the body.

hauṁ : The seed-syllable of Lord Śiva.

havana : Oblation in a fire-sacrifice.

haviṣyānna : Rice cooked with more milk, a little *ghī* and just enough raw sugar, eaten only once a day at noon or in the afternoon.

hiṁsā : Violence — mental, verbal or physical.

homa : The act of making an oblation to the gods by casting dehydrated, clarified butter into the fire.

hṛd : 1. The seat of feeling and emotion. 2. The seat of thought and intellectual operation. 3. The heart. 4. The *anāhata cakra*.

hṛdaya : See *hṛd*.

hrīṁ : 1. The seed-syllable of Mother Gaurī. 2. The seed-syllable of any Divine Mother.

huṁ : A mystical seed-syllable uttered in *mantra*s for protection. It is the *kavaca-bīja* (the *bīja* for protection).

hūṁ : The same as *huṁ*, but with greater force.

iḍā : The subtle lunar channel on the left of the *suṣumṇā* for the flow of *Prāṇa*.

indriya : The sensory and motor subtle organs, present in the subtle body.

iṣṭa : Wished, desired, liked, cherished.

iṣṭa-deva : The chosen, tutelary male deity.

iṣṭa-devatā : A chosen, tutelary deity; favourite god/ goddess; one particularly worshipped (male or female).

iṣṭa-devī : A chosen, tutelary female deity.

Īśvara : One who rules or controls; Almighty God who controls the universe.

Īśvara-praṇidhāna : Stay in God; complete absorption in God.

Īśvarī : Goddess; the Consort of God; *Māyā*.

jāgarita/jāgrata : Waking.

jalam : 1. Water. 2. The liquid state of matter.

janaḥ : 1. The world, present here and everywhere, with its specific subtlety and dimensions. 2. God who presides over the world of *janaḥ*.

jānu : Knee.

jānu-vṛtta : Patella.

japa : The silent, humming or vocal repetition of a *mantra* or God's name.

japa-thalī : See *gomukhī*.

jaya : Victory.

jijñāsu : One desirous of knowing.

jīva : An individual living being; an individual self.

jīvanmukta : Liberated, albeit still living with a body.

jīvātmā : An individual self.

jñāna : Knowledge.

jñāna-mudrā : The gesture of knowledge; the same as the *cin-mudrā*, except the palms facing downward.

jñāna-yoga : The *yoga* of *Brahma*-knowledge; the *yoga* of the realization of the Self.

jñānī : A highly enlightened person; a person with *Brahma*-realization.

ka/kaḥ : 1. See *Āpaḥ* or *Nāra*. 2. Hiraṇyagarbha or Brahmā.

kaivalya : A Sāṅkhya Yoga word for liberation which involves a complete disassociation (separation) of a *puruṣa* (individual self) from *Prakṛti* and the subsequent stay of the former in isolation in a higher realm, without further rebirth.

Kālī : The Power or Consort of Rudra-Śiva. The word is derived from *kāla* (time). She creates time when the universe is born and dissolves it in the total dissolution. She annihilates everything continually and finally. She is the same as Mother Gaurī with changes in form, colour and attributes.

Kālikā : See "Kālī."

Kāliśī : A worshipper who deifies his organs, tissues and cells and temporarily plays the role of the deity.

kāma : Wish, desire, longing.

kāma-bīja : The name of the *bīja* *klīṁ* and also of *laṁ*.

Kamalā : Mother Lakṣmī.

kāma-mudrā : A kind of *tāntrika* gesture, with which the seed-syllable *klīṁ* is uttered.

kāmanā : Desire.

kampana : Trembling, tremor.

kanda : 1. A bulb or tuber. 2. The source.

kaniṣṭhikā : The little finger.

kaṇṭha : Throat.

kaṇṭha-mudrā : A kind of gesture by which the throat is pressed.

kapālabhāti : A *haṭha-yoga* technique for cleansing the sinuses in the frontal portion of the head.

kara : Hand.

karamālā : The fingers of the right hand used as a rosary for counting any *japa*.

kāraṇa-śarīra : The causal body.

kara-pārśva-mudrā : A kind of gesture with the hands brought into contact at the sides of the little fingers and the lunar mounds.

karapṛṣṭha : The back of the hand.

karatala : Palm.

karma : 1. Action. 2. Mental prints of ideas resulting from actions and thoughts, otherwise called *saṁskāra*s.

karmāśaya : The reservoir of *karma*s; a subtle structure located in the subtle and the causal bodies to store *saṁskāra*s, including *vāsanā-saṁskāra*s.

karma-vāda : The doctrine of *karma*.

karma-yoga : The *yoga* of action, without attachment to the fruits thereof.

karṇa : Ear.

kaula-mārga : The path pertaining to *kula*.

kavaca : 1. Armour. 2. Any covering or jacket. 3. Anything inscribed with mystical words and carried about as an amulet. 4. A mystical syllable (such as *huṁ* or *hūṁ*) forming part of a *mantra* used as an amulet.

kha : *Ākāśa* or Space.

khecarī-mudrā : The tongue-lock seal.

kīlaka : 1. A bolt, wedge. 2. The inner cohesive force of a *mantra*.

kīrtana : Loud, rhythmic repetition of the name of God/Goddess, individually or in a group, generally with instrumental music.

kleśa : Affliction.

kleśahā-mudrā : A *tāntrika* gesture, shown while doing the *japa* of Kālī-*mantra*s, for avoiding or getting rid of calamities and afflictions.

klīṁ : The seed-syllable of Brahmā and also of any Divine Mother.

kothalī : See *gomukhī*.

kṛcchra : 1. Causing trouble or pain. 2. Bodily mortification, austerity, penance.

krīṁ : The seed-syllable of Mother Kālī.

kriyā : 1. Action. 2. A yogic or *tāntrika* technique.

kriyā-yoga : The *yoga* of *tapaḥ*, *svādhyāya* and *Īśvara-praṇidhāna*.

krodha : Anger.

krodha-bīja : The name of the *bīja* *huṁ*.

Kṛṣṇa : A celebrated *Avatāra* (God-Incarnate) of Viṣṇu, or Viṣṇu himself, born to Vasudeva and Devakī.

kṣraum : The *bīja* of Lord Nṛsiṁha.

kuja-mudrā : A kind of gesture, in which the fingertips press the Mars' troughs while both the fists are in contact.

kukṣī : Belly.

kula : A tāntric word, meaning "Divine Mother" or "Śakti."

kulīra-mudrā : *Kulīra means* "a crab." This *mudrā* is a gesture, in which the middle part of each sole is pressed by the fingernails of the respective hand in sequential spacings.

kumārī-pūjanam (*pūjā*) : The worship of Kumārī (Mother Durgā), performed by a ceremony on the occasion of the Durgā festival, when a girl between ten and twelve years old is placed on a pedestal as the representative of the Mother.

kumbhaka : The retention of breath.

kumbhaka-rahita : Without retention of breath.

kuṇḍala : 1. A ring-structure. 2. A coil.

Kuṇḍalinī : The Mother of the universe who dormantly rests in the *mūlādhāra-cakra* in the form of serpentine coils.

Kuṇḍalinī-Yoga : A highly specialized Yoga-school of the Tantra, concerned with *cakra*-meditation and the ascent and descent of Mother Kuṇḍalinī.

kūrcam : The mystical syllable *hūṁ* or *hrūṁ*.

kūrmaḥ : Literally a tortoise or a turtle. It is a kind of *mudrā* done before the Gāyatrī-*japa*.

lākh : An Indian number for 100,000.

lakṣa : The Sanskrit word for the Hindi *lākh* (100,000).

Lakṣmī : The Power or Consort of Viṣṇu. She nourishes the universe.

laṁ : The *bīja* of the *mūlādhāra cakra*, of the *pṛthvī tattva*.

likhita : Written.

liṅga : 1. Phallus. 2. The symbol of the Father of the universe. 3. Subtle.

liṅga-mudrā : The phallus gesture or seal, shown while doing the *japa* of the *mantra*s of Rudra-Śiva.

loka : 1. World. 2. Any one of the seven worlds: *bhūḥ*, *bhuvaḥ*, *svaḥ*, *mahaḥ*, *janaḥ*, *tapaḥ*, *satya*.

madya : Liquor; any intoxicating, alcoholic drink.

madhya : Middle.

madhyamā : The middle finger.

mahā : Mega; great.

mahaḥ : 1. The world, present here and everywhere, subtler than *svaḥ*, with its specific dimen-sions. 2. God who presides over the world of *mahaḥ*.

mahākrāntam : A kind of *mudrā* done before the Gāyatrī-*japa*.

Mahāmāyā : The Great *Māyā*, the Mother of the universe.

Maharṣi : A great seer.

Mahat : The Great; the Sāṅkhya equivalent of the Vedic *Virāḍ*; the first evolute evolved from *Prakṛti* or the Primordial Nature; the Cosmic Intellect; the Cosmic Mind or Supermind.

mahā-vyāhṛti : The three great *vyāhṛti*s; the three mystical utterances — *bhūḥ*, *bhuvaḥ*, *svaḥ*, personified as the daughters of Sāvitrī, Gāyatrī or Sarasvatī.

Maheśvara : 1. The Great Lord (God). 2. Rudrā-Śiva of the Hindu Trinity.

Mahimā : A *siddhi* (perfection) by which a *yogī* enlarges his body in any direction and dimension.

maithuna : Coitus, sexual intercourse; cohabitation; the intimate union of two.

makarāsana : A yogic posture; the crocodile pose.

mālā : 1. Rosary. 2. Garland.

māṁsa : Meat.

manas : 1. Mind in general. 2. An evolute of *ahaṅkāra*, involved in the coordination of sensory and motor functions.

mānasa : Mental.

mānasika : Mental, silent.

maṇḍala : A kind of mystical diagram used in invoking a deity; a *yantra*.

maṇipūra : The psychic centre in the navel region of the subtle body.

mantra : Derived from the Sanskrit verb-root √*man*, meaning "to think;" an instrument of thought.

marā : A corpse (derived from the verb-root √*mṛ*, meaning "to die").

māraṇa : The left-path *tāntrika* ritual to kill a person.

mārjana : 1. Wiping impurities off the body and the mind by sprinkling *mantra*-processed water on the body. 2. Purification by sprinkling or pouring water, while chanting *mantra*s. 3. Bathing a deity by sprinkling water.

mātā : Mother.

mātrā : 1. Measure. 2. Constituent units of a syllable or a word; a letter.

mātṛkā : 1. Mother. 2. Divine Mother. 3. Source, origin. 4. Any character of the Devanāgarī alphabet, written in *maṇḍala*s or *yantra*s, or imprinted on the petals of the six subtle *cakra*s.

mātṛ-mudrā : A kind of tāntric *mudrā*.

matsya : Fish.

matsyaḥ : Literally "fish." A kind of *mudrā*, done before the Gāyatrī-*japa*.

mauna : Silence.

Māyā : The Power of *Brahman*/*Īśvara*, the Primordial Nature or *Mūla-Prakṛti*; the Mother of the manifested universe/Nature, made up of matter and energy.

māyā-bīja : The name of the *bīja hrīṁ*.

māyā-mudrā : The same as the *mātṛ-mudrā*.

meru : 1. Pole. 2. The central bead, larger than the others, in a rosary. It is not crosed while counting. 3. Spine.

meru-agra-vakrāsana : A posture in a sitting position, in which the spine makes a convexity toward the front.

meru-pārśva-vakrāsana : A posture in which the spine is curved to the sides — right and left.

Mīmāṁsā : A philosophical school of ancient India. It gives importance on Vedic rituals; does not need God to explain cosmology; adheres to the concept of the steady-state-universe; and upholds the eternality of the Vedic words.

Mīmāṁsaka : A philosopher of the Mīmāṁsā School.

mīna : Fish.

mokṣa : Liberation; salvation; emancipation; release from bondage.

mṛga-mudrā : A tāntric *mudrā*, shown in the *japa* of *mantra*s or Rudra-Śiva.

*mṛtyuhara-bīja*s : Literally, the seed-syllables that remove death; they are *jūṁ saḥ*.

Mṛtyuñjaya : 1. God who conquers death. 2. God who protects a person from the danger of death. 3. Lord Rudra-Śiva.

mudgaram : Literally, a hammer, mallet, any hammer-like weapon or implement. A kind of *mudrā* done before the Gāyatrī-*japa*.

mudrā : 1. Coitus; sexual intercourse; coital postures. 2. Parched or fried grain. 3. A seal. 4. A symbolic gesture. 5. Mystical gestures shown in Yoga, Tantra and Hindu religious rituals.

mukha : Face.

mukta : Released; liberated.

mukti : Release or liberation from bondage; the release of the self; salvation.

mukulita : Fully open.

mūla : Base; root.

mūlabandha : The basal lock; a yogic *bandha* in which the muscles of the lower abdomen are pulled backward and upward.

mūlādhāra : The psychic centre which is the base or foundation; the lowest psychic centre of the subtle body, located two fingers above the anus and two fingers below the genital.

Mūla-Prakṛti : The Primordial Nature; the Unmanifest Power of *Brahman/Īśvara*.

mūrdhan : 1. The highest part; top; summit. 2. The topmost part in the roof the mouth.

mūrti : Idol; icon; image; picture; form.

muṣṭikam/muṣṭika-mudrā : A kind of *mudrā*, done before the Gāyatrī-*japa* (*Muṣṭika* = a fist).

muṣṭi-mudrā : A tāntric gesture with the fist, shown in the *japa* of Rudra-*mantra*s.

nābhi : Navel; umbilicus.

nāda : 1. A loud sound. 2. Any sound or tone, low or high.

nāḍī : A network of subtle channels in the subtle body for the flow of *Prāṇa*.

naivedya : Food-items offered to a deity during worship.

nakha-vidīrṇa-mudrā : A kind of tāntric gesture for chanting Nṛsiṁha-*mantras*.

nāma : Name.

namaḥ : Paying obeisance.

Nāra : The same as *Āpaḥ*.

Nārāyaṇa : Lord Viṣṇu; God who reclines in *Nāra* (*Āpaḥ* or the subtle Cosmic Fluid).

nāsāpuṭa : Nostril.

nāstika : An atheist.

nauli : A *haṭha-yoga* technique for massaging and strengthening the abdominal organs.

nava : Nine.

navākṣara : Nine-syllabled.

navārṇa : Nine-syllabled.

neti : A *haṭha-yoga* technique for cleansing the nasal passage.

netra : Eye.

netratraya : Three eyes. The two gross eyes and the third intuitive eye at the *ājñā cakra*.

nidhāna : A receptacle; a shelter.

nidrā : Sleep.

Nigama : 1. The Vedic scriptures. 2. What has been deduced. 3. What has come from the very source during meditation.

nīlakaṇḍhī-mudrā : A tāntric seal or gesture associated with *makarāsana*.

nirāśī : One who does not expect anything from others.

nirvāṇa : The act of being extinguished.

nirvāṇa-mudrā : A kind of *mudrā* done after the Gāyatrī-*japa*.

niṣkāma : Without desires; without worldly desires; without any desire other than liberation.

niṣṭhā : Sincerity with firmness and steadfastness; steadfast adherence.

nivṛtti-mārga : The path of self-abnegation and renunciation of worldly pleasure and attachment.

niyama : 1. The performance of actions prescriptive in *yoga*. 2. Rules.

Nṛsiṁha : 1. Literally, it means "man-lion" (*nṛ* = man; *siṁha* = lion). 2. Viṣṇu in his fourth *avatāra* (incarnation) with a hybrid form — partly human and partly lion.

nyāsa : The mental appropriation or assignment of various

parts of the body to *mātṛkās* and deities.

oṁ : The sacred monosyllable of the Hindus, designating *Īśvara/Brahman*; the primal vibration, *oṁ*, produced by the strings of the *vīṇā* of Mother Sarasvatī.

oṅkāra : The sound of *oṁ*; the *praṇava*.

pada : 1. Part of speech. 2. Footstep. 3. Foot.

pāda : 1. A quarter. 2. Foot.

pādāgni-mudrā : The same as the *kulīra-mudrā*.

pāda-ṭaṅka-mudrā : A kind of standing gesture, in which the mounds behind the toes are pressed.

padmāsana : A meditational, yogic posture known as the lotus-pose.

pālana : 1. Observance. 2. Nourishment; sustenance; protection.

pallavam : 1. A kind of *mudrā* done before the Gāyatrī-*japa*. 2. A sprout, shoot, twig, bud, blossom.

pañca : Five.

pañca-makāra : The five M's: *madya* (liquor), *māṁsa* (meat), *matsya* (fish), *mudrā* (coital pose) and *maithuna* (coitus), practised by the left-path *tāntrikas*.

pañcamakārārcanam : The *pañca-makāra-pūjā* of the left-path-*tāntrikas*.

pañcamukham : A kind of *mudrā* done before the Gāyatrī-*japa*. Literally, it means "five-faced."

pañcamukhī-mudrā : A kind of gesture shown in the *japa* of the *mantras* of Rudra-Śiva.

pañcopacāra : Five types of offering to a deity while worshipping (*gandha, puṣpa, dhūpa, dīpa, naivedya*).

paṅkaja-mudrā : A kind of *mudrā* done after the Gāyatrī-*japa* (*paṅkaja* = lotus).

Paramātmā : The Supreme Self; The Universal Self; God.

Parameśvara : The Great Lord; The Supreme Ruler/Controller; God.

Parameśvarī : The Consort or Power of *Parameśvara*.

parigraha : Propensity for the accumulation of more and more wealth; the acceptance of un-earned kind or cash.

parikalpanā : Imagination; conception.

pārsṇi-mudrā : A gesture of standing on the heels.

pārśva : Side.

parva/parvan : An internode.

paścimottānāsana : A yogic pose in which the back-muscles of the body are stretched. *Paścima* means "west." Here it means "the back of the body."

paśutva : Animality.

Pātañjala : Pertaining to Patañjali.

patra : Leaf.

pavana-muktāsana : A kind of yogic posture by which the colonic gases are expelled.

pāyasānna : Rice cooked with milk (*pāyasa* = pertaining to milk; anna = food).

pāyu : The anus.

phala : Fruit.

phaṭ : A mystical syllable used in incantations for paying obeisance.

piṇḍa : 1. The body. 2. A roundish lump of food. 3. Any round or roundish mass or heap.

piṇḍadā-mudrā : A kind of gesture which helps cardiac health.

piṅgalā : The subtle channel on the right of the *suṣumṇā* for the flow of *Prāṇa*.

pīṭha-pūjā : The word *pīṭha* means (1) "a seat," (2) "any one of 51 spots of religious temples of the Hindus." In Tantra, the *pīṭha-pūjā* is done by invoking deities on certain spots on the *yantra* and worshipping them there.

pracud : To inspire.

pradhāna : A substitute word for the Sāṅkhya *Prakṛti*.

prājña : The third quarter of *oṁ*; the state of the Self, active in the condition of deep sleep.

Prakṛti/prakṛti : 1. Unmanifested, insentient Nature of the Sāṅkhya; the evolvent of the world-evolute. 2. The totality of the world-stuff that is the product of the unmanifested Primordial Nature.

pralambam : A kind of *mudrā* done before the Gāyatrī-*japa*. The word literally means "hanging down," "pendent," "pendulous."

pramadā-pūjanam : Worshipping Mother Kālī in posture and gesture of protruding her tongue and vigorously dancing delightfully on the chest of Lord Śiva.

Prāṇa : An all-pervasive subtle substance that is the precursor of all the four fundamental forces and all forms of energy; it is the activating or energising principle; it is an evolute of *Āpaḥ*; it is the primal super-unified force and energy.

prāṇa : 1. The *Prāṇa* that dwells in the *anāhata cakra* and functions in the chest area in inhalation and generally in all areas in absorptive activities.

prāṇa-mudrā : A kind of gesture with the tips of the little finger, ring-finger and thumb.

praṇava : The same as *oṁ*.

prāṇāyāma : The yogic process of breath-control through which *Prāṇa* is collected, stored, restrained and harnessed (*Āyāma* = Stretching, extending, restraining, expansion).

praṇidhāna : Full stay, complete absorption; giving whole attention to; profoundly meditating upon.

praṇu : The same as *praṇava*.

prapañcopaśama : The cessation of the entire universe which is resolved into the fourth state of the Self.

prārabdha karma : The *karma* already initiated for fruition in this life.

prārthanā : Prayer.

prasāda-bīja : The name of the seed-syllable *haum*.

praśānta: Calm; serene; deeply peaceful; totally undisturbed.

pratīka : A symbol.

pratyāhāra : The withdrawal of the subtle senses into the *citta* or *buddhi*.

pravāla : Red coral.

pravṛtti-mārga : The path of propensities for worldly pleasure and possession.

prāyaścitta : Penance.

pṛṣṭha : Back.

pṛthivī/pṛthvī : 1. The earth. 2. The solid state of matter.

pṛthvī-bīja : The seed-syllable *laṁ*; also known as the *dharā-bīja*.

pṛthvī-mudrā : A yogic gesture shown by joining the tips of the little-finger and the thumb, facing upward.

pūjā : Worship.

pūraka : The filling of the lungs

by inhalation in the process of *prāṇāyāma*.

purāṇa : The Hindu mythology.

puras : In front; in advance; forward.

puraścaraṇa : 1. Rites preparatory or introductory to the actual tāntric *pūjā* and *mantra-japa*. 2. The tāntric *puraścaraṇa* comprises five components, namely, *mantra-japa, havana, tarpaṇa, mārjana* and *brāhmaṇa-bhojana*, which are post-*pūjā*. These two meanings and usages are different.

puraścaraṇa-japa : The repetition of a *mantra* as many times as the number of syllables contained in the *mantra*, multiplied with 100,000.

puruṣa : 1. The sentient spirits, innumerable in number, in Sāṅkhya and *Pātañjala Yoga*. 2. The self or the *ātmā* in the Vedānta. 3. The Universal Self, written with a capital P (*Puruṣa*).

puṣpa : Flower.

Rādhā : The name of a celebrated cowherdess or Gopī, beloved by Kṛṣṇa, the *āhlādinī Śakti* (gladdening or delighting Power) of Kṛṣṇa; the incarnation of Mother Lakṣmī.

rāga : Passion; vehement desire for material gain, power and sensual pleasure.

rajas : The string or strand of activity and motion.

rakta candan : Red sandalwood.

raṁ : The *bīja* of the *maṇipūra cakra* and that of *agni-tattva*.

Rāma : The incarnation of Lord Viṣṇu as the son of Daśaratha and Kauśalyā.

recaka : The exhalation of air from the lungs in the process of *prāṇāyāma*.

ṛṣi : A seer; a hermit; a saint.

Rudra : One and only one God who continually and finally annihilates the whole or part of the universe; one of the Hindu Trinity.

rudra-bīja : The name of the seed-syllable *hauṁ/hrauṁ*.

rudrākṣa : Seeds of *Elaeocarpue gannitrus*, used for making rosary.

śabda : 1. Word. 2. Sound. 3. Noise.

śabda-brahma : The universe manifested out of *oṁ*, the *nāda*, the primeval vibration.

śabdapūrvā : The word (*oṁ*) that precedes the creation.

Saccidānanda : Existence, Consciousness and Bliss; *Brahman*.

sad (*sat*) : Good.

sādhaka : A sincere, arduous, spiritual practitioner.

sādhanā : Sincere, arduous practice to gain perfecton.

saḥ : 1. He. 2. The *bīja* that designates *Īśvara/Brahman*.

sahasrāra : The thousand-petalled lotus; the seventh and highest subtle centre in the subtle body where Lord Śiva sits.

sakāma : With desires for worldly gains.

śakaṭam : A kind of *mudrā* done before the Gāyatrī-*japa*. The word literally means "a cart."

śākta : A worshipper or devotee of *Śakti*, the Divine Mother.

Śakti/śakti : 1. Power. 2. Consort. 3. The symbol of the Mother of the universe. 4. A female deity.

śakti-bīja : The name of the seed-syllable *hrīṁ*.

śakti-mudrā : A tāntric gesture with both fists, shown in the *japa* of the *mantra*s of Rudra-Śiva.

śaktipāta : Fall or transfer of spiritual power from a *guru* to a disciple.

śalabhāsana : A yogic *āsana* called the locust pose.

samādhi : The supreme yogic state devoid of thoughts, forms attributes, functions, dualities, pluralities and material existence in the mind; complete union or identification with *Brahman*; the yogic state in which the *buddhi* is completely absorbed in the self or Self.

samāna-mudrā : A kind of gesture of the hand with the tips of the four fingers and thumbs joined together.

samāna-nābhi-mudrā : A kind of gesture in which both hands in *samāna-mudrā* press the navel region.

samarpaṇa : Offering.

sammohana : A tāntric ritual to delude, infatuate or stupefy a person.

samprajñāta : 1. Distinguished, discerned, accurately known. 2. A *yogī*, in *samādhi*, who is still in a state of consciousness.

samprajñāta samādhi : A type of preliminary *samādhi*, in

which the consciousness of the *grāhya*, the *grahaṇa* and the *grahītā* does persist, and in which *vitarka*, *vicāra*, *ānanda* and *asmitā* operate.

sampuṭa : Literally, a hemispherical bowl.

sampuṭam : A kind of *mudrā* done before the Gāyatrī-*japa*.

sampuṭīkaraṇa : Enveloping or covering a nucleus-*mantra* with seed-syllables or with a *nāma-mantra*.

saṁśayavādin : A doubter.

saṁskāra : Karmic impressions printed in the *karmāśaya*.

saṁskāra-piṇḍa : The totality of the *saṁskāra*s imprinted in the *karmāśaya*.

saṁyama : *Dhāraṇā*, *dhyāna* and *samādhi*, done together.

sañcālana : Circulation; free flow; free motion.

sañcita karma : *karma-saṁskāra*s accumulated in the *karmāśaya* in the past lives.

sandhyā : The junction between two six-hour periods of a day of 24 hours (6 a.m., 12 noon, 6 p.m., 12 midnight).

sāndhya : 1. Pertaining to a junction. 2. Occult. 3. With apparent ambiguity in meaning.

saṅga : Attachment.

saṅga-varjita : One who has given up attachment; a detached person.

saṅkalpa: 1. A mental or verbal expression of the objective of a ritual, addressed to the deity. 2. A strong determination to get something done.

saṅkalpāyana : A yogic technique through which a resolve is introduced to the Unconscious; a yogic technique of auto-suggestion while in a state of yogic trance.

Śaṅkara : One who is benevolent; one who does good; Lord Śiva; *śam* + *kara* = *śaṅkara* (*śam* = good, auspicious; *kara* = to do).

śaṅkha-mudrā : A kind of *mudrā* with the hands that simulate the shape of a conch (*śaṅkha* = conch).

Sāṅkhya : An ancient school of Indian philosophy of dualism that accepts a single, insentient *pradhāna* or *prakṛti* and multiple, sentient *puruṣa*s. It is the most ancient philosophy of evolution.

ṣaṇmukham : A kind of *mudrā* done before the Gāyatrī-*japa* (*ṣaṭ* = six; *mukha* = face).

sannyāsī/saṁnyāsī : An ascetic; one who has renounced the usual worldly life.

śānta : Peaceful.

śāntiḥ : Peace.

śāntikarma : The tāntric ritual for peace, prosperity and avoidance of calamities.

santoṣa : Contentment.

sapta : Seven.

sarala-nāsā-śodhana-kriyā : A technique for the easy cleansing of nasal passages.

śaraṇam : Shelter; refuge.

sāraṅga-mudrā : See *mṛga-mudrā*.

saras : The flow of a fluid.

Sarasvatī : The Power or Consort of Brahmā, the creator God; Mother Creatrix; the Goddess of knowledge and wisdom.

śarīra : Body.

sarvajña : Omniscient.

sarvāṅga : All limbs of the body.

sarvatobhadramaṇḍala : A special *maṇḍala* or *yantra* used in certain Hindu worships.

sarveśvara : The controller and ruler of all.

ṣaṭ : Six.

Sat : Existence (derived from the verb-root √*as*, meaning "is," "to exist").

ṣaṭkarma : 1. The six purificatory actions of *haṭha-yoga*, viz., *neti, dhauti, nauli, basti, kapālabhāti* and *trāṭaka*. 2. The six rituals of Tantra, viz., *śāntikarma, vaśīkaraṇa, vidveṣaṇa, stambhana, uccāṭana* and *māraṇa*.

sattva : The string or strand of goodness and purity.

satya : 1. That which exists. 2. Truth; truthfulness. 3. The world, present here and everywhere, subtlest among the seven worlds, with its specific dimensions. 4. God who presides over the *satya-loka*.

satya-loka : The seventh and the final realm which is finest in subtlety among the seven worlds.

śauca : Cleanliness of body, mind, speech and environment.

śavāsana : The corpse-pose, a *yogāsana*.

Savitā : 1. The creator of the

universe. This word is mascu-line in gender and derived from the verb-root √*sū*, meaning to produce (*sū* + *tṛc* = *savitā*); 2. Our sun, the source of all the planets of our solar system.

Sāvitrī : Mother Sarasvatī, the Mother Creatrix. This word has been derived from the verb-root √*sū*, meaning "to beget, procreate, bring forth, bear, produce, yield." It is feminine in gender.

śāyana : Supine; pertaining to the lying position.

śeṣopacārāḥ : The rest of the rituals.

siddha : Perfected.

siddhāsana : A meditational posture known as the accomplished pose.

siddhi : 1. Perfection. 2. The action of exhibiting supernormal power. 3. The exhibition of miracles.

śikhā : 1. The crown of the head. 2. Peak, summit, pinnacle. 3. A tuft or lock of hair on the crown of the head.

siṁhākrāntam : A kind of *mudrā* done before the Gāyatrī-*japa*. This word literally means "attacked by a lion".

śiras : Head.

Sītā : The wife of Lord Rāma; the incarnation of Lakṣmī.

Śiva : God, the auspicious and benevolent Lord; the Father of the universe.

śiva : Benign; auspicious; benevolent.

Śivā : The Consort or Power of Lord Śiva; the Mother of the universe.

Śiva-Śakti : The Power and the Possessor of Power; the auspicious, benevolent Father of the universe and His Consort, the Mother of the universe.

śivo 'ham : I am Śiva; I am God; I am *Brahman*.

śloka : Verse; a scriptural verse.

smārta : Pertaining to *smṛti* or the Purāṇas (mythology).

smṛti : 1. Memory. 2. The Purāṇas.

so 'haṁ : He is I (*saḥ* = he; *ahaṁ* = I).

spandana : Vibration; pulsation.

sphaṭika : Quartz crystal.

sphoṭa : The eternal word or *śabda* that stands for *Brahman* in the philosophy of grammar of Bhartṛhari.

sraṣṭā : Creator (God).

sraṣṭrī : Creator (Goddess); the feminine form of *sraṣṭā*.

śravaṇendriya : The subtle, sensory organ of audition.

śrī : Light, lustre, radiance, splendour, glory, beauty, grace, loveliness.

śrīṁ : The *bīja* of Mother Lakṣmī.

Śrividyā : A special school of Tantra in which Mother Lalitā, with the *Śrīcakra*, is worshipped.

sṛṣṭi/sṛṣṭiḥ : Creation.

stambhana : A tāntric ritual to make a person rigid or immovable like a pillar.

stana : Breast.

stena : A thief.

steya : Stealing; misappropriation.

sthala : Place.

sthitadhī : Steady-minded; one with firm thought; one whose intellect does not vacillate in states of opposites. See *sthitaprajña*.

sthitaprajña : One who has given up all worldly desires, who is self-contented, unaffected by pleasure and pain, who is free from passion, fear and anger, who has equanimity in getting good and evil, who is free from agony and ecstasy, who has conquered and controlled one's senses and who is undisturbed and unperturbed in all circumstances — favourable or unfavourable — is a *sthitaprajña*.

sudhā-bīja : The name of the seed-syllable *vaṁ*.

sukhāsana : The comfortable pose.

sūkṣma : 1. Subtle. 2. Micro.

sumukham/sumukhī-mudrā : A kind of *mudrā* done before the Gāyatrī-*japa* (*su* = good; *mukha* = face).

sundara : Beautiful.

surabhiḥ : 1. A kind of *mudrā* done after the Gāyatrī-*japa*. 2. Sweet-smelling; fragrant. 3. The name of a fabulous cow in Indian mythology.

Sūrya : 1. Nārāyaṇa or God presiding in the sun. 2. The sun. 3. The *piṅgalā-nāḍī*.

sūrya-mudrā : A kind of gesture, in which each thumbtip presses the back of the respective ring-finger.

suṣumṇā: The subtle central channel along the spine for the flow of *Prāṇa*.

suṣupti : Deep sleep.

sūtra : 1. Aphorism. 2. Thread.

svabhāvataḥ : Naturally.

svadhā : Self-power; the Power or *Śakti* of *Brahman; Māyā* or the *Mūla-Prakṛti;* the *Śakti* which is inseparably contained in the Great Self.

svadharma : Own duties, Own properties.

svādhiṣṭhāna : The psychic centre in the subtle body, located two fingers above the root of the genital.

svādhyāya : 1. The study of scriptures dealing with liberation. 2. The *japa* of the *praṇava*.

svaḥ : 1. The *loka* (world), present here and everywhere, subtler than the *bhuvaḥ*, with its specific dimensions; it is shining, bright and lustrous. 2. God who presides over the *svarloka*.

svāhā : 1. Offering something to a deity with reverence. 2. Paying obeisance. 3. An exclamation used in making oblations to the gods. 4. The Mother of the universe, the Consort of God. 5. *su* + $\sqrt{}$*ah*, meaning "hail to."

svapna : Dream; sleep.

svarga : The world (*loka*) of light or lustre; the third world in increasing order of subtlety; with changed dimensions, it is here and everywhere.

svarūpa : Own form; own state.

svarūpa-śūnyamiva : One's own existence becoming void-like.

svastikāsana : A meditational posture known as the auspicious pose.

Śyāma : 1. Black, dark-blue, grey or green in complexion. 2. Lord Kṛṣṇa.

tāḍāsana: A kind of standing posture (*tāḍa* = palm tree).

taijasa : The second quarter of *oṁ*; the state of the Self, active in the dream condition.

tamas : The string or strand of inertia, impurity, darkness and ignorance.

tanmātra : Literally "that only." The five fields of the Sāṅkhya, each of which generates one state of the five *bhūta*s (material existences).

tanmayatā : The action of plunging or immersing into; the state of being absorbed in God.

Tantra : 1. An esoteric Indian system of philosophy and religious rituals for worldly attainments and spiritual liberation. 2. An advanced, ancient Indian science for controlling the web-structure of the subtle body and switching its special components for harnessing Nature.

tantra : 1. A loom. 2. A thread. 3. The warps or threads extended lengthwise in a loom. 4. The spiritual expansion of the body.

tāntrik(a) : 1. A person well-versed in the theory and practice of Tantra. 2. Pertaining to Tantra.

tanu : The body.

tapaḥ/tapas : 1. Austerities. 2. Heat. 3. The world (*loka*), present here and everywhere, subtler than *janaḥ*, with its specific dimensions. 4. God presiding over the world of *tapaḥ*.

tāra : The name of the *bīja oṁ*.

tarjanī : The index finger.

tarpaṇa : Satiating the deity by presenting him/her libations of water.

tat : That.

tattva : 1. True or real state; reality. 2. Any one of the five states of matter — solid, liquid, gaseous, energy and *ākāśa*. 3. That-ness.

tattva-mudrā : The same as the *jala* (*varuṇa-*)*-mudrā* except the fact that it does not face upward.

tattva-śuddhi : The purification of the body elements by sipping water sanctified by a *mantra*.

tejaḥ : Resplendence.

ṭhākura-ghara : See *deva-gṛha*.

trāṇa : Protection.

trāṭaka : A *haṭha-yoga* technique for fixed gazing at one point.

tri : Three.

tribījam : Three monosyllables — *hauṁ*, *jūṁ*, *saḥ*.

trimukham : A kind of *mudrā* done before the Gāyatrī-*japa* (*tri* = three; *mukha* = face).

trimūrti : The Hindu Trinity — Brahmā, Viṣṇu, Rudra (*tri* = three; *mūrti* = icons, forms).

trirūpā : Three forms, in feminine gender.

tryakṣara : Three-syllabled.

tryambā : Three Mothers; the

Consorts of the Hindu *trimūrti* — Sarasvatī, Lakṣmī, Kālī.

tryambaka : The Lord of the three *Śakti*s or the three Mothers.

tryambakā : The three Mothers — Sarasvatī, Lakṣmī, Kālī.

tulasī : The holy basil plant.

turīya : 1. Fourth. 2. The fourth state of the Self; the state of the Absolute *Brahman* — formless, attributeless, functionless, non-relational, non-dual and non-worldly.

tyāga : The act of sacrificing.

uccāṭana: A tāntric ritual to make a person violently excitable and incoherent.

udgītha : The same as *oṁ* or *praṇava*.

unmukhonmukham : A kind of *mudrā* done before the Gāyatrī-*japa* (*ut* = up; *mukha* = face).

upādhi : Limiting adjunct; U, the accessory one, is the *upādhi* of B, the real one, when the former confines the latter or the latter permeates the former.

upalabdhi : Realization.

upāṁśu : The method of *japa* with the movement of the lips in a whisper or humming.

upāsaka : Worshipper.

upāsanā : Worship.

upastha-mudrā : A kind of gesture in which the hind parts of the palms exert mutual pressure.

upāsya : One who is worshipped.

upavāsa : Fasting.

uras : Chest.

ūrdhvamukhī : Facing upward.

ūrdhvamukhī taḍāsana : A posture with backward bending while standing on the toes.

uru : Thigh.

Uṣṇik : The name of a Vedic metre.

uttarāraṇi : The upper friction-stick in the act of generating fire.

uttarīya : A shoulder-cloth used by the Hindu priest or worshipper.

vāc : Speech; word; *oṁ*.

vācaka : That by which somebody or something is named or designated.

vācya : Nameable; predicable.

vāda : Doctrine.

vādikā : A female who plays instrumental music.

vāgbīja : The name of the seed-syllable *aiṁ*.

Vāgdevī : The goddess of speech; Mother Sarasvatī.

vahni : Fire.

vahni-bīja : The name of the seed-syllable *raṁ*, the *bīja* of the *maṇipūra cakra/agni-tattva*.

vahnikāntā : A name of *svāhā*.

vaikharī : 1. The way of *verbally* pronouncing and repeating a *mantra*. 2. Pronouncing audibly.

vairāgya : Dispassionateness; aversion; freedom from all worldly desires.

vairāgya-mudrā : A kind of *mudrā* done after the Gāyatrī-*japa*. The same as the *jñāna-mudrā*.

Vaiśeṣika : An ancient school of Indian philosophy, the first one in the world to speak of atomism.

vaiśvānara : The first quarter of *oṁ*; the state of the Self active in the waking condition.

vajrāsana : A yogic posture known as the thunderbolt pose.

vakra : Curved.

vākya : A sentence.

vaṁ : The seed-syllable of the *svādhiṣṭhāna-cakra* and that of *jala-tattva*.

vāma : Left side.

vāmācārī : A follower of the left-path Tantra.

vāma-mārgī : One who follows the left path of the Tantra.

varāhakam : A kind of *mudrā* done before the Gāyatrī-*japa* (*varāha* = a boar).

vareṇyam : Adorable (in neuter gender).

varma : 1. Envelope. 2. Defensive armour. 3. Protection.

varma-bīja : The name of the seed-syllable *hūṁ*.

varṇa : 1. Any character of the Sanskrit alphabet. 2. Any letter of any alphabet. 3. Colour.

varṇamālā : Alphabet.

varuṇa-bīja : The name of the seed-syllable *vaṁ*.

vāsanā : A special type of *saṁskāra* that is more deeply buried in the Unconscious and more forcibly binding in nature.

vāsanā-saṁskāra : Mental prints of *saṁskāra*s of *vāsanā* type.

vaṣaṭ : An exclamation uttered at the end of a sacrificial or ritual verse.

vaśīkaraṇa : A tāntric ritual for subjugating or bewitching a person.

Vāsudeva : The son of Vasudeva; Lord Kṛṣṇa.

vauṣaṭ : An exclamation uttered at the end of a sacrificial or ritual verse.

vāyu : 1. The *tattva* of gaseousness. 2. Air.

vāyu-bīja : The name of the seed-syllable, *yaṁ*.

vāyu-mudrā : A kind of gesture done with the back of the index finger and the thumb.

veda : Knowledge; derived from the verb-root √*vid*, meaning "to know."

Vedānta : 1. The end of the Vedas. 2. An important school of Indian philosophy which centres around *Brahman*, the fundamental Reality. It has a number of sub-systems.

vicāra : Mentation.

videhamukta : Released after leaving the body.

vidveṣaṇa : A tāntric ritual to bring about hatred, enmity and hostility between two persons.

vidyā : Knowledge.

vidyā-dātrī : Giver of knowledge (in feminine gender); Mother Sarasvatī.

vīṇā : 1. A musical string-instrument of India. 2. The divine, musical string-instrument played by Mother Sarasvatī.

viniyogaḥ : The objective of application expressly stated.

vipāka : The fruition of *karmas*.

Virāḍ : Cosmic Mind or Supermind evolved from *Māyā* or the *Mūla-Prakṛti*; *Buddhi* or the Cosmic Consciousness, first manifested from the Mother Creatrix; the first manifested empirical Consciousness from which the whole universe evolved successively and sequentially. Literally this word means "Great," its equivalent word in the Sāṅkhya being *Mahat*.

virāma : Cessation.

vīrāsana/vīryāsana : A kind of yogic posture; the heroic posture; the seminal posture.

visarjana : Sending forth.

viśeṣa : Special.

Viṣṇu : 1. One who pervades all (derived from the verb-root √*viś*). 2. One and only one God who sustains and nourishes the universe; one of the Hindu Trinity.

vistāra : Expansion.

vistṛtam : Literally "well-spread." A kind of *mudrā* done before the Gāyatrī-*japa*.

viśuddhi : 1. The psychic centre in the subtle body at the level of the throat. 2. Purification.

viśvādhāra : The foundation of the universe; *Brahman*; God.

viśvarūpa : The world-image.

vitarka : 1. Alternative; same as *vikalpa*. 2. Hallucinatory experience.

vitatam : A kind of *mudrā* done before the Gāyatrī-*japa*.

vrata : The observance of vows.

vyāhṛti : 1. Utterance, speech, word. 2. Seven mystical utterances, namely, *bhūḥ*, *bhuvaḥ*, *svaḥ*, *mahaḥ*, *janaḥ*, *tapaḥ*, *satya*. These are the names of the seven worlds, everyone being present here and everywhere, with changes in dimensions and the degree of subtlety. The Hindu priest, while reciting the *vyāhṛtis*, pays obeisance to God who presides over these worlds.

vyāpaka : Extensive; spread-out.

vyāpakāñjalim : A kind of *mudrā* done before the Gāyatrī-*japa*.

vyāyāma : Exercise.

vyoma-bīja : The name of the seed-syllable *haṁ*.

yaḥ : Who (used in a clause).

yajña : Derived from the verb-root √*yaj*, meaning "to worship, adore, honour"; a self-less action for the benefit of others and the welfare of God's creation; any sacrifice, sacred gift and donation.

yaṁ : The seed-syllable of the *anāhata-cakra* and that of the *vāyu-tattva*.

yama : Restraint; self-control; non-performance of actions proscriptive in *yoga*.

yamapāśam : A kind of *mudrā* done before the Gāyatrī-*japa* (literal meanings; *yama* = the death-god; god who controls; *pāśa* = snare, noose, trap).

yantra : Mystic geometrical figures used in tāntric worshippings.

Yoga : An Indian system of philosophy that also prescribes physical and mental practices for the well-being of the individual and his spiritual liberation.

yoga : Derived from the Sanskrit verb-root √*yuj*, meaning "to yoke, to unite, to add." A special spiritual discipline to unite the individual self with the Universal Self. A discipline to keep the body, mind and spirit healthy.

yogāsana : Any yogic posture.

yogī : One who practises *yoga*.

yoni : 1. The female genital — vulva, vagina. 2. Source, origin.

yoni-mudrā : A kind of tāntric *mudrā*.

yoni-pūjā : A left-path *tāntrika*'s ritual worshipping the vulva of a woman (*bhairavī*), doing *mantra-japa* while holding the *bhairavī* on his lap with the interpenetration of the genital organs, and finally ending the ritual with sexual intercourse.

Bibliography

Acharya, S.A.T., 1998, *Nitya-naimittika-karmasamuccayaḥ (Brahmakarma-samuccayaḥ)*, Varanasi: Chaukhamba Vidyabhavan.

Atharvaveda Saṁhitā, The, with *Sāyaṇa-Bhāṣyam*, Varanasi: Chaukhamba Vidya-bhavan, 1997.

Avalon, Arthur (ed.), 1996, *Śāradā-tilaka-tantram*, Delhi: Motilal Banarsidass.

———, 1989, *Mahānirvāṇa Tantra*, with the Commentary of Hariharananda Bharati, Delhi: Motilal Banarsidass.

———, and Sarasvatī, A. (ed. & intro.), 1989, *Prapañcasāra-tantram of Śaṅkarācārya*, Delhi: Motilal Banarsidass.

———, and Shastri, L. (ed. & intro.), 1997, *Tantrarāja Tantra*, Delhi: Motilal Banarsidass.

Avasthi, S.S. (ed.), 1990, *Vākyapadīyam* by Bhartṛhari, Varanasi: Chaukhamba Vidyabhavan.

Bhagavad-Gītā, The (*Śrīśaṅkara's Gītā Bhāṣya*, tr. by Aiyar, C.V.R.), Mumbai: Bharatiya Vidya Bhavan, 1988.

Bhagavad-Gītā, The (*Śrīmad-Bhagavad-Gītā* with *Śāṅkara Bhāṣyam* and Hindi transln.), tr. by Goyandka, Sriharikrishnadas, Gorakhpur (U.P., India): Gita Press, *sam.*, 2053.

Bhagavad-Gītā, The (*Śrīmad Bhagavad-Gītā Bhāṣya of Śrī Śaṅkarācārya*), tr. by Warrier, A.G.K., Chennai: Sri Ramakrishna Math, 1983.

Bhāgavatam, The (*Śrīmad-Bhāgavata-Mahāpurāṇa*), vol. 1 & 2, Gorakhpur (U.P., India), Gita Press.

Brahma-Sūtram, The (*The Brahma-Sūtra Śāṅkara-Bhāṣya*), vol. 1 & 2, ed. by K.L. Joshi, Delhi: Parimal Publications, 1982 (1st publ. 1981).

Brahma-Sūtram, The (*The Brahma-Sūtra*), ed. by S. Radhakrishnan, London: George Allen & Unwin, 1960.

Danielou, A., 1973 (1st publ. 1949), *Yoga: The Method of Re-Integration*, London: Johnson Publications.

Devī-Bhāgavatam, Sabhāṣāṭīkam, part 1 & 2, Mumbai: Venkateshwar Press.

Durgā-Saptaśatī, with seven Sanskrit commentaries, compiled by V.H. Sharma, Delhi: Butala & Co., 1984.

Gheraṇḍa Saṁhītā (*Pure Yoga*), ed. by T. Rodriguez and Kansi Ram and comm. by Yogī Praṇavānanda, Delhi: Motilal Banarsidass, 1992.

Īśvara-Pratyabhijñā-Vimarśiṇī, with original text of *Īśvara-Pratyabhijñā-Sūtra* of Utpala, *Īśvara-Pratyabhijñā-Vimarśiṇī* Commentary by Abhinavagupta and *Bhāskarī* Commentary by Bhāskarakaṇṭha, ed. by R.C. Dwivedi, S. Ayer and K.C. Pandey, Delhi: Motilal Banarsidass, 1986.

Iyenger, B.K.S., 1992 (1st publ. 1966 by George Allen & Unwin, London), *Light on Yoga*, New Delhi: HarperCollins Publishers India.

———, 1981, *Light on Prāṇāyāma* (*Prāṇāyāma-Dīpikā*), London: George Allen & Unwin.

Jyotishacharya, M.V., 1988, *Karmaṭha-Guruḥ*, Delhi: Motilal Banarsidass.

Karanjia, R.K., 1977, *Kuṇḍalinī Yoga*, New Delhi: Arnold-Heinemann.

Keshavadas, Sadguru Sant, 1994 (1st publ. 1978 in New York), *Gāyatrī : The Highest Meditation*, Delhi : Motilal Banarsidass.

Malaviya, S. (ed.), 1997, *Mantramahodadhi of Mahīdhara*, Delhi: Chaukhamba Sanskrit Pratisthan.

———, (ed. & tr.), 1999, *Rudrayāmalam* (part 1 & 2), Delhi: Chaukhamba Sanskrit Pratisthan.

Māṇḍūkya-Kārikā of Gauḍapāda, The (*The Āgamaśāstra of Gauḍapāda*), ed. & tr. by V.S. Bhattacharya, Delhi: Motilal Banarsidass, 1989.

Mantramahārṇavaḥ, 1996, Mumbai: Khemaraj Shrikrishnadas, Sri Vekanteshvar Steam Press.

Manu-Smṛti, The, ed. by Pt. Rameshwar Bhatt, Delhi: Chaukhamba Sanskrit Pratisthan, 1998.

Mīmāṁsā-Sūtram of Jaimini: *The Wisdom of Mīmāṁsā*, part 1 & 2, ed. by K.P. Bahadur, New Delhi: Sterling Publishers, 1983.

Mishra, S.B. and Mishra, L.B., *sam.*, 2054, *Nityakarma-Pūjāprakāś*, Gorakhpur (U.P., India): Gita Press.

Mookerjee, A., 1982 (1st publ. in London by Thames and Hudson), *Kuṇḍalinī: The Arousal of the Inner Energy*, Delhi: Clarion Books.

Panda, N.C., 1996, *Mind and Supermind*, vol. 1 & 2, New Delhi: D.K. Printworld.

———, 2002, *Cyclic Universe*, vol. 1 & 2, New Delhi: D.K. Printworld.

———, 1999 (1st publ., 1991), *Māyā in Physics*, Delhi: Motilal Banarsidass.

———, 2000 (1st publ. 1995), *The Vibrating Universe*, Delhi: Motilal Banarsidass.

———, 2003, *Meditation: Science and Practice*, New Delhi: D.K. Printworld.

———, 2003, *Yoga-Nidrā (Yogic Trance): Theory, Practice and Applications*, New Delhi: D.K. Printworld.

Raju, P.T., 1985, *Structural Depths of Indian Thought*, New Delhi: South Asian Publishers.

Ṛgveda Saṁhitā, The, with *Sāyaṇa Bhāṣyam*, Varanasi: Chaukhamba Vidyabhavan, 1991.

Sāṅkhya Kārikā, See *The Sāṅkhya Philosophy* by Nandalal Sinha, 1979.

Sāṅkhya-Pravacana-Sūtra, See *The Sāṅkhya Philosophy* by Nandalal Sinha, 1979.

Sankhyatirtha, B.M., Bhattacharya, C. and Bagchi, P.C. (eds.), 1994, *Pūrṇānanda's Śrītattvacintāmaṇi*, Delhi: Motilal Banarsidass.

Sarasvati, Swami Satyananda, 1983, (1st publ. 1969), *Asana, Pranayama, Mudra, Bandha*, Munger (Bihar, India): Bihar School of Yoga.

———, 1984, *Kuṇḍalinī Tantra*, Munger (Bihar, India): Bihar School of Yoga.

———, and Sarasvati Swami Muktibodhananda, 1985, *Haṭha-Yoga-Pradīpikā of Svātmārāma*, Munger (Bihar, India): Bihar School of Yoga.

Sarva-Darśana-Saṅgraha by Madhvācārya, tr. by U.N. Sinh. Mumbai, Khemaraj Shrikrishnadas Prakashan, 1997.

Śatapatha-brāhmaṇa, The, with the commentary of Sāyaṇācārya and Harisvāmin, 5 vols., Delhi: Nag Publishers, 1990.

Saundarya-laharī of Śaṅkarācārya, tr. by V.K. Subramanian, Delhi: Motilal Banarsidass, 1990.

Shastri, J.C.B., 1995, *Sārasvata Kuṇḍalinī Mahāyoga Śaktipāta Śāstra*, 2nd edn., Lucknow: Nirmohibandhu Prakashan.

Singh, J., tr. & ed., 1991, *Spanda-Kārikā*, by Vasugupta, with *Spanda-Nirṇaya* Commentary by Kṣemarāja, Delhi: Motilal Banarsidass.

Sinha, Nandalal, 1979 (1st publ. 1915), *The Sāṅkhya Philosophy*, New Delhi: Munshiram Manoharlal.

Sivananda Swami, 1971, *Kuṇḍalinī Yoga*, Sivanandanagar (Tehri-Garhwal, Uttaranchal, India): The Divine Life Society.

———, 1972, *Japa Yoga*, Sivanandanagar (Tehri-Garhwal, Uttaranchal, India): The Divine Life Society.

Śiva Saṁhitā, The, tr. by R.B.S.C. Basu, 4th edn., New Delhi: Munshiram Manoharlal, 1990.

Spanda-Kārikā, by Vasugupta, with *Spanda-Nirṇaya* Commentary by Kṣemarāja, See Singh, J., 1991.

Śrīdurgopāsanā-Kalpadruma, 1997, Mumbai, Khemaraj Shrikrishnadas Prakashan.

Tripathy, R.D., 1997, *Mahāmṛtyuñjaya Sādhanā evaṁ Siddhi*, 3rd edn., New Delhi: Ranjan Publications.

———, 1997, *Rudrayāmala Tantra*, New Delhi: Ranjan Publications.

Udupa, K.N. and Prasad, R.C., 1985 (1st publ. 1978), *Stress and Its Management by Yoga*, Delhi: Motilal Banarsidass.

Upaniṣads, The Principal, ed. by S. Radhakrishnan, London: George Allen & Unwin, 1969 (1st publ. 1953).

Upaniṣatsaṅgrahaḥ, ed. by J.L. Shastri, Delhi: Motilal Banarsidass, 1984 (1st publ. 1970).

Vandana, Sister, 1984, *Nāma Japa* (*The Prayer of the Name*), Mumbai: Bharatiya Vidya Bhavan.

Vāyu-Purāṇa, The, vol. 1 & 2, tr. by G.V. Tagare, Delhi: Motilal Banarsidass, 1987.

Vidyaratna, T. (ed.), 1987 (1st publ. 1941), *Ṣaṭcakra Nirūpaṇa* and *Pādukāprapañca*, New Delhi: Aditya Prakashan.

Vivekacūḍāmaṇi of Śaṅkarācārya, tr. by P. Sankaranarayanan, Mumbai: Bharatiya Vidya Bhavan, 1988, (1st publ. 1973).

Woodroffe, S.J., 1975, *Śakti and Śākta*, 8th edn., Chennai: Ganesh & Co.

———, 1981, *The Serpent Power*, 12th edn., Chennai: Ganesh & Co.

Yajurveda, The (*The Śukla-Yajurveda-Saṁhitā*, with *Bhāṣya* of Ubaṭācārya and of Mahīdhara), Varanasi: Chaukhamba Vidyabhavan, 1996.

Yoga-Darśanam of Patañjali: Pātañjala-Yoga-Pradīpa, 14th edn., comm., by Sri Swami Omananda Tirtha, Gorakhpur (U.P., India): Gita Press, *sam.*, 2053.

Yoga-Darśanam of Patañjali: Sāṅkhya-Yoga-Darśanam, with classical commentaries, ed. by G.D. Shastri, Varanasi: Chaukhamba Sanskrit Samsthan, 1990.

Index

abhiṣeka, 60, 111

abhyāsa, 205

Absolute Bliss, 300

Absolute Consciousness, 300

Absolute Existence, 300

ācamana, 50, 60, 140-41, 159

acetylcholine, 80, 82

Adhomukham, 148

adhyakṣa, 36, 49, 108

adrenal cortex, 79, 80, 215

adrenal medulla, 79, 215

adrenaline, 79, 82, 213, 215, 257, 269

Ādyāśakti, 61

āgama, 60

agni, 172

agrasparśī tāḍāsana, 265

ahaṅkāra, 18, 133

ahiṁsā, 23, 99

aiṁ, 4, 62, 176-77, 194, 292

aṅga-nyāsa, 144

ājñā, 58, 227, 229, 292

ājñā cakra, 15, 144, 266

ajapā, 124

ajapā mantra, 124

ajapā-japa, 5, 20, 65, 110, 120, 124-25, 160, 220, 274

ajapā-japa so'haṁ, 201, 211

ākāśa, 5, 172

ākāśa-bīja, 247, 260

ākāśa-bīja (*haṁ*), 261-62

ākāśī-mudrā, 261

ākarṣaṇa, 75

Akṣara-Nyāsaḥ, 179

akula, 53

ālamba, 19

ālambana, 16, 122, 203

anāhata, 4, 58, 172, 227-29, 292

anāhata cakra, 237, 270, 273

anāhata-dhvani, 121

anāhata-nāda, 120, 266

antaḥkaraṇa, 8-9, 12, 14, 18, 21, 25, 44, 46, 55, 70, 73, 221

antarmātṛkā-nyāsa, 52

anterior pituitary, 79

antibodies, 216, 257

Anuloma-viloma-prāṇāyāma, 266

anuṣṭhāna, 120, 196-98

aṇimā siddhi, 74

Āpaḥ, 17, 133

apāna-mudrā, 287
aparigraha, 23, 99, 206
ardha-śalabhāsana, 254
ārogya-mantra, 295
arthritis, 244, 256
āsanas, 14, 22-23, 243
asmitā, 18
asteya, 23, 99
aśvinī-mudrā, 286
atherosclerosis, 213
ātmā (self), 17-18, 140-05
auditory degeneration, 247
aṣṭāṅga-yoga, 14
autoimmune reactions, 257, 263
autonomic nervous system, 78, 81, 215
āvaraṇa-pūjā, 58, 180
avatāra-vāda, 105
avatāras, 105
avidyā, 30
Avyakta, 133

bahirmātṛkā-nyāsa, 52
bīja krīṁ, 297
bīja vaṁ, 287
bīja-japa, 246
bīja-mantras, 265, 268, 276, 289
bīja-mantra laṁ, 237
bīja-mantra saṁ, 238
bīja-mantra yaṁ, 237
bījākṣara, 15
bījas, 4, 11, 13, 61, 73, 119, 172, 182, 184, 194-95, 227, 232, 249, 256, 258, 267-68, 276-77, 292
bandhas, 50, 55, 58, 256
Basti, 50
beta cells, 279
beta-cells of Langerhans, 274
bhūḥ, 126, 127, 172, 182, 227
bhadrāsana, 268, 269
bhakti, 70, 71
bhakti-yoga, 1, 13, 28, 31-32, 34, 40, 48, 63-64, 66, 68, 70, 72, 119, 123, 160, 203-04, 220, 229
bhūrloka-puruṣa, 127
Bhartṛhari, 131, 132
bhūta-śuddhi, 50, 58
bhuḥ, 182
Bhubaneśvarī, 47
bhujaṅgāsana, 251
bhukti, 44, 57, 60, 72, 123, 137, 299
bhuvaḥ, 126-27, 172, 182, 227
bhuvarloka-puruṣa, 127
bindu, 17, 266
blood-pressure, 222, 235, 236
Brahmā, 7, 16, 35-36, 48, 121, 130, 138, 176, 181, 224
Brahmā-Gāyatrī, 161
brahma-jñāna, 100, 205
brāhma-muhūrta, 94
brahma-nirvāṇa, 105, 137, 204, 221

brāhmī-sthiti, 16, 26, 100, 122
brahmacarya, 23, 99, 196
Brahman, 6-8, 12-13, 16, 18-19, 26, 29-31, 35-36, 41, 43, 45, 48, 53, 63, 65-66, 70-71, 100, 104-05, 107, 122-23, 126, 128, 131-32, 137, 202, 204, 224, 300
Brahman (*brāhmī-sthiti*), 136
Brahman/Īśvara, 109
brahmānubhūti, 103
brāhmaṇa-bhojana, 60, 111, 136, 176, 180, 191, 197
brahmāṇḍa, 53
brahmarandhra, 266
brain, 21
buddhi, 17-18, 26, 44, 70, 133, 137, 221, 224
buddhi-yoga, 26, 44, 66, 70, 224
buddhiḥ, 129

cakra-pūjā, 57
cakra-sādhanā, 57, 58
cakrārcanam, 54
cakras, 4, 50, 56, 58, 72-73, 78, 227, 229, 235-36, 268, 291
cakras ājñā, 4
calad-dhāraṇā, 292
Calcitonin, 242
Cāmuṇḍā, 174, 298
cāmuṇḍā-mantra, 174, 293
Cāmuṇḍā-sādhanā, 176
cancer, 213
Caṇḍī, 36, 47, 298
catecholamines, 81-82, 213, 269
Caturmukham, 148
cerebral cortex, 80, 81, 215
Cetanā, 155
Chinnamastā, 47
cholesterol, 213
chronic sinusitis, 266
cin-mudrā, 96, 123, 125, 245-46
citta, 15-16, 203, 224
citta-śuddhi, 221, 224
citta-vṛtti, 24
corticosteroids, 79, 213, 257, 269
Cosmic Consciousness, 19
Cosmic Egg, 17
Cosmic Mind, 17, 21, 133
Creator God, 301

(*Dakṣiṇācārī*) *Tantra*, 47
dakṣiṇa Kālī mantra, 174, 232
dakṣiṇa-mārgī, 48
dakṣiṇa-mārgī Tantra, 48
daridra-nārāyaṇa-sevā, 111, 136, 197
deep sleep, 31
degeneration of the auditory nerve, 249
degeneration of the intervertebral discs, 247, 251
detached action, 26
detachment (*anāsakti*), 26

deva-japa, 115

deva-mantra, 115

devatās, 62, 73, 107, 125, 133, 168, 170, 174, 181, 224, 276, 295

Dhūmāvatī, 47

dharā, 285

dharā-bīja (laṁ), 286

dhāraṇā, 11, 14, 18, 23, 203, 210, 214, 228, 231, 236-37, 246-47, 266, 268, 270, 273, 275, 278, 280-82, 285, 288, 290, 294

Dhauti, 50

dhenu-mudrā, 263

dhyāna, 11, 14, 16-17, 22-23, 45, 64-65, 71, 78, 82, 122-23, 137, 160, 176, 180, 195, 202, 206, 210, 228, 231, 236-37, 246-47, 266, 270, 275, 278-79, 281-82, 285, 287, 294

dhyāna-yoga, 63

diabetes, 274

diks, 126

dry joints, 242, 245

duṁ, 292

dualism, 28, 30-31, 43, 63-64, 66, 72, 106, 300

dualistic Vedānta, 300

Durgā, 36, 47, 56, 170-71, 174, 184, 230, 233-34, 276, 298

Durgā-Gāyatrī, 164

Durgā-kīrtana, 193

Durgā-mantra, 109, 173, 297

Durgā-Tantra, 47

dvādaśākṣara-mṛtyuñjaya-mantra, 184

Dvimukham, 147

dvināḍa-paṅkaja-mudrā, 289

endocrine glands, 79, 80, 213, 215

endocrines, 215

equanimity, 25-26, 70

essential hypertension, 211, 268

Freudian psychology, 57

frontal lobe, 215

gaṁ, 62

Gaṇeśa, 168, 184, 230

Gaṇeśa-Gāyatrī, 160

Gaṇeśa-kīrtana, 193

Gaṇeśa-mantra, 173

Gaṇeśa-Tantra, 47

Gauḍapāda, 9

Gaurī, 36, 48, 174, 276

Gaurī Mantra, 174

Gāyatrī, 121, 125-26, 129, 134-35, 138, 176, 224-25

Gāyatrī homa, 227

Gāyatrī-japa, 117, 119-20, 134, 137, 160, 178, 201, 228
- for arousing *kuṇḍalinī*, 227
- for avoiding accidents, 226
- for better cardiac and pulmonary heal, 227
- for better digestion, better eye sigh, 227

for curing sterility, 226
for getting rid of fear, 226
for strengthening the immune system, 226
for the better health of the excretor, 227
for the better health of the reproduc, 227
for the improvement of memory, 226
for the removal of poverty, 226
Gāyatrī-mantra, 110, 125, 127, 129, 134-35, 137, 145, 159, 224-27
Gāyatrī-mantra-japa, 142
Gāyatrī-sādhanā, 159, 160
glauṁ, 62
God, 1-2, 4, 7-8, 11, 16-17, 20, 22, 26, 28, 30-31, 33, 35-37, 40, 42-43, 45, 47, 53, 59, 62-65, 67-68, 70, 72, 94, 100-05, 107, 110-11, 123, 127-28, 130, 135-36, 140, 142, 160, 167, 170, 172, 182, 195-96, 203-04, 206, 210, 214, 218, 224-25, 232
God (Īśvara), 6, 70, 134
God (*brāhmī sthiti*), 24
God (*Brahman*), 220
God/Goddess, 108, 192-93, 299
Goddess, 36, 38-39, 47, 53, 59, 62, 64, 75, 102, 104, 130, 142, 160, 167, 225, 233, 296, 297
gout, 212, 239-40, 245, 253
Govinda, 169
grathitā mudrā, 264
Grathitam, 150
Great Self, 17
gross body, 78
guṇas, 7, 8, 108, 224
guru-mantra, 102, 107, 109, 230-31
guru-vāda, 103, 107
gurus, 101-07, 109, 135, 138, 159, 184, 198, 217-18, 231, 243

haṁ, 4, 62, 172, 226-27, 229, 237, 247-48, 260, 292
haṁ saḥ, 246
haṁ saḥ japa, 246
haṅkāra-japa, 262
haṅkāra-kriyā, 262
haṭha-yoga, 49
Hanumān, 170
Hanumāna-Tantra, 47
Hanumat-Gāyatrī, 164
Hari, 195
Hari-kīrtana, 195
Hasta-ṭaṅka-mudrā, 272
hauṁ, 182-83, 258, 265, 267, 276
hauṁ, hrauṁ, 62
havana, 59, 111, 136, 176, 197
havana-japa, 110
haviṣyānna, 99, 136, 196
histamine, 81
homa, 180, 191, 227

hormonal balance, 236, 258
hormonal imbalance, 257
hormones, 80, 215
hrīṁ, 62, 177, 258, 272, 276, 292
huṁ, 62
humoral balance, 222
Hypercholesterolaemia, 269
hypertension, 123-25, 211, 222, 234, 266, 268, 274, 279
hypothalamus, 78-79, 215

icon-worship, 33
iḍā, 50, 55, 73
immune system, 213-14, 216, 222, 232, 236, 247-48, 257, 261, 263, 294
immuno-fortification, 257, 261, 282
immuno-promotion, 257
immuno-suppression, 257
Indian Depth Psychology, 208
indriyas, 133
insulin, 274
ischaemic heart disease, 269
iṣṭa-deva, 71
iṣṭa-devī, 72
iṣṭa-devatā, 38, 71, 94, 102, 109, 184, 230-31, 298
iṣṭa-mantra, 197
Īśvara (God), 4, 8, 10-12, 16-19, 26, 30-31, 34-35, 48, 64, 71, 106, 108, 122-23, 126, 138, 202, 301
Īśvarī, 35, 64, 108
Īśvara-praṇidhāna, 10, 14-15, 24, 28, 100, 122
Īśvara/Brahman, 125, 128, 134

jñāna-mudrā, 96, 123, 125
jñāna-yoga, 19, 40, 63, 65-66, 119-20, 123-24, 160, 203-04, 220, 229
jūṁ, 182-84
jūṁ saḥ, 276, 278
jalam, 172
janaḥ, 126, 228
japa, 2-4, 10, 13-14, 16, 18-20, 24, 26, 28, 32, 37, 39-40, 43, 45, 59-60, 65, 67-68, 77-78, 82, 93-94, 96, 98, 100, 102, 107-08, 110-12, 115, 117-19, 122-25, 134-36, 145, 159-60, 167, 171, 176, 180-81, 189, 191, 196-97, 201-02, 205-07, 209-10, 214, 217-20, 222, 224-27, 230-31, 234, 239, 243, 246, 248-49, 251, 253, 256-59, 261, 263-64, 267-68, 270-71, 273, 275-77, 280, 282, 285, 289, 296-97, 299, 300
  in *Ūrdhvamukhī Tāḍāsana*, 249
  in *Bhujaṅgāsana*, 251
  in *Meru-Agra-Vakrāsana*, 250
  in *Meru-Pārśva-Vakrāsana*, 251
  in *Śalabhāsana*, 253
  in *Paścimottānāsana*, 255
  of *Sampuṭa-Mantras*, 296

with *bahupadī mudrā*, 281
with *kara-pārśva-mudrā*, 282
with pārṣṇi-mudrā, 290
with the *apāna-mudrā*, 287
with the *dvināḍa-paṅkaja-mudrā*, 289
with the *upastha-mudrā*, 288
japa-anuṣṭhāna, 197
japa-dhyāna, 65
japa-mālā, 112
japa-mantra, 16
*japa-mudrā*s, 282
japa-therapy, 211-13, 216, 226, 295
Japa-Therapy in Cancer, 291
japa-yajña, 3
japa-yoga, 1, 5, 23, 37, 46, 65, 69, 83, 101-02, 118, 192, 198, 205, 295, 300-02
jīva, 45
jīvanmukta, 66, 77, 104, 204, 221
jīvātmā, 8, 43

kaivalya, 106, 301
Kālī, 4, 36, 47, 48, 56, 108-09, 138, 170,-71, 174, 225, 230, 297
Kālī-kīrtana, 194
Kālī-mantras, 173, 297
kāliśī, 72
kāma-bīja, 259, 267
Kāma-mudrā, 259, 267, 294, 297
kāmanā, 109
kampana, 17, 121, 133
kanda, 50
Kaṇṭha-mudrā, 260-61, 294
Kapālabhāti, 50
Kara-nyāsaḥ, 143, 178
*kara-nyāsa*s, 143, 178
karamālā, 96, 116-17, 135, 181, 231
karamālā counting, 115
*karma-saṁskāra*s, 203, 209
karma-vāda, 44
karma-yoga, 41, 204
karmāśaya, 66, 68, 106, 203, 208, 221
karmāśaya (*sañcita karma*), 69
Kūrmaḥ, 152
*karma*s, 55, 68, 106
karmavāda, 68
kīrtana, 39-40, 120, 192-95, 220, 224
kaula-mārga, 53, 55-56
*kṛcchra-sādhanā*s, 27
khecarī-mudrā, 55, 261, 294
klīṁ, 62, 177, 259, 267, 292, 297
kleśahā-mudrā, 297
krīṁ, 4, 62, 226, 292
kriyā-yoga, 14
Kṛṣṇa-Gāyatrī, 162
kṣrauṁ, 62
Kuja-mudrā, 276
kula, 53
Kulīra (*pādāgni*)-*mudrā*, 277

Kumārī, 56
kumārī-pūjā, 56
kumārīpūjanam, 54
kumbhaka, 225, 228, 229
Kuṇḍalinī, 48, 50, 53, 56, 73, 228, 229, 292
kuṇḍalinī sādhanā, 227
kuṇḍalinī-arousal, 58
Kuṇḍalinī-Yoga, 53, 55
kuṇḍalinī-yogī, 48

Lakṣmī, 4, 36, 47-48, 138, 171, 174, 195, 225, 230
Lakṣmī-Gāyatrī, 165
Lakṣmī-kīrtana, 195
Lakṣmī-mantras, 109, 112, 173
Lalitā, 47
laṁ, 4, 62, 172, 227, 229, 268, 285, 289, 290, 292
liṅga, 36, 51
liṅga-mudrā, 190, 236, 239, 258, 265, 267, 276, 294, 298
Liṅgam, 157
Likhita-japa, 39
lokas, 126, 132
long-term memory, 21
lumbago, 248, 251, 255

madhyabhedī-prāṇāsana, 268-69
madya, 57
madyam, 55-56
mahā-mantra, 195
Mahā-mantra-kīrtana/mahā-nāma-kīrtana, 195
Mahā-mṛtyuñjaya-mantra, 109, 181-83, 189, 191, 232, 235-36, 239, 294-95
Japa-Sādhanā, 184
mantra-sādhanā, 191
mahā-nāma, 195
mahā-vyāhṛtis, 172, 182, 227
mahaḥ, 126, 228
Mahākālī, 180
Mahākrāntam, 152
Mahālakṣmī, 170, 180
mahāmantra, 170
Mahāsarasvatī, 180
Mahat, 17, 71
mahāvyāhṛtis, 126
mahimā, 74
maithuna, 56
maithuna-mudrās, 55
makarāsana, 247-48, 260, 262
mālā, 112
māṁsa, 57
māṁsam, 55, 56
mūla bandha, 287
Mūla-Prakṛti, 53, 133
mūlādhāra, 4, 48, 50, 53, 56, 58, 172, 227, 228-29, 235-36, 285, 288, 290, 292
Mīmāṁsā, 131-32
Mīmāṁsā School, 131

Mīmāṁsakas, 130-32
manas, 133, 221
mānasa pañcopacāra pūjā, 231
mānasa-pūjā, 171, 176, 231
mānasika, 10-11, 20, 118, 122
mānasika japa, 11
mānasika oṅkāra-japa, 19
mantra, 4, 6, 10-11, 13, 15, 17, 20-21, 38-39, 50, 59-61, 72-74, 93, 101-02, 107, 109-11, 117-18, 122-23, 125-26, 128, 134-35, 137, 140-41, 143-44, 160, 167-71, 174, 177, 181-83, 192-93, 195, 197-98, 201-02, 212, 220, 224-25, 227, 229-32, 234-35, 249, 253-54, 256, 263-64, 271, 274, 282, 288, 294, 296
  for *Japa*, 167
mantra oṁ, 122
mantra-japa, 3, 10, 12, 14-15, 22, 27-28, 38, 58-59, 61, 63, 71, 75, 93, 101, 111, 119-20, 136, 138, 145, 159, 176, 191, 198, 225, 230, 234, 236
mantra-kīrtana, 40
mantra-sādhanā, 60
mantra-siddhi, 60, 72
Mantra-Varṇa-Nyāsaḥ, 179
maṇipūra, 4, 58, 172, 227, 228, 229, 238, 246, 275, 278, 281, 292
maṇḍalas, 52, 58, 73, 188, 227, 256
māraṇa, 75, 77
mārjana, 50, 58, 60, 111, 176, 180, 191, 197
mūrti-pūjā, 58, 59
mātṛ(māyā)-mudrā, 234, 267
mātṛ-mudrā, 236, 258, 272, 276, 294, 297
Mātaṅgī, 47
mātṛkā, 51, 61, 72
matsya, 57
matsyaḥ, 55, 152
Māyā, 36, 42, 48, 108
māyā-bīja (*hrīṁ*), 258, 267
meditation, 275
memory, 21, 31
mental stress, 82
merus, 112, 115, 135
migraine, 266
mind, 21, 78, 82
mokṣa, 41, 43, 55, 66, 105, 109, 122, 196, 203
  yoga, 120, 124
Monotheism, 28-30, 34
Mother Creatrix, 130, 138
Mṛga-mudrā, 190
Mṛta-sañjīvanī-mantra, 182
Mṛtyuñjaya-mantra, 181-82, 184
mṛtyuhara-bījas, 183
Mudgaram, 152
mudrā, 96, 234, 258-59, 263, 265, 267, 270, 273, 276-77, 287, 289, 293

mudrā-japa, 263, 265, 274, 279, 281, 282
for Relief from Chronic Constipation, 283
for Relief from Hepatic Disorders, 280
mudrās, 50, 55, 58, 125, 142, 143, 145, 159, 239, 256, 258, 263, 267, 275
mukti, 44, 57, 60, 72, 123, 137, 299, 300
Muṣṭi-mudrā, 189
Muṣṭika-mudrā, 276
Muṣṭikam, 152

nāda, 17
nakha-vidīrṇa-mudrā, 298
nīlakaṇṭhī-mudrā, 248, 260-61
nāma-japa, 2, 13, 38, 101, 167, 191, 230
nāma-kīrtana, 40, 195
nāma-mantra, 170, 172, 230-32
nāḍīs, 50, 55, 236, 268
Nārāyaṇa, 168, 230, 234
Nārāyaṇa-kīrtana, 194
nāsāgra-dṛṣṭi, 268
Nauli, 50
nava-śakti, 180
navākṣara-mantra, 179
navārṇa-mantra, 174, 176, 180, 280, 292
Neti, 49, 266
neuroendocrine apparatus, 78
neuroendocrine system, 81, 82
neurohormones, 209
neurohumoral system, 81
Neurohumors, 80-81, 207, 213, 223
Nigama, 60
nirāśī, 206
nirdvandva, 25
Nirvāṇam, 158
niṣkāma, 67, 108, 218
anuṣṭhāna, 196
japa, 44, 67, 108, 201, 231
saṅkalpa, 141
nivṛtti-mārga, 203
niyamas, 6, 14, 22 24, 99, 100, 196
non-dualism, 28-29, 31-32, 43, 63-64, 66, 72, 300
non-dualism (Advaita Vedānta), 300
non-dualistic Vedānta, 300
noradrenaline, 78, 81-82, 213, 257, 269
Nṛsiṁha-mantra, 298
Nṛsiṁha-Viṣṇu, 298
Nṛsiṁha-Gāyatrī, 162
nyāsa, 51-52, 58-59, 61, 63, 142-43, 171, 176, 178, 180-81, 232, 236, 292
Nyāsaḥ, 185
nyāsas, 159, 188, 256

oṁ, 3-4, 7-9, 12, 14-17, 19, 24, 36, 39, 45, 61-62, 66, 100, 109-10, 120-21, 126, 132-34, 184, 192, 201, 210-11, 219, 227, 229, 268, 292
oṁ bhūḥ, 228
oṁ bhuvaḥ, 228
oṁ hrīṁ śrīṁ krīṁ, 63
oṁ janaḥ, 229
oṁ mahaḥ, 228
oṁ prāṇāya svāhā, 271
oṁ svaḥ, 228
oṁ tapaḥ, 229
oṅkāra, 5, 6, 7, 9
oṅkāra (*oṁ*), 64
  japa, 267
oṅkāra dhvani, 17
oṅkāra-(*praṇava*) *japa*, 119
oṅkāra-japa, 12-13, 15-16, 19, 63-64, 66, 110, 119-20, 122-23, 125, 160, 202, 204-06, 208-11, 215, 218, 220, 268
oṅkāra-japa-therapy, 213
oṅkāra-kīrtana, 219
oncogenesis, 217
osteo-arthrosis, 245
Osteoarthritis, 239, 255
osteoarthrosis, 239, 247, 253
Osteoporosis, 241, 247-48, 253, 255-56, 285
ovaries, 80, 215
pañca-bhūtas, 133
pañca-makāra, 46, 54
pañcamakārārcanam, 54
Pañcamukha-mudrā, 190
Pañcamukham, 148
pañcopacāra mānasa pūjā, 234, 236
paścimottānāsana, 255
paśutva, 55
Pada-ṭaṅka-mudrā, 272
padmāsana, 96, 123-24, 202, 220, 228, 267, 270, 280
paṅkaja-mudrā, 289
Paṅkajam, 157
pūjā, 58, 96, 138, 159, 171-72, 180, 198, 231, 234
Pallavam, 154
pancreas, 275, 279
pancreatic islets, 80
pīṭha-pūjā, 176, 180
pantheism, 29
Pāṇini, 131
pūraka, 229
Paramātmā, 2, 8, 17-18, 35, 43, 71, 106
Parameśvara, 35-36, 49, 64, 129, 224-25
Parameśvarī, 49, 64, 129, 225
Parameśvarī Mantra, 174
parasympathetic, 215
parasympathetic nervous system, 80

parasympathic system, 82
parathormone, 242
parathyroid glands, 242
parathyroid hormone, 242
parathyroids, 215, 247
Patañjali, 3-4, 6, 10, 14-15, 16, 19, 23, 25, 53, 64, 106, 119, 301
pavana-muktāsana, 285
piṅgalā, 50, 55, 73
piṇḍa, 53
piṇḍa-brahmāṇḍa, 53
Piṇḍadā-mudrā, 273
pituitary, 79
pituitary gland, 215
pluralism, 64
polytheism, 29, 31
post-*japa mudrās*, 154
pradhāna, 106
prājña, 8-9, 12, 17, 31
prakṛti, 106, 301
Pralambam, 150
pramadā-pūjā, 56
pramadā-pūjanam, 54
Prāṇa, 5, 17, 50, 55, 72, 236, 268
prāṇa-mudrā, 270
prāṇa-sañcālana-kriyā, 243-44, 249
praṇava, 4, 6, 9, 13, 15, 18-19, 24, 26, 28, 62, 66, 100, 109-10, 120, 201
praṇava (*oṁ*), 5, 13, 126, 195, 202
praṇava (*praṇu*), 14
praṇava-japa, 6, 11, 13-14, 16, 19, 24, 109, 119, 267
praṇava-japa (*oṁ*), 273
Praṇava-kīrtana, 192
prāṇāyāma, 14, 22-23, 50, 55, 58, 141, 222, 243, 268
praṇu, 5
prārabdha-karma, 66, 68
prasāda-bīja, 183
pratyāhāra, 10, 14-15, 23
pravāla, 112
pravṛtti-mārga, 203
prāyaścitta, 300
pre-*japa mudrās*, 145
prefrontal area, 78, 215
primal vibrations, 17
psychic centre, 78, 215
psychic stress, 82
Psychic trauma, 80, 82
psychosomatic diseases, 82, 124, 209, 211, 213
PTH, 242
pṛthvī, 172
pṛthvī-bīja, 285
pṛthvī-bīja (*laṁ*), 290
pṛthvī-mudrā, 285
puraścaraṇa, 58-59, 72, 93, 111, 180, 198, 232
Puraścaraṇa-japa, 99, 110-11, 117, 136, 159, 176, 180, 189, 191, 231, 236
    sādhanā, 191

Purāṇic Gāyatrī-Mantras, 160
puruṣa, 106, 301
Puruṣa (God), 127
puruṣa (*puruṣaviśeṣa*), 106
puruṣa-viśeṣa, 106
Puruṣottama, 127

Radhakrishnan, 6
rāga, 206
rajas, 7, 8, 108, 132, 138, 224
raṁ, 4, 62, 172, 227, 229, 238, 277, 292
ram, 268
Rāma, 169-70
Rāma-Gāyatrī, 163
Rebirth, 30
recaka, 229
releasing factors, 79
Rheumatoid arthritis, 239, 245, 248, 253
Ṛṣyādinyāsaḥ, 177, 185
Rudra, 35-36, 48, 53, 130, 138, 168, 176, 181
Rudra-Gāyatrī, 163, 189
Rudra-Śiva, 276, 295, 298
rudrākṣa, 135
rudrākṣa-mālā, 112
Rudrayāmalam, 55, 56

śabda, 130-31
Śabda-Brahma, 131
śabda-brahma-vāda, 132
Saccidānanda, 137
ṣaḍaṅga-nyāsa, 178
Ṣaḍaṅga-Nyāsaḥ, 144, 185
sadguru, 101, 102, 107
saḥ, 62, 182, 183, 184
sahasrāra, 48, 53, 56, 58, 74, 227, 229, 292
sakāma, 44, 67, 72, 102, 108, 110, 123, 217
sakāma anuṣṭhāna, 197
Sakāma bhakti, 44
sakāma japa, 63, 67
sakāma oṅkāra-japa, 218
Sakāma saṅkalpa, 142
sakāma-japa, 201, 230, 231
Śakaṭam, 149
Śākta-mantras, 112
Śāktas, 48-49
Śakti, 56-57, 61, 71, 73, 108, 130, 138, 302
Śakti-Gāyatrī, 167
Śakti-mudrā, 189, 276
śakti-japa, 115
śakti-mantra, 115
śaktipāta, 102
śalabhāsana, 253
samādh, 18
samādhi, 11, 14, 18, 23, 28, 65, 123, 125, 137, 160, 202, 207, 209-11, 214, 219, 221, 223, 229, 231, 239, 246, 266-67, 274, 279, 280

samādhi-yoga, 19
samāna-mudrā, 278
samāna-nābhi-mudrā, 279
sammohana, 75
samprajñāta, 18
samprajñāta samādhi, 18
sampuṭa, 232
sampuṭa bījas, 182
sampuṭīkaraṇa, 182, 232
Sampuṭam, 146
saṁskāras, 9, 12, 21, 30, 31, 43, 45, 55, 66, 106, 204, 208, 221, 301
saṁyama, 11, 18, 210
saṅkalpa, 110, 123, 141, 184, 201, 210-11, 214, 218, 222, 225, 231, 234, 236, 245, 247, 249, 251, 256, 258, 263, 267, 270, 275, 281, 291
saṅkalpāyana, 210-11, 214
Śaṅkara, 6, 31, 132
Śaṅkarācārya, 20
Śaṅkara's, 124
Śaṅkhaḥ, 157
śaṅkha-mudrā, 259, 267, 294
śānti-karma, 75
santoṣa, 24-26, 100
sapta-lokas, 127
Saptaśatī, 174
sāraṅga-mudrā, 190
Sarala-nāsā-śodhana-kriyā, 266
Sarasvatī, 4, 7, 16, 36, 47-48, 61, 120-21, 126, 129, 132-33, 135, 138, 170-71, 174, 194, 224-25, 230
SarasvatĪ-Gāyatrī, 166
Sarasvatī-kīrtana, 194
Sarasvatī-mantra, 173, 109
sarvāṅga nyāsa, 292
Sarvāṅga-saṁyama with mantra-japa, 280
sarvatobhadramaṇḍala, 180
sat, 300
ṣaṭkarmas, 49
sattva, 7-8, 108, 132, 138, 224
satya, 23, 99, 126
Satya-Loka, 107, 127
satyam, 228
śauca, 24, 100
śavāsana, 123-25, 202, 206-08, 210-11, 214, 219, 222-23, 267-68, 273, 291
savitā, 128, 135
Sāvitrī, 121, 126, 134-35, 138, 224-25
Sāvitrī-mantra, 125
śayāna vyāyāma, 244
sciatica, 248, 251, 255
self, 8, 12, 18, 30-31, 35, 43, 64, 66, 123, 196, 204, 207, 221
self (*ātmā*), 2, 6, 8
Self (*Brahman*), 204
self (*jīvātmā*), 12
senile degeneration of the auditory nerve, 261

serotonin, 81
sex, 24
sex-libido, 57
siddhāsana, 96, 123-24, 202, 220, 228, 267, 270, 280
siddhi, 74
singularity, 17
sinusitis, 263
Sītā, 169
śiva-mantra, 111
Śiva, 32, 35, 47-48, 53, 56-57, 61, 73, 108, 111, 168, 172, 181, 191, 224, 230, 233-34, 237-39, 302
Śivā, 47, 302
Śiva-kīrtana, 193
Śiva-mantras, 112, 298
Śiva-Śakti, 36
Śiva-Tantra, 47
śivo'haṁ, 224
smṛti, 9, 12
Ṣoḍaśī, 47
so'haṁ, 20, 65, 123, 160, 220, 274
so'haṁ japa, 20, 124-25, 221, 267
so'haṁ-kīrtana, 223
Sos in Yoga-Tantra, 295
Space, 5
Space (*Ākāśa*), 5, 127, 133
spandana, 17, 61, 121, 132
special *puruṣa*, 301
sphoṭa, 131, 132
sphoṭa-vāda, 131, 132
spondylosis, 248, 251
śravaṇendriya, 249
Śrībagalā, 47
Śrīkṛṣṇa, 169
Śrīrāma, 169
Śrīvidyā, 47
śrīṁ, 4, 62, 195, 226, 292
stambhana, 75, 76
sthitaprajña, 26
stress disorders, 81
string-theory, 16
subtle body, 51, 78
sukhāsana, 96, 123-24, 202, 221, 250-51, 267, 270, 280, 287, 289
Śukrācārya, 182, 232, 235, 294
sūkṣma śarīra, 51
sumukhī-mudrā, 264
Sumukham, 145
Super-Self, 2
super-strings, 16
Supermind, 21, 133
superstring theory, 7
Supreme, 6
Supreme (*paramātmā*), 6
Supreme Self, 12, 19
Surabhiḥ, 155
suṣumṇā, 50, 55, 56, 73
suṣumṇā nāḍī, 268
suṣupti, 8, 9
Sūrya-Gāyatrī, 163

Sūrya-mudrā, 276
svaḥ, 126, 127, 172, 182, 227
svādhiṣṭhāna, 4, 58, 172, 227-29, 238, 283, 287, 290, 292
svādhyāya, 6, 14, 24, 28, 100, 196, 198
svādhyāya-anuṣṭhāna, 197
svapna, 8
svarloka-puruṣa, 127
svastikāsana, 96, 123-24, 202, 221, 267, 270, 280
Symbol-Worship, 32-33
sympathetic, 215
sympathetic system, 82
sympathetic nervous system, 78
synovial fluid, 242, 243, 245

taijasa, 8-9, 12, 17, 31, 63
tamas, 7-8, 108, 132, 138, 224
tanmātras, 133
Tantra, 13, 46-47, 49-50, 53, 56-58, 60-61, 63, 72-74, 77, 120, 171, 180, 232, 296, 299, 300-01
Tantra-Yoga, 55, 58
Tāntric Mantras for Japa, 173
tāntrika mantras, 119, 232
tāntrika puraścaraṇa, 111
tanu, 49
tanu-vistāra, 49
tapaḥ, 14, 24, 27, 100, 126, 196, 228, 299
Tārā, 47, 62
tāram (*oṁ*), 182
tarpaṇa, 59, 111, 176, 180, 191, 197
tat, 300
tattva-śuddhi, 50
tattva-mudrā, 293, 294
testes, 80, 215
thyroid, 80, 215, 242, 247
Trāṭaka, 50
Trāṇa (Sos)-*Mantras*, 297
trāṇa-mantras, 299
trauma, 82
tri-ambās, 108, 138
tribījam, 182
trimūrti, 35, 108, 138, 181
Trimukham, 147
Tripurabhairavī, 47
Tripurasundarī, 47
tryakṣara-Mṛtyuñjaya-Mantra, 184
tryambā, 36
tryambaka, 181
tryambaka-mantra, 181
tulasī, 135
tulasī-mālā, 112
tumour, 213
turīya, 8-9, 12-13, 18, 31, 64
Tyāga, 299

uccāṭana, 75, 76
udgītha, 4, 6
ujjāyī prāṇāyāma, 222, 268

Unconscious, 208
Unmukhonmukham, 150
upāṁśu, 10, 12, 20, 118, 122
upāṁśu japa, 11
upādhi, 108
upastha-mudrā, 288
Upavarṣa, 132

vaṁ, 4, 62, 172, 226-27, 229, 238, 259, 283, 289-90, 292
vaṁ (*varuṇa-bīja*), 267
vaśīkaraṇa, 75
vacuum, 5
Vāgdevī, 121, 130
vahni, 172
vahni-bīja, 279
vahni-bīja (*raṁ*), 246
vaiśvānara, 8-9, 12, 17, 31, 63
vaikharī, 10-11, 20, 40, 118, 122
vaikharī-japa, 192, 262
vairāgya, 205
Vairāgyam, 156
vajrāsana, 96, 123-24, 202, 221, 246, 268
vam, 268
vāma-mārga, 301
vāma-mārgī tāntrikas, 56
vāma-mārgīs, 46, 56
vāmācāra, 57
vāmācārī, 46
vāmācārī Tantra, 47
Varāhakam, 152
vīrāsana, 244, 245
Varṇa-nyāsaḥ, 186
varuṇa-bīja, 283
varuṇa-mudrā, 293
varuṇa-mudrā (*jala-mudrā*), 282
vīryāsana, 268
vāsanā-saṁskāras, 21, 44, 208
vāsanās, 43, 46, 55, 66, 208
Vāsudeva, 168
vāyu, 172
vāyu-bīja (*yaṁ*), 272, 273
vāyu-mudrā, 271, 273
Veda-mātā, 133
Vedāntic kīrtana, 192
viśuddhi, 4, 58, 172, 227-29, 237, 247-48, 258, 260, 282, 292
viśva-rūpa, 34
Viśvāmitra, 125
videha-mukti, 204, 221
videhamukta, 104
vidveṣaṇa, 75, 76
Viral hepatitis, 280
Virāḍ, 71, 133
Vistṛtam, 147
Vitatam, 146
Viṣṇu, 35-36, 48, 130, 138, 140, 170, 176, 181, 195
Viṣṇu Gāyatrī, 161
Viṣṇu-Tantra, 47

vivarta, 131
void, 5
vyāhṛtis, 126, 127, 182, 228
Vyāpaka-Nyāsaḥ, 179
vyāpakāñjali-mudrā, 282
Vyāpakāñjalim, 149

yaṁ, 4, 62, 172, 227, 229, 273, 292
yajña, 3
yama, 14, 23
Yamapāśam, 149
yamas, 22, 99, 100, 196
yantra, 58,
yantra-pūjā, 58, 59, 176, 180
yantras, 52, 58, 73, 180, 189, 198 256
yoga, 4, 10, 13, 22-23, 25, 31, 40, 98, 101-02, 195, 199, 257, 266, 280, 300
Yoga metaphysics, 301
yoga-nidrā, 209, 275
yoga-tantra, 258, 263
Yoginī-Hṛdaya Tantra, 61
yoni, 36, 156
yoni-pūjā, 57